THE ULTIMATE CHALLENGE

The Centenary of the Isle of Man Parish Walk

Dermot O'Toole

ACKNOWLEDGEMENTS

Although the Parish Walk has captured the public's imagination like no other for the best part of 100 years, it was not until 2004 that the rich history of this unique happening was first told. Since then, another nine events have taken place and many records broken, most notably Derek Harrison's long-standing course record of 27 years, finally eclipsed in 2006 with Sean Hands breaching the fabled 15-hour barrier for the very first time.

No goal in life is ever achieved alone and as I begin to reflect on the magnitude of this project, I am reminded of the unfailing support from a whole host of behind-the-scenes people who have helped to make this possible - especially Anne, my soul mate of many years who never doubted my determination to finish this project on time as promised.

Although not intended as a sequel to 'A Walk Through Time,' this book has enjoyed a long life from conception to completion for I began developing its basic ideas many years ago. Since then it has become a labour of love and taken the combined resources of many people to finally bring it to fruition.

Nonetheless, in order to preserve its historical facts, some early text from 'A Walk Through Time' was deemed necessary for inclusion thus making this version a complete and up-to-date definitive history that hopefully will be savoured for many years to come.

Although too numerous to mention in detail there are many people who deserve my gratitude, especially Manx National Heritage who steered me on a true course throughout and provided many of the historic images that make this book Thanks to Paul Weatherall and his helpful team at the musuem..

My thanks to Murray Lambden for so generously allowing access to his amazing Parish Walk website of statistics that makes compulsive reading and surely provides enough substance for another book in the future!

Special thanks also to race director Ray Cox for providing history on the organising committee, who over the last twenty-two years, have worked tirelessly to make this great event what it is today.

I am indebted to John Watterson of Isle of Man Newspapers for giving up valuable time to write a much-needed Introduction that only he could have written so eloquently. John also supplied considerable photographic material as did my friend freelance journalist Bill Dale who magically produced pictures whenever they were required!

My sincere thanks are also extended to Matthew Biggart, consultant anaesthetist at Nobles Hospital. Local historians have also played an important role, particularly Peter Kelly, John Wright and Stan Basnett - all of whom shared their specialist knowledge in making this book that more interesting.

Further afield, my thanks are extended to Chris Flint, Richard and Sandra Brown, past winners of the Parish Walk who graciously provided history on many of the past and present ultra- distance race-walking events held both in Great Britain and the near Continent.

Thanks are extended to 17-year-old Alex Eaton - the present fastest Manxman over 20 kilometres, who I am sure one day, will also enter the Parish Walk Hall of Fame to be up there with the very best. Alex spent many hours putting his IT skills to good use in the layout of this extended manuscript and I am grateful for his contribution. My finally thanks to Manx Telecom for all their support, especially Margaret McGee.

Last but not least, the final word must go to Miles Cowsill (Lily Publications Ltd) for his brilliant publishing skills and fine handling of this enormous undertaking that at times seemed never-ending and must have tested his patience to the limit.

First published in the
Isle of Man in 2013 by
Lily Publications
PO Box 33
Ramsey
Isle of Man IM99 4LP

Best wishes,

Dermot. B. O'Toole.

Contents

Foreword

No event captures the imagination of the Isle of Man's general public quite like the Parish Walk. Each year, hundreds of individuals collectively cover thousands of miles on foot to prepare themselves for the rigours of one 24-hour period in late June. Such is the challenge of the event that most of the people who enter never complete the full 85 miles, indeed most don't make it to half-distance.

In recent times, the Parish Walk has become the island's very own 'London Marathon'. It's an event for the masses with only a select few likely to feature in the top echelon.

Every single starter has a goal, whether it's to reach the most southerly parish church of Rushen or the imaginary half-way at Peel. Most of those who do go beyond the true midway point at Ballaugh generally continue all the way back round to Douglas to successfully complete all 17 parishes within the stipulated 24 hours of starting.

On such a long course with high peaks and exposed coastal stretches, weather conditions can have a profound effect on walkers and their ability to overcome adversity. In 1977, scorching temperatures accounted for all bar one of the 90 starters failing, while 31 years later the 2008 event will be remembered as the wettest and arguably the toughest of all. Heroically, 121 of the original 1132 starters completed the event.

It's a race with an intriguing history dating back to its origins in 1913. After a sporadic period of 47 years, in which only two more similar events were held, the Parish Walk was revived in 1960 when 35 starters (many of them ill-equipped and ill-prepared) whittled down to three finishers inside the time limit.

The walk has grown significantly since then, attracting entries in excess of 1,000 for the past decade or more, with the backing of corporate sponsors and a hard-working, stable committee.

Since 1960, 52 events have produced 21,754 starters, 2,113 finishers and 28 individual winners.

Although retired postman John Cannell holds the record number of six wins, another Douglas man of the same name became the first person to visit all the island's parish churches within a 24-hour period. He completed the feat in July 1852 on horseback, covering a shorter 77-mile distance than the current route, in a time of 15 hours.

Two men jointly hold the record number of 34 starts, although David Collister is the most prolific finisher with 30 in succession.

After completing the wet 2008 event, Douglas woman Bethany Clague carried on to become the first person to complete two laps of the Parish Walk back-to-back, doing it in less than 48 hours. The oldest finisher to date was 74 years of age at the time.

While this great event can be compared to the London Marathon for its interest and atmosphere, similarities can also be drawn with the world's greatest annual sporting occasion, the Tour de France. Both events were inspired by newspapers. The first Parish Walk comparable to that of today was organised by *The Isle of Man Times* in 1913. The Tour's founding newspaper, *L'Auto*, was printed on yellow paper – which explained the colour of the race leader's jersey. Its front page on the opening day of the maiden event in July, 1903 carried a map of the route.

The Parish Walk is now an intrinsic part of the Isle of Man's diverse sporting and social history.

In the words of the author: 'Records and hearts will continue to be broken in this popular happening that has captured the public's imagination like no other.

John Watterson
November 2013

The National Sport Centre in Douglas is the starting point for the annual classic.

A sovereign dependency of the British Crown but not part of the United Kingdom, the Isle of Man lies midway between the shores of England and Ireland, from where all four kingdoms of Britain can be seen on a clear day.

The beauties of the approach to this island have been often described but rarely effectually. Onboard the Royal Yacht *Victoria and Albert* during the Royal Visit in 1902, Edward VII said of his visit to Douglas: 'All islands are beautiful when viewed from the sea but I know nothing as lovely as this.'

Self-governing, with Tynwald the oldest parliament in the world, this enchanting island of 226 square miles remains steeped in folklore and legend – the mythical Manannan, Lord of Mann, was once said to keep watch over the Island and repel invaders with his cloak of mist.

From earliest times, its people have lived mostly as farmers, crofters and fishermen – a way of life from a distant past.

Overrun at times by its powerful neighbours, the Island has been successively Irish, Scandinavian, Scottish and English, and yet today is politically independent of them all. 'Quocunque jeceris stabit' says its coat of arms. 'Whichever way you throw me I shall stand' – a proud boast but justified by events.

Famous for its motorcycle races, Manx kippers and cats without tails, the Isle of Man has for the past century and a half played host to a secular event that centres on all of its 17 parishes, yet the churches themselves are not the centre of attention. In fact, little is made of the role they play in this increasingly popular happening that continues to capture the public's imagination like no other.

The event of course is the Parish Walk – a physically demanding 85-mile foot-slog that requires those brave enough to contemplate such an undertaking, to visit each of the Island's 17 parish churches within a 24-hour period.

From its humble beginnings in 1913 when just 12 people took part, this eagerly awaited highlight in the Manx athletic sporting calendar, has in recent years gone from strength to strength with entry numbers regularly exceeding 1500.

So why then, do close-on two per cent of the Island's population participate in an event of such Herculean demands that only the fittest and most mentally disciplined will succeed? Personal achievement and the unlikely possibility of finishing are perhaps the dominant driving forces, however the event has in recent years become part of Manx culture and very much 'the thing to do' with many seeking financial sponsorship for their chosen charity.

To find the answer to this much asked question, we need to look into the past to understand what was happening in Britain and how walking evolved from a daily chore to a fulfilling pastime enjoyed by so many.

THE GOLDEN AGE

In the midst of the most critical time in the country's history, with war never far away, the nineteenth century began with Britain being the most powerful and influential country in the world. George III was King and William Pitt, Prime Minister.

The first general census of Great Britain and Ireland taken in 1801 revealed a population of 16 million; this was a period when England was changing from being predominantly agricultural, with most of her population living in the country, to becoming a predominantly manufacturing nation. Migration into the towns came about with the rapid invention and development of machinery, enabling manufacturers to produce large quantities of goods more cheaply and quickly than they could be produced in the villages. During the first half of that century, Britain became the workshop of the world with factories, smoking chimneys and powerful machines fuelling an Industrial Revolution that radically changed society, bringing with it immense prosperity, but also war, to an expanding empire upon which the sun never set.

This was undoubtedly Britain's golden age. It was a time of great change, with rapid expansion of the railways and waterways soon replacing the established turnpikes and packhorse coach routes of bygone years. For the very first time, travel was affordable to the working classes, many of whom thought nothing of spending half a day walking to work and back – often from one town to another in all kinds of weather. Sadly, there is no one alive today to recall those momentous events in what was undoubtedly Britain's greatest-ever century.

Photography has only been with us since 1843 so before that time dependence was placed on artists of the day to paint and sketch the scenes around them. Luckily, Manx newspapers dating back to 1794 are preserved in the archives of the Manx Museum and from this collection it has been possible to reference many of the Island's historic sporting events which otherwise would have been lost forever.

Perhaps the earliest reference to an unusual demonstration of prowess is that of a man named Kinry, who sometime before 1760 took a bet on himself that he could run from Douglas to Bishops Court and back, stark naked. The circumstances of the bet are unclear but it may have been as a result of a drinking session in a Douglas tavern. Undeterred by the heavy snow storm, Kinry made his way from Douglas to Cronk Breck, probably via the Strang and the road above Crosby. Running alongside Greeba, Slieau Ruy and Lhergy Ruy, all of which lay to the left of his route, he crossed the Brandywell road beneath Sartfell, taking the well worn Baltic track to Slieau Curn before descending into Bishopscourt, home of the Bishop of Sodor and Man.

Retracing his steps back to Douglas, Kinry collapsed in the vicinity of Lhergy Ruy and died. When he was discovered some days later, a cairn of quartz stones was erected and the spot ever since has been known as Lhiaght-ny-Kinry or Kinry's grave. The tracks today are clearly marked as public footpaths, however in those days they would have been packhorse routes used mainly by traders travelling the Island with their wares.

In 1848 the *Manx Sun* published an account of Harry Kermode, who walked from Patrick to Ramsey and back again. The distance was 48 miles which in those days was quite an achievement for a man aged 84 years.

Some years later, in an undated newspaper, John Corlett of Andreas claimed he could remember living under five monarchs and being baptised 92 years before when he was just a few years old. It was his custom until three years before his death to frequently walk to Douglas – a round trip distance of some 36 miles.

THE BELLE VUE AND THE GREAT EXHIBITION

Although the Manx population more than doubled in the 100 years after 1800, the Island was not completely without athletic facilities during that period. Occupying the site upon which today stands Pulrose power station, the National Sports Centre and numerous commercial outlets, the Belle Vue complex of the late nineteenth century encompassed an extensive rectangular area bordering Quarter Bridge in the north to Pulrose Road in the south, and Peel Road in the east to Groves Road in the west.

In 1885, Jonathan White Johnson, a mineral water manufacturer from Dalton-in-Furness, Lancashire purchased Ballaughton Mill, its dam, race and meadows from the eminent businessman, George William Dumbell for £2,000. Johnson used the mill for mineral water production, however two and a half years later in March, 1888, he extended his property by purchasing the adjoining Ballabrooie Meadow from the estate of John Moore of Pulrose for £1,860. He bought the land with the intention of emulating the success of the Falcon Cliff as a sports centre, but also to combine this with a pleasure ground to capitalise on the tourist boom which was now ever-expanding on the Island.

During 1889, a major transformation of the land took place including the re-routing of the River Glass. A four-acre boating lake was then created by damming the confluence of the Dhoo and Glass rivers. A wooden pavilion to accommodate 'thousands' was constructed along with a bicycle and running track together with facilities for lawn tennis, archery, football, cricket and bowls. This was all achieved in a little over a year, but as with the Loch Promenade and Victoria Pier projects of the early to mid-1870s, the era was one of long hours and low pay.

Opened on Tynwald Day 1892 by the Island's Lieutenant Governor, Spencer Walpole, the complex was named Belle Vue Gardens, possibly after the Belle Vue in Manchester. A Parisian circus with trained animals was introduced the following year plus a switchback railway, claimed to be the largest of its type in the world.

On the sports track, the Douglas Harriers staged a world record attempt at the 440 metres hurdles attracting athletes from far and wide. There were ten

flights of hurdles three feet high to tackle, requiring timekeepers from Salford Harriers and Douglas Harriers to be in attendance and ratify the time. Starting off with a number of competitors lined up at ten-yard intervals, New Zealander Godfey Shaw stormed around the track overtaking all but one by the 300-yard mark. With Manxman Silas Christian the only one standing in his way, Shaw went on to win by ten yards in a world record time of 57.4 seconds.

The success of the Belle Vue prompted the Manx government to use the premises for its planned International Exhibition of Industry, Science and Art.

The architect of the buildings was Joseph Douglas who, like his brother, designed and built houses in Woodbourne Square, Kensington Road and Brunswick Road. The special construction covered in nearly 2,000 square feet in three different sections. It was claimed correctly to be the largest covered floor-space on the Island. The building spanned three sides of a square with the floor raised four feet to allow for ventilation and water pipes which acted as fire extinguishers. The roof was rolled plate-glass to afford the maximum light in daylight hours.

After paying an entrance fee of 6d, visitors to the building passed a statue of the artist Raphael before entering an exhibition whose contributors were a mixture of international, British and local establishments. The British companies included Singer, Rowntree, Bovril, Lever Brothers and Frys – the latter described in the brochure as 'the most attractive of the exhibition'. Other exhibits included a type of early alarm clock, lead pencils, Everton Toffee, oil and gas engines, pianos, bicycles, telephones and a working dairy. Local companies were well represented including Cubbon's Rock, Keigs Photographics, Cottier and Cubbon the Drapers and Kirwin and Mullen who made carriages and dog carts.

Perhaps the 'jewel in the crown' of this extraordinary exhibition was the almost full-size replica of HMS Victory, the original of course preserved in Portsmouth harbour. A painting depicting the Battle of Trafalgar by the German artist Philip Fleischer was also on show. The massive work measured 105 feet by 310 feet and could be viewed from a central platform three tiers in height. The famous battleship which had previously been exhibited at the 1891 Royal Naval Exhibition had been purchased by the organisers for £4,000. Nelson's deathbed scene was meticulously recreated with all the prominent characters present – Nelson, Captain Hardy, Doctor Beatty, Lieutenant Quilliam, Lieutenant Burke and Doctor Scott, the ship's chaplain. At the opening ceremony, the Victory was manned by the Douglas Corps of Volunteers, their uniforms making a pleasant contrast against the ship's black and white hull.

The circus was another popular attraction with seating for a thousand. Close by was a four-acre lake site complete with imitation gunboats and a fort on the island, on what is now the site of the new swimming pool.

At the Dancing Pavilion, a continuous series of artists

performed throughout the day. Other attractions included a recreation of the Deadwood Stage Robbery plus bucking broncos from Buffalo Bill's London Wild West Show.

Despite the presence of Keigs and other photographers, there is hardly any photographic evidence of this great spectacle. There is however, an anonymous painting which depicts the layout of the exhibition and for many years this hung behind the counter of a small shop at Spring Valley. It is now in the store rooms of the Manx Museum.

Although the Great Exhibition was short-lived, Johnson opened for the 1893 season with the same attractions he had managed in the years prior, with the notable addition of Victory, which by now had been purchased by a three-man consortium. The site also reverted back to a sports stadium after a year of suspension. However, as well as the Falcon Cliff having a running track, there was also the nearby Olympia, now a rival having been established the previous year. Sadly, each venue was built to cater for huge crowds and the Island was unable to support three stadia, forcing the Olympia to close in 1896 after a very short life.

With little happening towards the end of the decade, the appointed caretaker at Belle Vue, Joseph Cowley, had the task of maintaining the premises and making sure they were not damaged by vandalism. By now the Victory had become a decaying hulk and a shadow of her former self.

One Sunday in January 1899, the superintendent of Douglas Fire Brigade was informed that a fire had broken out at the Belle Vue. By the time the firemen arrived on the scene the Victory was ablaze. Despite having their hoses connected to the water supply in Ballabrooie their efforts were in vain. Soon, all that was left of the 226-foot vessel was charred timber and sheets of galvanised iron.

Although no one was injured onboard the replica, it was obvious what had caused the fire. The caretaker had left the grounds at about 5:30pm on Saturday and had noticed nothing amiss. The following morning, while clearing up in the aftermath of the fire, he found a half empty whisky bottle with a glass upturned over the top. An employee of the Railway reported that on a number of occasions he had seen vagrants crossing the lines in that vicinity at first light and that it was well known that during the winter months they made their home on the vessel. Their presence and smoking onboard probably contributed to accidentally setting it alight.

With closure of the Falcon Cliff Sport's track, the Belle Vue was left as the only sports venue on the island however enthusiasm was waning and fewer events were held by the turn of the century.

A DAY AT THE RACES

A new age was, however, to dawn for the huge park, giving it once again a place in the hearts of locals and visitors alike. In 1912, a Manchester company bought and developed the site as a horse racing venue. The course prospered during the bumper season of 1913 holding meetings every Tuesday and Thursday, with day trippers from across the water more than eager to pay the 1s 6d entrance fee. The outbreak of the Great War closed the course for four years, however it re-opened in 1919 being as popular as ever.

The excursion trippers attended the twice-weekly meetings coming over in droves on the Fleetwood steamer. The main entrance was a half-timbered Victorian-styled building situated near the rail crossing on the site of the present car park. The horses were stabled in Spring Valley Lane at the back of what is now Mylchreest Motors. At the time the Manx Spinning Company Woollen Mills occupied what had been Johnson's pop works, and flies were a nuisance for the workers during the hot summer months therefore a reward was offered for anyone swatting a thousand flies. During the winter months, the horses were stabled at Court Farm, Santon. Among the regular riders was Jimmy Hogg who rode Lucky Jim and Lady Astor, owned by Mr. Atkinson of The Howe and three Irish brothers by the name of McArdle. The bookmakers during the halcyon days of the twenties included Mr. Corlett of Douglas and Mr. Bernard Murphy of Liverpool.

During the hot summer of 1921 it was necessary to artificially flood the course to make the going softer. The season also saw the first fines for 'crooked riding' which led to the course developing a tarnished reputation.

Pleased with their continued success, in 1927 the organisers proposed four meetings a week during the season, two horse racing and two greyhound meetings. But the sport was riddled with 'crooked riding,' The *Isle of Man Times* writing: 'It is exceedingly difficult to know when horses are run honestly. A horse is not always fit, and consequently takes part in a race more as exercise than of making a serious attempt. The same thing exactly happens under rules. The chief people responsible for crooked racing are the professional backers. These men have more control over jockeys than the owners themselves. The names of the professional backers are well known, their tactics are well known and these deserve no consideration whatsoever.'

The course closed for the last time in September 1931. A plea for a five-year extension fell on deaf ears against the views of Douglas Town Council and the police who felt that despite four cases in the last season for 'dubious riding', the meetings compared favourably with those run in England. Nevertheless, Tynwald refused any reprieve and the Belle Vue closed down as a race course. The remaining equipment was then sold off, the grandstand realising £30 and the horse boxes £6 each. The expected decline in tourism failed to materialise and charabanc drivers reported that if anything business was better.

KING GEORGE V PARK

With horse racing no longer a proposition, Belle Vue

Colonel William James Anderson. b.1831 d.1912.

was sold to the Douglas Corporation in April 1932 for £6,250. The transaction was described as being 'a very sound piece of business' on the part of the Town Council. The intention was to convert it into a park which would do credit for the town.

The first part of the plan was to raise and level the area by six feet and thus avoid further flooding by the adjacent rivers. This was carried out by transporting 50,000 of tons of waste from the Foxdale mines by rail to the park. It was then rolled, soiled and reseeded under the supervision of Eric Coward, the newly appointed Corporation gardening superintendent.

Fully landscaped and renamed King George V Park after the late king who had died just before preliminary work had begun, the scheme envisaged by the Town Council was to have a children's play area and pets' corner, a boating lake, bowling greens, tennis courts, sports pitches, refreshment pavilion, grandstand and dressing rooms with public conveniences.

Estimated to cost in the region of £52,000, the scheme was put before the Douglas Town Council in May 1938, and other than one dissenting voice, it was passed unanimously. Nevertheless, a month later the Council did an abrupt about face after finding the cost had increased to £72,000.

The outbreak of the Second World War put an end to any ideas of resurrecting this grandiose undertaking and it was not until 1947 that the Town Council expressed a wish to go ahead with the scheme it had previously rejected. The cost was now £53,581 and would provide work for 120 men for six months. However, once again the plans were held in abeyance, this time by Governor Bromet who decided how much of that amount would come out of government funds. But with many housing developments in progress, severe weather and a cement shortage, nothing more was done although the sports pitches were now available for use. The cement shortage also halted the important work of walling up the banks of the River Dhoo to prevent the perennial problem of flooding. Despite this, the Corporation used the old stables as rented housing. One family that lived there was the Gibb family who subsequently moved to Willaston and later found fame as the Bee Gees pop group.

In November of the same year, the newly formed Manx Amateur Athletic Association lobbied for an athletics and cycle track. Eric Coward, parks superintendent for the Corporation came up with suggestion that a tarmac track should be built on the ground adjoining the park so as not to interfere with football and hockey matches elsewhere. This area which later became The Bowl was used as a 300-metre track for the Manx Games during the 1980s. The approximately 800 metre tarmac track encompassing the perimeter of the park was laid about the same time.

In September 1950, Douglas Town Council announced plans to develop the area between Pulrose Bridge and the River Glass into a cycle and athletics track. The estimated cost was £3,200, subject to an application to Tynwald to borrow some of the money to use as a grant to provide work for the unemployed.

In May 1953, a further £1,500 was found to complete the 'football area' with seven rows of terraces. At a cost of £4,700, the new stadium was completed in April 1954 thus effectively finishing work on King George V Park, which had been planned from the time the grounds had been purchased in 1935. Over the next five decades many international events were staged at the King George V Park. The sports complex also served as the main venue throughout the year for football, hockey, and cricket.

The Bowl has played host to former England captain Bryan Robson who made his return from injury playing for Manchester United Reserves against the Isle of Man senior side. The 800 metre tarmac track has seen champion cyclist Reg Harris and international runners, Jeff Norman and Don Macgregor all make a good account of themselves. On the home front Derek Harrison, Graham Young, John Cannell and Steve Partington have all served their apprenticeship well and gone on to make household names of themselves.

Perhaps the most outstanding record to be made came in February 1971 when Boundary Harriers promoted an event that saw British International Paul Nihill take on the Island's athletes over ten miles. Nihill's time was exactly 69 minutes knocking 38 seconds off the previous world best of Olympic gold medallist Ken Matthews. The achievement was all the greater because Nihill's great rival Ron Wallwork was unable to make the trip and only Allan Callow was able to provide a realistic challenge. The time was a world best due to world records only being recognised over metric distances.

In 1987, the Island's sporting and recreational areas were reviewed by an independent commission with a view to siting a multi-million pound National Sports Centre. As many as ten sites were studied, of which the four considered most suitable were Nobles Park, King George V Park and Bowl, Onchan Park and Mooragh Park in Ramsey.

The report concluded that the most suitable location for an all-weather facility incorporating a hockey and football pitch should be Nobles Park. It was also recommended that an aqua leisure centre and competitive swimming pool should be sited at the Villa Marina. The report was released on January 1988 amid a storm of protest from the Nobles Park trustees who felt that it had infringed the covenant of their benefactor Henry Bloom and from politicians who felt that the poor tourist figures and the size of the local population would mean that it was too ambitious a project to be financially viable.

The commission examined the King George V Park, The Bowl and the area of waste ground that was previously covered by the Groves Road rubbish tip. This second report was published in April 1989 having examined the area geologically. It concluded finding that the rivers Dhoo and Glass flood plain was the ideal location for the all-weather facilities as the site was not too exposed to south-west winds. To combat the problem of flooding, defences had to be built to solve the age-old problem that had dogged the area ever since it had been used as an entertainment venue. This was done by deepening the bed of the River Dhoo and strengthening its banks. The first phase of development involved relocating Cronkbourne Cricket Club, somewhat appropriately, at Tromode overlooking the former residence of its founder, A.W. Moore, SHK.

On a wet day in September 1991, phase one was opened by Olympic 800 metre gold medallist Steve Ovett and the inaugural athletics match was a keenly contested affair. The first wet day for weeks ensured the all-weather track was thoroughly tested.

Phase two was completed in February 1998, the swimming pool declared open by Tourism minister David Cretney, MHK (Member of the House of Keys). The complex boasted two 25-metre pools with moveable floors, two flumes and a fun pool thus replacing the ageing Aquadrome at Derby Castle. This was followed some months later by a sports hall and fitness centre. Thus the area occupied some one hundred years earlier by a boating lake was now home to water sports of a different kind.

In March 2001 the second sports hall was opened, which included a bowls hall and six squash courts thus completing the final phase of this ambitious project which cost in excess of £16,000,000.

ATHLETIC TRADITIONS

Although not a walking event, The Peel to Douglas road race remains the oldest athletic event in the Manx sporting calendar and was first run in 1909.

With closure of the Belle Vue, the Falcon Cliff and the Olympia stadium during the 1890s, the Island was left with little in the way of facilities to carry on the tradition of athletics that had produced a British four-mile champion in 1872. Across the water in England in 1908, athletics was creating a lot of interest for a number of reasons. The Olympic Games had been held in London that year and the climax had been the marathon in which the American Joseph Hayes scored an unpopular victory when the leader Dorando Pietri, a pastry cook from Capri, collapsed within sight of the finish but was then helped over the line and disqualified.

The British sense of fair play, to say nothing of getting back at the Americans, was boosted however by victory in a marathon race in Madison Square Gardens when Alf Shrubb, a professional and therefore banned from the Olympics, beat the American Tom Longboat. Like most races in those days a lot of money was riding on the athletes.

The *Isle of Man Weekly Times* came up with the idea of promoting a marathon of their own, running from west to east along the Peel to Douglas main road. Commencing at Peel Football Club the ten-mile race terminated at the Palace on Douglas Promenade. The route was almost identical to that of today and there are many other similarities that would surprise those who thought athletics in those days was rather haphazard. First, all competitors were required to produce a medical certificate and proof that they had run at least four races previously. They were also allowed a trainer who could follow on a bicycle and offer refreshments when required.

The event caused huge interest with trains taking supporters to the start at Peel, later returning them to Douglas in time to see the competitors descending Railway Hill.

Hailed by the *Isle of Man Times* as the greatest event in the annals of Manx sport, the event attracted an entry of 32 people, all of whom passed the strict entry regulations. They set off from Peel amid hundreds of supporters on April Fools' Day, 1909. The returning trains to Douglas stopped at all stations on the way, with a man from the telephone company providing up to date information for race officials at the finish line outside the Palace.

Wasting no time, 21-year-old Joseph Karran of Douglas took an early lead and was never seriously challenged. He made it to St Johns in 12 minutes, Greeba Bridge 22½ minutes, Corlett's Halfway House, 31 minutes, Union Mills Post Office 45½ minutes, Quarter Bridge 54 minutes, Royal Hotel 62 minutes and the finish in 70½ minutes.

At Lazy Hill, next to the Brown Bobby, Karran's mother came out to see him and he responded, 'Its all right mother, I'm going through'. While descending Railway Hill a dog came at him but was quickly driven off. On reaching the finish, he entered the ballroom looking fresh as paint to win by nearly four minutes. Daniel Lawson of Hope Street Douglas was second and 17-year-old George Shimmin third.

Karran's story explaining his preparations and problems during the race is quite interesting. He ran the distance three times at fortnightly intervals, otherwise running two, four and six miles every day. At Union Mills, he felt a nail coming through his shoe which irritated his foot on every stride. Referring to the incident on Railway Hill, he said, 'If my pace had been any slower the dog would have had my leg off.' As to his fluid intake prior to the race, which began at 6 o'clock in the evening, Karran downed an Oxo drink which he found invigorating and stimulating.

The second race in the series was held in late May in conjunction with the Auto Cycle Races. Karran was no longer invincible having been beaten in the Ramsey to Andreas miniature marathon and the Laxey Good Friday race by Thomas Evans of Ramsey. The northsiders were down in force to support their favourite who must have fancied his chances as Karran had sprained his leg at an earlier meeting. In addition, a national walking champion working at Cunningham's Camp named Robert Wilkinson had entered amid controversy that he was not a permanent Manx resident. Although his entry was eventually accepted, officials stuck strictly to the rules and barred one competitor for not producing a medical certificate.

On a hot sultry night, 26 runners started from the football ground. Hundreds of cyclists followed, including a large contingent from Ramsey hoping for a northern victory.

Karran, Wilkinson and Evans tracked the race leader, Alfred Kennish as they headed for Ballaleece Bridge. At St Johns, Evans stumbled on a loose stone, twisting his ankle and was dispatched back to Ramsey on the train. At Ballacraine, Karran and Wilkinson overtook Kennish and raced each other along with Walter Teare of Castletown, however the dusty roads and inconsiderate motorists made life difficult for the runners.

Wilkinson took a slight lead at Quarter Bridge while Karran began to feel the effects of his sprained leg, nevertheless, he stayed in close proximity until the railway station where again he was chased by a dog. Despite the distraction, Karran gained slightly on his opponent at the Jubilee Clock, however on reaching Broadway, Wilkinson sensed victory and went on to win in a shade under 69 minutes.

A glance at the Karran Cup shows that there are remarkably few different names on it. There are serial winners like Abba Taylor in the 1920s and 30s, Peter McElroy in the 50s and 60s, Peter Harraghy in the late 60s and the incredible Steve Kelly in the 70s and 80s. For instance, Dave Newton and Graham Clarke, two of the fastest men over the course, only have their names on the trophy once and twice respectively. Karran would have been amazed to see runners breaking the hour for the distance, but then the roads are much better surfaced now.

Another talented Manx athlete, running during the nineteenth century, was James Edgar. Born in Douglas in 1851, he stood nearly six feet tall and weighed about 10½ stones. He shot to prominence in August 1869 at an athletics meeting at Kirby, Braddan (home of the Drinkwater family, as it still is today), when the 18-year-old lined up with three other locals, together with some visitors from England in a scratch two-mile race. In those days, runners were bet on like horses and greyhounds, and odds were offered of ten to one against a local victory. Patriotically, some people bet on Edgar who had only recently bought his first pair of pumps to train in earnest. The track was 440 yards in length and after the first lap he was up with leading English runners Joseph Snow and Charles Kenyon. Lapping the circuit in 67-second intervals, he soon took the lead and went on to win by 60 yards in 10 minutes 11 seconds.

He did not race again that year, but was invited to meetings in England in 1870, the first time he had ever left the Island. He ran a two-mile handicap event at Ormskirk, took the lead but then retired with a stitch after completing about three-quarters of the course.

He returned to Ormskirk in 1871, winning the mile in the slowish time of 4 minutes 57 seconds and then completed his afternoon's work by winning a half-mile steeplechase in 2 minutes 20 seconds. He returned to the Island to compete in a mile race at the Douglas Sports, beating J. Scott of London, holder of the prestigious four-mile Championship, so this was a significant scalp.

By now his fame had spread and Edgar was being trained by well-known professional runner Willie Long, who himself had taken part in some famous running duals some years earlier.

In 1872, Edgar went to London and won the four-mile Championship by over 70 yards in the slow time of 21 minutes 31 seconds. Later on that year he won the two-mile and half-mile races, beating his old rival Warburton in 10 minutes 39 seconds in the former and C.H. Mason of London Athletic Club in 2 minutes 11 seconds in the latter.

Twelve months later, he ran in the Douglas Autumn Sports at the new race course above the Strang, winning the half-mile and quarter-mile handicaps. In the latter event, he conceded 20 yards to a runner from Derby but was still first over the finish line in 53 seconds.

Announcing his retirement at the ripe old age of 22, Edgar then returned to his job of post office clerk, being the first in a tradition of athletic postmen who would later dominate the Island's premier walking event, the Parish Walk. He was often called upon to start races such as the inaugural Peel to Douglas road race in 1909, followed by an international race in 1911 at the Douglas Recreational Grounds, later to be known as Nobles Park.

However, by the time of his death in 1929, James Edgar was long forgotten by the local athletic community, the bald statement in the *Isle of Man Examiner* for 2nd August read: 'The funeral of Mr. James B. Edgar, formerly of "Keithock," Cronkbourne Road, Douglas, took place at Allerton Cemetry on Tuesday last.' He was 78-years-old.

THE EARLY DAYS

Although the history of the Parish Walk and events of similar nature have been well documented since 1913, at least two eminent gentlemen from the late nineteenth century also accomplished the feat of having walked the 17 parishes within 24 hours however, until recently, little was known about their exploits.

In 1848, the Island's premier newspaper *The Manx Sun*, published the account of Harry Kermode who walked from Patrick to Ramsey and back again. He estimated his distance to be 48 miles which in those days was quite an achievement for a man supposedly 84-years of age!

Four years later in July, 1852, the *Mona's Herald* published an article entitled 'A Summer's Day Journey' which recorded the exploits of John Cannell of St. Barnabas Square, Douglas. His undertaking was to visit every parish church throughout the Island on the same day.

Setting off from Douglas at 7 o'clock in the morning on Friday 23rd July, the Coroner for Middle walked as far as the parish of Maughold, calling at Onchan and Lonan for light refreshment. Here, his servant was in attendance with a horse and gig, and proceeding from the parish church, he soon made light work of the onward journey to Ramsey, Lezayre, Bride, Andeas,

Jurby, Ballaugh, Michael and German. Obtaining a fresh horse at the western capital, he continued to Patrick, Rushen, Arbory, Malew, Santon, Marown and Braddan accomplishing his journey in 15 hours. This included stoppages and refreshment for himself and his horses. More extraordinary still, he proceeded on foot six weeks later for the southern side of the Island, touching all the parish churches, thus reversing the route and completing his journey so far as Laxey by 11 o'clock on the same night.

A year later on September 17th 1853, John again attempted to visit all the Island's parishes on foot. Setting off from Douglas half an hour before midnight and proceeding northward, he visited all the parishes and the four towns of the Island within 24 hours. The newspaper report of the time claimed an 'extraordinary distance' walked by Mr. Cannell of 86 miles but this was probably an exaggeration, the real distance was nearer to 77 for he almost certainly took the shortest off-road route between churches.

SETTING OFF AGAIN

The next attempt at this grandiose undertaking, a quarter of a century later, was by Lieutenant Colonel William James Anderson, MHK and Receiver-General. Recently retired after 30 years of service with the 1st Battalion Duke of Cornwall's Light Infantry, the 50-year-old colonel set off on foot from Patrick in 1879 and he too visited all 17 parish churches, however his time went unrecorded.

Ten years later, the colonel attempted another assault on the 17 parishes, on this occasion covering an estimated 73 miles and seven furlongs. Setting off from Glenaspet, Patrick at 2:40pm, his journey took him north to German, Michael, Ballaugh, Jurby, Andreas, Bride, Lezayre and Ramsey, arriving at the most northerly town at 10:25pm where he stopped for 35 minutes. Reaching Maughold shortly before midnight, he continued on through Lonan and Onchan, stopping for ten minutes at the third milestone on the Douglas to Peel road. Braddan was reached at 3:31am and Santon at 5:50am at which point he stopped for half an hour. With daylight well advanced, he pressed on through Malew and Arbory to reach the southernmost church at 7:57am.

Although the colonel had undergone no training whatsoever his time of 2 hours 50 minutes from Rushen to Patrick, cumulating in an overall time of 19 hours 39 minutes, was nothing short of phenomenal. Still to reach the Psalmist's span of life – three score years and ten, he had maintained extraordinary vigour. His tall and somewhat stooped form was tough as steel, giving him the powers of endurance which were the envy of men in the prime of life. As a pedestrian he was simply marvellous. With him a walk of 50 miles without stopping for refreshment was a mere nothing, and on leaving the army, he undertook to emulate a feat which up to then had only been achieved by one man – John Cannell. Nevertheless, unfatigued after his near 20-hour ordeal, the colonel was up in time the

The Palace Gates were the starting point for the 1913, 1923 and 1924 events.

following morning to attend the Agrigculture Show.

As the nineteenth century drew to a close, much of the Island's infrastructure underwent radical change. Mainly due to the indefatigable resolve of Henry Loch during his 19-year tenure as Lt. Governor, much of lower Douglas was rebuilt with new piers, a magnificent promenade and plush hotels, hastily erected in anticipation of an expanding tourist trade and becoming a vibrant centre of commerce.

The idea to promote a walking race through the Island's 17 parishes was first conceived during the winter of 1913 – a time when European leaders were soon to embark on the bloodiest and senseless of all wars.

In March of that year, the *Isle of Man Examiner* published an interesting account by Mr. Fred Clucas about the past exploits of John Cannell and Colonel Anderson, both of whom during the late nineteenth century, accomplished the remarkable achievement of travelling on foot to each of the Island's 17 parish churches. The descriptive article gave details of these great walks and inspired a committee of Douglas gentlemen, under the chairmanship of Mr. C.T. Cowell, to promote a race under the conditions which had governed the walks of the two men. Unknown to the committee at the time, these preparations were in fact the building blocks to an event that would stand the test of time for the next one hundred years.

The day chosen for this unique undertaking was Wednesday 28th May 1913, with the all-male contest due to start at 7:00pm outside the Palace gates on Central Promenade. In those days of Edwardian etiquette, discrimination between genders was quite normal and it was unusual for women to participate in any activity that required excessive stamina. It was also a time when mixed bathing in public was outlawed.

Initially heading west along the promenade, the 12 competitors turned up Broadway, following York Road and Stoney Road to Quarter Bridge and on to the first church at Braddan. From here, competitors could choose any route they wished providing they reached the parish churches in sequential order and their arrival

Setting the Scene

was witnessed by the vicar and a registration card signed by the duty constable.

The early walkers arrived at Rushen in the black of the night having taken 3 hours 42 minutes to cover the first 19 miles. Ahead of schedule and with no officials in attendance, they had to wait over half an hour at the church to be registered.

The long haul over the Sloc to Patrick took the leading man 2 hours 24 minutes. So thick was the fog on the mountain that several missed the road altogether, ending up in the bog.

At Peel, the three leaders, Harry Bridson, A. Hawley and E. Garrett, arrived together at 5:06am as dawn was breaking. They had arranged to rest for half an hour for breakfast but owing to a misunderstanding, Garrett got away first and did something unusual by dipping his feet into cold water, thus allowing the other two to regain the lead.

Garrett reached Kirk Michael at 6:49am, one minute ahead of Bridson with Hawley a minute back. The fast pace was beginning to tell with back-markers already two hours behind.

At the halfway mark Hawley was forced to give up, leaving Garrett and Bridson to contest the lead. They were so far ahead at this stage that several competitors at the rear of the field went unreported at Jurby.

Setting off from the whitewashed church overlooking the sea, Bridson's choice of cross-country route to Andreas paid dividends for he reached St. Andrew's church at 9:40am with a twelve-minute lead. The field by now was spread far and wide with the last man arriving at this point four hours later. Only eight made it to Bride, with Bridson the first to touch the church door at 10:35am – his lead now extended to 15 minutes.

At Lezayre, his lead had stretched to 25 minutes over Garrett with the remaining three walkers a further two hours back and still to reach the most northerly church.

Public interest in the race among Ramsey residents waxed during the earlier part of the day, however this enthusiasm was soon short-lived. You cannot keep excitement at boiling point all day with intervals of two hours or more between competitors. Bridson arrived at the Public Office at 12:13pm and promptly retired into the Central Hotel for refreshment. He was on his feet again nine minutes later, proceeding along Parliament Street at a fine swinging pace with his closest challenger Garret 20 minutes behind as a result of stopping at his relatives for a midday meal and then taking a wrong turning at Lezayre church and missing the town altogether.

Crowds turned out to welcome Bridson as he passed through Ramsey in great style. Taking the road to Maughold, he lost no time on the climb to Port e Vullen, that quintessential seaside hamlet where the telegraph from Cumbria once came ashore.

Stopping briefly at the hill above Lonan for refreshment with Canon Quine, Bridson remarked that his speed had been measured as 4.75 mph by the speedometer of a passing car.

With bunting out and flags raised, he was cheered on to the finish by hundreds of spectators gathered outside the Palace gates on Douglas Promenade and eager to witness this one-off spectacle. Feeling as fresh as paint, Bridson reached the winning post at 4:56pm, his overall time of 18 hours 56 minutes a remarkable achievement and one beyond all expectation.

Of the five who finished, two were well outside the time limit, arriving back in Douglas having been on their feet for 27½ hours and too late for the grand presentation which by now was well and truly dusted.

After the race, many competitors reported being in difficulty on Dalby mountain. Some missed the turning at the Round Table and continued on to Foxdale before retracing their steps, while another was accused of riding a bicycle between Colby and Rushen.

At the time this event was unfolding, Douglas chemist John Young was making history by completing the same journey on four legs rather than two. Not wishing to bring his horse to the crowded start, he joined the race some 20 minutes later as the walkers headed west from Quarter Bridge. In poor conditions, his ascent of the Sloc was slow and difficult for it was a dark and misty night and poor eyesight made the thoroughbred extremely nervous.

Passing the leading walkers with night turning to day, John reached the western town of Peel at 5:15am only to discover his mount had developed a loose shoe that would soon need repairing. At Kirk Michael the horse was shod and fed before continuing to the most northerly parish, a point he reached at 12:55pm. Poor weather throughout severely hampered progress, the two eventually reaching the finish on Central Promenade at 9:15pm but in time for the presentation conducted by the Island's Chief Constable, Colonel Henry William Madoc.

During his 23-hour equestrian journey, John pulled up several times to converse with farmers and the many spectators lining the route. He did not push the horse hard and was confident he could have out-paced the walkers but for the delay incurred at the ninth church.

A RE-RUN

The outbreak of the Great War the following year brought to an end any idea of re-running the event in the immediate future. During the four years of hostilities many of the Island's finest young men were needlessly sacrificed in a war supposed to end all wars. As a consequence, most sporting events were abandoned during that period and not until a decade later was the event considered worthy enough to be re-run.

Held in 1923, the Isle of Man Times sponsored event failed to attract more than two entrants so the occasion became a challenge rather than a race, between Harry Bridson, winner of the inaugural event a decade earlier and namesake Gerald Bridson from Baldrine.

Their surname may have been the same but there the similarity ended. Harry was a typical working-class man while Gerald was the son of wealthy parents and a member of government since 1919.

There were differences too in their racing kit. Harry was dressed in a dark tweed suit, while the flamboyant Gerald, with his bushy ginger beard flowing in the breeze, wore a large pair of white shorts and a waistcoat. He was also equipped with one pound of tobacco and plenty of matches for his anticipated long journey.

On a bitterly cold early morning on 17th May, 51-year-old Harry and 31-year-old Gerald came to the start line outside the Palace gates on Douglas Promenade. The promoters however had not anticipated bad weather and a full gale from the north-west with showers of hail made it seem more like January.

Sent on their way by Mr. C.T. Cowell at 1:00am, the pair was soon on their way up Broadway, along Stoney Road, past Quarter Bridge and on to Braddan church, arriving there in just 27 minutes.

Marown church was reached by Harry Bridson at 1:59am, followed two minutes later by Gerald. For some unexplicable reason, Harry made a grave mistake in the darkness and instead of taking the road to the Braaid went on to St. Marks. The error cost him dearly for he trailed Gerald by 19 minutes at Santon from which point he never really recovered. Falling behind even further at Arbory and with his son acting as support and riding a motor bike from behind, Harry was forced to take refuge in a nearby ditch to avoid the heavy downpours threatening his progress. Reaching Rushen at 4:04am and showing little sign of fatigue, Gerald Bridson was met at the church gate by the vicar who kindly offered some refreshments.

The demanding climb over Cronk-ny-arry-Laa was made even more difficult with a strong headwind accompanied by driving rain which seriously hampered progress. Recalling his experiences many years later, Gerald Bridson said: 'I do not remember much about it but I can recall getting wet through with snow on that part of the journey.'

The pair plodded on, Gerald the first to Patrick shortly before 8 o'clock in the morning, Harry 47 minutes later.

Arriving in Peel at 8:23am, the leader was welcomed by his Labour Party colleague in the House of Keys, Mr. Christopher Shimmin and given breakfast. Twenty-two minutes later, he was on his way to Kirk Michael leaving Harry, who also took a substantial breakfast at the Peveril Hotel, more than an hour behind.

Extending his lead to 1 hour 37 minutes at Jurby, Gerald Bridson forged on to Andreas, the country road in poor condition hampering progress and taking an hour and a half to negotiate. Reaching Bride at 2 o'clock in the afternoon, he then turned for Lezayre, a distance of five and a half miles where he was met by Cannon Kermode.

A crowd of well-wishers greeted the MHK as he made his way into Ramsey. He was limping slightly and later complained of a blister on the tiring road to Maughold where he was supplied with further

Fifteen year old Marshall Braide faced an unfair challenge.

sustenance from the vicarage.

Meanwhile, Harry was falling further and further behind, arriving at Lezayre church shortly after 5pm, a point reached by his adversary an hour earlier. To the surprise of onlookers, Harry, instead of going through Ramsey, took a narrow lane to Ballure Bridge and then promptly retired. He returned to Douglas by electric tram, slept all the way and had to be awakened on his arrival at Derby Castle.

Leaving Maugold alone at 5:08pm, Gerald pressed on for the penultimate church at Lonan, eight miles distant and a point he reached in 17 hours 43 minutes 32 seconds.

Onchan was the final church on his agenda however, instead of using the steep Burnt Mill Hill to drop into Douglas, he chose Royal Avenue as the route of least resistance leading to Port Jack and Douglas Promenade. Met by two fellow MHKs and a cheering crowd at the finish line outside the Palace, his time of 20 hours 23 minutes was nothing short of remarkable.

DEFENDING THE TITLE

The following year, Gerald was called to defend his title in another challenge match, this time against 15-year-old schoolboy Marshall Braide, the son of George Braide, custodian of Castle Rushen. But there was much public disapproval of this apparently unfair match and only after an intense medical examination did officials allow the boy to take part.

The race began in good weather outside the Palace gates on Douglas Promenade at 1:00am on Thursday 5th June. Bridson was dressed in his famous white shorts and shirt, complete with walking stick, pipe and tweed sports jacket draped over his arm. Shaking hands and wishing each other good luck, they set off together reaching Braddan in 28 minutes.

Through the moonless night, they stayed together, the boy marginally ahead at Arbory but his lead

Setting the Scene

increased to three minutes at Rushen. Forcing the pace even harder on the back-breaking climb to the Round Table, Braide reached the summit 15 minutes in front to clock in at Patrick church at 7:20am.

Both competitors stopped at Peel for a substantial breakfast and it was at this point that the accompanying support teams were replaced.

At Ballaugh, the gap began to close with Bridson only 15 minutes behind. He reached the halfway mark in 9 hours 49 minutes and briefly stopped to bathe his feet in the river. Continuing north, Braide checked in at Jurby church in 10 hours 24 minutes. Now taking a direct route to Andreas, he piled on the pressure to arrive at the twelfth church an hour and a quarter later, his lead stretched to 26 minutes over his opponent who stopped here to change into more comfortable boots.

But the strain was already beginning to tell on the boy. At Bride, he received a massage and was given a stick to help him on his way.

Clocking in at Lezayre church at 3:25pm with a lead extending to over a mile, Braide stopped for further refreshment at the vicarage allowing Bridson to take the lead for the first time. Although showing signs of fatigue, the youngster closed the gap on the journey to Maughold and was the the first to touch the church door having been on his feet for over 15 hours. Never an easy section to negotiate, the uphill climb to the Hibernia took its toll with both men looking tired and weary at Glen Mona but the end result was too early to call at this point.

The next three miles were not easy ones for the young pretender who was now exhausted and unable to maintain any form of tempo. Now a forlorn figure and beyond redemption, he struggled on to the Dhoon where his father reluctantly persuaded him to give up.

Continuing alone at a more relaxed pace, Bridson found time for cold tea and sandwiches at the penultimate church high above the hill over Lonan.

With a growing time of 19 hours 38 minutes to St. Peters church in Onchan, he struck out for the finish, arriving some 22 minutes later as the clock struck nine.

Recording an overall time of exactly 20 hours, Bridson's journey was 23 minutes quicker than his last attempt, for which he was awarded a silver cup and gold medal for his remarkable achievement.

Without doubt one of the great characters on the Manx sporting scene, Gerald Bridson lost his seat in the Keys later that year but remained a determined person and a pillar of society. He contested a total of nine general elections, six for middle, two for Garff and one for Rushen, with his home close to the MER tram crossing at Lonan. Gerald and his wife took on the role as Justice of the Peace for many years. Guest starter for the 1960 Parish Walk, Gerald died in 1967 aged 88.

BREAKING THE RECORD?

Although the two challenge matches were successful in their own right, lack of interest for a third meeting the following year failed to materialise forcing

promoters to withdraw their support and the event was abandoned indefinitely.

Nevertheless, the next attempt at this grandiose undertaking was made by Harry Coulston, a sturdy New Zealander who arrived on the Isle of Man in July 1933 with the sole intention of breaking Harry Bridson's Parish Walk record set 20 years earlier.

An intrepid traveller undertaking a seven-year hiking journey around the world on foot, Harry had left New Zealand penniless two years earlier with the self-imposed conditions that he neither beg, steal or borrow but instead pay his way by lecturing in schools and universities eager to share in his adventures. His ubiquitous journey over the past two years had taken him to Australia, Fiji, Samoa, Tahiti, Hawaii, Canada, USA, England, Scotland, Ireland, Wales, Orkney, Shetland and the Hebrides.

After two weeks of intense training, plus the use of a car to aquaint himself with the 'short cuts' necessary for success, Coulson began his task on the evening of Monday 31st July 1933.

With boy scouts of the 1st Douglas Group posted at each of the parish churches to see that conditions were complied with, Harry set off from the Palace gates on Douglas Promenade at 6 o'clock in the evening. He soon discovered however, that there was more to this than first met the eye. The weather was unsuitable and the strong westerly gale largely contributed to his undoing. He lost no time in reaching the south of the Island by way of Braddan, Marown and Santon, Malew and Rushen, however the journey to Patrick proved a daunting task. It was almost impossible to walk upright without being blown over and his hard toiling on the Sloc Road blistered his feet so much that he could not resist an invitation to rest in the home of a Kirk Michael resident.

This was about 4:30am on Tuesday morning, however after a much-needed rest followed by considerable sustenance, he continued his journey later that afternoon but aware that his much-publicised attempt on the record was doomed to failure.

Plodding on northwards through the hours of darkness was not made easy for the 25-year-old who, unacquainted with the roads, didn't arrive back at his starting point in Douglas until early on Wednesday morning after a trying but no doubt, unique adventure.

MANX AMATEUR ATHLETICS ASSOCIATION

Towards the end of the 1920s, the seeds to worldwide economic disaster were well advanced. The Wall Street Crash in 1929 followed a year later by the Great Depression, which devastated economies both rich and poor. No country was spared – the Isle of Man in particular experienced hardship with considerable damage done to its tourist and farming industries.

A slight improvement to the economy during the late 1930s raised hopes of resurrecting the Parish Walk in 1939 however events in Europe later that year saw the Isle of Man once again making preparations to sacrifice its young men in another war not of its making.

There was victory for Gerald Bridson in 1923 and 1924.

With normality slowly returning after six years of conflict, many returning servicemen to the Island turned to sport as therapy to re-build their war-torn lives. Nevertheless, facilities to indulge in recreational pastimes were few and far between. Other than the few established football and cricket clubs, walking activity was mainly restricted to events on the TT course organised by nursing, farming and educational institutions.

At the time, the Island remained without an officially recognised athletic club, meaning Manx athletes and their counterparts on the mainland were unable to compete in each other's events. 'Recognised' meant an organisation affiliated to the Amateur Athletics Association and one that required a permit to function legally.

Determined to take Manx athletics by the scruff of its neck and shake it out of post-war lethargy, Arthur Currie and the legendary runner Bill Kelly worked tirelessly together in 1947 to form the Manx Amateur Athletics Association. An application for formal affiliation was then made to the Northern Counties Athletics Association and in May of that year their request was granted.

The object of the exercise was to bring the Isle of Man to the British athletics arena from which it had for so long divorced itself and to therefore put the sport on a proper basis. The idea was essentially to make the Island a member of the British Athletics Fellowship and at the same time offer the opportunity for young Manx athletes to participate in national events off island.

Arthur Currie was a wonderful athlete from Lancashire who took up the position of secretary to the Liverpool Boundary Harriers between 1929 and 1939. Like other young men of his age, he served in the Royal Air Force during the war years and was later demobbed, moving to the Island where he went into partnership with his brother Donald as a painter and decorator in Douglas.

During the club's early years, great difficulty was experienced in getting Manxmen interested in athletics. About 95 per cent of the club's membership consisted of painters and decorators hence it became known as the 'Painters Club'. The club had little money at its disposal so Arthur and Bill donated some of their own trophies as prizes.

The first event of the newly formed running club was the Round the Houses Marathon Race. Starting on Douglas Promenade, the 55 starters ran their way up Port Jack, Royal Avenue, Glen Crutchery Road, Down Bray Hill, Quarter Bridge Road, Station Hill, North Quay, Promenade, into Regent Street to finish inside the Palais-de-Dance on Strand Street. As expected, the club's chairman Bill Kelly won the bazzar event convincingly in 38 minutes 49 seconds.

Undoubtedly the Island's best distance runner ever, Bill Kelly enjoyed considerable success with outstanding performances against the very best British marathon runners of the 1950s.

Bill's success in winning the 1954 London to Brighton road race convinced Arthur of a need to organise a similar event over the famous TT course the following year.

Sponsored by the Isle of Man Tourist Board and scheduled for a Whit Monday start, the event attracted an entry of 15 with much interest focused on 1948 Olympics marathon silver medallist, Tom Richards of the South London Harriers whom Bill had beaten in a previous London to Brighton meeting. Unfortunately, Bill had to settle for the runner-up spot on this occasion completing the near 38-mile circuit in a little over four and a half hours.

Widely acclaimed for his sporting achievements both home and away, Bill's greatest moment came in 1958 at the British Empire Games in Cardiff when he finished the marathon in seventeenth place. It was a proud moment too for Arthur whose sheer dedication and organising skills as team manager earned him the title 'Mr. Athletics.'

By late 1959, race walking fever was making a huge impact across England. National Service had been abolished and Doctor Barbara Moore was making all the news with her epic walk from Edinburgh to London. By early 1960, the 57-year-old had become a household name by walking from one end of Britain to another – a journey of 900 miles that took the best part of 23 days to complete. Months later, she walked from San Fransisco to New York in 46 days.

The publicity generated from these courageous walks soon prompted committee members of the Manx Amateur Athletics Association to consider reviving the Parish Walk last held in 1924.

At a meeting convened in Douglas on 10th March 1960, the committee chaired by Arthur Currie, Hadyn Wood and Tom Lewthwaite announced plans to reintroduce the event and form a sub-committee of travelling judges, travelling stewards, a chief timekeeper and race controller. A souvenir programme costing six pence was then printed in which contained a list of entrants, instructions and a full description of the route as follows:

Starting at the junction of Hope Street and Myrtle Street, Douglas, follow Upper Church Street to its junction with Circular Road, keeping to its right-hand side and continuing along Peel Road, past Quarter Bridge to BRADDAN CHURCH. Proceed along the TT course to MAROWN CHURCH at Crosby. Reverse course to, and along Glendarragh Road, over railway lines, turn left at the 'Y' junction leading to Ellerslie Farm and proceed to Braaid Chapel. Continue in same direction over crossroads and take first turning on left leading to Clanagh Road, Santon, joining main Castletown Road near Lancashire Hotel. Turning right in southerly direction to and along Oatlands Road, then by way of the Old Castletown Road to SANTON CHURCH (100 yards left off roadway)

From Santon church, return to and along the Old Castletown Road to the Blackboards turning left and proceeding south to Ballasalla. Turn right at the Whitestone Inn and follow the main road to Cross Four Ways, then turning left continue to MALEW CHURCH. Retrace steps to Cross Four Ways then turning left

Johnny Quine played a pivotal role in reviving the Parish Walk in 1960.

Setting the Scene

proceed along main road south by way of Ballabeg to ARBORY CHURCH, thence by main road through Colby, turning left at the crossroads in direction of Port St Mary to RUSHEN CHURCH. Retrace steps to crossroads and take the mountain road in Peel direction skirting Cronk-ny-Iree-Laa to Round Table cross roads; thence by way of Niarbyl, through Dalby and Glen Maye. Continue to Patrick village, turning right at Clauge's shop and proceeding for about 100 yards to PATRICK CHURCH.

Retrace steps to main road, turning right in direction of Peel, over Glenfaba Bridge, down Patrick Street in to Peel Market Place. Turn right at the Post Office, left into Michael Street continuing to Athol Place before touching the entrance door to ST. GERMAIN'S CHURCH. Retrace steps to main road turning right and then left down Church Street into Peveril Road on the main Peel to Ramsey Road. Continue past Knock Sharry, Devil's Elbow and Glen Wyllin to join the TT course at KIRK MICHAEL CHURCH. Continuing along the TT course to Ballaugh, turn left at the humped-backed bridge proceeding over railway lines to BALLAUGH (NEW) CHURCH. Continue along Ballaugh to Jurby Road coastwise to the 'T' junction leading up to JURBY CHURCH, the gate being about 450 yards from the main road.

Retrace to main road and continue along coast road to the Lhen. Follow most northerly road through Smeale to BRIDE CHURCH. Leave village by way of West Kimmeragh and Burma Road to ANDREAS. (The unmade road and gateway leading up to the church is about ¼ mile bearing left from the elementary school entrance.) Retrace steps to main road and bare left out of Andreas along main road to Sulby Bridge joining the TT course again and proceeding towards Ramsey by way of LEZAYRE CHURCH. (Taking the loop road leading off the TT course, touching the church gate and rejoining the TT course 200 yards further on. Follow the main road into Ramsey's Parliament Square, thence head for the Laxey coast road by turning left into Albert Road before the bus station.

Continuing past Ballure, turn left at the 'Y' junction through Port Lewaigue to MAUGHOLD CHURCH. From Maughold by way of Ballajora, continue to main Ramsey to Douglas road at Hibernia, turn left and follow the bus route to and through Laxey (new road) past South Cape and Fairy Cottage before turning sharp right at Ballacannell and proceeding half a mile uphill to LONAN (NEW) CHURCH. Retrace steps thence main Laxey to Douglas road by way of Garwick, Baldrine, White Bridge hill to Onchan. Turn left opposite war memorial proceeding down hill 200 yards to ONCHAN CHURCH. Retrace steps to Onchan main road and turn left down Royal Avenue along left-hand side of Royal Avenue West to Port Jack. Take seaside pavement along Douglas Promenade to finish 20 yards inside the Broadway entrance to the VILLA MARINA.

Notes and instructions:
It is hoped to have the route indicated by direction arrows painted on the roadway at certain crossings and

road junctions. These arrows are readily visible both during daylight hours and the hours of darkness.

Procedures at church gates:
On arriving at the church main gate, each walker must touch the gate and hand in competitor's card to the official in charge who will punch it in the appropriate space and then hand it back. It must be carried at all times between churches by the competitor.

Retirements:
The organisers must be notified of all retirements, and a competitor having retired from the event must arrange for his registration card to be handed in at the church nearest to the point of retirement. The race number may be handed in to the church official or surrendered to the organisers at reception and distribution of prizes function on the Sunday evening when a refund will be handed to the Walk Secretary at the end of the event.

First aid:
The St. John Ambulance Brigade has very kindly agreed to give First Aid coverage during the Walk.

Time schedule:
No allowance for time lost through stoppages en route will be made, neither for food taking, rests or other causes. Official timekeepers will record starting and finishing times and also the times of arrival at churches.

ROAD SAFETY REGULATIONS:
1. Competitors must walk on the RIGHT-HAND SIDE of the road, (i.e. facing oncoming traffic) at all times, except when crossing the road at junctions. Foot paths on the right-hand side must be used where they exist. From Port Jack to the finish, the seaside footpath along the Douglas Promenade may be taken.
2. Competitors may not walk two or more abreast. Any attendant walkers must walk behind competitors.
3. Competitors are advised in the interests of safety to wear white clothing above the waist at all times, both during daylight hours and the hours of darkness. This is a request made by the Road Safety Officer. In addition, competitors wearing dark trousers or slacks are advised to attach patches of white material both back and front, especially when continuing to walk after dark. The wearing of reflective and fluorescent strips on caps, clothing or shoes are recommended as additional safety precautions. Reflective patches attached to the competitors individual numbers both back and front will be provided by the organisers of the event. Competitors must ensure that these are not obscured at any time, especially after dark. Walk numbers with reflective patches must be returned to the organisers on retirement or after completion of the walk when the 50p deposit will be refunded. Attendant walkers should take appropriate and similar safety precautions, especially during the hours of darkness.
4. Vehicles found moving slowly near competitors will

be discouraged by the police in order to avoid traffic conjestion which can be dangerous.

DESCRIPTION OF ROUTE

In a walk as in life, one should always have a definite objective. It is much more satisfying to reach a target by personal effort than to wander aimlessly. An objective is an ambition and life without ambition is not worth living.

So let's take time out to describe the route taken in this most eagerly awaited and demanding athletic event on the Manx sporting calendar, an occasion that has captured the public's the imagination like no other and one that only the physically fittest and mentally ablest will complete.

Throughout this demanding 85-mile journey, the countryside traversed is beautiful almost everywhere yet extremely varied in character. Mountains and hills, valleys and rivers, heather and moors add to a pastoral landscape as far as the eye can see.

Usually held over the weekend of the summer solstice, this extraordinary journey through the Island's 17 parishes commences at the National Sports Centre in Douglas, initially heading west through Braddan and Marown before back-tracking for Santon and all churches south.

With Marown the only parish not bordering the sea, the tough climb from Glen Darragh to the Braide and beyond to Mount Murray is an early test of resolve for those wishing to complete this Herculean task.

Turning south onto the main Douglas to Castletown Road at Newtown, the delapitated Lancashire Hotel is not passed unnoticed as we head south to Oatlands, soon exchanging the new road for the old.

Although lovingly tranquil, the route from Santon to the Blackboards, Orrisdale and Ballasalla should not to be taken lightly. Thirteen miles may be behind us but many are already succumbing to the pain barrier and unlikely to reach Rushen, a point at which one-third of the entry will fail to continue.

Although the pavement is narrow and the road heavy with traffic, a steady pace can managed between Malew and Abory – the whitewashed church at Rushen our next calling point before taking on the infamous Sloc and all churches north.

Already it seems ages since leaving the capital, and with 19 relatively easy miles behind us, there now follows a lofty ascent of the Sloc massif – a tedious four-mile slog to the highest point of the course 1,180 feet above sea level. Enveloped in mist and rain for much of the year, the retrospective views from here are simply breath-taking – the open farmland and majestical sweep of the Langness peninsular combining to a pageant of colourful scenery far below.

The pace now easier for the remaining miles to Peel, the dramatic scenery in this most desolate place is soon replaced by lush farmland – the quintessence of Dalby and Glen Maye apparent as we march on relentlessly to the most westerly town where only one-third of the field will take up the challenge to continue.

One of four original towns, Peel is place unlike others. Once a thriving fishing port, its narrow streets, quaint stone buildings and a castle dramatically poised above the cliffs are reminders of times long past.

An obvious staging-post for licking wounds and making preparations for the long night ahead, the historic town is soon left behind – the journey to Kirk Michael following the winding coast road for the best part of six miles. From here the views are nothing short of spectacular – the Mourne mountains to the west and the Galloway peninsular to the north clearly visible on a distant horizon.

Devil's Elbow will not be passed unnoticed – the great gash within the sea cliffs savaged by countless years of erosion that continues to devour this fragile coastline at a seemingly alarming rate.

Probably the most scenic part of the entire journey, the beauty of the west coast is firmly before us. A quilted patchwork of fields bordered by hedgerows and stone walls gracefully reach out to the ever-changing coastline – the whitewashed church at Jurby standing like a sentinel, precariously perched high above the cliff tops and soon to become another victim of this windswept region.

After a short but tiring climb out of Glen Wyllin, the road from Kirk Michael to Ballaugh is simple and the way obvious. Making brief use of the famous TT course, the 40-mile mark at Bishop's Court is quickly reached as we trudge on to the famous humped-backed bridge before turning for the halfway mark, a point midway between the new church and the old.

For those with a passion of walking on high ground, the northern plain will seem the dullest and most monotonous part of the entire journey. Polished smooth by an ice age that ravaged this area 9000 years ago, the countryside is totally rural and pleasantly arranged with unrestricted views far and wide.

This is the start of the long monotonous journey across the northern plain. For the best part of 18 miles, it is a route uninhabited, remote from industry and noise and free from traffic.

Although it is usual for two-thirds of the entry to have dropped out at this point, the time is not right for celebration. More difficult miles lie ahead, and with darkness still to come, the only way forward is to remain positive.

St. Patrick's church in Jurby is our next point of call. Occupying a commanding position overlooking the deserted airfield, the lonely church offers a panaroma far wider than its modest elevation would suggest. Reaching out to the Point of Ayre, the broad expanse of this fertile land is seen without interruption – the eastern side of North Barrule still to be passed but many hours away.

With the sun low in the west, quaint sounding places like the Lhen, Smeale and Ballaghennie pass by like ships in the night. For over seven miles, the road has seemed endless, winding its way along the 30-metre contour as we wearily trudge on to the most northerly church.

With nearly 52 miles completed, St. Bridget's

Setting the Scene

church, Bride is not seen until the last moments of approach. The builders of these ancient churches were not only experts in a craft now extinct, but landscape artists too for they favoured pleasant rural surroundings to make this one of the most quintessential villages on the Island.

The brief but strenuous climb from this charming and secluded place is testament to just how weary and fragile our bodies have become since setting off half-a-day ago. With the gradient beginning to ease along the Burma Road, the journey to Andreas is short and straightforward – the defunct World War 2 airfield passed unnoticed as we toil on to the thirteenth church.

Resisting the temptation to stop for sustenance at the only public house in the parish, the journey from Andreas to St Judes is easily accomplished, the winding road following the same contour through fertile land not seen elsewhere.

After crossing the dismantled railway track at Sulby, the route rejoins the TT course from where it aims for the church at Lezayre, two and a half miles further on. With darkness well advanced and the bulk of walkers still to reach this point, the way forward demands the greatest respect. Even at this late hour, the dark tree-lined road is heavy with traffic, headlights often on full beam and a pavement uneven making this the most dangerous section of the entire journey. Locating the nineteenth century church during the black of night is not easy. Set back from the road and hidden from view it is easily passed unnoticed by those unfamiliar with its surroundings.

Christened Royal Ramsey in recognition of Prince Albert's visit in 1847, the most northerly town is our next port of call. Out-and-about and in high spirits, late night revellers in Parliament Square bid farewell as we set out for the lonely road to Maughold.

Although the gradient leaving Ramsey is moderate, the climb to Ballure is testing. Not since leaving Bride three hours earlier has such exertion been required. Most will undertake this tiring journey during the black of night when the dense canopy of trees blocks out light making progress slow in this quietest of places.

Leaving the A2 coast road at its junction with the road to Maughold, the descent to Port Lewaigue is far from easy. Swollen feet pushed forward in their cosy enclosures soon awaken maturing blisters making advance painfully difficult on the descent to the tram track that marks the 65-mile mark.

Situated in idyllic surroundings with extensive views to the Lake Districk, Port e Vullen marks the beginning of a six-mile, back-breaking climb to the Hibernia. Once a thriving community of 30 or so dwellings, it was here in 1860 that the electric telegraph came ashore from the Lake District. The old cable house has long since gone however a roadside tablet promently displayed close to the now defunct Port e Vullen Hotel reads: 'It was at this point on the 18th July, 1644 that nothing happened.'

A place to be reached for there to be any chance of making the finish, the journey from the lowest part of the course to Maughold is far from easy. With the most easterly church, overlooking the tiniest village green, this is a place like no other. Words cannot adequately describe its charm, a centuries-old village in a pleasant rural setting with far-reaching views that are dominated by the graceful outline of North Barrule in the far distance.

From here to Ballajora, the route is neither straightforward or foolproof. An ultimate test of mental ability and physical endurance, it is a back-breaking climb of four miles or more should a wrong turning be taken. A lonely twisting road with a narrow strip of tarmac for the occasional motorist, the way forward is slow and difficult – the thick canopy of trees blocking out all but the faintest of light for the vast majority of walkers who will transit this most tranquil place during the hours of darkness.

Merging with the main Ramsey to Douglas coast road at the 71-mile mark, this is the long-awaited and final stage of our journey, a splendid high level coastal march by way of Laxey and Onchan.

One of 16 public houses en route, the Glen Mona Hotel is quickly reached however only those at the head of the field will be in time for last orders, back-markers instead preferring to take on sustenance at the Dhoon cafe – open until dawn when the last walker goes by.

Although the going from Bulgan becomes easier, the winding road above Laxey seems endless. A pleasant place with charm and character, the old mining town is a mixture of old and new, the giant waterwheel unnoticed as we head for the penultimate church two miles distant.

Only those fronting the field will reach this point before sunset, the journey to Fairy Cottage tedious and the climb to the chuch above the hill punishing.

An excellent vantage point for monitoring those in front and behind, Lonan is the final hurdle to confront with just six miles the difference between success and failure. Nevertheless, they are difficult ones, the terrain undulating with the difficult descent of the White Bridge immediately followed by a back-breaking climb to the seventeenth and final church.

Even at this late stage finishing is by no means certain. Only the strongest and most enterprising walkers will complete this incredible journey on the same day it started. For the rest, the long haul through the night is a daunting prospect and many will fall by the wayside long before dawn.

Nevertheless, for those soldiering on, the painful journey will have been worthwhile, the going now easier as we strike out for Port Jack and the lonely promenade that seems never ending. A lifeless place at dawn but a mecca for all weary pilgrims, it is here at journey's end that we finally find time to shed a tear and celebrate an achievement never thought possible.

1960

Few promotions in the Isle of Man have aroused such public interest as the revived Parish Walk in 1960. Scheduled for an evening 7 o'clock start on Friday 13th May, the long-awaited event saw 35 come to the start line, seven of whom were women.

Young men at the time, Stanley Cleator, Jim and Henry Harvey, Noel Cringle, Bernie May, Michael Gray and Peter Lewthwaite were totally unaware of the demanding physical and mental requirements needed for this Herculean task to walk to all 17 parish churches within a 24-hour time limit. It was a journey into the unknown but also one that would capture the public's imagination like no other.

The drama of the day was the tremendous courage of 16-year-old James Alfred Harvey of Ballamenagh farm, Abbeylands. Entering the race merely to keep his 26-year-old brother company, this slight schoolboy figure with the mop of dark-brown hair was undoubtedly the sensation of the race. 'Fantastic' was how 30-year-old race winner Stanley Cleator described him as the boy walked at Cleator's mature and experienced pace for much of the day. The Douglas postman whose job takes him 16 miles every day was no stranger to foot-slogging and on this occasion the farmer's son stuck to him like a leech. Leading the race, they walked together through night and day.

The appearance of young Harvey was deceptive. He ambled rather than walked, and to spectators lining the roadside, he seemed fragile and destined to retire at any moment.

Excitement was running high on Upper Church where several hundred spectators had gathered at the junction of Hope Street and Myrtle Street eagerly awaiting the start of this extraordinary event last held in 1924.

Most came to the start line straight from work. The three Harvey boys left their farm late that evening and only made it to Douglas with minutes to spare. However, much unwelcome attention focused on 16-year-old Hilary Copner when official starter, and twice-winner Gerald Bridson, protested over her decision to walk barefooted.

The Reverend Bertram Kelly awaited the leaders at Braddan, farmer, Donald Parsonage of Clayhead, Baldrine, the first to arrive in just 21 minutes.

The heavens opened on the climb to the Braaid where Hilary Copner's gallant effort came to an end, the vicar's daughter from Lonan the first of 31 that would eventually call time. From this moment on, the rain just got heavier and what began as a carnival tramp, soon developed into a serious foot-slog.

The flags were out at Santon where the vicar had set out a welcome table of food and drinks. Parsonage was first there in a little over two and a quarter hours, already 11 minutes up on Lewthwaite, Cringle and Gray, still together at this point.

Reaching the most southerly church in 3 hours 55 minutes, Parsonage was the first to tackle the back-breaking climb to the Round Table, a journey of five miles that took the Baldrine farmer 1 hour 11 minutes to complete. Cringle and Gray reached the summit four minutes later with Lewthwaite a further five minutes back.

Truly all seasons in one day, wind, rain and darkness made this most difficult part of the course unpleasant. It was undoubtedly a tough and long haul with only 16 walkers making it to Patrick where the vicar waited patiently. Parsonage was first here in 6 hours 41 minutes but Cringle was on his heels and less than two minutes behind.

One of the finest gestures that evening was at Patrick where Mrs. Lily Clague, of the village corner shop, opened her house and offered appetising food to all and sundry. Both Gray and Lewthwaite stopped here for sustenance leaving Parsonage to romp on to Peel where he arrived at six minutes past two. Cringle touched the church door at St. Germain's four minutes later, his lead over third-placed Gray now extended to eight minutes. Lewthwaite, young Jim Harvey and Stan Cleator were next to reach the eighth church – a mile or so back but seemingly well prepared for what lay ahead.

The pace was punishing on the tiring, twisting road to Kirk Michael where both Parsonage and Cringle were forced to throw in the towel having led for nearly all the way. Leading the race for the next six miles with badly blistered feet, 26-year-old Gray was forced to give up leaving the door firmly open for Cleator and Harvey to take control from this point on.

Welcomed by the pealing of church bells Cleator and Harvey reached the most northerly church in 12 hours 5 minutes – already an hour ahead of Lewthwaite holding third spot but looking unlikely to continue much further. Only eight were left in the race at this point, two of whom were three hours behind and still to reach Jurby.

The Reverend Charles Cannan awaited the arrival of Cleator and Harvey at Andreas.

Together, the pair had walked the Burma Road in 47 minutes, extending their lead over Roscow and Henry Harvey to over an hour. Nearly two hours back,

Upper Church Street, Douglas was the starting point for the first five events of the 1960's.

1960

Top: Henry Harvey and James Roskow leaving Ramsey in 1960.

Below: Stanley Cleator on Douglas Promenade and close to victory in 1960.

Lewthwaite and Eric Culpan were the last of six to reach this point, however the Douglas electrician was a casualty here leaving only five left in the race.

Losing his way soon after Port e Vullen, Cleator eventually turned up on the Old School Road at Dreemskerry. Fortunately, a passing motorcyclist noticed he was missing, the Onchan postman rejoining the road at Ballajora but adding another mile to his already painful journey.

The Reverend George S. Duckworth welcomed the leaders to Maughold – Cleator and Harvey both arriving together in 15 hours 30 minutes. With his card signed and victory just 18 miles away, Cleator struck out alone leaving the boy to make his own way home, scarcely believing he was second on the road with his brother Henry two hours back.

With the sun making its first appearance after hours of torrential rain, Cleator reached Laxey at 12:54pm to lead the race by 16 minutes, this increasing to 19 at Lonan. Young Harvey was still in second place but struggling and looking unlikely to complete the full distance. His brother Henry was still maintaining third spot, some two hours further back, while fourth and last on the road was 45-year-old Culpan, who although walking well, looked doubtful to finish within the 24-hour time limit.

Covering the last six miles in an hour and a half, Cleator was met by a cavalcade of Post Office

motorcycles on Central Promenade. To salutations from hundreds of spectators, he was escorted to the Villa Marina gates by police sergeant Trevor Rimmer, crossing the finish line at 2:05pm having completed 85-miles in 19 hours 50 minutes 30 seconds.

Struggling along Queen's Promenade – so named because it was completed in the year of Queen Victoria's Diamond Jubilee, young Harvey was down to little more than funeral pace and having difficulty in putting one foot ahead of another. Aided with a walking stick and guided by his concerned brothers and sisters, he quickened his pace at the bottom of Broadway before turning into the Villa Marina gates to claim a richly-deserved second place and finish over an hour ahead of his brother.

The fourth and final finisher was Eric Culpan who had walked alone for much of the day. Crossing the finishing line at 7:20pm, his time of 24 hours 20 minutes 30 seconds was outside the limit but in spite of his late finish, he still had time to attend the prize presentation held later that night at the Villa Marina Royal Hall.

An employee of the *Isle of Man Times*, Eric had not trained for this event, and like all others, was unprepared for what lay ahead. Cheerful, Eric had told his wife that he wanted to go on a long walk around the Island because he liked long walks and this was his opportunity to do something other than strolling around Douglas Bay!

The likeable character walked merrily throughout the day and night without the slightest sign of distress or unevenness of pace. He almost appeared to make light work of the whole affair. The reason why he did not win will always remain a mystery. Perhaps he stopped for too many chats, perhaps he spent too much time helping others, or perhaps the moment he took the wrong turning at St. Judes, adding a further two miles to his journey, ruined his chances.

A MEMORABLE DAY

This was a truly memorable day with everyone heroes. All credit must go to the Manx Amateur Athletics Association's president Hadyn Wood for suggesting it and to Arthur Currie and John Quine for promoting it.

For days, if not weeks later, the euphoria of this extraordinary event refused to go away. It was the talk of the Island and no wonder, for it produced demonstrations of courage and determination far exceeding anything ever seen in the Manx sporting calendar.

Although the competitors showed plenty of enthusiasm and a happy spirit throughout, few were experienced in marathon events and nearly all were unaware of the punishing task that lay ahead. Inadequate training took a heavy toll, nevertheless no one gave up without a fight and some of those personal battles were inspiring.

Nearly all were poorly equipped for 20 hours on the road in all weathers. Most had come to the start line with unsuitable clothing and footwear and lacked any understanding of diet and nutrition. Advice on completing the gruelling 85-mile event was not available because no one had ever walked such a long distance before. It had always been assumed that heavy walking-type boots were the key to success, a theory soon dispelled by Michael Gray who pulled out at Jurby with badly blistered feet. Hilary Copner chose not to wear footwear of any kind and spent weeks hardening her feet with methylated spirits only to see her folly end at the seven-mile mark. Peter Lewthwaite's choice of walking in his wedding trousers could have been better, while Sister O'Kane's diet of glucose tablets supplemented with hot coffee and brandy was a recipe for disaster.

But there was no lack of cheerfulness and the quality that is best described as sheer guts was in plentiful supply. The youngsters in the race were a credit to their generation with Graham Young not even 15, a boy in a man's race!

And not only did the competitors display a degree of sportsmanship which is all too rare in these days. Men and women too, from all walks of life, rallied to the aid of the competitors. Workmates, friends and neighbours joined in to keep them company through the long night, some for short distances in relays, others for longer spells on the lonely roads.

But when it was all over and a young postman won in convincing style, there were grouses, not from the competitors but from the onlookers. The prizes should have been worthy of the occasion it was said.

It is doubtful that competitors entered with any thought of reward. They took part because the event represented a challenge to the youth of the Island, and some not so young, who acquitted themselves with credit. They accepted that challenge gladly, gallantly, and it matters not if most fell by the wayside. The spirit was there, though the flesh may have been proven too weak for so tough an endurance test.

A few days later, John Quirk, sports correspondent for the *Isle of Man Times*, light-heartedly wrote:

Well, I walked ... and ... walked ... and walked. Past the Quarter Bridge and along the Braddan straight, light of step and full of the joys of spring. On to Union Mills and Crosby, thoroughly enjoying the new road surface which made walking a pleasure. That is until I came to the turn for the long haul up the Glen Darragh Road and on to the winding Clannagh Road at Santon. Tired? Not a bit, Blackboards, Ballasalla, Four Roads, Arbory and Rushen – all were passed with ease before taking the back-breaking climb to the Sloc and on to the Round Table for a welcome cup of soup and a cigarette.

The blinding rain deterred me not, nor the cold tugging at my plastic coat as I stepped light-heartedly down the hill to Juan-y-Clarey's Bridge in the direction of Dalby, Glen Maye, Patrick and Peel.

As the sun climbed the eastern sky, it warmed me on my journey northward through Kirk Michael, Ballaugh, Jurby, Bride and Andreas with another welcome pause for refreshments prior to the long journey home and still fresh as a daisy with ten minutes in hand.

Parish Walk? Up to then one of the easiest walks I have had with people dropping out all over the place with fatigue, sprains, pains, boredom arching muscles, rheumatism, lumbago and a host of other minor ailments!

As for my companions and me, we never felt better as we set off laughingly for Lezayre and the winding road through Ramsey to Maughold, Ballajora, Cornaa and up the steep incline to the Hibernia joining the road leading to the church high on the hill above Lonan.

A glorious day and still fit for another 85 miles! By this time of course, the field had thinned down considerably, but those of us left strode resolutely onwards, keeping in view the tall and welcome spire of Onchan church which we soon passed as we hurried down Royal Avenue towards the Villa Marina and on to success.

Thus my companions and I finished the long journey without one ache, pain, or sign of fatigue. After all, why should we? The only way to do the Parish Walk is the way we did – sitting in a comfortable seat in a local hostelry with pints of foaming beer on the table and our imagination running riot!

I now look forward to the next marathon affair – a walk to all the pubs around the circuit, organised I hope by the Licensed Victuallers Association. With the prospect of visiting 45 public houses this should literally be a staggering affair!

1961

With the overwhelming success of the revived Parish Walk still fresh in the memory of many, the Manx Amateur Athletics Association, under the leadership of its president, Hadyn Wood, unaminously agreed to stage the event again in 1961.

On this occasion prizes would be awarded to the top three placings in both the men's and ladies' classes. Seven guineas, five guineas and three guineas was a considerable sum in those day's and comparable to a labourer's weekly wage. A prize for the greatest mileage covered by a team of four was also introduced.

Starting from the junction of Hope Street and Myrtle Street on Friday 28th April, the event attracted an entry of 89, 24 of whom were women.

Sent on their way by the Mayor of Douglas, Alderman T.K. Quirk at 7:00pm prompt, the leaders wasted no time, reaching the first church at Braddan six minutes ahead of last year's time. Leading the field were Herbert Cannell of Trollaby Farm, Union Mills, W.E. Harvey, William Cain and Rodney Castle, already two minutes ahead with Donald Parsonage, Henry and Jim Harvey next. Cleator was three minutes back, while Helen Callow led the girls in thirteenth place.

Maintaining the pace to Santon, Cain reached St.

1961

Top: First of three victories for Abbeylands farmer Henry Harvey.

Below: Henry Harvey under the watchful eye of Philip Caley.

Santain's parish church in just under two hours, some 20 minutes quicker than last year. Castle and W.E. Harvey were with him followed by Cannell who had dropped to fourth place three minutes in arrears. Brothers Henry and Jim Harvey were next to reach the 11-mile with Parsonage a further six minutes behind. Cleator and Stephen Christian arrived next but over a mile behind the leader. The leading girls, Barbara Stacey, Betty Coward and Heather Lewin were also losing ground at this early stage having been on the road for 2 hours 21 minutes.

With darkness well advanced, Parsonage stopped at the Blackboards for warm clothing. Cain, Castle and W.E. Harvey were the leaders through Malew in a time of 2 hours 38 minutes, which was 21 minutes up on last year. Cannell was on his own in fourth place and four minutes behind, with Henry and Jim Harvey 16 minutes back. Cleator and Christian were joint seventh, 19 minutes in arrears. Behind them came J. Brown, D. Dow, Parsonage and Bernie May.

Cain and Harvey were first through Arbory in 3 hours 2 minutes with Castle a minute back followed by Cannell four minutes later. Henry and Jim Harvey were a further 17 minutes in arrears followed by Cleator and Christian five minutes later. Parsonage was now ninth but his brief stop cost him dearly for he now trailed the leaders by 24 minutes.

With three retirements registered already, the 81 who made it to the most southerly parish were greeted at the church gate by the Reverend William George Squire. Cain and Harvey were first to this point in a time of 3 hours 34 minutes, some six minutes ahead of Trollaby farmer, Herbie Cannell who clearly looked like a man on a mission. Castle arrived a quarter of an hour later followed by Henry and Jim Harvey at 18 minutes with Parsonage and Cleator at 25 minutes. The first girl there was Pat Leather in twenty-sixth place with a time of 4 hours 17 minutes 30 seconds.

The punishing climb over the Sloc took its toll on Cain and Castle, both slowing considerably on the long haul to the Round Table. W.E. Harvey then took the lead and joined Cannell on the winding road to Patrick. They arrived at the seventh church in 6 hours 05 minutes with a 14-minute lead over Henry and Jim Harvey. Cleator was fifth, seven minutes behind, then came May, Christian, Kewley Quayle, Castle and Lewthwaite. Over an hour separated the first 11

walkers. Many of the girls declined the challenge of the Sloc leaving Standen, Cowell, Corkill, O'Kane and Morrison to continue the female competition.

Ending his ordeal at Patrick church after eight hours, 61-year-old Edward Moore was the the oldest walker in the race.

At Peel, Cannell and W.E. Harvey clocked 6 hours 25 minutes with the Harvey brothers 17 minutes back. Cleator was the next to enter the western capital at 22 minutes followed by May, Kewley, Quayle and Castle – the latter man over an hour back.

Cannell continued to lead at Kirk Michael, reaching that point in the black of night at 2:42am. In second place, Henry Harvey was now making his bid having reduced the deficit to 13 minutes. But the punishing pace was too much for his brother, W.E. Harvey, who called time at Devil's Elbow leaving Cleator to take up third spot, 24 minutes in arrears. In fourth spot, 15 minutes back, Jim Harvey was being pressed hard by May, Quayle, Kewley and Gray soon to reach the 39-mile mark.

The pattern of the race was now set. Harvey and Cannell were clearly out to demolish the Cleator challenge, but the postman, for the most part unaccompanied in contrast to the others who usually had friends walking alongside, gallantly forged on half expecting that the tremendous pace of the leaders would bring them to a halt.

Cannell was first into Jurby where he arrived in 8 hours 58 minutes. He had a 12-minute lead over Henry Harvey and was now half an hour ahead of Cleator, with Jim Harvey fourth and May fifth.

The punishing walk through the most northerly parish took its toll on Cannell. He arrived at St. Bridget's Parish Church at 5:25am but only leading by five minutes. With the skies brightening to the east Harvey quickened his pace as if he were hurrying to catch the last train. Cleator was 38 minutes behind at this stage but well ahead of his 1960 time with Jim Harvey, Quayle, May and Kewley arriving next.

Cannell went slower and slower along the monotonous Burma Road leading to Andreas. Dawn was breaking as the Trollaby farmer touched the gate to the thirteenth church at 6:01am. He was now only six minutes ahead of Harvey with Cleator a further 36 minutes behind.

The 'galloping' Harvey now took the lead through Lezayre where he arrived at the fourteenth church in 12 hours 17 minutes and leading Cannell by eight minutes. Cleator was going well in third place, half an hour behind the leader with Jim Harvey now fourth.

At Maughold, Henry Harvey led comfortably having walked the 67 miles in 13 hours 24 minutes. His lead had grown to 13 minutes over Cannell and 36 over Cleator – the postman reaching this point at 9:00am.

Although a considerable distance back, the ladies were still circulating with Kathy O'Kane the first of the fairer sex to reach the 71-mile mark at the Hibernia. Sadly, her hopes were dashed four miles on at the

Dhoon where her gallant effort came to an end.

Harvey hurried on to Lonan, arriving at the sixteenth church at 10:50am and nearly an hour ahead of Cannell who was now barely moving. Cleator was still in good shape, overhauling Cannell who seemed beyond redemption on the approach road to the penultimate church.

But time was finally up for the Trollaby farmer. Bleeding and unfit to continue, his courageous effort came to an end at the church high on the hill above Lonan. Kewley and May were also in trouble leaving only nine in the race.

Harvey reached Onchan in 16 hours 45 minutes and the finish line at the Villa Marina gates 27 minutes later. To his surprise few had turned out to meet him for he arrived two hours earlier than expected!

Stanley Cleator was next over the finishing line, his time of 18 hours 18 minutes 01 seconds nearly an hour and a half quicker than his winning time last year.

Claiming the coveted third spot with a superb time of 20 hours 29 minutes 45 seconds, 17-year-old Jim Harvey made it two finishes in a row, comfortably edging out Daryl Gribbin by nearly an hour.

There were also first-time finishes for Michael Gray, Allan Corlett, Douglas Vernon, James Corlett and Terry Crellin – the latter man unfortunately exceeding the 24-hour time limit by nearly five minutes.

After the huge success of the 1961 event, the committee of the Manx Amateur Athletic Association decided to run a junior relay event over the same distance four weeks later. Competitors were split into two sections – 14 years of age and under 17, and 17 years of age and under 20. The event was open to youth club teams of four including boys, girls and mixed. The first team member took the leg from St. George's Church in Douglas to Rushen church in the south – a distance of 19 miles. For the second member, a gruelling back-breaking climb over the Sloc had first to be undertaken before embarking on the relatively easy downhill section from the Round Table to Patrick, St. Germain's and Kirk Michael – a distance of 20 miles. A longer, but easier journey of 24 miles faced the third member of the team who set off from the 39-mile mark, proceeding north to Ballaugh, Jurby, Bride, Andreas, Lezayre, finishing at the Northern Youth Centre in Ramsey.

Considered to be the most difficult section, Ramsey to Douglas was usually set aside for the team's fittest walker. The 22-mile leg took in the parishes of Maughold, Lonan and Onchan to finish at the war memorial on Douglas Promenade.

Unlike the Parish Walk, the junior relay race allowed pacers and proved popular until 1968 when a fatality forced organisers to abandon the event. The deceased, a 17-year-old youth from Douglas High School, had been acting as a pacer when he was struck by a passing car while walking alongside a competitor on the Peel to Kirk Michael coast road

Henry Harvey receiving the winner's trophy from Manx Amateur Athletics Club President Haydn Wood.

1962

near Ballakaighen Farm, German.

With the overwhelming success of the first two events, race walking quickly became flavour of the month. Walking clubs began forming – Onchan United Harriers were the first but were soon followed by Boundary Harriers, Laxey Heralds and Malew Beagles.

The idea of Braddan farmer Herbet Cannell, the Boundary Harriers was founded by breakaway members of the Manx Amatuer Athletic Association. At their inaugural meeting at the Quarter Bridge Hotel in November 1961, a committee was elected consisting of brothers Tom and Peter Lewthwaite, Herbie Cannell, Michael Gray, Allan Corlett, Terry Crellin and Fadge Christian.

After referring to a dictionary for correct definition, the Lewthwaite brothers took credit for chosing the name Boundary Harriers because it sounded sporty and athletic. Peter also liked the word boundary as many members were expected to join from outside Douglas.

Within weeks of formation, their first event was the Peel to Douglas Walk, held in December 1961. The ten-mile road race started at Peel Town Hall and finished at the Quarter Bridge. Bernie May, of Onchan United Harriers, was first over the line in 1 hour 32 minutes 10 seconds, some 12 minutes quicker than Joan Cannell of the Boundary Harriers and winner of the ladies' event.

The was quickly followed up in February 1962 by the Boundary Stroll, a supposedly sedate ten-mile walking event that started at the Legion Hall, Pulrose and followed the New Castletown Road to the Cooil, Braaid, Foxdale, Ballacraine, Quarter Bridge to end back at the starting point. The Lewthwaite brothers may have chosen the name but stroll it was not. It was infact a back-breaking slog that tested the very best.

The club then participated in inter-club walking events such as the End to End Walk, Parish Walk Relay, TT Course Relay, Harvest Moon Race, Mountain Marathon, TT Course Walk, Peel Hill Run, Greeba Fell Race, Wheel Barrow Championship and Lhergy Cripperty one mile Hill Climb – all of which contributed to the demise of the Manx Amateur Athletics Association who then reluctantly merged with their rival in 1967.

1962

In a bid to attract even greater attention, the Manx Amateur Athletics Association gave the Parish Walk a new look in 1962 with the ladies starting at 6:30pm followed by the men an hour and a half later.

In a display of race walking intelligence at its very best, Henry Harvey, the lean fast-striding farmer from Ballamenagh, Abbeylands, annihilated all opposition to win his second record-breaking Parish Walk convincingly. However, the 28-year-old was a reluctant hero and came close to retiring at St. Patrick's Parish Church, Jurby when contesting the lead with Leece Kneale of Laxey.

After his runaway victory, Henry recalled the moment he was close to defeat. 'Dawn was breaking and I just felt fed up and wanted to pack it in' he said. Nevertheless, with the family honour at stake he was persuaded to continue by his 20-year-old brother, Edwin.

None of the ladies managed to complete the course – the best effort coming from Nurse Sadie Goldsmith who reached the 71-mile mark at the Hibernia before admitting defeat.

Not only in the men's race was the pace a devastating one. In the ladies' event, 17-year-old Jane Waters, of Victoria Avenue, Douglas led the field until her retirement at Patrick. From there to Andreas, 19-year-old Irene Cottier of Patrick and Ivy Griffin of Crosby dominated the race.

This year, weather conditions were more favourable with the event getting underway on the evening of Friday 27th April. Nineteen girls had taken up the gauntlet, their hairstyles as varied as their outfits. One girl sported a large bouffant, which later sagged noticeably.

Eighteen-year-old Hazel Taubman of Nobles Hospital was the first to reach Kirk Braddan. In a time of only 22 minutes, she had covered the two miles pressed hard by Jane Waters of Onchan United Harriers, just ten seconds back. The 17-year-old was walking in tandem with Mrs. E. Forsythe, a 54-year-old grandmother from Jurby with little experience at walking any distance, let alone 85 miles.

The two WRAF girls from Jurby, Eunice Davies and Pat O'Sullivan, were next to check in at the first church with the rest not far behind. Taubman took 56 minutes to reach Marown but hot on her heels came Waters, Forsythe and the two WRAF girls, followed by O'Kane, Cottier and Griffin – a trio representing the Boundary Harriers 'A' team.

By the time the 64 men started at 8:00pm, both sides of Circular Road leading to the Brown Bobby were lined with spectators by the hundreds, eagerly

A second win for Henry Harvey.

awaiting this great spectacle to unfold. Cars by the dozen choked the Peel Road which looked like the road from Brighton to London on a bank holiday. Everything and everyone was moving out of town!

At Quarter Bridge, the field was already beginning to spread out with Trollaby farmer Herbie Cannell of the Boundary Harriers 'A' team, first to touch the church door at Braddan in 17 minutes 25 seconds. Charles Cannell of the Malew Beagles, and Ballabeg farmer Noel Cringle were next to the two-mile mark quickly followed by Stanley Cleator of the Onchan United Harriers – winner in 1960 and runner-up last year.

The leading group were together on the Old Castletown Road. Henry Harvey, last year's winner and member of the Manx Amateur Athletic Club's team, finally drawing level with his old rival Cleator on the approach to Santon church, a point he reached in 1 hour 53 minutes. Two minutes later came Jim Harvey, second in 1960 and third last year. The 18-year-old-year had a two-minute lead over Leece Kneale and strode along with effortless style.

The great motorcade of cars followed the walkers on the short leg from Santon to Malew. Although the ladies had started 90 minutes earlier, the leading trio of Jane Waters, Ivy Griffin and Irene Cottier were being pressed hard by the men with Harvey and Cleator the first to check in at Malew at 10:50pm. Jim Harvey was now third followed by Leece Kneale, Norman Senogles and Herbie Cannell.

Two miles further on at Arbory, the order of the first four ladies had not changed. Waters checked in at 10:10pm, Griffin and Cottier at 10:12pm and O'Kane at 10:14pm.

Harvey and Cleator checked in to the fifth church together at 10:50pm – their lead over Kneale and Jim Harvey stretched to five minutes. Senogles was five minutes further back followed by sixth-placed Cannell who touched the church door at one minute past 11.

The leading ladies reached Rushen in total darkness. Waters arrived at 10:45pm with a two-minute lead over Cottier and Griffin. O'Kane was fourth at 10:51pm, Goldsmith at 10:59pm and Taubman 11:04pm. Jurby's youthful grandmother, 54-year-old Mrs. E. Forsythe was striding out determinedly in eighth place, 25 minutes down on the leader, however the two-girl team from RAF Jurby halved at this point when blistered feet forced Pat O'Sullivan out of the race.

Even at this late hour, all roads leading to the southernmost church were choked with cars, vans, motorcycles, cyclists and pedestrians – all eager to witness this incredible happening.

Cleator and Harvey continued their elbow-to-elbow duel, and it was reflected in their pace. At Rushen, they were 12 minutes up on schedule, arriving at 11:18pm and now ahead of the slower ladies. Kneale was holding third place, six minutes behind, with young Jim Harvey a further three minutes in arrears. Senogles touched the church door at 11:32pm closely followed by Cannell in sixth place.

But there were many retirements at the 19½-mile mark with James Russell, Robert Cowley and William Skillicorn all ending their ordeal and going no further. Sixteen-year-old Brian Rae checked in at the sixth church at 11:47pm, continuing on to Ballakillowey but then returning at 12:20am to announce his retirement.

Although well past midnight, stragglers were still wending their way to Rushen where the Reverend William George Squire continued to wait patiently. Ernie Broadbent of Droghadfayle Road, Port Erin, was one of the last to arrive at this point but still had a band of loyal supporters to cheer him all the way to the church door.

A total of 50 men and 17 women made it to the most southerly church, however the hardest section was soon to follow. For many, the killing climb to the Round Table and beyond was nothing short of torture. Tired and weary with endless miles of dark, uninviting countryside ahead, many of those continuing from this point were forced to admit defeat long before daylight.

Harvey took over the lead at Ballakillowey and hurried on to Patrick arriving at the seventh church in 5 hours 29 minutes, already half an hour ahead of schedule. He had taken 2 hours 44 minutes for the 11-mile uphill slog and was leading Kneale by three minutes with Cleator a further minute behind.

Reaching the western capital 21 minutes later, Harvey was first to the door at St. Germain's church where he was met by a large reception committee of young people eager to greet the early walkers. Although walking in an assuming and effortless way, only four minutes separated the leading trio making this a difficult race to call at this stage.

Overtaken by the leading men at Eary Cushlin, the two girls, Irene Cottier and Ivy Griffin, were next to

Henry Harvey congratulating Stanley Cleator who was the runner-up.

Start of the 1962 Parish Walk Relay.

Nancy Harvey keeping a watchful eye over brother Henry.

1962

reach the eighth church – 18 minutes adrift and unable to reduce the deficit.

Relentlessly, Kneale whittled down Harvey's hard-won lead. At Peel it had been two minutes; by Kirk Michael the margin was down to a minute and it seemed that the Laxey flier must catch the record holder in the next mile or two.

But Harvey found a champion's reserve of energy and pulled out that little bit extra to stretch his lead to two minutes at Ballaugh. Kneale was not to be denied however, and at Jurby he caught and stayed with Harvey, checking in at the lonely church of St. Patrick at quarter past four with daybreak still an hour away. Cleator was holding a secure third place with no one near enough to worry him. Bernie May lay fourth, with Jim Harvey and Norman Senogles marching step by step but nearly an hour down on the leader.

Irene Cottier and Ivy Griffin continued to lead the ladies' race, both reaching the 45-mile mark at 5:20am. Although chased hard by the gallant ward sister from Nobles Hospital, O'Kane lost her 'third time lucky' bid to become the first woman to complete the course, when she was forced out at Jurby. Her surprise departure elevated Eunice Davies into third place, however the WRAF girl was trailing far behind and unlikely to close the gap.

As night turned to day, only half the field remained. Stragglers were spread far and wide with many still to reach the halfway mark at Ballaugh.

At Jurby, the sun rose like a giant fireball warming the walkers after their long overnight ordeal. Dawn chorus filled the still morning air as early risers peered along the road from their doorsteps wishing the walkers well for the long and painful journey ahead.

Overhauling Harvey on the tiring road to Bride, Kneale was first to the most northerly church in 9 hours 45 minutes. Harvey was nine minutes back with Cleator next to the church as the clock struck six.

May was next to check in at the 52-mile mark but his legs were in poor shape and from this point on he went no further. Joint third, Jim Harvey and Norman Senogles looked like going the full distance but both still 35 minutes down on the leader.

With the clock showing 6:19am outside the primary school at Andreas, Kneale was now holding a 14-minute lead over Harvey who lost considerable time on the Burma Road re-fastening his shoes. Cheered on by his many admirers, the Abbeylands farmer increased his pace on the way to Sulby Bridge, managing to cut the deficit to 11 minutes at Lezayre.

People were up and about in Ramsey as the leaders passed through Parliament Square en route to the fifteenth church. Kneale was still in the lead and giving little indication of what was soon to come. Harvey was next to leave Ramsey, followed by Cleator, Senogles, and young Jim Harvey. However, the youngster was in trouble with badly blistered feet, his gallant walk coming to an end on the Ballure Road.

At Maughold church, Leece Kneale had his card

signed by the Reverend George Duckworth. Then, to the surprise of the spectators, suddenly announced, 'that's it – I've had enough' and then promptly retired, his badly blistered feet making it impossible for him to continue. At the time, he had been leading Harvey by ten minutes but the Abbeylands farmer now had a new lease of life, and changing into shorts and a vest, upped his pace on this most difficult section to arrive at Lonan five minutes ahead of nearest challenger Cleator.

Behind the postman followed the fair-haired Senogles, in third place and going well on his own, having covered most of the walk in the company of Jim Harvey.

Harvey hurried on to Onchan where he touched the door at St. Peter's parish church at three minutes past noon. Retracing his steps to the top of Royal Avenue, he wasted no time on the fast descent to Port Jack where a large group of onlookers cheered him on to the finish no more than a mile away.

Greeted by the Mayor, Alderman T.A. Quirk at the Broadway entrance to the Villa Marina, Henry had little to say although it was obvious by looking at the faces of his brothers and sisters crowding round him that the family were justly proud of his brilliant win. Completing the 85-mile course in 16 hours 25 minutes 40 seconds, he beat his previous winning time by nearly three-quarters of an hour. In recognition of his superb performance, Henry was also awarded the prize for the first male competitor to catch up with the leading woman who had started 90 minutes earlier.

Cleator was second to finish in 17 hours 22 minutes 16 seconds followed by Norman Senogles over an hour later. Seventeen-year-old David Brew of Ballaugh was fourth in 19 hours 55 minutes with Peter Lewthwaite fifth. His third attempt in as many years and his shoes in pieces, Peter reached the ultimate goal at 7:45pm but was too tired to attend the presentation held shortly after in the Villa Marina Ballroom.

In sixth and final position, 24-year-old Bob Kewley completed his epic journey but over one hour outside the time limit. It was a great personal triumph for the Santon farmer, who two years earlier was seriously injured in a motor accident, breaking a leg in three places and sustaining other significant injuries.

The chances of one of the women competitors finishing the course for the first time diminished at Andreas as lady race-leader, Irene Cottier, was forced to a standstill at 8:05am by an extremely painful leg muscle strain. This left Ivy Griffin and Eunice Davies to dispute the lead. However, they too stopped at the 69-mile mark leaving Sadie Goldsmith as the only contender until her retirement two miles further on at the Hibernia.

1963

The daunting task of walking through the Island's 17 parishes was not made easy in 1963 when the coldest winter in living memory seriously disrupted training routines for the forthcoming event.

Four men who had dominated the first three places in the Parish Walk since 1960, Henry Harvey, Stanley Cleator, Jim Harvey and Norman Senogles, all failed to make their mark in the 1963 event, held over Friday and Saturday 26th and 27th April.

The race was the second fastest ever and won by Joe Brown of Menorca, Laxey in a time of 17 hours 04 minutes 09 seconds.

By far the outstanding performances of the day were those from Flight Sergeant Eunice Davies of Jurby and Irene Cottier of Patrick, who became the first women ever to complete the exhausting 85-mile journey. Eunice completed the course in 20 hours 51 minutes 24 seconds and Irene in 22 hours 54 minutes 10 seconds.

Runner-up to the strongly finishing Joe Brown was Willie Kneale of Ballasalla in 17 hours 20 minutes 31 seconds and third-placed man was Douglas Corkill also from Ballasalla, in 19 hours 11 minutes 28 seconds. Fourth and final place went to Mitch Joughin of Spring Valley in 20 hours 41 minutes 45 seconds.

The veterans' relay walk, for those aged 45 years or more, was won by George Stacey, George Craine, Arthur Jones and Eric Culpan in a time 19 hours 11 minutes 28 seconds.

It was a race of which every finisher could feel intensely proud. It was also a race that eliminated the top stars before the three-quarter distance mark.

If any or all of the competitors had called it a day after groping their way through the mist shrouded Sloc, or indeed suffered the soaking of the incessant rain in the early hours of the morning, they would have heard no words of recrimination from those who followed this 1963 epic walk.

Rain clouds were gathering as the 12 lady competitors left St. George's Church, Douglas at 6:30pm prompt. Flight Sergeant Eunice Davies was first to reach Braddan church, some three minutes up on Joan Cannell and Irene Cottier who both stayed together in their attempt to overhaul the fleet-footed Flight Sergeant.

At 8:00pm, and with the leading lady fast approaching the eight-mile mark on the Clannagh Road, 62 male competitors were sent on their way by the Speaker of the House of Keys, Mr. H.C. Kerruish.

Much interest was shown in the Scots Guards contingent as they marched in close formation along the Peel Road, their royal blue tracksuits giving them equal conspicuousness as their 'regulation paced' progress.

The soldiers did not appear to be hurrying as they marched on to the first parish. At Braddan church, the swift-moving, lithe John Tasker of Ballasalla and his Malew Beagles colleague, Brian Shooter, were already a minute up on Joe Cain. The next to this point were Ken Sloane, Joe Brown, Henry Harvey, Herbie Cannell, Ken Christian, Norman Senogles, Leece Kneale and young Jim Harvey.

Tasker was the first of the men to reach Marown, arriving at the new church at 8:39pm having completed four miles and already one minute ahead of his nearest challenger, Brian Shooter.

Nevertheless, the pace was already beginning to tell for at Santon, Tasker complained of stiffness in his thighs. He was not aware at this time that his colleague Brian Shooter had retired and that the slender, bespectacled Leece Kneale of Laxey was but three minutes behind him. Retirements were few and far between at this point. However, Cecil Keig went no further than the Braaid while Joe Cain ended his

Joe Brown of Laxey was first to the finish line in 1963.

1963

ordeal on the road to Arbory.

Tasker continued to lead the field through the southern parishes, but his pain increased making him the first casualty at Arbory.

Kneale took over the lead at the 16-mile mark but not far behind came Laxey Herald's representatives, Joe Brown and Norman Senogles. Henry Harvey was next to this point, followed by Willie Kneale, Stanley Cleator, Willie Cain, Alf Crowe, Ken Sloane and Bernie May.

Eunice Davies continued to lead the field, reaching the whitewashed church at Rushen shortly after 10:30pm. Nevertheless, her starting advantage of 90 minutes soon eroded as Leece Kneale made his challenge on the leadership. It had been a fast pace on the journey south with Kneale the first man to arrive at the most southerly church at 11:15pm. Joe Brown was next to reach this point, fractionally ahead of Norman Senogles and the much-fancied Henry Harvey who seemed content with his pace and progress. Willy Kneale, Stanley Cleator, Willie Cain, Ian Turnbull and Alf Crowe were the next walkers to reach the 19½-mile mark, however the many retirements at this point included Ian Turnbull, John Comaish, Donald Johnson and Vivien Pedder.

Despite bad weather across the Island, large numbers of spectators braved the elements to cheer on those undertaking this daunting task. The Scots Guardsmen were still together and marching with precise regularity. They were a pleasure to watch, and their smart footwork overshadowed the performance of the RAF quartet who seemed content to take it easy knowing there was still a long way to go.

In atrocious weather conditions, Eunice Davies led the field over the infamous Sloc. By midnight, the uphill, twisting road was aglow with the headlamps of service cars making their way to the summit in rain and swirling mist. It was cold and miserable with the walkers eager to press on to Patrick where conditions were better. Nevertheless, the climb to the Round Table took a heavy toll on those who were unprepared.

Though tipped by many as capable of gaining a hat-trick of wins, the quiet and genial Henry Harvey was a retirement at Patrick church where he returned his card and race number to surprised officials. The Abbeylands farmer had felt unwell since leaving Rushen and severe dehydration forced him to go no further than the 30-mile mark.

There were retirements too for Joyce Crellin, Eddie Arrowsmith, Douglas Airgy, Alf Crowe, Pat Caine, Dave Shimmin, Bernie May, Ed Kennaugh, detective Alan Killip, Peter May and postman Charles Gale.

Eunice Davies was the first to check in at the eighth church and without doubt the heroine so far, and already an hour ahead of Joan Cannell and Irene Cottier. Her effortless striding through the mist, rain and darkness had captured the hearts of many and she never lost one whit of her charm or cheerfulness.

Leece Kneale was second to arrive at Peel at 1:50am and only 17 minutes adrift of the leading

Top: Eunice Davies was the first ever lady finisher.

Above: Approaching Lonan, 19-year-old Graham Young was the second of six finishers in 1964.

lady. Willie Kneale was a further five minutes in arrears, then came Norman Senogles, Stanley Cleator, Daryl Gribbin, Willie Cain, Herbie Cannell and young Jim Harvey.

But Kneale was in a bad way on the A4 coast road to Kirk Michael. His badly blistered feet prevented him from going beyond the ninth church where the Reverend John Foster waited patiently. Norman Senogles was another casualty at this point leaving Joe Brown to take control.

With the road to Ballaugh free of traffic, Joe was the first to reach the halfway mark as the skies brightened in the east. The Laxey painter checked in at the 42-mile mark at 3:42am, some eight minutes ahead of Willie Kneale and Eunice Davies, now walking together.

Brown and Kneale continued as front-runners to St. Patrick's Church, Jurby with the leading lady not far behind. Many colleagues from the RAF camp turned out to greet her, and although tired, Eunice set off cheerfully on the long seven-mile journey to Bride with dawn soon to break.

Despite the coming of the morning light, the rain persisted in making life miserable for the leading trio now well on their way to Bride. In hot pursuit and eager to win this event for a second time, Cleator soldiered on bravely however blistered feet forced the Douglas postman to throw in the towel at the most northerly church.

The weather continued to take its toll on the dwindling field with only two of the five Guardsmen reaching the 39½-mile mark at Kirk Michael. For those fortunate to be still going, the early morning opening of the Lhen café was a welcome sight, however Joan Cannell was a casualty here, leaving Irene Cottier to continue alone.

Torrential rain swept across the northern plain and few people waited at Andreas to see the leading trio through. Brown checked in at the 55-mile mark at 6:26am, Kneale at 6:43am and Davies at 7:29am. Brown was definitely quickening his pace towards St. Jude's for he was now 19 miles ahead of the last man on the road who checked in at Kirk Michael as the clock struck seven.

Brown was first to Maughold, reaching the most easterly church at 8:55am and 12 minutes ahead of Willie Kneale. He in turn was slightly over an hour ahead of Eunice Davies and Douglas Corkill, both contesting third place. Only 15 walkers remained in the race – 12 men and three women.

With weather conditions improving at the 67-mile mark, Mr. H.C. Kerruish, Speaker of the House of Keys, had an 'open house' with tea and coffee served to race officials and early leaders as they progressed south to the penultimate parish.

Brown reached Lonan church at 11:35am. By the time he rejoined the main Laxey to Douglas road, his nearest challenger, Willie Kneale, was walking up to Fairy Cottage and most unlikely to mount a serious challenge at this late stage.

In the meantime, Eunice Davies had arrived at

A third victory for Henry Harvey in 1964.

1964

Bulgham, the furthest any lady competitor had travelled in a Parish Walk to date. Walking quite effortlessly with her assistant, Sergeant Radcliffe, she gave a smile to all who wished her well. With no change in the leader board from this point on, Brown pressed on to the finish to claim a well derserved victory in 17 hours 04 minutes 09 seconds.

Kneale crossed the finish line at the Douglas War Memorial 16 minutes later but nearly an hour and three-quarters ahead of third-placed Douglas Corkill.

Occupying fourth spot in 20 hours 45 minutes 45 seconds, Michael Joughin had to work hard over the closing stages to hold off Eunice Davies, the first woman ever to finish this event, her time of 20 hours 51 minutes 24 seconds over two hours quicker than Irene Cottier who was sixth. Soaked to the skin at the penultimate church, Irene had been close to throwing in the towel and only words of assurance from husband, Dickie, persuaded her to continue.

Welcomed at the Villa Marina by the Mayor, Councillor T.A. Corkish, JP, MHK, the six finishers received a standing ovation from the many well-wishers gathered. Mr. J.H.T. Wood, President of the Manx Athletic Club, presented the awards later in the evening with assistance from club chairman, Mr. A.J. Currie.

In spite of appalling weather through much of the day, the event had run smoothly and much credit must go to Mr. Brian Whitehead, Secretary of the Manx Amateur Athletic Club and controller of the race, along with his large group of helpers.

Later in the year at the Annual General Meeting of the Boundary Harriers, new officials were appointed. Arthur Currie took up the post as president, with Dennis Lace the chairman. Ian Turnbull and George Bannan put their administrative skills to good use as joint secretaries, while George

Quayle assumed the role of treasurer. Founder member Herbie Cannell took up the position of club manager while Mitch Joughin and Irene Cottier were elected for dual captaincy.

1964

Now in its fifth year and easily the most anticipated athletic event in the Manx sporting calendar, the Parish Walk of 1964 attracted its biggest entry to date with 85 competitors setting out on the well-trodden route. A new starting time of 7:00pm was introduced for the ladies with the men following an hour later.

After last year's disappointing race, Henry Harvey shattered all opposition to score his third Parish Walk win in four years with a new record time of 16 hours 21 minutes 06 seconds.

In contention with the leaders during the early stages, the Abbeylands farmer walked the race his way – storming to the front on the lower slopes of the Sloc and stretching his lead to nearly one hour at the halfway stage.

The race fell to pieces in the latter stages with previous winners Stanley Cleator and Joe Brown both falling by the wayside.

Nineteen-year-old Graham Young was the runner-up, some three hours later, with Ken Christian a further 33 minutes back in third spot.

Only six completed the gruelling 85-mile circuit within the 24-hour time limit with Northern Ireland's John Adair, Clarence Cheney and Heather Murphy completing the leader board.

The junction of Hope Street and Myrtle Street was packed to capacity on the evening of Friday 17th April. From the time Councillor J.H.T. Wood lowered his flag at 8:00pm to start the men's event, the early pace was set by George Bannan using rather similar

1964

Above: George Bannan leading the way before retiring on the Sloc.

Below: Douglas postmen John Cannell and Graham Young were victorious on eight occasions.

tactics to those of John Tasker the previous year.

Even at this late hour, the road to Quarter Bridge was heavily congested with vehicles barely moving in order to catch a glimpse of this great happening that had caught the public's imagination as never before.

Bannan was the first to arrive at Braddan church and was already a minute up on Bobby Kaneen, Doug Allan and Ulsterman Clarence Cheney. He continued his incredible pace to Marown church, clocking in at 8:38pm and already five minutes in front of a leading pack headed by Cheney, Kaneen, Brown, Cleator and Kneale. Next to the second church were Henry Harvey and John Cannell, with Eddie Kennaugh a further minute back.

Setting his sights on all churches south, Bannan's ultra fast pace of 6 mph was having an adverse effect on the leading men. They were keen to stay with the leader and prevent him from opening a bigger gap but this played havoc with their schedule of arrival times at the various churches.

But things did not go exactly to plan for Bannan either. In his haste to reach Santon church, he went astray shortly after New Town and missed the turn-off for Oatlands, the road that joins the new with the old. Correcting his mistake, he still managed to reach St. Sanctain's parish church at 9:45pm, and in the process, increased his lead to seven minutes. Nevertheless, the fast pace began to take its toll on the young pretender who checked in at Malew parish church at 10:24pm but now only five minutes ahead of Willie Kneale.

Even at this late hour, traffic was still heavy along the road to Ballabeg where the entourage of accompanying vehicles illuminated the busy scene tracking west to the fifth church.

At Arbory church, the 17-mile mark, Willie Kneale

had cut the leader's advantage to less than five minutes with Cleator hot on his heels a minute further back. Next on the road in close company were Bobby Kaneen, Joe Brown, Doug Allan, Henry Harvey and John Cannell. But hero of the 1960 Parish Walk, Jim Harvey, was struggling at this point – his race over for another year.

Bannan was first to reach the southernmost church at 11:20pm but only a minute ahead of second-placed Kneale who was a similar margin ahead of Cleator. However, the pace was too fast for even those at the back of the field – both George Quayle and Bill Corkill ending their ordeal at the 19½-mile mark.

Followed closely by Kneale, Bannan led the procession to the Ballakillowey crossroads before turning north towards the formidable Sloc – a test of resolve for even the most seasoned athlete.

As in previous years, the punishing climb to 'Tom the Dippers' corner took a heavy toll on those unprepared, including the leader, Bannan. Often referred to as 'Heartbreak Hill,' this wrecker of hopes and dreams again lived up to its reputation with many failing to reach the 25-mile mark at the Round Table.

Frank Oates failed to make it to the control point at Patrick where retirements came thick and fast for Herbie Cannell, Michael Gray, William Skillicorn, John Comaish, Joe Brown, John Cannell, Robert Cowley, Bobby Kaneen and Sefton Dent.

If the Sloc proved an obstacle for many, it gave Henry Harvey his opportunity to draw ahead. In exceptionally fine form, he attacked the heights effortlessly in the dark, setting a pace that brought him to the seventh church at 1:31am simultaneously with Cleator who had won the event four years previously. However, Harvey established his

1964

superiority and soon drew away from Cleator who was beginning to feel the after-effects of his quick pace through the southern parishes in his bid to stay with Bannan.

Harvey was the first to arrive in Peel where he was given a standing ovation as he made his way along Derby Road to the check-in point at St. Germain's Church. Commissioners chairman Mr. W. Faragher was present to greet the remaining walkers, but there were many stoppages here including Alan Hayward, David Boyle, Tim Wood, Doug Allan, Charles Gale, Dave Beattie, George Bingham and William Conway.

Nevertheless, there was sensation here at the eighth church when officials discovered that the latter three had missed the turning at the Round Table and had gone straight on towards Foxdale – a mistake that eliminated them from the event.

With Cleator in trouble and later calling time at Glen Willyn, Harvey hurried on to Kirk Michael leaving Kneale as his main challenger.

The brightening skies in the east saw Harvey reaching the halfway mark at 3:37am and still walking in fine fashion. Kneale reached Ballaugh some 18 minutes later but all was not well with the Ballasalla lad as he continued to lose time on the leader – reaching the white washed church at Jurby half an hour in arrears and showing serious signs of wear and tear.

Kneale carried on a few miles further but stopped soon after Smeale. It was a bitter blow to those who had admired his tenacity and his retirement left Henry Harvey in undoubted command of the race.

The Reverend Wilfred George awaited the 14 walkers approaching Jurby including 18-year-old Heather Murphy, now the only remaining lady in the race. Harvey continued his fast pace through the northern plains, his lead now one and a half hours over John Kneale. However, the two-time winner pulled a calf muscle on the road to Lezayre and was forced to stop for medical attention administered by the accompanying Mr. Fred Ward.

Ken Christian was in poor shape too but decided to continue. He was in fourth place and not far behind 19-year-old Graham Young who was comfortably holding third place through Ramsey. Behind them were John Adair, Clarence Cheney and a tired and weary Heather Murphy.

Henry Harvey checked into the fifteenth church at 8:37am. There was no doubt that he was out to secure his third victory as he strode along the arduous road to Maughold where the vicar, the Reverend Duckworth, welcomed him at the church gates. With his check-in card signed, and only 18 miles to go, Henry set off in the direction of the Hibernia, watched by Joe Brown, Bobby Kaneen, John Cannell and Herbie Cannell who had all thrown in the towel and were now just spectators.

The landslide on the Bulgam coast road necessitated a detour at Ballaragh. Unperturbed, Harvey set his sights on Laxey and was now over three hours ahead of the nearest challenger. Meanwhile, the gallant walk of John Kneale through the northern parishes ended in disappointment at the 67-mile mark leaving Ken Christian and Graham Young to contest second place. Cheney, Adair and Heather Murphy, were next on the road, followed a long way back and unable to beat the 24-hour deadline by T. Crellin, E. Kennaugh and E. Whiteside.

Urged on by his brothers, Harvey cleared Baldrine, perspiring freely in the hot sunshine as 'manager' and younger brother W.E. Harvey coaxed him on to the finish. Also in company was 16-year-old Post Office messenger, Colin Morling, who had set out earlier in the day on his bicycle to accompany Stanley Cleator and other postal colleagues. However, on their retirements, Colin stayed with Henry through the

There was no Parish Walk in 1965, however Graham Young and John Cannell (pictured top left and far right) both took part in the Island Games held at King George V Park.

1964-1967

night urging him on to the finish.

Unchallenged and with the finish now in sight, Harvey negotiated the difficult White Bridge, his shoes in pieces. Cheering spectators lined the pavements of Royal Avenue and Douglas Promenade as he sprinted to the finish, reaching his goal at the Villa Marina gates at 12:21pm. It was his third win in four years. His record time of 16 hours 21 minutes 06 seconds was to stand the test of time for years to come.

The ladies' 32½-mile race to Peel was won in magnificent style by 18-year-old Lilian Murphy of Ballymacash, County Antrim, Northern Ireland. Third at Braddan church in the preliminary stages, following closely behind Irene Cottier and Ivy Griffin, the slim bespectacled Irish girl out-paced and outclassed all the ladies to finish at St. Germain's Parish Church in a time of 6 hours 37 minutes 07 seconds – some 32 minutes ahead of the schedule set by the race organisers. Continuing on, Lilian became only the third lady ever to complete the gruelling course in 22 hours 27 minutes 35 seconds.

Irene Cottier, heroine of last year's event, was the second lady to finish at Peel, nearly eight minutes behind the Irish victor. The Knockaloe girl and pride of the Boundary Harriers later admitted that Lilian had been hard on her heels at Marown and had taken the initiative over the Braaid.

Cottier and Griffin were first to arrive at Braddan church, however the teenager was not far behind. She in turn was followed by Audrey Simpson, Lillian Gale, Pauline Armstrong and Caroline Corteen.

Irene and Ivy were together at Marown, arriving at the second church at 7:45pm and just a minute or so ahead of the eventual winner.

The picture changed along the Clannagh Road when the Irish girl took the lead and the race was in the bag from that point onwards. She upped the pace on the long haul south and brushed off all opposition with her tenacious attack of the Sloc and the downhill leg to St. Germain's and victory.

1965

With no Parish Walk scheduled in 1965, local athletes turned their attention to the 37 ¾-mile TT Course Walk held on Saturday, 21st August. Mayor of Douglas, Councillor J.H. Moore set off the 33 starters from the TT Grandstand at 10:00am in wet conditions, which improved as the day wore on.

Guy Goodair of the Wakefield Harriers set a cracking pace from the start and went on to win the event in a record time of 5 hours 55 minutes 22 seconds. John Cannell of the Boundary Harriers was the only real challenger but the fast pace troubled him at the nine-mile mark and he dropped back only to retire soon after. With Stanley Cleator and Willie Kneale non-starters, Albert Johnson of the Boundary Harriers took up the challenge to finish in second place, eight minutes in arrears. He later said: 'I was walking in borrowed shoes which were rather too big

and caused blisters. I never expected to beat Guy Goodair but I'm quite surprised to have made second.' There were 24 finishers with the Boundary Harriers team of Albert Johnson, George Bannan, Henry Harvey and Ian Turnbull winning the team prize.

1966

Lack of resources and unrest between the officials of the Manx Amateur Athletic Club continued into 1966 and for the second consecutive year, the Island was without its premier walking event.

Many local athletes turned their attention elsewhere, a few representing the Island in the British Empire and Commonwealth Games held in Jamaica later in that summer.

Haydn Gawne, Phil Bannan and Albert Johnson took part in the 20-mile walk however the heat took its toll on many and after initially performing well, Haydn collapsed with just six miles to go. Ron Wallwork, former winner of the TT Course Walk, went on to take the gold award, outwalking the great Don Thompson in a creditable time of 2 hours 44 minutes 43 seconds. Nevertheless, the Manx contingent put in a fine performance with Phil Bannan taking seventh spot in 3 hours 06 minutes 11 seconds, some two minutes ahead of Albert Johnson.

The TT Course Walk held in August attracted an entry of 27 of which 20 were club walkers from England.

Boundary Harriers fronted a strong team, which included Albert Johnson, Graham Young, Ian Turnbull, Doug Allan and John Cannell.

Albert Johnson led the field for 18 miles but he retired soon after Ballaugh and it became very much a two-horse race between G.W. Barrass and Doug Allan. Barrass of the Wakefield Harriers was first to reach the TT Grandstand in 6 hours 01 minute 03 seconds, just two minutes ten seconds ahead of Allan who made a gallant bid to win the event during its final stages. Last year's winner, Guy Goodair, took the third spot while local postman, Graham Young, finished fifth in 6 hours 22 minutes 25 seconds.

1967

As the 1960s progressed, so too did the popularity of the Parish Walk with entry numbers increasing throughout the decade. In general, sporting activity across the Island was on the increase and much reference made to it in the *Green Final*.

After an absence of three years from the Manx sporting calendar, the Parish Walk made a welcome return in 1967 with Boundary Harriers taking over its administration under the strong leadership of Dennis Lace, Edwin Dudley, Johnny Quine, Bill Turnbull and Kevin Madigan.

Held over the weekend of Saturday and Sunday 6th/7th May, the event attracted 57 starters, 11 of whom were members of the Northern Ireland

Top: Albert Johnson won the 1967 event to become the first man to break the 16-hour barrier.

Above: Start of the 1967 ladies race.

Walking Club.

A new starting point at the Villa Marina Arcade confirmed the course distance as 84.95 miles with competitors now required to touch the church gate instead of the church door as in previous years.

In weather conditions unfit for a walk of this nature, the eight ladies set off from Douglas Promenade at 6 o'clock in the evening followed by the men five minutes later.

The legendary Albert Johnson, followed by John Cannell, headed the field west to Braddan, reaching the two-mile mark in just 20 minutes and already ahead of the earlier lady starters.

Daryl Gribbin was next to the first church, closely followed by Leece Kneale, E. Kennaugh,

Johnson set a blistering pace on the climb out of Union Mills, reaching Marown in 45 minutes – already two minutes up on Cannell and four on Kneale. Behind the leading trio came Ian Hodgkinson, Irene Cottier, John Tasker, Peter Lewthwaite and Herbie Cannell.

However, Johnson was a man on a mission for he reached Rushen at 9:11pm – his lead over Cannell now extended to 15 minutes.

Leece Kneale was next to the whitewashed church – four minutes back but comfortably ahead of Ian Hodgkinsn, Willy Kneale, Jim Harvey and John Tasker, all contesting fourth spot but nearly two miles in arrears.

Day was turning to night as the leaders set their sights on Ballakillowey and the punishing climb to the Round Table. Rain was now falling with a quarter of the field venturing no further than the 19½-mile mark. John Tasker of the Malew Beagles was a surprise retirement here, so too were Willy Kneale and Parish regular, Daryl Gribbin.

The rain and mist on the tortuous ascent to the Round Table made conditions unbearable. Undeterred, Johnson hurried on to Patrick, arriving at the seventh church at 11:17pm and leading the race by 21 minutes. It had been an extremely fast pace for he reached St. Germain's church in 5 hours 30 minutes to record the fastest time ever to this point.

The waning moon was a sight most welcomed by those still to reach the Round Table. With a ten-minute advantage over his nearest challenger, Kneale was second to the western capital arriving just before midnight having got ahead of Cannell on the tiring twisting climb out of Glen Maye. The Douglas postman in turn enjoyed a 50-minute advantage over fourth-placed Ian Hodgkinson.

Irene Cottier had walked a splendid race too – arriving in Peel at 12:50am to secure fifth place and the ladies' prize for her class.

Less than half of the 56 starters made it to the most westerly point with only 16 continuing to Kirk Michael. But there was disappointment for Ian Hodgkinson and Peter Lewthwaite whose brave efforts ended three miles further on at the halfway mark.

Already 20 minutes up on record time, Johnson's lead had increased to 40 minutes at Jurby. Here at the lonely church overlooking the Irish Sea, parish regular Michael Gray was an early casualty – his painful journey finally ending after 10 hours 39 minutes.

At the northernmost church, Johnson touched the church gate at 3:26am – 29 minutes ahead of Kneale and now nearly an hour ahead of third-placed Cannell.

Heavy downpours at dawn reduced the pace with Johnson slowing appreciably and losing considerable time in Andreas where he took a wrong turning. Here at the 55½-mile mark, he was so far ahead that stragglers were still reaching Kirk Michael 16 miles back!

Realising he was close to exceeding the time limit, Frank Oates called time at Andreas, having been on his feet for over 14 hours.

Maintaining his lead through the northern plain Johnson reached Maughold at 6:25am where pools of mist drifted serenely beneath a golden sunrise. Nevertheless, the 'blistering' overall 5 mph pace was too hot for Kneale and he retired at the Dhoon with severe cramp leaving only nine left in the race.

Two miles back at the Corrany, 23-year-old Jim Harvey was another to call time having walked several miles in severe pain with a twisted ankle. Meanwhile at the rear of the field, Terry Crellin was the final retirement of the day, stopping at Lezayre after 15 hours 48 minutes but more than happy with his performance.

1968

Well on course for the first-ever sub-16-hour circuit of the 17 parishes, Johnson wasted no time on the final push to Douglas. Accompanied by two cyclist attendants throughout, he hurried on to the finish arriving at the war memorial in a time of 15 hours 54 minutes 51 seconds, knocking over 26 minutes off Henry Harvey's 1964 record time.

John Cannell walked a very steady and sensible race, achieving yet another ambition by finishing second and completing his first Parish Walk in a time of 17 hours 42 minutes 36 seconds. His apprenticeship over the gruelling course now served, the Douglas postman would go on to become the most successful Parish Walker of all time.

Walking a steady and sensible race, W. McFall was on his own from Rushen but still managed third spot in 22 hours 50 minutes. Northern Ireland visitors John Adair and Victor Richardson walked the entire course together to record joint fourth place in a time of 20 hours 48 minutes while joint sixth were J. Smyth and H. Shaw, both exceeding the time limit by 47 minutes.

1968

Towards the end of the 1960s, a new breed of walker was beginning to emerge with household names such as Graham Young, John Cannell and Derek Harrison dominating the scene. Between them, the trio won 13 Parish Walks from 1971 to 1994 with Derek's phenomenal 1979 absolute race-record of 15 hours 20 minutes 51 seconds not broken until 2006.

One of two years that produced two winners, the 1968 Parish Walk was overshadowed with controversy when the winner was announced as 25-year-old Ian Turnbull who finished second out of a field of 44 starters.

Leece Kneale, a 34-year-old building worker from Lonan, was first man over the line, recording a time of 16 hours 05 minutes 52 seconds, however the result did not count as he was entered in the 'C' event, which was a purely social class for 'non-road walkers' wishing to tackle the course.

Event 'A' was the category for recognised walkers belonging to athletic and walking clubs and Turnbull was the No. 1 walker in a team entered by the Boundary Harriers. His time of 18 hours 50 minutes 44 seconds was nearly two hours slower than that of Kneale, however by race rules he was classed the winner and was awarded the Gerald Bridson Trophy at a presentation held in the Bowling Green Hotel later.

There was much bad feeling at the time with press and radio reports favouring a Leece victory. Mr William Turnbull, Ian's father and a member of the Boundary Harriers organising committee for the event told the *Examiner*: 'We want to make it quite clear that by race rules, Ian is the winner and I'd stand by that for anyone in his position. There's been an awful lot of loose talk about this business throughout the Island and it's time the record was put straight.

There's been too much talk of it being a fiddle and this sort of thing could lead to the end of the event.'

Ian Turnbull said: 'I won according to the rules which are there to protect people who are registered members of the Amateur Athletic Association. It's not a satisfactory way to win – Leece had a great race and beat me fair and square. I'm sorry that it's had to turn out this way but there seems to be nothing anyone can do.'

Kneale was more than disappointed and was quoted as saying: 'It seems as though it's a bit of a closed shop. They've given me a trophy but I'm told they had to knock up a jeweller on Sunday morning to get one when it was obvious that I was going to get to the finish first.'

Boundary Harriers was deeply embarrassed by the result and distanced themselves from the growing imbroglio that refused to go away.

There were 44 starters in this controversial race, four of whom were women.

Skies were grey on 4th May as Mr Eric Brown, President of the Boundary Harriers, raised the small Manx flag at 6:55pm to send the four ladies on their way, followed five minutes later by 40 men, Bernie May leading the way onto Circular Road.

A large crowd had gathered at Braddan church and first to arrive were Irene Cottier and Ivy Griffin. The men came next, led by Ian Hodgkinson, John Cannell and fast-moving Leece Kneale. At this stage, it was unusual for Leece to be so far ahead. He had determination written all over his face and it became obvious that he was making an attempt on Albert Johnson's race record time set the year before.

Heavy rain at the beginning of a Parish Walk is never good; Peter and Bernie May were early casualties at the Union Mills Railway Hotel, their race run for another year.

With weather conditions far from ideal, Ian Hodgkinson, closely followed by Leece Kneale and Irish walker Rob Storey were the first to the Braaid crossroads. Behind them came Irene Cottier and Ivy Griffin but John Cannell was losing ground at this point and appeared in trouble

Next through the road junction came ex-TT course record holder Willie Kneale – now making a comeback and exhibiting, as always, his near perfect race walking style. Mitch Joughin was not far behind and was doing his best to impress Centurion and Parish debutant, Charlie Draper.

There was no change on the leader board at Santon, however Cannell was now four minutes adrift of the leader and struggling at this point to stay in contention.

Ivy Griffin was struggling too, her race coming to an end on the Clannagh Road, leaving leading lady Irene Cottier to go it alone.

In tandem throughout Malew, Kneale and Hodgkinson arrived at the church gate in 2 hours 33 minutes. Northern Ireland's Rob Storey appeared two minutes later, soon followed by the brightly coloured figure of Cannell who had sensibly stopped and

Top: Ian Turnbull was the second to finish but awarded the winner's trophy.

Below: Leece Kneale was first over the line but denied victory.

changed his clothing with darkness now approaching.

First lady to the 15-mile mark, Irene Cottier, was already well ahead of Willy Kneale and the colourful Ian Turnbull, next to this point having spent considerable time changing into overnight clothing for the long slog ahead. Jim Harvey made it to the church at 9:50pm and behind him came Peter Lewthwaite, sensibly attired in a Colin Cowdrey cap, full of smiles and ready for supper.

The pace quickened through Arbory with Cannell moving into third spot some six minutes down on the leaders but comfortably holding off Storey, Kneale and Turnbull, battling it out for fourth place.

Both Kneale and Hodgkinson arrived at Rushen church as daylight was fading. It was now 10:20pm with 19½ miles already covered.

Cannell was moving better through Colby but was still nine minutes in arrears at Rushen where he sensibly stopped to change into something warmer in preparation for the treacherous mountain climb soon to come. Irene Cottier was still holding fourth place at this point with Willie Kneale fifth.

There was a good crowd of onlookers gathered at the most southern parish and much applause was given, even to the retirements, of which there were many, including Rob Storey who stopped with severe cramp.

The tiring ascent of the Sloc contributed to many casualties with Jim Harvey and Mitch Joughin succumbing to the elements, as did Willie Kneale at Glen Maye.

Although the time was well past midnight, a large crowd had gathered outside the seventh church to greet the leaders of this apparent two-horse race.

Town clerk, Leslie Kelly greeted the leaders at Peel Town Hall – both arriving at 12:48am having completed 32½ miles in 5 hours 48 minutes. It had been a relentless pace with Kneale bettering his own record by nine minutes. Cannell was still holding third place with Turnbull fourth and Irene Cottier, winner of the ladies' section to this point, fifth.

At Kirk Michael, the clock chimed two as Kneale and Hodgkinson stopped to change socks. Leece was the quicker and was soon 200 yards along the Ballaugh road with Ian following in hot pursuit.

The pace quickened from Ballaugh to Jurby where Kneale increased his advantage to nearly five minutes.

Raining heavily and with dawn soon to break, the leaders reached the northernmost church at 4:25am with Kneale holding a 15-minute advantage over Hodgkinson. With Cannell a surprise retirement here, Turnbull took up third spot but failed to make any impression on the leaders who by now were well advanced on the Burma Road.

Cold and wet, Kneale approached the waterlogged path leading to Andreas church – his lead now stretched to 20 minutes with Hodgkinson falling further and further behind and unable to make an impression.

Having stopped at Sulby Bridge for a well-deserved change of clothes, the now brightly dressed Kneale checked in at Lezayre church only four minutes down on Albert Johnson's 1967 record time. He was leading Hodgkinson by 26 minutes with only eight walkers now left in the race.

With a new record now a strong possibility, Kneale upped his pace yet again to reach the fifteenth church at Maughold two minutes earlier than Albert Johnson's time of the year before. It was raining heavily and he was acutely aware that the approaching miles had forced his retirement on two previous occasions.

But drama was unfolding on the road to Port e Vullen with 18-year-old Hodgkinson down to a funeral pace on the difficult climb to the most easterly church. He had walked 67 wet and miserable miles but could go no further. There were tears in his eyes as he admitted defeat. Turnbull was now in second place, but many hours behind.

His lead now unassailable, Kneale hurried on to the finish where the crowds were the biggest ever known. His winning time of 16 hours 05 minutes 52 seconds was just 11 minutes outside the absolute race record and to the shock of the crowd, he announced his retirement from race walking.

Turnbull was the next to arrive at Douglas in 18 hours 15 minutes 44 seconds followed by V. Richardson in 21 hours 29 minutes 45 seconds with V. Thompson the fourth and final finisher in 23 hours 19 minutes 30 seconds.

PARISH WALK TRAGEDY

Despite the large turnout, the year was marred by the tragic death of a 17-year-old youth acting as a pacer in the Parish Walk Relay event held earlier in the week.

This was the first known accident to take place in the eight years that the walk had been held. The event was for teams of six with the rules allowing pacing, however competitors walking two abreast would be disqualified. It was also a rule that competitors must walk on the pavement and obey all road safety instructions.

On the day of the event and throughout the race, Manx Radio had issued announcements to motorists informing them the race was taking place. Competitors wore white and carried a red reflector triangle on their backs, easily picked up by car lights. The organisers, however, had no jurisdiction over the clothes of team helpers as this was the responsibility of the team manager, but it was recommended that they too should wear distinctive clothing. Individual walkers were left to choose their own pacers and at a meeting before the race it was suggested that light-coloured clothing should be worn.

The deceased was acting as a pacer when he was struck by a passing car while walking alongside a competitor on the Peel to Kirk Michael road, near Ballakaighen Farm, German.

Constable J.A. Nelson was on motor patrol during

1969

Top: Ian Hodgkinson (No. 12) sets off from the Villa Marina.

Below: Ian Hodgkinson at Laxey on his way to becoming the youngest ever finisher.

the early hours when he came upon the scene of the accident. It was raining heavily and visibility for driving was poor. During the race he had warned nine of the walkers on the offside of the road to cross over. In one case he had narrowly missed three of them who were in the path of his police car. The competitors in their whites could be easily seen, but many of the pacers were wearing dark clothes and were difficult to identify. In his opinion, the walkers had been a danger to other road-users while walking on the offside of the road.

At an inquest in Douglas, the Coroner recorded a verdict of death by misadventure and felt that rules and regulations covering the clothing of walkers should in future also be extended to those acting as pacers.

1969

By the end of the decade, interest in the Parish Walk was on the decline with much absenteeism from the Northern Ireland and overseas contingency that had been loyal to the event since its revival. Media publicity was also minimal with newspapers losing interest in an event that had once filled front pages. Also, the timing of the race coincided with the TT races, which traditionally received maximum newspaper coverage throughout the June fortnight.

With no previous winners entered, the Parish Walk of 1969 was a wide-open affair with Irene Cottier firm favourite in the ladies' class to Peel. In the men's class, Doug Allan, Mitch Joughin and Peter Lewthwaite, treasurer of the Boundary Harriers, were once again prepared for an assault on the 17 parishes, as were hopefuls Brian Speedie and Tony Temple.

The veterans' section was well represented too with four members of the Northern Ireland Walking Club in participation. Charles Draper, winner of this class last year, was again hopeful of victory but stiff opposition was expected from fellow visitor Cyril Evans and Arthur Jones, chairman of the organising

committee.

Scheduled for a 7:00pm start on Saturday 31st May, the final event of the decade, although run in excellent weather conditions, attracted a poor turnout with only 54 men and six ladies setting off from the Villa Marina Arcade.

Leaders on the road at Marown, after just 48 minutes, were Ian Hodgkinson and Doug Allan. Retracing their steps to the Glen Darragh Road, the pair led the field up the tiring section to the Braaid and on to the third church, Santon, where Hodgkinson held a two-minute lead over Allan.

Indeed, the pace was 'blistering' with the duo reaching the 11-mile mark in less than two hours. George Bannan was third to Santon at 9:04pm, quickly followed by Mitch Joughin, Frank Oates and John Adair.

Retirements were thick and fast with Charlie Draper a surprise casualty at Rushen. Here at the most southerly church, Doug Allan had taken control of the race with a three-minute advantage over Hodgkinson. Mitch Joughin, R. Kaneen and Cyril Evans, were joint third, ahead of Northern Island's John Adair. Looking relaxed, leading lady Irene Cottier was seventh to this point and seemed well prepared for the back-breaking task soon to come.

Darkness was well advanced as the leaders pushed on to the Round Table, eager to complete this daunting and difficult section of the journey. But the punishing climb took a heavy toll with Bannan an early casualty. Others to succumb to the pain barrier were W. Brown, J. Quilleash, W. Callister, T. Cowin, G. Lawson, A. Bridson, J. Corlett, B. Speedie, C. Morling, E. Beattie, A. Caine plus ladies J. Corlett and J. Evans.

Doug Allan was first to reach Peel, arriving at St. Germain's Parish Church at 1:01am and four minutes ahead of his nearest rival Ian Hodgkinson. Roy Kaneen followed 16 minutes later but then announced his retirement. Cyril Evans checked in at 1:31am with fifth-placed Mitch Joughin a further two minutes in arrears. Next to reach the western capital and in sixth place was Irene Cottier. She covered the 32½ miles in 6 hours 41 minutes and was one of only three ladies to complete their class.

Here at the eighth church, 12 retirements were recorded, including police constable Albert Lowe and Tony Temple. In the veterans' section, Arthur Jones walked a superb race to this point in just over seven hours.

Only 16 walkers continued beyond Peel, however Parish regulars Peter Lewthwaite and David Christian were casualties at Kirk Michael, a point reached by Allan in 7 hours 23 minutes. Hodgkinson remained in second spot two minutes back, with Cyril Evans third.

Wasting no time on the road north, Allan checked in at the halfway mark in 8 hours 03 minutes and was somewhat surprised to see Hodgkinson now only 50 yards behind.

Behind the leading pair, Evans was holding third place, but 30 minutes in arrears.

By now, the field was spread far and wide with Mitch Joughin fourth but over an hour behind the leaders. Frank Oates and John Adair were joint fifth with only 14 now left in the race.

The sky was brightening in the east as the leaders sprinted on to Jurby. Hodgkinson and Allan were together on the approach track leading to the whitewashed church. However there was drama at this point when Allan announced his retirement due to badly blistered feet which had slowed him considerably since leaving Peel.

Now alone, Hodgkinson set out on the long, soul-destroying road to the northernmost church, arriving at 5:20am as the sun began its climb over the eastern horizon. Evans was next there, some 33 minutes in arrears but still three miles in front of third-placed Joughin who was fading badly at Smeale crossroads and destined to retire soon after.

In tandem Dalby, Frank Oates, John Adair and Victor Richardson touched the gates of St. Bridget's Parish Church, Bride as the clock struck seven. They had been on the road for 12 hours exactly. With Mitch Joughin a retirement at this point, Terry Crellin moved into sixth place over an hour ahead of John Bradley, W.T. Thompson and John Smyth – all together and destined to finish in that order. Only two more walkers were to reach Bride. W. Stevenson arrived in 14 hours 06 minutes followed by H. Shaw 12 minutes later.

Meanwhile, Hodgkinson was fast approaching the 72-mile mark at Glen Mona, now four hours ahead of Shaw who bravely continued to the penultimate church before calling time high on the hill over Lonan.

After last year's disappointment, Hodgkinson hurried on to the finish, touching the Memorial Mine on Douglas Promenade shortly after noon to record a well-deserved victory in 17 hours 11 minutes 25 seconds.

Visiting walker, Cyril Evans was second in 17 hours 59 minutes 07 seconds with joint third place going to Frank Oates, John Adair and Victor Richardson

nearly three hours later.

Terry Crellin completed the course for a second occasion. His time of 22 hours 39 minutes, nearly an hour ahead of seventh placed W. Stevenson.

Together over the closing miles, visiting walkers W. Thompson, J. Smyth and J. Bradley were the last to finish in joint eighth place.

The Boundary Harriers won the team award with walkers Frank Oates, Terry Crellin and Ian Hodgkinson all completing the full distance.

The ladies' race to Peel was won by Irene Cottier with Marilyn Rooney second and Ruth Watt third.

1970

Only the second overseas visitor ever to claim victory in the Island's most demanding athletic event, Dudley Seddon of the Sutton Coldfield Walking Club won the 1970 Parish Walk at his very first attempt. One of only seven finishers, Seddon had twice competed in the TT Course Walk but this was his first major win and he took great pleasure in his triumph.

Held over the weekend of 23rd and 24th May, the classic annual event attracted 43 starters but was restricted to men aged 18 to 60 and women aged 18 to 50.

The two local stars expected to take the honours, record holder Albert Johnson and Leece Kneale, both retired during the race leaving Stanley Sille of the Boundary Harriers to claim the runner-up spot with Derek completing his first walk and taking third place.

As was expected, Albert Johnson, former winner and race-record holder, set the pace, reaching the first church in 19 minutes 45 seconds. George Bannan and D. S. Christian were next to the two-mile mark, a minute in front of a chasing pack led by Derek Harrison, Mitch Joughin and Leece Kneale.

The weather on the journey south was favourable with a light westerly wind allowing Johnson to extend his lead to ten minutes at Arbory, a point he reached in just 2 hours 43 minutes. Here at the 17-mile mark, Castletown's Juan Kermode was one of three retirements as was Bannan, three miles further at Rushen.

Johnson was first to tackle the back-breaking climb to the summit of the Sloc but was losing ground quickly because of badly blistered feet .Nevertheless, his nearest challenger, Leece Kneale, continued at a punishing pace covering the 11-mile section from Rushen to Patrick in just 2 hours 10 minutes.

Eventually overhauling the leader at the seventh church, Kneale hurried on to Peel with a comfortable four-minute advantage. For many, the western capital was the final goal and finishes were recorded for Peter Lewthwaite, Charles Draper and Albert Lowe. With Johnson unable to continue beyond this point, Kneale began to pull away from Dudley Seddon, now occupying second place and seemingly unconcerned at the Herculean task that lay ahead. Even at this early stage, the field was spread far and wide with only 13

Douglas Seddon was the first of seven finishers in 1970.

1971

walkers setting out for Kirk Michael.

Through the dark moonless night, Kneale continued to extend his advantage. At Ballaugh the difference was 27 minutes, Jurby 30 minutes and Bride 38 minutes.

But the long trek through the northern plain to Bride took a heavy toll on Kneale. With dawn breaking in this most beautiful part of the Island, he retired midway along the Burma Road leaving Seddon in the lead but chased hard by Derek Harrison and Stanley Sille.

Harrison was the next in trouble and lost considerable time between Andreas and Lezayre with Sille finally overhauling him to become second on the road. Nevertheless, Harrison very pluckily carried on to the finish despite considerable discomfort.

There were no further changes in the leader board from this point on, and unchallenged, Seddon, went on to claim a well-deserved victory in 17 hours 21 minutes 49 seconds. Sille was second in 17 hours 45 minutes 35 seconds and Derek Harrison third in 18 hours 30 minutes 25 seconds. Finishing fourth for the fourth consecutive year, John Adair of the Northern Ireland Walking Club led home final finishers and clubmates John Bradley, William Stevenson and Ralph Whyte.

Other meritorious performances were by Terry Crellin of Douglas and David Corrin of Castletown who both walked 67 miles to Maughold, D.C. Christian who reached Andreas and C.D. McGrath, who made it to the halfway mark at Ballaugh.

In the ladies' race over 32½ miles to Peel, the lead was shared for much of the distance by Irene Corlett and Gladys Teare. Although just recently married, Irene was in trouble after Rushen and retired on the Sloc leaving Gladys to win in a time of 6 hours 50 minutes. Marilyn Rooney was second to reach the western capital in 8 hours 30 minutes with Mrs. J.A. Corlett in third place, a further five minutes in arrears. They were the only three finishers in this class.

In the veterans' race over the same distance, Cyril Evans of the Leicester Walking Club went unchallenged to win for the second successive year in 6 hours 33 minutes.

Irishman John Bradley was second in his class to reach Peel in 7 hours 15 minutes with Arthur Jones of Boundary Harriers third in 7 hours 32 minutes. Charles Draper was fourth in 7 hours 40 minutes, followed by three Irish walkers, John Smyth, Harry Shaw and William Thompson, the last two crossing the finish line at St. Germain's church together.

The Northern Ireland Walking Club 'A' team regained the club team prize of the G. & R. Ridgway Shield, which they had relinquished to Boundary Harriers last year. The members of the winning team were John Adair, John Bradley and William Stevenson. Onchan Parish won the Parish Team Trophy for the second successive year, this time by Tony Temple, David Brown and Bernard Kelly.

1971

Although mainland competitors were well represented in the 1971 Parish Walk, the annual classic quickly developed in to a two-horse race between Graham Young and Derek Harrison, two of the Island's most respected athletes.

In spite of poor weather over the weekend of Saturday 22nd May and Sunday 23rd May, the event was the most exciting to date with only 54 seconds separating first and second place.

Out of 44 male starters, 10 finished the overall distance, with first man home being Manxman Graham Young. His time of 15 hours 43 minutes 12 seconds was nothing short of phenomenal, easily beating Albert Johnson's all-time record set in 1967 by 11 minutes.

But it was by no means an easy win for Young. It was very close going, as second man home, Derek Harrison, led the field for practically the entire walk and may have gone on to victory had more distance been available.

With the race getting underway from the Villa Marina Arcade at 7:00pm, there was early disappointment for Philip Bannan whose dream of winning this race ended prematurely at the four-mile mark after just 48 minutes.

Albert Lowe was the next to throw in the towel. The Douglas policeman, who did his training while on the beat, announced his retirement to timekeepers at Santon with only 11 miles completed.

Irene Corlett (née) Cottier was a surprise retirement at Rushen where she headed a list of 14 to go no further, including Peter Lewthwaite, Peter Oates, Trevor Taubman and Juan Kermode.

The last year's runner-up Stan Sille was the first of 14 to stop at the eighth church, a point from where only 17 continued. Retirements were thick and fast through the night with only 18 left on the road by dawn.

Not relishing the thought of the endless and painful miles ahead, Geoff Kennaugh and George Peach of Castletown brought an end to their 12-hour

Graham Young (No.35) setting off from the Villa Marina Arcade in 1971.

40-minute ordeal at the lonely whitewashed church at Jurby. David Corrin continued to Bride before yielding to the elements, while A. Kewley managed to go that bit further before stopping at Andreas at 9:24am. The final retirement of the day was that of William Stevenson who called time at 12:45pm, just 18 miles from the ultimate goal!

There was no let up in the pace with Harrison and Young clocking less than ten-minute miles. Only 150 yards separated the Island's very best as they passed the grammar school on the outskirts of Ramsey.

But the Douglas postman was not yet ready for a 'fight to the finish.' Easing his pace at Ballure, he afforded Harrison the lead in a bid to save his energy for later. With no time to take in the pleasant views in this most picturesque part of the course, Harrison increased his lead to 17 minutes on the tiring, twisting uphill road to Ballajora and from this point looked a certain winner.

But Young was not yielding yet. Although a mile back, he stopped briefly at the Hibernia to remove his tracksuit and then pressed on relentlessly for a final challenge on the lead.

The two were neck and neck on the Everlasting Bend above Laxey with Young finally edging out Harrison close to the old school house at Garwick.

The Douglas postman's advantage increased to three minutes on reaching the seventeenth and final church at Onchan, and with victory in sight, he sprinted to the finish to record the fastest-ever circuit of the 17 parishes.

But it was a close-run thing, with Harrison digging into his final reserves and reducing the deficit to just 54 seconds along the promenade to finish only 300 yards behind.

Third place was a tie between last year's winner, Dudley Seddon, and Ray Manning of Newcastle who both finished in 18 hours 10 minutes, almost three hours after the leading pair.

There were seven entrants in the men's veteran class to Peel which was won by 58-year-old Worcestershire man, Cyril Evans, who also completed the course to finish fifth overall. John Adair from Northern Ireland finished in sixth place with joint seventh place going to Irishman John Bradley and Castletown's Steve Gardner. Twenty-one-year-old Steve was competing in his first Parish Walk, however this up-and-coming shy, young athlete would make major athletic headlines in the years to come. Ninth place went to local walker, Ken Cross, with Irish veteran William Thompson completing the course for a third time to secure tenth spot.

The ladies' race to Peel was won by local competitor, Roberta Moore of Douglas, in 7 hours 45 minutes. Only five of the eight ladies finished.

In the team section for walking clubs, the three members from the Northern Ireland 'A' team won the award for completing the full distance.

The trophy for non-walking clubs went to the Post Office Sports 'A' team, which included Graham Young – the ultimate winner. A special award was

1972 saw the first of five wins for Derek Harrison.

also presented to Northern Ireland walker, John Adair, who finished sixth overall. It was his fifth consecutive finish.

1972

Determined to overturn last year's disappointing result, Derek Harrison was very much hot favourite for the 1972 Parish Walk, held over the weekend of 20th and 21st May

Starting at 6:55pm at the Villa Marina, the nine ladies were away first followed by 46 men five minutes later.

Wasting no time in taking the lead, 38-year-old Harrison swept aside all opposition to win convincingly by over two hours in a time of 16 hours 19 minutes 15 seconds. He was literally miles ahead of runner-up John Adair who recorded a personal best for the 85-mile event

But even these great performances were overshadowed by Irene Corlett (née Cottier), who won the ladies' race to Peel in a record time of 6 hours 32 minutes 50 seconds – eight minutes faster than the previous best for this event.

For the early part of the race, Irene had allowed her five-minute lead to slip away. She later walked one minute per mile quicker than her nearest challenger and by fighting back, astounded the male competitors who had overtaken her earlier. Winning the 32½-mile ladies' event to Peel by 32 minutes, she was second on the road behind overall winner, Derek Harrison.

Cyril Evans of Leicester won the veterans' race to Peel for the third successive year and continued the remaining 52½ miles in wet and misty conditions to finish in fourth place overall and within half an hour of Birmingham walker, Dudley Seddon, who finished third in 19 hours 26 minutes 50 seconds.

John Bradley, of Northern Ireland, who was second in the veterans' race, also kept going for the full 85 miles but failed to pass Cyril Evans, finishing

1973

fifth overall.

Castletown's Steve Gardner and Ken Cross of Douglas also had good outings, finishing in sixth and seventh in 21 hours 17 minutes 52 seconds and 21 hours 44 minutes 15 seconds respectively.

Other than a brief mention in the *Isle of Man Courier*, the event was poorly covered by the media with newspapers preferring instead to report the latest happenings in the annual TT races, which were taking part at the same time.

This was quite an 'about turn' when compared to the first event in 1960 that captured the public's imagination like no other. Then, both the *Isle of Man Times* and the *Isle of Man Examiner* gave the event extensive coverage on their front pages as well as a detailed and humorous account written by the respected sports correspondent of the time, John Quirk.

1973

Although into its second decade, the Parish Walk was beginning to look tired and worn out by 1973 with limited media coverage and a general lack of interest contributing to the second poorest turnout since its revival in 1960.

Starting an hour later at 7:55pm on Saturday 12th May, conditions for this eleventh event were far from ideal with steady drizzle that later turned to rain.

Wasting no time, last year's winner, civil servant Derek Harrison, took an early lead, forging away from the rest of the field to stamp his authority and never to be seriously challenged.

As ever, the race was a gruelling one with only six of the 46 starters completing the testing course.

Both Harrison and former winner, Graham Young, set a killing pace to lead the race at Rushen by seven

minutes. Nevertheless, the Douglas postman burnt himself out on the tiring climb to the Round Table and he retired at Dalby leaving Harrison on his own for the remainder of the race.

Chairman of the 'Castletown Ale Drinkers' Society,' Steve Gardner, moved into second place and continued a lonely walk, his lowest ebb being at 5:00am when the after-effects of staying up all night began to take effect.

Only 18 competitors continued through Peel and they dropped out at intervals between there and Maughold, a point reached by only the six eventual finishers.

Harrison's winning time of 16 hours 36 minutes 04 seconds was over two hours quicker than second-placed man, Gardner, who completed the course for a third consecutive time in 18 hours 58 minutes 45 seconds, having done less training than in previous years.

John Adair completed the course for a sixth time, finishing third in 20 hours 52 minutes 07 seconds. Fourth place went to Bernard Kelly in 21 hours 55 minutes 50 seconds and equal fifth were W. Thompson and J. Bradley, a further hour behind.

The 32½-mile ladies' race to Peel attracted a poor entry with just four ladies coming to the start line. An equally impressive Irene Corlett won the race, but at a much slower pace than last year in 7 hours 08 minutes 40 seconds. She was almost two hours ahead of P. Collister who just finished inside the nine-hour limit. With Jill Colebourn retiring at Malew and M. Leah-Hughes at Rushen, the poorly contested class produced only two finishers.

The veterans' race to Peel was well contested with Arthur Jones the victor by ten minutes. William Stevenson of the Northern Ireland Walking Club claimed the runner-up spot in 7 hours 18 minutes 55

Committee members of the Boundry Harriers, including Dennis Lace and Edwin Dudley.

In 1974, there were no finishers in the ladies entry.

seconds with W. Thompson and John Bradley finishing joint third, a further 36 minutes in arrears. Charles Draper was fifth, arriving at the western capital at 4:24 am as dawn was breaking.

Despite the late finish, and managing little sleep, race secretary, Arthur Jones was up and about at 10:00am for worship at All Saint's Church, Douglas.

1974

The Island's very best race-walkers, Allan Callow, Graham Young and Derek Harrison did themselves proud at the 1974 Commonwealth Games. Months of strenuous labour proved fruitful for Graham Young who put in a magnificent performance in the 20-mile walk held in Christchurch, New Zealand.

Having gone through a bad patch early on, the Douglas postman moved into sixth position at the 15-mile mark and, with a superb display of race walking ability, he just missed out on the bronze award by 47 seconds. His time of 2 hours 42 minutes 55.2 seconds was a personal best, finishing two minutes ahead of Ian Hodgkinson.

A former Parish Walk winner in 1969, Hodgkinson represented Australia on this occasion, and was a little disappointed with fifth place, having recently recorded a fine 2 hours 39 minutes over the same distance. Allan Callow also put in a brilliant performance, finishing eighth and some distance ahead of Derek Harrison, who failed to maintain his early pace, finishing twelfth.

A record entry of 107 – nearly twice last year's number – entered for the 1974 Parish Walk, including three former winners.

In a bid to restore the annual classic to its former glory, race secretary Arthur Jones attributed the increase in interest to the fact that the start had been brought forward to 2:55pm for the women with the men starting five minutes later. It was a controversial decision and one not favoured by everyone.

Held over the weekend of 25th and 26th May, the gruelling 85-mile race was won by Paddy Dowling by more than 25 minutes. Because of race commitments

in Bradford the following day, the Irishman collected the winner's trophy on Douglas Promenade, went back to change in his hotel and was on the morning boat for Liverpool before the third man had finished!

Dowling, who walked for Sheffield Harriers, took command of the race shortly after Peel where the much-fancied local hope, Derek Harrison had retired, feeling unwell after a recent bout of flu.

Harrison had walked most of the 32½ miles to Peel with his clubmate Graham Young, however the Douglas postman had intended going only as far as Peel and, although he was first on the road, it was Harrison who was first to leave. Nevertheless, within a few miles Harrison was forced to retire, leaving Dowling to go it alone.

Fifty-eight walkers in all made it to Peel but only 26 of the original 94 starters continued beyond that point with Dowling well in front but chased hard by previous winner Ian Turnbull and Ron Ronan of the Boundary Harriers.

In all, 21 walkers reached Kirk Michael, however the much-talented teenager Murray Lambden was one of five calling time at this point having clocked a creditable 8 hours 25 minutes for the 39 miles.

The long haul to the most northerly church was far from easy and by Bride there were only seven walkers left in the race, a figure reduced to three by dawn – everyone else having called it a day.

The experienced Dowling had a comfortable lead of almost half an hour over Turnbull as the walk went into the early hours of the morning. Almost three miles ahead in actual distance, Dowling kept up the pressure to finish on Douglas Promenade some 26 minutes ahead of his nearest rival at 7:40am. Turnbull's time was 17 hours 06 minutes 52 seconds with Ronan a very tired but pleased third in 20 hours 40 minutes 34 seconds.

Boundary Harriers won the team award, John Corrin, Ron Ronan and Ian Turnbull receiving the G.&R. Ridgeway Shield. Castletown Ale Drinkers 'B' team won the award for the best non-walking club with two walkers reaching Bride and another to Jurby.

But the most remarkable feat of the day was in

Top: Eric Brown with John Corrin, Ian Turnbull and Ron Ronan who took the team award.

Below: Awaiting starters orders.

1975-1976

the ladies' section with every one of the seven starters completing the course to Peel. The winner was Heather Staley in 7 hours 17 minutes 10 seconds, followed by past winner Roberta Moore in 8 hours 13 minutes 45 seconds.

Norma Gardner from Castletown was third in 8 hours 25 minutes 30 seconds while two pairs of girls finished together to take joint fourth and sixth places. Jennifer Corlett and Marilyn Hughes crossed the finish line in 8 hours 42 minutes and Maureen Turnbull and Sylvia Walmsley in 8 hours 56 minutes 40 seconds.

In the veterans' race, only three of the four starters made it to Peel. Cyril Evans took the honours in 7 hours 04 minutes 35 seconds, some five minutes ahead of runner-up, Arthur Jones. Northern Island's William Thompson was third in 8 hours 37 minutes.

1975

The success of last year's event with its new start time of 3:00pm convinced race organisers to repeat the same in 1975. Although the afternoon start was not advantageous to everyone, it certainly made life more bearable for those seeking cooler conditions during the early stages. With Derek Harrison taking part in the Northern Area 50-kilometre Championship in Bradford and Manx stars Graham Young and John Cannell both non-starters, only five from a field of 90 completed the testing 85-mile circuit, with members of the Leicester Walking Club again dominating the event and taking first, second and fourth places.

In one of the slowest-ever circuits of the 17 parishes, Ed Warner completed the 85 miles in 18 hours 49 minutes 52 seconds, some three hours slower than Graham Young's 1971 record time. Veteran William Roe was second in a fraction over 19 hours, while best-placed local was Steve Gardner of Castletown. Walking for the Boundary Harriers, he completed the course for a fourth time in 19 hours 38 minutes 47 seconds. Veteran Cyril Evans, winner of the shorter race to Peel in the previous year was fourth in 20 hours 08 minutes 48 seconds, managing to hold off John Corrin, who took the fifth spot a further seven minutes in arrears.

With the month of May being the warmest and driest on record, the Meteorological Office at Ronaldsway predicted fine weather for the afternoon of 24th May – good news indeed for the 74 men and 16 women assembled at the Villa Marina Arcade on Douglas Promenade.

Mr. Fred Ward, starter for the fourteenth event, sent the ladies on their way at 2.30pm with the men following half an hour later.

The eventual leaders were prominent in the early stages but there were many retirements too, with one-third of the field failing to proceed beyond Rushen.

Stan Sille of Douglas was the first to reach the 25-mile mark at the Round Table. Maintaining his lead, he arrived at the eighth church in 6 hours 22 minutes only to retire soon after.

Nineteen walkers proceeded beyond the western capital with the front-runners taking turns to lead the field on the long journey north.

Darkness was the order of the day at Kirk Michael with 18-year-old Murray Lambden an early arrival and very much in contention. Nevertheless, the long haul to the most northerly church had taken its toll on the young pretender, and although he had established a comfortable lead, he was forced to throw in the towel shortly after two o'clock in the morning.

With dawn soon to break, only six of the field were still circulating. One of only three to finish last year, Castletown's Ron Ronan struggled on to Andreas with badly blistered feet. Officiating timekeeper Allan Callow did his best to keep him going, however beyond redemption at this point, Ronan called time shortly before dawn.

The leading pair was through Maughold just after daybreak, however third-placed Steve Gardner had slowed considerably over the northern plain, trailing the leading duo by more than three miles at Laxey.

Warner and Roe hurried on together with neither able to gain any real advantage over the final miles. They both arrived together at the penultimate church however Warner was the stronger and went away to win by ten minutes.

The story of the veterans' race to Peel centred on John 'Paddy' Dowling who missed the 3:00pm start because his inbound steamer was late docking. He was whisked over by taxi to the Villa Marina but was the best part of an hour and a half late in starting.

Dowling, a member of Sheffield United Harriers and winner of the previous year's 85-mile classic, quickly began carving his way through the main field. Allowing for his late start, his walking time to Peel was 5 hours 55 minutes 15 seconds, which would have made him a comfortable winner if the start rule had been relaxed. It was a superb walk and his effort won him an award for the most meritorious performance.

The ladies' 32½-mile event to Peel was more open than in previous years with multi-time winner, Irene Corlett, and present title holder, Heather Staley, both non-starters. The winner was Susanne Lardner-Burke of Castletown in 7 hours 05 minutes 35 seconds, which was over 40 minutes ahead of second finisher, Caroline Convery.

1976

After many years of trying, John Cannell achieved a lifetime ambition in 1976 by winning his first Parish Walk in a time of 17 hours 28 minutes 12 seconds.

A career in athletics stretching back to the very first End to End Walk in 1961, John was undoubtedly one of the finest walkers ever to set foot on the Island. He will be remembered in history alongside such great athletes as Albert Johnson and Graham Young, past winners of this event, but will also be remembered by friends and fellow athletes for his sheer guts and determination, the two important qualities that make him the man he is.

During the year, John had been suffering from a mystery illness for some time and had spent more time in hospital than in training. But he always returned to the track, for walking was what he lived for. He is the kind of person everyone admires and likes, and there could not have been a more popular winner of this year's event. His emotion showed clearly at the presentation buffet in the Douglas Head Hotel where he received the coveted trophy after finishing almost 1½ hours ahead of Kirk Michael's Murray Lambden.

With 80 starters setting off from the Villa Marina Arcade at 3:00pm on Saturday 22nd May, the annual 85-mile foot-slog around the 17 Parishes soon developed into a two-horse race spearheaded by Castletown's Steve Gardner and Douglas postman John Cannell.

Cannell took over leadership at the top of the Sloc when he overhauled a tired Gardner who had led from the start. The weather was poor on this section of the course and Gardner said later that he had gone through a bad patch and was unable to recover enough to catch Cannell. Eventually, John Corrin and Murray Lambden both caught and passed Gardner as the walk went on into the night.

By daybreak, Cannell led on the road from Lambden, with Corrin third. Gardner, now going through another bad spell, was fourth and struggling to put one foot in front of another.

With no change in the leader board, Cannell, Lambden, Corrin and Gardner were the only four finishers in the senior men's class. At the evening presentation, Cannell certainly looked fitter than the others who had obviously suffered in the latter stages of the walk.

Arguably the toughest event on the Manx sporting calendar, just completing the Parish Walk is a fantastic achievement in itself. For nineteen-year-old Murray Lambden it was even more credible, making him the fourth youngest walker ever to finish the event.

Cannell was not one of the listed pre-race favourites but said afterwards that he did not feel like retiring at any stage. 'I was having slight trouble with my shoes,' he said, 'there was some blood but no blisters and retiring never crossed my mind except when I saw Steve Kelly standing with a pint of beer outside the Waterfall Hotel in Glen Maye.'

There were four male finishers out of 70 starters, six lady finishers out of eight starters and one veteran finisher out of two starters. The ladies' race to Peel was won by Brenda Kneale of the 'Castletown Ale Drinkers' Society' while Cyril Evans of the Leicester Walking Club again won the veterans' class.

1977

In weather conditions more akin to the Sahara desert than the Isle of Man, 28-year-old Steve Gardner of Castletown was the sensational and only finisher of the Boundary Harriers 1977 Parish Walk, held over

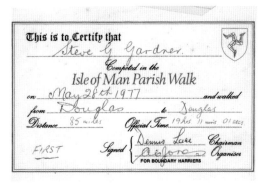

the weekend of 28th and 29th May.

In blistering hot conditions, his time of 19 hours 11 minutes 01 second was more than commendable but fell short of Graham Young's all-time record set six years earlier. Soaring temperatures throughout the afternoon and early evening made the going difficult and only half the 90 starters made it to Peel.

The entry of 72 men and 18 women was very much on a par with recent years. However, in the veterans' class for those aged 45 years or more, only two had entered for the shorter distance to Peel. There were many entries from the Castletown area including those of five-time finisher Steve Gardner, his sisters Brenda and Norma, plus Jeff Clayton, Kevin Walls, George Peach and Paul Baker.

With years of experience behind them, last year's winner, John Cannell, and race-record holder, Graham Young, were firm favourites for the honours. With Centurion and Commonwealth Games status already behind them, the Douglas postmen were no strangers to distance events and both were aware of the daunting and demanding task that lay ahead.

As in recent years, the ladies were away from the Villa Marina Arcade at 2:30pm, followed by the men 30 minutes later.

Wasting no time on the Peel Road, Cannell and Young were soon setting the standards for others to follow. Averaging a fraction under 6 mph, the pair hurried south to Rushen to arrive at the 19½-mile mark just after a quarter past six.

Above: Steve Gardner was the only finisher in 1977.

Below: Pictured soon after the 1976 event, left to right Dennis Lace, Murray Lambden, John Cannell and Ian Turnbull

Below: There was only one finisher from 90 starters in 1977.

1977-1978

Nevertheless, the scorching afternoon temperature took a heavy toll on those who came unprepared, with 43 walkers going no further than the sixth church. With Cannell a casualty at this point, Young led the way over the Sloc, the most demanding and tiring section of the entire course. He was first to Peel in a superb time of 5 hours 37 minutes however, as in previous years, the Douglas postman was only using the 32½ miles as a training session and at this point he promptly retired.

Pamela Reynolds was second into Peel, arriving at the Town Hall at 9:14pm, 21 minutes ahead of third-placed Steve Gardner. John Curphey and Tony Varley were next to the check-in point at 9:50pm followed by Simon Capelen ten minutes later.

With darkness not far away, Gardner was the first of 25 to head north out of Peel. There were six more retirements recorded at Kirk Michael, while James Thompson, Richard Sanderson and Gregory Joughin were more than pleased to end their painful ordeal three miles further on.

Only nine made it to Bride, with Kevin Walls, George Peach and Leslie Austin all stopping at the most northerly church as night was turning to day.

John Curphey and Tony Varley had pursued Gardner throughout the hours of darkness however, after a gallant performance through the northern plain, they were unable to reduce the 20-minute deficit and called time at Andreas, leaving Simon Capelen as the only serious challenger.

David Christian was next to call it a day, reaching the 62-mile mark at Lezayre in 15 hours 17 minutes – his furthest distance ever in four attempts.

With Capelen stopping at Maughold soon after sunrise, only two were left in the race, Jeff Clayton some 14 miles in arrears of the leader and looking unlikely to continue much further. Nevertheless, in spite of walking an extra three miles as a result of getting lost between Bride and Andreas, the 'Castletown Ale Drinker' bravely struggled on to Maughold where he was posted as the final retirement shortly after noon.

Alone from Maughold, Gardner confronted the back-breaking, tiring uphill road to the Hibernia unaware he was the only competitor left in the race. Undeterred, he pressed on to the finish, arriving at the Douglas War Memorial at 10:11am having been on the road for 19 hours 11 minutes 01 second.

A more than delighted Gardner said later: 'I was unaware the field had completely diminished. My mind just drifted from one thing to another. Although tired with tender feet, I was not exhausted and could have managed a few more miles had it been required.'

It was a wonderful achievement for the chairman of the Castletown Ale Drinkers Society. This was his sixth finish with more still to come. It is said that records are made to be broken, but this is one guaranteed to stand the test of time!

1978

Derek Harrison missed the 1978 Parish Walk having just returned from France where he broke the world record for miles walked in 24 hours. The brilliant Manx athlete who only turned to race walking a few years before, covered an incredible 136½ miles in front of thousands of cheering French walking enthusiasts. His amazing achievement received huge press and media coverage both on and off the Island making him our first-ever world champion.

The event took place in Rouen on the weekend of 20th and 21st May, and from a field 60 world-class walkers, only 30 finished the testing event.

Hundreds turned out to witness the evening start and although Derek set off at around 6 mph he still had about 20 competitors ahead of him during the early stages. As the night wore on, Derek gradually moved towards the front of the field to take the lead after three hours, a position he maintained to the finish. His only stoppages were to change clothes during the early hours when it became cold. Most of the other competitors stopped for occasional rest periods and were surprised at Derek's non-stop performance. Luckily, his wife, Sylvia worked tirelessly to support him throughout.

Although the Island's most respected athlete was a non-starter for the 1978 Parish Walk, Murray Lambden of Kirk Michael made up for his absence by winning the event in 16 hours 19 minutes 37 seconds. It was a race that only produced eight finishers and the fifth fastest time ever recorded in the history of the event. Lambden took the lead at Bride and went on to win by more than 1½ hours from Geoff Dowling and Britains's first female Centurion walker – Ann Sayer.

Scheduled for a 3:00pm start on Saturday 20th May, the entry of 85 included 17 teams with 19 walkers representing the 'Castletown Ale Drinkers' Society'. Race secretary, Arthur Jones, was chief organiser of the seventeenth event which started outside the Villa Marina Arcade on Douglas Promenade.

Weather conditions couldn't have been better as the 17 lady starters set off at 2:30pm followed by the 68 men 30 minutes later.

Early leaders through the southern parishes were Doug Allan, John Cannell, Graham Young and Murray Lambden. Cannell was the first to Rushen, however 18 retirements were recorded at this point including former finisher Jim Harvey, who reached the whitewashed church in 3 hours 57 minutes.

Cannell led the way up the Sloc with a four-minute advantage over Lambden and Young. Doug Allan was now fourth and just ahead of English visitors Geoff Dowling and Ann Sayer. Others going well were John Curphey, Tony Varley, Simon Capelen, Steve Gardner and Peel footballer Eddie Convery.

At Peel, the 32½ mile mark, the leading positions changed marginally with the premature retirement of Doug Allan. Here, at the eighth church, the retirement list continued to grow with another 19 falling by the wayside.

Douglas postman, Graham Young was the first to call time at Kirk Michael having entered the race as a training run for the Commonwealth Games later in August. George Peach of Castletown also stopped here, while at Ballaugh, three miles on, Kevin Brennan, Richard Sanderson and Gregory Joughin ventured no further.

Simon Capelen reached Jurby in 10 hours 18 minutes but then retired at this point along with Peter Lee, Barry Corris, James Thompson and Peter Lace, the latter arriving late at twenty past three in the morning.

There were retirements too for Michael Morling, Derek Corkhill and David Collister at Bride where Lambden had overtaken Cannell and now led on the road with Dowling third and Ann Sayer fourth, just a minute down. Behind the early leaders came John Curphey, Tony Varley and Brian Richmond from England.

Cannell was the first casualty at Andreas having reached the thirteenth church in only 10 hours 24 minutes and over four hours ahead of Keith West and Leslie Austin, also destined to stop here. Castletown's Jeff Clayton was going well at this point and put in a fine performance before surrendering at Lezayre shortly before 7 o'clock in the morning.

The race carried on through the early hours of daylight with only 11 walkers reaching Maughold. Albert Kermode, David Christian and Eddie Convery were all casualties here having walked 67 miles in a little over 17 hours.

Positions from here to Douglas were unchanged and it was Murray Lambden of the Boundary Harriers who crossed the finish line first, recording a magnificent time of 16 hours 19 minutes 37 seconds which put him in the record books along with all the other great walkers of this testing event.

In second place, but only just, Geoff Dowling from Yorkshire made it back to the finish in 17 hours 50 minutes 21 seconds. Ann Sayer was third, taking over three hours off the ladies' record. Fourth place went to John Curphey who, after a slow start, walked steadily throughout the night to put in a fine performance. Douglas fireman, Tony Varley, completed his first-ever Parish Walk finishing fifth, while Brian Richmond from England was sixth. Steve Gardner finished seventh but more than two hours slower than last year. In eighth and final place, Ivor Mellor was just pleased to get back to Douglas relatively unscathed in a time of 23 hours 13 minutes 07 seconds.

The ladies' race to Peel had 17 starters of which 11 completed the 32½ miles. Brenda Kneale was the early leader until retiring at Malew. Caroline Convery then took command of the race to reach Peel in 6 hours 58 minutes 47 seconds, ahead of Stephanie Quirk who was second and Barbara Moore third.

The Boundary Harriers 'A' team consisting of Murray Lambden, John Curphey and Tony Varley won the overall team prize while the ladies' section was won by the 'Castletown Ladies' Football Club' consisting of Barbara Moore, Jennifer Saunders and Susan Peach.

There were only three veterans entered in the 32½-mile race to Peel. It was won by Geoff Dowling in a record time of 6 hours 23 minutes 45 seconds. Fellow visitor Douglas Galloway was runner-up and Cyril Evans third.

1979

Derek Harrison returned to France in May 1979 but was unsuccessful in his defence of the annual Rouen 24-hour race, which he had convincingly won last year.

By invitation only and limited to 50 competitors of which four were women, Derek led the field during the early stages but was soon overhauled by the Dutch walker Jonge who went on to win by recording a new world record distance of 221.65 kilometres. Derek was second-placed, covering 219.23 kilometres – 370 metres less than his world record performance 12 months earlier.

Millennium year in 1979 saw the Isle of Man celebrating 1,000 years of self government. It was also a year that saw Steve Kelly become the first runner to record a sub-60-minute time over the ten-mile Peel to Douglas road race.

However the ultimate athletic performances of the year were those of Derek Harrison and Irene Corlett who shattered all records in the Parish Walk. Harrison bettered Graham Young's 1971 record time by 22 minutes and Corlett took 41 minutes off the ladies' record to Peel.

Entries were on a par with last year with 24 ladies taking part. Mylchreest Motors sponsored the event which Mr. Brian Mylchreest started at 5:30pm on Saturday 12th May from outside the Villa Marina Arcade.

Irene Corlett from Crosby immediately went to the front and soon built up a considerable lead, which by Peel, was well over one hour. Irene had produced one of her finest performances ever and reduced the record by 41 minutes 46 seconds. It was a superb performance for she reached Peel in 5 hours 51 minutes 04 seconds, averaging 5.55 mph for the 32½ miles.

Barbara McDermott was second in 7 hours 07 minutes 09 seconds with third place going to Afton Wray in 7 hours 15 minutes 39 seconds. There were only 13 finishers in this race which was held in poor weather conditions with reduced visibility on the Sloc to Round Table section making life even more difficult for those still in the race.

The men's race started 30 minutes later with Lt. Col. J.B. Mylchreest sending the 59 starters on their way at 6:00pm prompt.

Derek Harrison was the early leader, setting the pace from a group of three led by Murray Lambden, John Cannell and Graham Young.

Derek and Sylvia Harrison celebrate his 1978 world champion status for walking over 136 miles in twenty-hours.

1979

Derek Harrison with the Millennium Baton at Buckingham Palace.

Young may have been the early leader at Arbory but 25 minutes later, he was the first of 17 to retire at the most southerly chuch. Roy Corlett, John Moss and Albert Lowe also stopped at this point leaving Harrison to power his way up the mist-covered Sloc chased by Lambden and Cannell.

Harrison was first on the road into Peel, leading by 2 minutes 40 seconds from Lambden with Cannell a further 12 minutes behind.

Geoff Dowling was the first of the veterans' to reach the most westerly town in a creditable time of 6 hours 23 minutes 33 seconds. Bob Baxter was next in 6 hours 38 minutes 15 seconds followed by regular visitor Cyril Evans in 7 hours 10 minutes 12 seconds.

With darkness well established at Jurby, the leading duo was only three minutes apart, timekeeper Mitch Joughin checking them in at the whitewashed church before heading off on the lonely road to Bride.

Harrison quickened his pace on the long journey north leaving both Lambden and Cannell even further behind. Nevertheless, it was a pace too hot for Lambden and he stopped at Lezayre having reached the fourteenth church in 11 hours 13 minutes 32 seconds. This was also the stopping point for David Christian and Derek Corkhill and as daylight

approached, only six of the 83 starters were left on the road.

From Ramsey, positions changed little with Harrison pressing on for home in great haste. He crossed the finish line shortly after 9:20am on Sunday morning in a record time of 15 hours 20 minutes 51 seconds to beat the previous best set by Graham Young in 1971 by 22 minutes 21 seconds.

Second, but over an hour later, John Cannell improved on his previous best by 66 minutes to finish in 16 hours 22 minutes 03 seconds. Third place went to Paul Briggs of Bradford in 18 hours 07 minutes 06 seconds. John Curphey completed his second Parish Walk finishing in fourth place in a personal best time of 18 hours 28 minutes 16 seconds. Fifth was Castletown's Steve Gardner finishing for the eighth time in 21 hours 34 minutes 20 seconds while sixth and final place went to Castletown newcomer Jeff Clayton in 22 hours 23 minutes 50 seconds.

1980

Derek Harrison continued his rigid training programme throughout the winter months of 1979 and 1980 in preparation for the coming season of many long-distance walks. He trained daily during the comparatively mild winter, usually in the early morning at about 6:30am which did not interfere too much with family life. During the early months of winter, he would cover 60 to 70 miles a week, but increase this to around 100 miles as the season progressed. His intensive training had been designed to build up to the 24-hour long-distance race in Rouen where he was was again bidding to regain his world record of walking more than 137 miles in 24 hours.

A special diet was introduced seven days prior to the event and Derek ate nothing other than high protein foods such as meat, fish, cheese and eggs, switching to a high carbohydrate diet of rice and porridge just before the event. It was what Derek called 'going by the book' and designed to super-charge his body for the 24-hour race. He had used the remedy two years before when he broke the world record.

Derek was also careful with his food when not racing. He ate lots of fruit and vegetables but never cake or sweets.

But it was not just his gruelling training schedule and diet that helped him in his record bid. Mental approach was just as important. It is so easy to relax during a long-distance event and say to yourself 'I'll call it a day'. You have to stick at it and push yourself mentally as well as physically.

Nevertheless, the hundreds of hours of training were not quite good enough and windy conditions at the Rouen track may have prevented the record being broken. His third attempt at the world record was still a magnificent performance and Derek finished a close second, covering 134 miles in the 24-hour period.

Turning his attention to events closer to home, Derek was again favourite for the first Parish Walk of the new decade, an event he had already won three times.

With a June start and entry numbers exceeding 100 for the very first time, Mylchreest Motors again sponsored the event, held on the weekend preceding the summer solstice.

However, weather conditions were far from ideal with mist, heavy rain and flooding making life miserable for the seven who persevered to the finish.

Harrison won the race in a time of 16 hours 13 minutes 10 seconds, and although the conditions prevented him breaking the course record or getting close to the 15-hour mark that was hoped for, he still made the record books by winning for the fourth time, bettering Henry Harvey's achievement by one.

The real record-breaker in the race however, was Irene Corlett who knocked ten minutes off the ladies' record when she amazed even some of her greatest admirers by completing the course in 17 hours 41 minutes 40 seconds. Who knows what Irene could have achieved had weather conditions been better.

Scheduled for a 2:30pm start from the Villa Marina Arcade, the 31 ladies were away first followed by the

79 men half an hour later.

Extreme weather conditions through the early stages cut the field with much-talented Murray Lambden and John Curphey both going out at Rushen. Brian Leece, Tony and Bill Dale also called time here having underestimated the ingredients required for this Herculean task.

Tony Barfoot was another who failed to take the event seriously. With no training whatsoever, the Douglas Town Clerk was the last to reach the southernmost church having been on the road for well over five hours. However, the punishing climb to the Round Table was a walk too far for the 26-year-old. Consumption of large quantities of whisky to numb his pain had dehydrated him to such an extent that race officials requested a police van to convey him to Patrick village for medical observation.

The pattern of the race was set by Peel, the 32½-mile mark. Harrison had taken the lead at about 24 miles when the early pacemakers retired. He led previous winner, John Cannell, by 15 minutes who in turn was followed by Irene Corlett, Graham Young, Noel Cringle, Ian Turnbull and Roy Corlett.

But the weather had been unpleasant on the descent to Peel where stoppages were recorded for Bob Baxter, Cyril Evans, John Moss, Anthony Kneale, Allan Corlett, Simon Capelen and Graham Young – the Douglas postman and past winner reaching this point in 6 hours 13 minutes. Only 24 walkers continued beyond the most westerly town with Noel Cringle calling time at Kirk Michael shortly after 11 o'clock in the evening.

The second half of the walk saw Harrison surging ahead as others began to fall by the wayside. Cannell was now adrift of the leader by 30 minutes at Jurby where he surprised timekeepers by announcing his retirement despite reaching this point in 8 hours 47 minutes.

Parish regulars, Roy Corlett, Jeff Clayton and David Cain were the only retirements at Bride, the latter man barely moving, having been on his feet for 14 hours 10 minutes. Only ten walkers proceeded beyond this point with Leslie Austin ending his ordeal at St. Andrew's Parish Church, Andreas shortly after 6 o'clock in the morning and daylight well advanced. Nevertheless, back-marker Stephen Evans continued that bit further, reaching the 62-mile mark at 7:38am where he was posted as the final retirement of the day.

Graham Crowe produced a splendid performance too, and with little or no training, reached the fifteenth church in exactly 15 hours before calling it a day.

Harrison led the seven survivors out of Maughold to comfortably win his third event in ten years. Over an 1½ hours behind, Irene Corlett claimed the runner-up spot with Ian Turnbull third.

Despite the atrocious weather conditions Eddie Convery, Ivor Mellor, James Thompson and Roy Cooil all kept going to the end, the latter completing the course for the first time in 22 hours 47 minutes 38 seconds.

Derek Harrison was the first of only seven finishers in 1980.

1981-1982

1981

Although well disciplined with a punishing training schedule the envy of many, Derek Harrison failed to make an impact in the 1981 Parish Walk which was won convincingly by Douglas postman John Cannell. It was his second victory in six years, knocking nearly seven minutes of his 1976 time and completing the gruelling 85-mile course in 16 hours 15 minutes 11 seconds.

Unlike some competitors who thrive on competition, John's best performances in the 'Parish' have been when he could relax and walk at his own pace. This year he was in his element in the near perfect overnight conditions and finished at the war memorial on Douglas Promenade at quarter past seven in the morning on the longest day of the year. His time was the sixth fastest, behind Derek Harrison, Graham Young, Albert Johnson and Leece Kneale.

Many of the Island's leading walkers, Graham Young, Murray Lambden and Steve Gardner, were missing from this year's event and only 56 men came to the start line at the Villa Marina Arcade. Celebrating its twenty-first birthday, the event was held over the weekend of the summer solstice, the 29 ladies were first away at 2:30pm followed by the men 30 minutes later.

Derek Harrison's attempt to record the first-ever hat-trick and his fifth win in total ended shortly after reaching Peel. The former 24-hour world record holder, who was competing in his last major race, took the lead on the bottom of the Sloc after pacemaker, Robbie Lambie, retired.

Harrison continued to Peel at a very fast pace, recording the quickest time ever to this point of 5 hours 39 minutes. He led overall at this stage by five minutes from Willie Corkill with Cannell a further minute behind. But the pace proved too much for the Douglas civil servant, and although on a record schedule he stopped soon after the eighth church.

Eamonn Magee was fourth into Peel, along with unofficial Andrew Garrett whose entry was refused because he was almost three years short of the 18-year-old age limit!

Next to arrive at the Commissioners Offices was Frank Dolan and then veterans Noel Cringle and Bob Baxter who took the second and third places in that class. There were 17 retirements at this point including the young teenager Garrett who was not credited with a finishing time.

Dolan got ahead of Magee on the coast road to Kirk Michael while 'Parish' icon Noel Cringle made his way painfully to the ninth church only to retire after 8 hours 06 minutes.

The list of retirements continued to grow as the race neared the halfway mark with Robert Burnett, Derek Lewney, Allan Corlett, Juan Walters and Eric Costain all calling time at Ballaugh.

Tony Barfoot, Leslie Austin and Anthony Kneale reached Jurby in a little over 11 hours before retiring while Thomas Kelly and Alan Pilling stopped at Bride

as daylight approached.

Cannell was well in front after leaving the northernmost church but second-placed Corkill was fading fast and was the first retirement at Andreas having walked 55½ miles in 11 hours 01 minutes,

Dolan now moved into second place but added an extra four miles to his journey when he missed the Lezayre church turn-off. Eamonn Magee was the final and only retirement at this point having covered 62 miles in an excellent time of 12 hours 27 minutes.

Only nine competitors checked into the fifteenth church, and from here to the finish there was no change in order. Roy Corlett was suffering from a painful back and for some time looked unlikely to finish. He and Roy Cooil were equal third and walked the final miles together, overtaking a determined John Smith who finished fifth.

Sixty-eight-year-old Cyril Evans from Coventry was sixth and became the oldest person ever to complete the course. Making his Parish Walk debut, David Ronan was seventh. Having damaged a hamstring at Lezayre, David was forced to walk the final 23 miles dragging his foot along the road. There was little of his shoe left at the finish where he was greeted with great applause.

Joint eighth place went to last year's finisher, Eddie Convery, with Eric Nelson finishing for the first time in 23 hours 29 minutes 32 seconds.

The ladies' race to Peel was completely dominated by Irene Corlett, now at the pinnacle of her career, who took eight minutes off her own record and was only three minutes slower than Derek Harrison's time to this point. Her time of 5 hours 42 minutes 22 seconds was nearly one hour quicker than second-placed Gladys Crellin who was making a welcome return after some years of absence.

1982

Now in its third decade and slowly returning to its former glory, the Parish Walk of 1982 produced its highest entry to date with a record number of entrants eager to take up the challenge of walking to each of the Island's 17 parish churches within a 24-hour period.

As in previous years, the contest produced its usual records, high standards and gutsy performances from many of the 120 starters lined up at the Villa Marina Arcade on Saturday, 19th June. Irene Corlett led the 32 ladies away at 2:30pm followed by the men 30 minutes later.

Douglas postman John Cannell was the popular winner, recording the fifth fastest time ever over the gruelling 85-mile circuit. His time of 15 hours 59 minutes 33 seconds was over two hours quicker than his nearest rival, Roy Corlett. Brother-in-law to Irene, Roy completed the course for a second time in 18 hours 31 minutes 43 seconds, nearly half an hour ahead of Thomas Kelly who was third. Thomas celebrated his twenty-first birthday on the weekend of the race and was later awarded the Murray

Lambden Trophy for the best under-21 performance. Of the 88 starters in the main event, only eight completed the full distance.

Cannell stamped his authority on the men's event from the start and soon pulled ahead of the field as he challenged Derek Harrison's 1979 course record. Although this was to slip from his grasp, John hurried on to the finish to become only the fourth person to record a sub-16-hour time. Although his time was exceptional, the race in general was slower than in previous years with former Commonwealth Games competitor, Allan Callow, completing the 85 miles for the first time, in a creditable 19 hours 40 minutes 15 seconds.

In securing fifth place, Roy Cooil recorded his third finish. It was a brave effort for he struggled many miles with a groin injury to finish just outside the 20-hour mark. Steve Gardner of Castletown was sixth. His time of 20 hours 55 minutes 14 seconds added another finish to his total of nine.

Chris Keown was ecstatic at his first circuit of the 17 parishes in what was his first full year of race walking. Inspite of a lack of training, John Smith showed great character to pace himself to the finish, arriving opposite the Gaiety Theatre to secure the eighth and final place in a time of 21 hours 57 minutes 51 seconds.

As expected, former Parish Walk winner, Derek Harrison, dominated the veterans' race to Peel, completing the 32½ miles in 5 hours 47 minutes 41 seconds. John Curphey was second in 6 hours 29 minutes exactly and Noel Cringle third in 6 hours 34 minutes 01 seconds. Seventy-year-old Arthur Jones had a good walk too, reaching Peel in 7 hours 30 minutes 50 seconds. He finished sixth in this class, also making the record books as the oldest man ever to complete the 32½ miles.

In the ladies' race to Peel, Irene Corlett broke all records, beating her own record time by 19 minutes and reaching the eighth church in an incredible time of 5 hours 23 minutes 16 seconds. The amazing 40-year-old covered the 32½ miles at an average speed of 6.03 mph to finish nearly one hour ahead of nearest challenger, Anne Cain.

1983

Having triumphed in all of the Island's race walking events over the last two decades, John Cannell made it three wins in a row by winning the 1983 Parish Walk in a time of 16 hours 31 minutes 38 seconds. It was the first-ever hat-trick of wins in the testing 85-mile event and one that gave him great pleasure.

The annual foot-slog held over the weekend of 18th and 19th June was one of the best for years although no records were broken in any of the three classes. Entries were on a par with last year with 109 taking part including four-time winner Derek Harrison entered in the veterans' class to Peel only.

Sponsor of the event for the fifth year, Mr. Brian Mylchreest sent the 24 ladies on their way at 2:30pm

Charlie Weston and John Cannell approaching Rushen. It was a third victory for John in a race that produced only eight finishers.

followed by 85 men half an hour later.

Although the weather was kinder than in recent years, the temperature had reached 18 degrees centigrade by mid-afternoon making life uncomfortable during the early stages.

Cannell started steady in the heat-wave conditions but there were many retirements on the tiring haul south with Noel Cringle the first of 15 to stop at the most southerly church.

Cannell built up a lead from Tom Kelly during the evening, extending it to almost an hour by the halfway mark. Willie Corkill was third with 24 walkers continuing past this point.

There were further retirements at Lezayre with David Collister, Gary Heron, Juan Walters, Leslie Austin and Tony Barfoot all calling it a day, the latter man in poor shape having reached the fourteenth church in 17 hours 35 minutes.

Dawn was well advanced as the leaders approached Maughold. Cannell was the first to the church gate and he was given plenty of encouragement from the few spectators up and about at this unearthly hour. Michael Watterson, Gary Gamble and David Cain all stopped at this point, the latter arriving in 18 hours 14 minutes with no enthusiasm to continue.

Only ten walkers continued past the 67-mile mark with no change in the leader board from that point on. Last year's runner-up Roy Corlett, was fourth and Chris Keown fifth. Experiencing his longest walk ever, Tony Kneale managed to hold on to sixth spot, while Derek Corkill and Steve Gardner walked the latter stages together to claim joint seventh place. It was a first-ever completion for Derek after many previous attempts, but not for Steve Gardner who completed the walk for the tenth time, but at a much slower

Above: Roy Corlett was runner-up in 1982.

Below: A third finish for Roy Corlett in 1983.

1983-1984

Steve Gardner completed the course for the tenth time in 1983.

time of 22 hours 30 minutes 46 seconds. Husband and wife, Eddie and Caroline Convery, completed the finishers in a time of 23 hours 06 minutes 46 seconds and 23 hours 36 minutes 46 seconds respectively. It was Eddie's third finish and Caroline's first after many years of trying – a wonderful performance from both.

With last year's winner and record holder, Irene Corlett, off the Island, the ladies' race to Peel was very open and only decided over the closing miles with eventual winner Gladys Crellin overtaking Rose Clark less than two miles from the finish. Gladys had taken the lead early on and had built up a gap of almost ten minutes by Malew, however the intense heat affected her performance and Rose closed and passed her on the Sloc. Nevertheless, with eight miles to go, Gladys appeared to recover and re-took the lead on the Patrick road, reaching Peel in 7 hours 01 minute 46 seconds. Rose finished second, two minutes later, with Jean Oldroyd third.

There were many other fine performances recorded in the ladies' race which produced 17 finishers. Fourth-placed was Barbara Kniveton, fifth Angie Aire and sixth Caroline Convery, the latter reaching the Town Hall in 7 hours 55 minutes 18 seconds.

Derek Harrison won the veterans' race to Peel, just four minutes slower than last year in 5 hours 44 minutes exactly. A worthy performance was recorded by Arthur Jones too. The 71-year-old organiser of the event, who completed 32½ miles in 7 hours 43 minutes 45 seconds to establish himself once again as the oldest-ever finisher of this class.

1984

Proving the old adage that life begins after 40, Derek Harrison swept all opposition aside in 1984 when he won the Parish Walk for a fifth time to become the oldest-ever winner of the modern event.

Derek, who had just celebrated his fiftieth birthday, completed the 85-mile event in 16 hours 10 minutes 17 seconds. It was one of his best walks ever,

finishing over 1½ hours ahead of his nearest rival Roy Corlett. Only seven of the 105 starters made it back to Douglas, four of whom were newcomers.

As in previous years, the race began from the Villa Marina Arcade on Saturday 16th June in warm conditions with the 20 ladies away at 2:30pm, followed by the men 30 minutes later.

Previous four-time winner, John Cannell, was missing from this year's event due to taking part in the 100-mile Centurion event in Leicester. Also not contesting the race were 1978 winner, Murray Lambden, and ten-time finisher, Steve Gardner. The race was more open than in previous years with few retirements in the early stages thanks to favourable conditions.

Making his first appearance, but well experienced at distance events such as this, Mick Holgate was one of ten to retire at the most southerly church, a stopping point for those using the event solely for training purposes.

Harrison was never really challenged, taking an early lead from Willie Kneale, Ian Turnbull, Brian Richmond and last year's finishers, Roy Corlett and Tony Kneale.

Twenty-seven continued beyond Peel including Rose Clark, and with the conditions being favourable, it looked likely that there would be a good number of overall finishers.

As darkness set in, Harrison moved away from the field with second place hotly contested between Willie Corkill and Chris Keown. Only 17 walkers continued past the most northerly church however, Corkill was an early retirement at Andreas, a point he reached in 11 hours 23 minutes. Harrison continued his relentless pace through the northern plain and by daybreak he was 17 miles ahead of the remaining stragglers.

Chris Keown, Keith Davies and Michael Watterson all stopped at Lezayre, but behind them and last on the road, were Tony Barfoot and David Collister. The two had been together since Union Mills, but now moving at a funeral pace over the Sulby Bridge and aware that the 62-mile mark had been their stopping point 12 months earlier.

The sun was well up when the pair reached the fourteenth church, however Collister was in poor shape and took time out on the roadside bench before announcing he was going no further. It was his fourth attempt at the 'Parish' and surely couldn't all end here. Determined to keep him going, Barfoot and the support team gave Collister a 'good talking to' and reluctantly, he rose to his feet to continue along the road to Ramsey, but at a greatly reduced speed.

The five miles to Maughold were not easy ones for Collister who was now on his own and over 7 hours behind the leader. Ivor Mellor and Derek Lewney were the only retirements at Bride where Barfoot quickened his pace, desperate to reach the finish within the 24-hour time limit. Nevertheless, the 30-year-old Douglas Corporation clerical officer struggled on through the picturesque parish with badly

It was a 3 O'Clock afternoon start in 1983.

blistered feet that made life difficult on the tiring, uphill road to the Hibernia.

There was no change in position from here to the finish on Douglas Promenade where both Harrison and Corlett had arrived some three hours earlier and now well in to a good night's sleep!

Tony Kneale finished third in 18 hours 47 minutes 28 seconds, but behind him, the remaining four, James Anderson, David Cain, Tony Barfoot and David Collister were strung far and wide along the Ramsey to Laxey coast road.

The early finishers were 'up and about' when Collister crossed the finishing line at the Douglas War Memorial soon after 4 o'clock in the afternoon. His time of 25 hours 08 minutes 25 seconds was outside the set limit, but this was of no importance at the Villa Marina presentation held later that night where he received tumultuous applause for his gallant effort.

The ladies again performed well with 16 of the 20 starters completing the 32½ miles to Peel. After a number of attempts, Irene Kelly of Baldwin easily defeated the pre-race favourite Ann Kelly in a very respectable time of 6 hours 35 minutes 51 seconds. Indeed, Ann only just held off a challenge from Rose Clark, last year's runner-up, in the closing stages.

The veterans' race also finished at Peel and it was Derek Harrison who was first to reach the line, but, because he carried on to complete the whole distance, he was ineligible to take the award. The winner was therefore Ian Turnbull, a former winner of the event, in a very creditable time of 6 hours 08 minutes 31 seconds. Brian Richmond from Barrow was second and Keith Davies third.

As expected, 72-year-old Arthur Jones again put up an amazing performance, finishing eighth in this class to complete the 32½ miles in 7 hours 45 minutes 52 seconds.

A fifth and final win for Derek Harrison in 1984.

1985

Although John Cannell, Graham Young and Derek Harrison had dominated the Parish Walk in recent years, time stands still for no one, and by 1985, a new generation of walkers were making themselves known.

There were a record 15 finishers in this year's event which attracted the largest entry ever. Willie Corkill of Colby was victor on this occasion, completing the annual foot-slog around the Island's

Soaking up the sunshine on the way to Marown.

1985

Left: Seventy-three-year-old race secretary Arthur Jones would regularly walk to Peel in a pair of sandals.
Right: A first victory for Willy Corkill in 1985.

17 parishes in a creditable 16 hours 29 minutes 31seconds, comfortably ahead of visiting competitor, Charlie Weston.

The race, normally held over the weekend of the summer solstice, was a week earlier this year and held on Saturday 15th June.

Starting at the Villa Marina Arcade in Douglas and again sponsored by Mylchreest Motors, the 30 ladies started at 2:30pm and the 91 men half an hour later.

The early leader was Charlie Weston from the Highgate Harriers, London, who raced away from the rest of the field with only previous winner, John

Cannell, in contention. On schedule for a course record time, Weston reached Peel in a very brisk 5 hours 35 minutes 08 seconds, but only 38 seconds ahead of race favourite Cannell. Derek Harrison was not far behind with Willy Corkill in sixth place and moving strongly through the field.

The pace continued along the coast road to Kirk Michael where Cannell briefly took the lead. Unfortunately, his feet were in a poor state and he was an early retirement three miles further on at the halfway mark.

Harrison continued to close on Weston through

Journey's end and a fifth finish for Roy Corlett.

1985-1986

the dark hours with Corkill some way back but making good progress and holding his own. As in previous years, Harrison's feet blistered badly on the coast road to Bride and he was an early retirement soon after, leaving Corkill in second place and catching the leader fast.

The weather conditions were ideal for Corkill to take control of the race and he caught and passed Weston on the Lezayre road from which point he was never seriously challenged, finishing on Douglas Promenade at half past seven on Sunday morning, nearly half an hour ahead of Weston.

Last year's runner-up, Roy Corlett, overcame the usual difficult times and finished third, a further 1½ hours behind Weston, but in a creditable time of 18 hours 32 minutes 46 seconds.

Regular finisher, Chris Keown, was fourth and in equal fifth place were Chas Pimblett and Douglas postman, Ray Hughes, who completed the walk for the first time in 19 hours 20 minutes 40 seconds.

Tony Kneale was next to finish in 19 hours 38 minutes 36 seconds with Peter Halsall finishing in eighth place, just beating the youngest finisher, Andrew Garrett, who won the Murray Lambden Cup for the best under 21 performance in a time of 20 hours 10 minutes 08 seconds.

Castletown's Dave Wilkinson was next over the line in tenth place, followed some time later by final finishers, Steve Evans, Norman Christian, Tony Kerruish, Leslie Austin and David Collister – all of whom showed exceptional courage in pushing themselves to the ultimate limit.

1986

For the first time in its long history, the Parish Walk had a new starting time of 12 noon in 1986 with the race getting underway outside the Villa Marina Arcade on Saturday 21st June, the longest day of the year.

Colby's Willie Corkill was a delighted winner of the Mylchreest Motors sponsored event in which only 14 finished. Corkill completed the tortuous 85-mile circuit in a time of 17 hours 3 minutes 45 seconds, over two hours ahead of Douglas postman, Ray Hughes. Mick Holgate took third place while Rose Clark and Allan Callow were the respective victors in the ladies' and veterans' classes to Peel.

A record entry of 157 walkers started the event in ideal conditions with the temperature soaring to 20°C by mid-afternoon. It was a second win and third finish for Corkill who preserved his energy during the early stages of sweltering conditions.

John Cannell set the early, fast pace, building up a five-minute lead over the opening miles. But he slowed on the Sloc climb allowing Allan Callow to take the lead, which he held to Peel. His time of 5 hours 29 minutes 50 seconds was the fastest-ever recorded to this point and just one minute ahead of three-time winner Cannell. Charlie Weston was the third veteran to finish at the eighth church, arriving in 5 hours 54 minutes 30 seconds.

With the top three veterans' stopping at Peel, Corkill moved into second place 15 minutes behind five-time winner, Derek Harrison, who was now leading on the road. Corkill reduced the deficit to six minutes at Jurby but then promptly retired having been in contention for 45 miles or so.

Chris Keown who had been holding third position was a casualty at Kirk Michael which elevated youngsters, Steve Taylor and Steve Brennan, into second place at Jurby. Soon after, they were overtaken by three-time finisher, Tony Kneale, who maintained second position until retiring at Maughold with injury problems.

Thirteen hours of sunshine were recorded on this, the longest day of the year. Nevertheless, conditions deteriorated overnight, which slowed Corkill and the remaining field, now a long way back.

Neither Ray Hughes nor Mick Holgate featured among the early leaders but Ray used last year's experience to improve by three minutes, recording a time of 19 hours 17 minutes 44 seconds but over two hours behind the leader.

Mick was the first veteran home, a further half an hour behind. He judged his pace well to record a first-time finish in 19 hours 46 minutes 31 seconds.

'Parish' regulars, Dave Wilkinson and John Wright walked the latter stages together, finishing in joint fourth place in 20 hours 42 minutes 30 seconds. John was also completing the course for the first time.

Next to finish were Norman McKibbin and Mick Rodger. Then, to everyone's surprise, in joint eighth place, came Steve Taylor and Steve Brennan, both 20 years of age, who shared the Murray Lambden Cup for best performance by an under 21-year-old.

Walking in company, David Hall and Fintan Suddards recorded their first finish, Norman Christian his second. Also completing the course for a first time after six attempts was Colin Hodgkinson followed by David Collister at the rear of the field, finishing for a third year in succession but at a slightly slower time than last year.

In the ladies' race to Peel, Ann Cain set a fast pace early on but paid the penalty later when she was forced to retire on the Sloc. The remarkable veteran, Jean Oldroyd, briefly took the lead but was later passed by Rose Clark who went on to win in a time almost half an hour faster than last year. Her 70 miles a week training programme certainly paid off for Rose reached the eighth church at Peel in 6 hours 33 minutes 06 seconds – a very creditable time indeed.

Derek Harrison's wife, Sylvia, also had a good outing, reaching Peel in third place in 6 hours 50 minutes 25 seconds.

Every team needs its captain and the Boundary Harriers were deeply indebted to Arthur Jones who had acted as their most efficient captain and race organiser over the years. Seventy-four-year-old Arthur was one of the Island's most respected sports administrators but due to his many commitments was unable to contest this year's event

Steve Taylor finished in 1986 in 21 hours 33 minutes and 49 seconds.

1987

A second win for Willy Corkill.

1987

Media coverage of this great event had much room for improvement during the late 1980s with newspaper coverage sparse. Only the *Isle of Man Courier* and the *Manx Star* covered the event in any detail with assistance from enthusiastic part-time correspondents Kevin Madigan and Derek Harrison.

The Isle of Man Weekly Times and *Manx Star* ceased publication in 1987 to be replaced by the *Manx Independent*. John Watterson was their chief sports correspondent and his enthusiastic and comprehensive reporting of the event certainly helped with its resurgence.

The second person ever to score a hat rick of wins, Colby's Willie Corkill was a popular winner of the 1987 Parish Walk. Not only did he complete the 85-mile course in 16 hours 58 minutes 33 seconds, he also improved on his 1986 winning time by almost five minutes.

In the ladies' 32½ mile race to Peel, Rose Clark chalked-up a similar hat rick after leading from start to finish.

Due to increased numbers and concern for road safety, this year's start was switched to the Villa Marina Gardens with the main event getting underway at 12 noon on Saturday, 20th May.

In warm, sunny conditions, the 36 ladies and 107 men were sent on their way by starters Mr. and Mrs. J. B. Mylchreest, sponsor of the event for the eighth year.

Former winner Charlie Weston of Highgate Harriers set off at a quick pace and was almost five minutes ahead of fellow veteran, Allan Callow, after just seven miles. Andrew Garrett was in third place through the early stages with Willie Corkill, pacing himself well for the full distance and fourth.

Inevitably, 50-year-old Weston slowed dramatically on the punishing climb over the Sloc and was then passed by Allan Callow and Frank Huntley on the downhill winding road to Dalby.

At Glen Maye, Callow and Huntley were striding out in front, having also overhauled the leading lady walkers who had started 30 minutes earlier. Weston was really paying the penalty for his early lead and it looked for a while as though the Highgate man would not reach Peel.

Callow was the first arrival at the eighth church, his

Left: Willy Corkill makes it a hat trick of wins.

Right: A tiring climb to Glen Maye.

time of 5 hours 44 minutes 22 seconds, some five minutes ahead of schoolmaster, Huntley, so repeating his veterans' class success of the previous year. Next home was Allan Kelly who just dipped under 6 hours for the 32½ miles. Corkill reached Peel very comfortably where he touched the timekeeper's table at the Town Hall before continuing on the long haul north to Kirk Michael and beyond.

However, Weston was in trouble at this point and stopped to repair his damaged feet. After a brief respite, and with much renewed confidence, he set about the mammoth task of reeling-in the Manxman. He covered the long coastal route through Kirk Michael, Ballaugh and Jurby in determined style, chasing Corkill to the finish, the gap between them hardly varying over the final 40 miles.

At Maughold, Weston had drawn back to within 15 minutes of Corkill but the Boundary Harriers stalwart hung on grimly, to cross the finish line on Douglas Promenade at 5:00am, some 19 minutes in front of Weston.

Martin Lambden was comfortably in third place through the northern plain but fatigue took its toll on the dairyman and he retired at Lezayre after 62 miles.

Norman Christian finished his third successive Parish Walk in a time of 18 hours 09 minutes 40 seconds, an amazing three hours quicker than last year. In fourth place and recording a personal best time of 18 hours 49 minutes 17 seconds, Ray Hughes caught Tony Kneale over the closing miles, finishing 31 minutes ahead.

Castletown's Dave Wilkinson completed a hat-trick of finishes with sixth spot and ahead of Don Bottomly, Laurie Gale and Bob Baxter, all completing the course for the first time.

Norman McKibbin completed the course for a second time. It was a fourth successive finish for David Collister who took nearly two hours off last year's time, finishing in 21 hours 48 minutes 58 seconds, just 28 seconds ahead of final placed Don Higgins.

Rose Clark's winning time to Peel was just a shade over 6½ hours, with Jean Oldroyd of Onchan runner-up for the second year in succession, some 11 minutes in arrears. Linda Gelling and Sue Quine walked the entire distance together while Joyce Stigant and Anne Lewin completed the top six.

The Murray Lambden Cup for the most meritorious performance by a competitor under 21 years of age went to Steven Cain who reached the eleventh church at Jurby, in 11 hours 29 minutes.

There was a welcome return for the event's secretary, 75-year-old Arthur Jones, who again completed the 32½ miles to Peel in a spritely time of 7 hours 42 minutes 52 seconds.

1988

Never short of surprises, the Parish Walk produced a most unlikely winner in 1988 with 35-year-old Braddan dairyman Martin Lambden claiming the honours by just 15 minutes in the second closest finish ever.

His victory was remarkable and it marked an unprecedented family double as his brother Murray was a winner ten years earlier. Never had two brothers won the event before, the nearest coming during the early 1960s when the Harvey boys of Abbeylands dominated the event.

Held over the weekend of 18th and 19th June, this year's event was wide-open as John Cannell, Allan Callow and Willie Corkill were only contesting the veterans' 32½-mile race to Peel.

For the second year in succession, the Villa Marina

Above: On this occasion, Willy Corkill only went as far as Peel.

Left: Steve Partington was first to Peel, however his time of 5 hours 02 minutes was un-recorded.

Right: At only his third attempt, Martin Lambden won the 1988 Parish Walk in 17 hours 12 minutes 01 second.

1988

Above: The tough Sloc soon to be negotiated.

Below: Tony Kneale earned a well deserved third place in 1988.

Gardens was the venue for the start with the 37 ladies away at 11:30am, followed by the 85 men at 12 noon.

The first to arrive at Peel, by a long chalk, was the Island's leading walker, Steve Partington. Literally striding out over the Sloc, the 18-year-old showed no signs of weariness after his continental debut seven days earlier in Luxembourg. He reached the Town Hall in an incredible time of 5 hours 01 minute 59 seconds, however as this was merely a training session, his time went unrecorded.

Meanwhile, two miles back, the battle for veteran honours continued. John Cannell and Frank Huntley were the main protagonists after former double winner Allan Callow pulled up at Rushen suffering further problems with his hamstring.

Huntley was leader through the first two parishes but Cannell drew level at the Braaid crossroads. By the time the pair reached Malew, John had the marginal advantage. Nevertheless, the Douglas postman was having stomach problems and all but gave up on the return to Cross Four Ways. 'I felt terrible,' he admitted later, 'and just stood at the roadside for several minutes before continuing.'

Continue he certainly did, however by this time he was some eight minutes down on Frank with both Allan Callow and Willie Corkill also leap-frogging ahead.

Cannell found an extra gear on the Ballakillowey ascent and by the time he got to 'Tom the Dipper's' corner, he had Huntley firmly in his sights, determined to grasp his first Parish veterans' win.

Inevitably, at such a pace, Cannell strode past Huntley at the Round Table and by the time the pair reached Glen Maye, John was some four minutes clear pulling out more than ten minutes over the tops.

The remaining three miles into Peel were a formality for Cannell, and with Allan Callow's 1986 record in sight, he pressed on to better that standard by some three minutes, touching-in with a time of 5 hours 26 minutes 32 seconds to record the third quickest time ever to this point.

Huntley made it home to Peel, over five minutes down on Cannell, while Corkill, fourth on the road behind Partington, Cannell and Huntley, gained third spot in his first veterans' event, having opted out of the full 85-miler in preparation for the National 100-mile Championship in August. The Parish Walk winner for the past three years was clearly not at his best over the shorter 32½-mile section to Peel.

Next on the road, and a clear distance ahead in the ladies' event was Ann Cain who, after slipping two minutes behind pre-event favourite Rose Clark in the early stages, took control before Malew for a well-earned success. It is possible that Clark went off too quickly. After gaining a two-minute lead in less than ten miles, she appeared to lack her usual drive over the hills towards Dalby and was some six minutes adrift at Glen Maye. This was Ann's first finish since 1985 when she was runner-up to Irene Corlett and she was absolutely delighted with her success.

By now, the long-haulers and all-nighters were beginning to filter through with the amazing Charlie Weston out on his own, some 16 minutes clear of local man Martin Lambden. Tony Kneale was the only other walker to go through Peel in less than six hours, in turn some five minutes down on Lambden. On the Kirk Michael stretch, Weston was saving himself for the long haul ahead, enabling both Lambden and Kneale to reduce the deficit.

Further back, nineteen-year-old Lee Cain had reached Peel and had very nearly called it a day, but was persuaded to continue after a ten-minute break, clearly with the intention of going for the Murray Lambden Cup, awarded for best performance of an under 21-year-old.

Cain was closely followed on the road by Douglas postman, Ray Hughes, who had been placed fourth the previous year. His main rival, Norman Christian, had retired on the Sloc when well placed. Norman was forced out of the race by the pain of his injured right knee and ankle, an injury incurred during an argument with a beer barrel at work before Easter. Parish Walk regular, Chris Keown, was another man saving his resources for the National 100-miler and was a retirement at Peel, the 32½-mile mark.

The last to reach the eighth church was Port Erin's Trevor Belcher who checked in to the Town Hall shortly before 9 o'clock in the evening. By now, the field was well spread, with leader Weston some 17 miles ahead and rapidly approaching the quintessential village of Bride.

Darkness was descending as the long-haulers reached this most northerly point, 52½ miles out. Weston was on his own some 16 minutes clear of Lambden, with Tony Kneale a further 45 minutes in arrears.

Lambden continued and, slowly but surely, reduced the deficit. By Ramsey, the gap was less than 13 minutes, and on reaching Maughold, he was only 11 minutes behind the Highgate Harrier. Going into Laxey, he was just one minute behind and by the time the pair headed out of the old mining town towards the penultimate church at Lonan, the Manxman had raced ahead to take control.

Lambden crossed the finishing line at the war memorial on Douglas Promenade an exhausted, but clearly delighted winner in a time of 17 hours 12 minutes 01 second. He was 15 minutes in front of Weston who had walked a near flawless race.

Tony Kneale kept his weary legs in motion to gain a best-ever finish in third spot, just over an hour behind Weston. Fourth place, for the second year in succession, went to Ray Hughes with veteran Norman McKibbin fifth. Completing the course for the fifth consecutive time in 22 hours 42 minutes 25 seconds David Collister was the sixth and final finisher, Lambden the only one not to have gone the full distance before.

There were 13 finishers in the ladies' 32½-mile race to Peel. Ann Cain was first to reach the eighth church in a time of 6 hours 29 minutes 59 seconds.

Last year's winner, Rose Clark, was second in 6 hours 42 minutes 25 seconds and Judith Corkish third in a time of 7 hours 19 minutes 20 seconds.

1989

Eclypsing Derek Harrison as oldest-ever winner of the Parish Walk, 55-year-old Charlie Weston won the 1989 event in 18 hours 17 minutes 55 seconds. It was the fourth slowest time ever recorded over the 85-mile course but one that gave the regular visitor much satisfaction.

Many previous winners had not entered this year, including four-time winner John Cannell who gave the event a miss in preparation for the forthcoming National 100-miler. The previous year's winner, Martin Lambden, was also missing due to work committments and shortage of preparation. The much-experienced Steve Gardner, winner in 1977 and ten-time finisher had also entered after a six-year lay off, however personal injury forced him to withdraw at short notice.

Eleven of the original 124 starters went the full 85-mile distance in the Mylchreest Motor's sponsored walk, but the most significant overall factor was the sheer tenacity shown by the lady competitors, three of whom made it back in determined style.

Pre-walk favourite, Weston, made no pretence about his ambition of an overall victory after being 'bridesmaid' on so many occasions. He set off from the Villa Marina at 12 noon on Saturday 17th June and was only matched for strides in the early stages by Frank Huntley and Chris Keown, both of whom were using the event for mere training purposes. Frank stopped at Ballabeg while Chris went on to Peel in 6 hours 14 minutes 48 seconds.

There were 23 retirements at the most southerly church, including 77-year-old Arthur Jones who was making his nineteenth appearance in the annual Manx Classic.

Charlie soon caught the ladies who had started 30 minutes in advance. He finally moved ahead of Ann Cain and Rose Clark on the Sloc ascent. Ann and Rose had matched each other stride for stride throughout and had decided well in advance of the finish to cross the line in tandem at Peel, the termination of the ladies' event.

'I gave Ann a lift up the hills and she helped me on the final stretch to Peel,' admitted three-time former winner, Clark, later. The pair crossed the line in a time of 6 hours 40 minutes 14 seconds, over 20 minutes clear of twenty-third birthday girl, Ann Marie Kelly, of Colby. Twenty-nine of the 38 women starters made it to Peel.

It was blistering hot by late afternoon with temperatures as high as 21 degrees at the airport. There was no breeze on the Sloc with melting tar making walking conditions difficult and progress slow for many.

Weston was first to reach the crossroads at the foot of South Barrule with the two leading ladies now

some way back. Huntley was an early retirement at Arbory while the much-talented Chris Keown lost considerable time on the punishing Sloc climb.

Weston eased the pace on the descent to Dalby and was first to Peel, thereby claiming a right to the veterans' prize, which eventually went to southside farmer, Alan Clucas – the first finisher to that point.

Nevertheless, Weston was more interested in lengthier achievements. After a ten-minute stop to burst a blister or two, he continued on his way. His lead at the eighth church was 45 minutes but this reduced to 35 minutes allowing for stoppage time.

Weston wasted no time on the road to Kirk Michael, his lead over Tony Kneale stretched to 40 minutes. Veteran, Jean Oldroyd, was going well too, in third place and one of only four women to proceed beyond Peel. Not far behind was former Commonwealth Games hurdler Dave Anderson's brother, John, chased by fellow veterans Willie Kneale and Peter Dougherty.

Determined to maintain a low body heat in the sultry evening sunshine with temperatures easing to 18°C, Weston received regular half hour liquid intakes and a refreshing dousing with a wet sponge. By dusk, he was tracking far north, through the lonely lanes and quaint villages of Bride, Andreas and St. Judes where the overnight temperature had now cooled to a more comfortable 12°centigrade.

Weston reached Bride close on 2 o'clock in the morning still maintaining a 45-minute advantage over Tony Kneale who was nearly an hour ahead of third-placed John Anderson. Early morning dawn saw him soldiering on through Laxey from where he enjoyed the company of Boundary Harriers club secretary, Joan Powell, for the final eight-mile slog to Douglas.

Weston's winning time of 18 hours 17 minutes

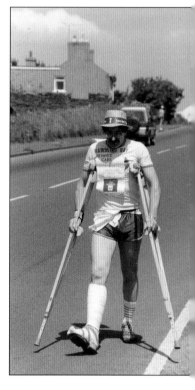

Left: After many attempts, Charlie Weston achieved his first victory in 1989.

Above: Twenty-two-time finsher Ray Hughes was unsuccesful on this occasion.

1989-1990

55 seconds was considerably down on Derek Harrison's all-time record of 15 hours 20 minutes 51 seconds,
but still quite outstanding considering the extremely warm conditions.

'I'm thoroughly delighted with the win,' announced Charlie later that day. 'I love the Island and its people – it's a smashing event and certainly a victory I'll always treasure.'

Tony Kneale crossed the line shortly after 7:00am having completed a steady walk throughout. Blisters on his heels gave him quite a lot of aggravation at mid-distance. He 'tightened-up' coming out of Maughold before battling back to his hometown for a 6th finish in ten attempts.

John Anderson was not too far adrift at the finish either and he was more than happy with his first finish in three attempts, raising cash for the worthy Voluntary Service Overseas effort in the process.

Other first-time finishes came from Andrew Quayle and Phil Readshaw, both finishing strongly after brave performances throughout.

Veteran Jean Oldroyd at more than 50 years of age, was a fine sixth overall and only the third local woman ever to go the distance behind record holder Irene Corlett and, more recently, Caroline Convery.

Ralph Martin was suitably elated with his first-ever finish, while Dave Wilkinson was nonchalant as ever crossing the line for his fourth finish.

John Ronan and David Collister completed the course close together in eighth and ninth positions, John suffering somewhat in the latter stages while David chalked-up his sixth consecutive finish.

The last word has to go to Maureen Cowbourne and Vivienne Hooper who walked every inch of the way together, finishing just one minute inside the 24-hour limit for a richly deserved joint finish – both raising funds for people suffering from Parkinson's disease.

Sponsored by Clerical Medical International for the first time, Gordon Vale won the 1990 Parish Walk at his first and only attempt.

After equally determined walks to Jurby last year, Vivienne and Maureen had battled on regardless to become only the seventh and eighth women to go the full distance in 29 years!

The Murray Lambden Cup for the best performer under 21 years of age went to Peel footballer, Lee Cain, who was following in the footsteps of his brother, Stephen who had won the cup the previous year. Lee retired at Lezayre at 3 o'clock in the morning after literally falling asleep on his feet!

1990

It is most unlikely that the Parish Walk would have reached today's level of participation and success without some form of sponsorship. The event, although popular in the 1960s and 1970s, failed to attract great numbers and it was not until 1979 that a major sponsor was found, guaranteeing its future success. Mylchreest Motors had funded the event throughout the 1980s however, after 11 years of dedicated sponsorship they announced their withdrawal from the event in 1990 on review of their marketing policy, which favoured motor sport events and other organisations.

With the coming Parish Walk only months away, this was a huge body blow to the organising committee of the Boundary Harriers. Committee member, Murray Lambden, had to move fast and identify a sponsor who would benefit from a commercial return. Murray approached Clerical Medical International in February 1990, full of enthusiasm and determination to make the Parish Walk bigger and better than ever. His presentation to the would-be sponsor was unique. Few would have thought it possible to depart from tradition, but Murray's well thought-out recommendations were appealing to both parties and a five-year sponsorship with Clerical Medical International was born.

Gordon Vale, a school teacher at St. Mary's Primary School, Foxdale, was first across the finish line in the Clerical Medical International 1990 Parish Walk, winning the event at the first attempt. The former Great Britain Junior Race Walking International completed the punishing 85-mile course in just over 17 hours 55 minutes, which was more than two and a half hours outside Derek Harrison's long-established record set in 1979. But conditions definitely played a part in slowing down the field, and only six competitors managed to finish out of a record entry of 155.

'I used the Ballajora Hill for training,' explained Gordon at the finish having completed a full circle of the Island's 17 parishes. He finally overhauled last year's winner, Charlie Weston, in the vicinity of the Dhoon at around 3 o'clock in the morning and from there pulled out an amazing 54 minutes over the remaining ten miles to Douglas.

Held over the weekend of 16th and 17th June, the 60 or so ladies left the Villa Marina Gardens at 11:30am, followed by the men 30 minutes later. Last year's winner, Charlie Weston, of Highgate Harriers, started as the favourite and after a slow start began to move up through the field.

Claiming the veterans' prize to Peel, Allan Callow was the first to that point in 5 hours 35 minutes 24 seconds. The former Commonwealth Games representative shared the lead in the ealy stages but built up a substantial lead in the south of the Island to arrive at Rushen some six minutes ahead.

Callow was simply superb over the Sloc, attacking the climb and pulling out another seven minutes on Cannell before arriving at Patrick. His blistering pace over the Sloc certainly told on him, and after being seven minutes quicker than anyone else on the longest and toughest stint, he was incredibly one of the slowest on the two-mile section into Peel from Patrick.

Allan Kelly was third into Peel in 6 hours 01 minute 21 seconds, 13 minutes ahead of Weston who in turn was one minute up on Chris Keown who was using the event as a training session. Two-thirds of the field reached the most westerly church but only 31 continued.

The twisting road to Kirk Michael took a heavy toll on those continuing. Alan Clucas, Ian Dunbar, Barbara Mason and Alan Corran all called time at the 39-mile mark, as did Peter Dougherty, Craig Phillips, Phil Readshaw, David Radcliffe, John Storrie and Mark Phillips at the halfway mark at Ballaugh. There were only 21 walkers past this point with Carl Faragher, John Norrey, Kathy Lambie and Steven Small all stopping at Jurby.

At Bride there were retirements for Philip Ashworth, Daniel Kneale, Terry Moore, Denis Quaggin and Juan Callow, the latter two reaching the church gate in 13 hours 40 minutes. Newcomer Brigitte Lanskoy, a visitor of French origin, was also a casualty at this point as were last year's finishers, Maureen Cowbourne and Vivienne Hooper, both reaching the twelfth church together in 14 hours 24 minutes.

Three-time finisher, Tommy Kelly, was an early retirement at Andreas, as was Gary Poole some two hours later.

Only seven hardy souls reached Lezayre. Six-time finisher, Tony Kneale, was in poor shape on the approach to Maughold where he waved the white flag having walked 67 miles at close on 5 mph throughout.

Weston was tiring too and his 15-minute lead at Ramsey was dramatically cut to five by the rapidly approaching Vale who drew level at the Dhoon to take command of the lead.

The final miles were difficult for Weston and it was a close-run thing to the finish. Nevertheless, the 1989 champion hung on by the narrowest of margins to claim the runner-up spot from Douglas Rugby Club Captain John Anderson who finished third for the second consecutive year.

Onchan landscape gardener, David Collister, claimed a new record by finishing for the seventh consecutive time while last man to make it back to Douglas on two feet was Malcolm Whelan, claiming his first-ever finish in a time of 22 hours 39 minutes 43 seconds.

Ann Marie Kelly convincingly won the ladies' race to Peel in 6 hours 15 minutes 49 seconds. It was the eve of her twenty-fourth birthday and she had plenty of reason for an early celebratory drink. Denied the glory several years ago when she competed in the event and won just a few days short of the minimum eighteen-year-old age limit, Ann Marie looked supremely confident throughout, casting aside any worries she may have had because of a painful ankle injury suffered in her final training session. Once on her favourite stretch above Ballakillowey, there was no way former winner, Rose Clark could reduce the deficit and Ann was sixth overall to reach Peel.

Rose Clark was happy enough with second place having done little training through the winter. Ann Oates of Ballasalla was third, completing the 32½-mile event in 7 hours 01 minute 20 seconds and just 1½ minutes ahead of swimming instructor, Ros Macaulay.

1991

Throughout its long history, the Parish Walk has attracted members from all sides of the community, the young and the old, the rich and the poor. Distinguished members from the political arena have competed too. Colonel William Anderson was the first in 1878, followed by Gerald Bridson in 1923, Noel Cringle, and Bernie May in 1960 and Hazel Hannan a year later.

The involvement of a major sponsor had a significant impact in the 1991 Parish Walk with a record entry of 176, many of foreign origin, promising to make this the best and most successful event yet. Nevertheless, former Commonwealth Games representatives John Cannell and Allan Callow plus last year's winner, Gordon Vale, were missing from the line-up and, unusually, the race was wide-open.

Tony Kneale and John Anderson were the main contenders with the fast walking Kevin Walmsley a dark horse and more than capable of taking up to the challenge. Last year's winner Charlie Weston was also making an appearance but unlikely to feature with age now very much against him. It has to be remembered, of course, that the vast majority of those who set out never intend to complete all 17 parishes. Indeed, for many, the goal is Peel, the 32½-mile mark, which is the official finish for the ladies and veteran men.

The Met Office at Ronaldsway forecast unsettled weather for the weekend of 22nd and 23rd June thus making choice of clothing difficult for the 160 starters gathered in the Villa Marina Gardens for an 11:30am start.

In a slightly quicker time than last year, Charlie Weston surprised everyone by winning this classic for a second time in as many years. Tailing Chris Keown

1991-1992

CM
172

Right: In 1991 Charlie Weston won his second Parish Walk in 17 hours 46 minutes 48 seconds.

over the difficult section to Peel, the 57-year-old Londoner slowly pulled clear on the flat stretch towards Jurby during the early hours of Saturday evening, maintaining station throughout the hours of darkness to arrive back in Douglas some 18 minutes ahead of his rival in a time of 17 hours 46 minutes 58 seconds.

Only nine of the 38 were continued beyond Peel completed the distance including two women. Veteran Jean Holroyd of Onchan finished for the second time in three years, some two and a half hours ahead of last-but-one finisher Maureen Cox.

Ray Hughes finished third, completing the well-trodden circuit for a sixth time with fellow veteran Mick Holgate, reported as being most relaxed in the final stages, taking fourth place.

Lee Cain, the Marown footballer and local farmer, was fifth. His 'amble' around the 85 miles was a first,

Kevin Walmsley, (No. 72) and Peter Dougherty at Eairy Cushlin.

arriving back on Douglas Promenade shortly after 8 o'clock on Sunday morning.

David Collister lived up to expectation by completing his eighth successive finish despite experiencing the worst of the early morning rain showers in the north of the Island.

The final finisher was Bob Baxter, who in company with Maureen Cox, managed to walk an extra two miles when he missed the turn-off at Maughold church.

The shorter race to Peel for veteran men and ladies was won for the first time by Ballasalla's Allan Kelly. Pacing himself well during the initial parishes of Marown and Santon, Allan overhauled first-time veteran, Tony Kneale, on the climb out of Rushen. Appearing out of the mist at the Round Table, 49-year-old Kelly was leading on the road by some five minutes, stretching this advantage to more than 11 minutes at the termination of the race in Peel.

Third veteran to reach the eighth and final church was eventual overall winner, Charlie Weston. But there were excellent walks behind from seasoned campaigner Brian Brough and Juan Callow.

Liz Corran was also a first-time winner in the ladies' event. Out of training for most of the winter following an operation at the end of last year, the Onchan walker overhauled former winner, Rose Clark, in the final six miles to beat Linda Kelly by just under four minutes, to add Parish glory to her recent success in the End to End.

Veteran, Jean Miller, again looked quite comfortable on her way to success when she was fifth woman to reach Peel behind Ann Marie Kelly, recording a time of 7 hours 00 minutes 19 seconds for the 32½ miles.

1992

One of only three men to dominate Manx race walking since 1960, Graham Young won the 1992 Parish Walk for a second time after a long absence from the event. A Commonwealth Games representative and iconic figure from bygone years, Graham swept all opposition aside to finish some 73 minutes ahead of his nearest rival and work colleague, Ray Hughes. His time of 16 hours 38 minutes 27 seconds was almost an hour slower than his epic performance in 1971 when he beat Derek Harrison by just 54 seconds in the closest finish to date.

Jim Harvey was another making an appearance after a long absence. However, the Abbeylands farmer, a two-time finisher during the 1960s, found this a walk too far and was one of 17 to stop short at Rushen.

Blustery weather and cool temperatures made for reasonable walking conditions in an event that saw a record number of starters and finishers. The 11:30am start on 20th June saw 176 hardy souls leave the Villa Marina Gardens on a journey around the 17 parishes in which only 16 finished.

Liz Corran and Linda Kelly making easy work of the notorious Sloc. They were joint winners of the ladies race to Peel.

1992

Douglas postmen, Young and Hughes paced themselves superbly. The former winner was equal sixth on the punishing climb to 'Heartbreak Hill', keeping pace with Marown footballer, Lee Cain. Ahead of them was Allan Kelly, four-time finisher, Chris Keown, leading ladies, Liz Corran and Linda Kelly, and twice former winner, Charlie Weston.

Training partners Liz and Linda had in fact led the entire field through Rushen, having dictated the pace from the start. On reaching the third church at Santon, the two girls had covered 11 miles and were roughly one minute ahead of Weston. They were eventually hauled in and passed by Allan Kelly and Chris Keown on the start of the punishing climb to 'Tom the Dipper's' corner, that remote spot on the lower slopes of the Sloc some 650 feet above sea level.

Looking fit and fresh throughout, 50-year-old Kelly went on to win the veteran men's event to Peel in a time of 5 hours 58 minutes 13 seconds. 'I was really in my element on the climb over the Sloc' admitted Allan later, when reflecting upon his second successive veterans' win. 'For the first time ever, I didn't suffer any cramp – it felt good.' It was indeed an impressive performance from the all-round athlete who lost three whole months of training during the winter and put on a stone in weight!

Former Peel resident Chris Keown was next to reach the eighth church. He was still looking good for the overall honours but was hard chased by the young pretender, Lee Cain.

In joint fourth spot to Peel, Liz Corran and Linda Kelly crossed the line hand-in-hand after walking every inch of the way in tandem. They only decided to finish together after passing through the 31-mile mark at Patrick. Both were given identical times of 6 hours 03 minutes 54 seconds for what was a most impressive race. It was the second occasion in recent years that two women had shared the honours – Ann Cain and Rose Clark finishing in similar circumstances in 1989.

Graham Young was now in 'overdrive' after stopping to change shoes at the 25th milestone on the descent from the Round Table to Dalby. He was looking extremely fit and was the people's choice to take the overall honours as he passed through Peel in a shade over 6 hours 04 minutes, just three minutes down on Chris Keown. Only minutes separated the leaders into and out of Peel with 40 walkers

Right: After a absence of many years, Graham Young won the 1992 Parish Walk in 16 hours 38 minutes 27 seconds.

Below: The Villa Marina Gardens was the starting point for the 1992 event.

continuing beyond this point.

Keown and Cain were leaders on the coast road to Kirk Michael but the Braddan farmer was in serious trouble and destined not to reach the ninth church where there were retirements for Carl Faragher, Bernard Corlett, Donald Brown, John Kelly and Mike Craig.

Chris Keown was struggling on the approach to Glen Mooar where he forfeited the leading role to the galloping postman who had advanced an amazing 16 minutes between Peel and Ballaugh.

A finisher in 1981, Frank Dolan was the first retirement at St. Mary's Parish Church, Ballaugh. Others to throw in the towel at this point were George Hall, Mick Rodger, David Tasker, Peter Caine, Brian Beattie, David Boorgaize and Duncan Robertson.

At Jurby, the 45-mile mark, there were further retirements with Colin Hodgkinson, Steven Small, John Tyson and David Butterworth all calling it a day – the latter man having been on his feet for nearly 12 hours at which time the leaders were fast approaching Ramsey.

Only 28 walkers continued beyond the disused airfield as darkness descended. Simon Shaw was the first to stop at Bride, reaching the church gates of St. Bridget's in 11 hours 30 minutes exactly. John Norrey also called it a day as did Alan Kneen who exceeded the time limit, arriving at the most northern church in 14 hours 09 minutes 00 seconds.

Much-talented and twice finisher, John Anderson, was struggling too. Severe cramp along the Burma Road put an end to his challenge and he stopped at the 55½-mile mark, along with Manx Radio's John Moss, Carla Thompson, Les Brown, Craig Phillips and Barbara Mason.

Lezayre was the stopping point for Charles Pimblett and Peter Corlett. Phil Ashworth went the extra five miles to Maughold where he was the last retirement of the day having been on his feet for 15 hours 49 minutes.

Throughout the hours of darkness, Young reeled off the parishes of Andreas, Lezayre and Maughold, well and truly in the driving seat, arriving at Lonan as night was turning to day.

He eventually crossed the finishing line shortly after 4:00am to claim victory for a second time in 21 years. It was a remarkable achievement and perhaps one unexpected – his time of 16 hours 38 minutes 27 seconds down 55 minutes on his previous best.

Work colleague, Ray Hughes, had his legs working overtime during the hours of darkness, pulling through the field from fifth place at Ballaugh to overhaul Charlie Weston and Chris Keown and claim the runner-up spot and his seventh finish.

Veteran Weston again got the better of Keown to finish third, his lowest-ever position in the Parish. In eight attempts, he was victor twice, runner-up on four occasions and once only contested the veterans' race to Peel.

Tony Kneale, another seasoned campaigner had a

lonely walk to record his seventh finish, while Mick Holgate took sixth place in front of David Collister who completed the course for the ninth consecutive time.

Former finishers, Bob Baxter and Don Higgins, were eighth and ninth respectively, while the amazing 60-year-old Jean Oldroyd was the only woman to go the distance, completing the 85 miles in a time of 21 hours 22 minutes 39 seconds.

Tommy Kelly was the only other experienced hand to go the distance. The remaining five finishers, Anthony Rickaby, Winston Lui, Laurence Maddrell, David Woolnough and Mark Phillips, were all first-timers – the latter two improving on last year's performance when they both retired at Lezayre.

There were notable performances in the veterans' classes to Peel with Brian Brough, Kevin Madigan and George Callister taking fifth, sixth and seventh places respectively.

Maureen Cox, who had completed the full distance the previous year, was more than delighted with her performance. She crossed the line in tandem with fellow veteran, George Callister, in 6 hours 36 minutes 24 seconds, just 1½ minutes ahead of third-placed veteran, Diane Humphries.

1993

With last year's winner Graham Young absent from the start line, the 1993 Parish Walk had all the ingredients of becoming a two-horse race between past winners John Cannell and Charlie Weston.

Cannell, the postman from Douglas, was making a bid to draw level with Derek Harrison for the all-time number of Parish Walk wins. Between them, the two had won nine of the 31 events staged, Derek having retired from the sport some years ago.

Twice-winner Charlie Weston was also looking to increase his tally of wins, while in the ladies' event, Liz Corran, Ann Marie Kelly and Rose Hooton nee Clark, were all looking favourite for the honours.

The Villa Marina Gardens was the venue for the thirty-second event, which got underway at 11:30am on Saturday 19th June.

Manx Harrier's Race Secretary, Liz Corran, led the field of 204 through the streets of Douglas at a scorching pace in the early stages. Douglas building surveyor Allan Callow took over on the Peel Road to lead thereon and claim the veterans' record for the shorter Douglas to Peel course with a new record time of 5 hours 18 minutes 16 seconds.

'Everything went well,' admitted Allan later. 'I was scared of pushing too hard into the strong wind and frequent rain showers, so backed off for a while in what was a very lonely walk.' Liz actually stayed within sight of Allan until reaching the Oatlands Road about eight miles out and was only passed by John Cannell on the approach to Arbory.

Cannell had great ambitions and pressed on to Peel, arriving at the Town Hall steps in 5 hours 42 minutes, some 15 minutes ahead of Chris Keown,

Left: John Cannell well out in front at the half-way mark.

Right: Liz Corran and Simon Cox on the road to Dalby.

Top: John Cannell receives the trophy for a fifth time.

Middle: Allan Callow receives the veterans' prize to Peel with a time of 5 hours 18 minutes 16 seconds - a time not beaten for another ninteen years.

Bottom: Liz Corran made it a hat trick of wins in the ladies race to Peel.

third to this point and runner-up in the veterans' class.

Liz Corran made it a hat-trick of wins in the ladies' event in spite of being sick on the way out of Rushen. She took it easy on the climb to the Round Table, eventually catching up with Simon Cox. The two walked in tandem to Peel, equal fourth on the road and recording a time of 6 hours 02 minutes 08 seconds for the 32½ miles.

Maureen Cox reached the Town Hall in 6 hours 20 minutes 37 seconds to secure second place in the ladies' veteran event. Behind her came Anne Somer, Anne Oats, Rose Hooton and Sue Partington.

Pioneers of the first event in 1960, Jim Harvey and Noel Cringle, were two of the 11 finishers at the eighth church while Dermot O'Toole used his first-ever training session to Peel as experience for a future assault on the full 85 miles.

Cannell was certainly moving well on the way out of Peel and several minutes ahead of his nearest rivals, Lee Cain and Simon Shaw, both looking relaxed on the coast road to Kirk Michael. Behind them, was seven-time finisher Tony Kneale, Charlie Weston, Frank Dolan and regular finisher and runner-up last year, Ray Hughes.

But double winner Weston was in trouble having stopped with severe cramp on the lower regions of the Sloc and in obvious agony as he checked in at the Peel Town Hall. 'My thighs are tied in knots – it's the first time I've suffered cramp like this,' said the 59-year-old Highgate Harriers man as he asked for some salt tablets.

But there was controversy at Peel when three times former finisher Bob Baxter was asked to hand over his race number having past the official maximum age limit of 60 for the full course last year. The determined campaigner he is, Bob continued with companion John Moss and indeed went on to complete the distance, albeit unofficially, in a sub-23-hour time.

George Callister was the first of seven to stop at Kirk Michael as Cannell hurried on to the halfway mark at Ballaugh, arriving there some five minutes before the official timekeepers. He was so far ahead by the time he reached Ballaugh Old Church that the second and third-placed men were barely at Kirk Michael, some four miles behind.

Cannell kept up his blistering pace, arriving at the lonely Jurby church in 8 hours 20 minutes and much to the surprise of time keeper Mitch Joughin who said he wasn't asked to set up post until 8:15pm!

Cain and Shaw were still together at Ballaugh while Tony Kneale took his time sipping a cup of coffee as he donned his tracksuit bottoms and an extra top for the cool and long journey ahead. Brian Brough was next to arrive at the halfway mark with Frank Dolan and Charlie Weston a further three minutes down after keeping pace together since Peel. Nevertheless, the ever-popular Weston was over an hour behind the leader and quite literally on his last legs. There was no disguising his anguish. 'The mind says yes, but my body says no,' said Charlie somewhat despondently. 'I've managed to win this great event twice, been second four times and third once, but I reckon I'll have to admit defeat this time.' Charlie's final attempt at the full distance ended soon after when he was the first of four to call time at the half way mark. Three miles on at Jurby, there were stoppages for Brian Goldsmith, Bill Morton and Tim Layhe, all ending their ordeal after 45½ miles.

Frank Dolan was the first retirement at Bride, touching the church gate of St. Bridget's four minutes short of 12 hours. There were further retirements here for Nigel Whitehouse and Bernie Corlett, while Ann Marie Kelly reached her farthest point ever in 13 hours 50 minutes.

John Moss called it a day at Andreas having

1993-1994

Brian Brough approaching Peel.

reached the thirteenth church some 44 minutes quicker than last year. Also stopping at this point was the incredible Brian Brough, Stuart Sayle, David Tasker and Gary Poole.

Simon Shaw was the first of five to call time at the 62-mile mark, Lezayre, arriving over three hours ahead of Alan Kneen, Billy Brown, Colin Hodgkinson and the only remaining woman, Barbara Mason.

Dave O'Sullivan was the only retirement at Maughold. He was the last person not to go the full distance, reaching the fifteenth church in total darkness at just after half past two on Sunday morning.

By now, John Cannell was well on his way to the finish, crossing the line on Douglas Promenade shortly after half past three on Sunday morning, having carefully negotiated the departing revellers outside the Palace Hotel and Casino. His official time of 16 hours 11 minutes 11 seconds was the sixth quickest of all time and his own second best. It was his fifth win in seven attempts at the full distance having finished runner-up in his debut race in 1967. It was also John's first attempt at the full circuit since 1983 and he was actually using the occasion as training for the National 200-kilometre event in August.

Second on the road leaving Ramsey, Lee Cain had difficulty in identifying the route to Maughold. In an incident similar to Stanley Cleator's of 30 years past, the Trollaby farmer missed the Port Lewaigue turn-off for Maughold, continuing along the B19 for a further two miles to Dreemskerry. Lee's concerned father, Brian, eventually tracked him down, recommending he 'run' the two miles down to Ballajora and on to Maughold for further advice. On realising Lee's dilemma, Martin Lambden, chief timekeeper at the fifteenth church, gave permission for the distressed farmer to return to the original turn-off and then retrace his steps to Maughold. The 40-minute detour

was costly, dropping him from second to fifth spot and adding another four miles to an already long journey.

Recovering well from his misfortune, Cain wasted no time on the winding coast road to Bulgam. He overhauled a surprised Ray Hughes in Laxey village to regain the second spot, and finished for the second time in as many years, some eight minutes ahead of the Douglas postman who was third.

Mick Holgate completed the event for a fourth time, sandwiched in fourth place between two men recording their eighth Parish finish, 'Rambling' Ray Hughes and Tony Kneale.

However, even they could not match the incredible David Collister who literally strolled in to record an unbelievable tenth consecutive finish with, as always, a permanent smile etched upon his face.

Alan Clucas, a former winner of the veterans' race to Peel completed the full course for the first time. He was equal seventh with walking companion, Leonard Gaunt.

Regular race-walker, Phil Ashworth, had a lonely walk, improving on his previous year's performance when he stopped 18 miles from the finish. It was Phil's first full distance, finishing ninth in 21 hours 36 minutes 59 seconds, over 20 minutes in front of Gymns' footballer, Michael Dougherty, who completed the course at his first-ever attempt!

Allan Corran and Steven Small were the only two other men to go the full distance, the latter struggling across the finish line close to the war memorial at half past ten on Sunday morning, precisely 23 hours after he'd left the start.

1994

Vandalism and age finally took its toll on the Charity Collecting Mine, which had adorned Harris Promenade for decades. The large red mine, thought to be a relic of the First World War, had been used for years to collect donations for the Shipwrecked Fishermen's and Mariner's Royal Benevolent Society. It was also a welcome landmark for the fortunate few reaching the finishing line at the end of the gruelling 85-mile Parish Walk. About £60 was collected every year by the Douglas Coast Guards who had taken responsibility for the mine's upkeep. However, it was broken into and pushed over on so many occasions by vandals that in 1994, the Department of Highways Ports and Properties disposed of it forever.

Although the smooth and efficient running of the Parish Walk is attributable to a dedicated few, the event is not always without problems. In 1994, a clash of sporting events presented race director Ray Cox and his organising committee with a logistical nightmare. Both the Parish Walk and Peel Kart Races had been scheduled for Saturday 18th June. However, due to Peel town centre being closed during the early evening, Manx Harriers was forced to divert the route on reaching Patrick church.

The detour of Peel required competitors to follow

the Patrick road to St Johns, Tynwald Mills and the Switchback to its junction with the Peel to Kirk Michael coast road.

The temporary and revised 86-mile route, passing 16 parish churches, attracted 223 starters with John Cannell becoming the most successful competitor ever, recording his sixth win in the 34-year history of the modern event. In a near re-run of last year's event, John completed the extended circuit in a time of 16 hours 13 minutes 46 seconds, some 1½ hours ahead of his nearest rival, Lee Cain, who had also been runner-up last year.

Setting off from the Villa Marina Gardens at 11:30am precisely, the early leader out of Douglas on wet roads was all-rounder, Simon Cox. The only local finisher in the recent TT Marathon, Simon was only aiming for the veterans' distance to St. John's, as was his wife, Maureen, who was keeping pace with eventual winner, Cannell, and the jovial Les Brown.

Simon Shaw and Lee Cain were equal fifth at Marown, while Jane Quirk of the Isle of Man Newspapers was an impressive sixth, but set to burn herself out by Rushen.

Cox and Cannell were level-pegging along the flats at Colby. However, the Douglas postman pulled clear on the demanding climb out of Ballakillowey and was the first to tackle the infamous Sloc.

Roy Cooil was the first retirement at Rushen but windy conditions made the going difficult and another 49 followed his example by venturing no further.

By the Round Table, Cannell was over five minutes clear of his nearest challenger Cox, a margin he had stretched to more than ten minutes by the time he reached the official veterans' mark of 33 miles at St. John's.

Les Brown was third to pass the Farmers Arms with Lee Cain close behind, followed by a relaxed looking Phil Ashworth, the second of 117 to stop here.

Sixth on the road and glad to end her lonely journey, Maureen Cox claimed the ladies' veteran title in 6 hours 22 minutes 54 seconds. Rose Hooton crossed the finish line 11 minutes later to hold off the strong finishing Anne Oates for the runner-up spot, while Sue Partington was the fourth lady home in 7 hours 09 minutes 51 seconds after a superb climb up the tortuous Sloc.

With John Cannell well on his way to Kirk Michael, the honours in the men's veteran category were automatically passed to Simon Cox, so producing the first-ever husband and wife success over the shorter distance.

Brian Brough was next to stop at St. John's, followed two minutes later by twice-winner, Charlie Weston, who on this occasion, went no further.

Other notables to stop at the 33-mile mark were Noel Cringle, Jim Harvey, Gordon Corran, Ralph Martin, Adrian Earnshaw, and at the rear of the field as darkness descended, Claire Walmsley who had been on the go for 9 hours 11 minutes 51 seconds.

A sixth and final title for John Cannell.

Of the 40 walkers to go beyond St. John's attempting full distance, only two were women. Caroline Kennaugh and Kathryn Egerton maintained their progress over the Switch Back climb but called it a day at Kirk Michael after 11 hours on their feet.

Chris Lyons of Union Mills was another to surrender at the ninth church, as did David Bawden, Ron Chadwick, Robbie Moore, Roy Gelling and brothers, David and Luke Bourgaize. It was a fine performance from the under 21-year-old Luke who won the junior award, reaching the 39-mile mark in ten hours exactly.

Andreas stalwart George Callister reached the near halfway mark in slightly over eight hours, retiring there with Hadyn Cubbon, Barry Cowin and Stephen Hinds.

Frank Dolan was the first of six to call time at the whitewashed church in Jurby, arriving in 10 hours 05 minutes exactly. Meanwhile, Chris Keown failed in his charity attempt at full distance, stopping at the northernmost church with fellow Manx Harrier, Brian Goldsmith.

St. Andrew's Parish Church, Andreas was the end of the road for Bill Morton, Mark Harvey, Michael Dougherty and Allan Kneen. Tired and weary, Mark Bridson and Craig Phillips continued another five miles to Lezayre before throwing in the towel – the latter man recorded as the final retirement of the day.

Cannell was now so far ahead that by the Dhoon, 74 miles out, his nearest rival Lee Cain was still attacking the Ballajora climb to Hibernia some six miles adrift.

With daylight approaching and looking fresh as paint, Cannell hurried along Douglas Promenade shortly before 4 o'clock on Sunday morning, claiming a sixth outright success and one more than race-record holder, Derek Harrison.

Lee Cain was next into the Island's capital, arriving

1995

1½ hours later and 43 minutes ahead of third-placed Ray Hughes who completed his 9th finish in ten years.

It was a first-ever finish for Les Brown in fourth, while Manx Harriers club chairman, Ray Cox, took fifth spot, making his debut in the event and doing it all in aid of the Cystic Fibrosis Charity.

Tony Kneale made it home for what was his 9th time in 12 years while Centurion Mick Holgate, Alan Clucas and Leonard Gaunt all repeated their success of last year.

The amazing David Collister completed the course for the 11th consecutive time finishing in tenth place while veterans, Dave Tasker and Dave O'Sullivan, completed the full distance for the first time, the latter man having come to within six miles of success last year!

1995

After the last year's enforced detour of Peel, the Parish Walk reverted to the well established route in 1995. The thirty-fourth event since 1960 attracted many entries from Great Britain including twice-winner, Charlie Weston, regular finishers, Leonard Gaunt and Frank Dolan, as well as Centurions Brian Ashwell, and Jill Green. Six-time winner, John Cannell, was absent because of injury and Arthur Jones, stalwart of the organising committee for many years, stood down as race secretary with Liz Corran as his replacement.

This year's event saw a new start time of 12 noon with a record 239 starters setting off from the Villa Marina Gardens on Saturday 24th June.

In a truly amazing display of race walking intelligence, 62-year-old Brian Ashwell of Leicester, became the oldest-ever winner of the event, recording a time of 16 hours 37 minutes 47 seconds – nearly 1½ hours ahead of his nearest rival, Ray Hughes.

Early leaders onto the Peel Road were Allan Callow, Lee Cain and Maureen Cox, the former Commonwealth Games walker soon clocking sub-ten-minute miles and the first to reach Peel in 5 hours 38 minutes 32 seconds.

Last year's junior champion to Peel, Luke Bourgaize, was an early retirement at Santon. By the time the field had cleared at Rushen, close on one-quarter of the entries had dropped out including regulars John Moss and Frank Dolan.

The uncomfortably hot conditions made walking difficult for those tackling the Sloc and by mid-afternoon, the temperature had reached 22°centigrade. For many, the 1,100-foot ascent to its summit was unbearable with the light easterly breeze affording little relief on one of the warmest June days ever recorded.

Eminent government minister, Noel Cringle notched up another finish to Peel, as did Tony Bates, George Callister, David Tasker and the intrepid Jim Harvey. Race Secretary's husband, Gordon Corran, also completed the veterans' race for a second time

while Michael and Brenda Kneale along with Kevin and Margaret Tasker checked in late at the Town Hall, one place ahead of final finisher to that point, Brenda Charlton.

A total of 33 walkers ventured beyond Peel, but there was disappointment for Roy Gelling, Mark Harvey, Dennis Quaggan, David Bourgaize, Margaret Bridson and James Lomas, all stopping at Kirk Michael, the 39-mile mark.

Peter Cain, Kath Quirk, Geoff Barfoot and Chris Lyon all reached the halfway mark before calling time, while David Bawden, Jayne Cubbon, Catherine Moore and Tony Barfoot went that bit further to St. Patrick's Church, Jurby as darkness rapidly set in.

Dermot O'Toole and Melanie Kermeen were barely moving on the lonely road to Bride. Stopping at the Lhen to attend to his badly blistered feet, the Glen Vine man lost valuable time in his quest to beat the cut-off time at Bride, a point he reached as the church clock struck two in the morning. However, there was controversy here when he was asked to return his number, having supposedly exceeded the time limit. Chief timekeeper, Martin Lambden, had misread the race programme, which clearly stated 2:20am as the deadline. After much deliberation, Dermot was allowed to continue. Meanwhile, Melanie Kermeen was the last to the most northerly church, the 21-year-old in a poor state having been sick for much of the day. Unable to proceed further, she ended her gallant journey after being on her feet for 14 hours 10 minutes.

Previous finisher, Phil Ashworth, only made Andreas on this occasion. Ian Watson also stopped at the thirteenth parish and was the final retirement of the day.

Commonwealth games representative and two-time winner, Graham Young, was supposed to be looking after Brian Ashwell through the night. The Leicester Centurion was leading on the road, but overshot the Lezayre church turn-off. Lee Cain, not far behind, sportingly called him back. Later, at Parliament Square Ramsey, a similar mistake occurred with Ashwell briefly continuing on the mountain road to Douglas.

Dermot O'Toole struggled on through the early hours of daylight, arriving in Parliament Square Ramsey at half past five in the morning. His service team, consisting of John Howie and the recently retired Tony Barfoot, had arrived some time earlier having boiled a pan of water to sterilise the Swiss army knife used to lance his marble-sized blisters. The bizarre operation caused considerable bewilderment with the late-night revellers. When Dermot finally continued on his way, he was so far in arrears that the leading walkers had arrived in Douglas and already gone to bed!

Setting a relentless pace through the northern parishes, Ashwell and Cain maintained close company to Maughold where the Foxdale AFC footballer finally conceded defeat shortly after 1:00am leaving the wily veteran to continue through the night alone.

George Callister on the Sloc.

Left: Sixty-two-year-old Brian Ashwell is the oldest ever winner of the Parish Walk.

Right: Brian at the highest point of the course.

1995-1996

Only 11 walkers survived the night with Ashwell crossing the finish line at the Douglas War Memorial shortly after half past four on Sunday morning. It was a magnificent achievement for the near 63-year-old who later admitted the Parish Walk was the toughest thing he'd ever done. 'I feel as though I've been in a fight,' said the former world indoor 1,500 metres and over 50's record holder, who reckoned he had lost seven of his toenails.

'Rambling' Ray Hughes, the Douglas postman went one better than last year to finish runner-up for a third time, just eight minutes ahead of Tony Kneale who completed the course for a tenth time. Past Centurion, Mick Holgate was fourth, finishing the course for a sixth time, ahead of Rushen rambler Alan Clucas.

Leonard Gaunt made it a hat-trick of finishes in sixth place, while the only woman to complete the full course was Centurion Jill Green of the Isle of Wight, finishing a superb seventh in her Parish debut.

David Collister, the man who claims to never train, was the first finisher under the age of 40, completing an astonishing 12 Parish Walks in succession.

There were first-time finishes for Allan Corran, Simon Shaw and Dermot O'Toole, the latter man on his feet for very nearly 24 hours, finally crossing the line in blazing heat at 11:12am on Sunday.

1996

After last year's extraordinary Parish Walk which produced the oldest winner ever, the 1996 event was won at a more sedate pace with twice runner-up, Lee Cain, finally securing victory after five previous attempts. Lee claimed to have only done about six miles actual walking prior to the race. 'I keep fit with my football training and working on the farm,'

admitted the 26-year-old farmer and part-time footballer from Braddan, who completed the gruelling 85-mile event shortly before half past five on Sunday morning. His time of 17 hours 26 minutes 29 seconds was slower than in recent years and over two hours off Derek Harrison's 1979 course record time.

Tony Kneale of Douglas produced an excellent performance to claim the runner-up spot, just under half an hour later in 17 hours 56 minutes 03 seconds. It was his twelfth finish in 14 years.

Last year's runner-up, Douglas postman Ray Hughes, made a strong challenge for the second spot, missing out by just three minutes. Alan Clucas was fourth, with Mylchreest Motors service manager, Phil Readshaw fifth. Only 19 of the 304 starters completed the full distance – testament to just how difficult this event is.

Held in excellent weather conditions over the weekend of the summer solstice, the thirty-fifth event had some notable stars missing. Middle-distance walkers Allan Callow, Simon Cox and Liz Corran were away in Belgium competing in the World Veterans' Championship, thus leaving the annual classic to as far as Peel wide-open.

With race director Ray Cox getting the event under way from a packed Villa Marina Gardens at 12 noon, the leaders wasted no time in negotiating their way along the busy Peel Road leading to Quarter Bridge.

Tackling the physically demanding event for the first time, John Reynolds led the field to this point. It was only his second major race walking event ever, having won the End to End race last year. He set a blistering pace throughout and was soon a minute clear of Terry Bates and ladies' race winner, Maureen Cox. The last they saw of him was approaching Marown church where John was doubling back to

1996

Above: Ninth place for Peter Kaneen.

Far right: Robbie Callister leaving Glen Vine.

Below: Petrol prices were much lower in 1996!

1996

Left: Jackie Bairstow was second woman to Peel.

Right: Lee Cain receiving the richest prize in Manx Athletics.

join the demanding Glen Darragh climb to the Braaid crossroads.

Reynolds and Bates, better known for their achievement on the running circuit, both received warnings from race judges in the early stages for poor technique. Nevertheless, they completed the shorter distance to Peel without further controversy, neither looking like being challenged by any of the 300 or so walkers behind them.

Reynolds kept to his plan well, arriving at the southernmost parish 17 minutes ahead of his schedule and four minutes ahead by the time he reached Patrick. 'That was tough,' gasped the 44-year-old former hockey player after clocking in at the Town Hall in 5 hours 39 minutes 14 seconds to win the veterans' race in one of the quickest times ever. 'I went off too fast and my legs cramped on the Sloc climb, then going to jelly on the descent to Dalby.'

Bates had a lonely walk after leaving Maureen Cox and arrived in the western capital some 22 minutes later and just outside his six-hour target. 'That was good fun,' he said at the finish. 'A nice walk, but I fell asleep at Dalby.'

Almost 20 minutes down on Terry, Tony Kneale was the next veteran to reach Peel, but he, like Alan Clucas behind him, went on to complete the full distance.

Robbie Callister was just seven seconds behind Alan at Peel, in turn over five minutes ahead of Liz Corran's husband, Gordon, who was delighted to break the seven-hour barrier. 'I was set to retire on the Sloc, but John Curtis wouldn't let me in the car,' he said. Gordon reached the eighth church with Jon Clucas for the second year running. Jon was the winner of the under-21 category by almost half an hour from Peter Dixon and Mathew Callister.

For Maureen Cox, it was her third win in the ladies'

race in as many years. Over 14 minutes down on her winning time 12 months earlier, Maureen led throughout and was two miles clear of Manx Harriers' rival, Jackie Bairstow, at Rushen. With a superb walk over the Sloc, Jackie cut the lead to just three minutes at the finish, recording a time of 6 hours 28 minutes 15 seconds over the 32½ miles.

Kate Cain had a tremendous walk to comfortably beat Tricia Gelling into third place. 'It's something I've always wanted to do,' said Kate while taking a breather in Peel before heading northwards for a failed but brave attempt at the full distance.

For Tricia it was a fourth finish to Peel and her first time under seven hours. She finished more than a quarter of an hour ahead of Donna Davies and Cathy Reynolds, whose husband, John, had sportingly held on for an hour and a half to applaud his wife home before retiring to the Whitehouse for a well-earned, cool pint of Guinness.

Linda Morrison and Caroline Dawson were the first retirements of the day, both calling time at Marown church after 1 hour 20 minutes. A further 243 retirements were posted at Peel with only 59 walkers, including eight women, continuing on into the evening.

After a brief stop to change into warmer clothes, Lee Cain cracked on alone from Peel with Tony Kneale and Alan Clucas in hot pursuit. Simon Shaw and veteran campaigner, Charlie Weston, were the next to depart from the most westerly town however the local law student was suffering from thigh strains and raised the white flag later at the midway mark.

Shaw's departure at Ballaugh elevated first-time finisher, Phil Ashworth, up to fourth place but the pace was unsustainable and Phil was the first to retire at the northernmost church.

Charlie Weston, Ray Hughes and George Callister

Grid lock on Finch Road.

were next to arrive at the 42-mile mark, but the Andreas veteran was in poor shape and stopped at 9:30pm, three miles further on at Jurby.

With darkness descending, Hughes and Weston pressed on to the finish, Ray for the eleventh time in 12 years, while two-time winner, Charlie, recorded his eighth finish in 11 attempts.

Throughout the night, Cain and Kneale maintained station. Tony virtually had his rival in his sight on the long straight roads of the northern plain, but Lee eventually stretched his lead again to a winning margin of 29 minutes 34 seconds.

It was another solid performance from Tony Kneale, his twelfth finish in 14 years and one better than last year when he took third spot behind fellow veterans, Brian Ashwell and Ray Hughes. On this occasion, Ray had to settle for third place, eight minutes slower than last year. Wily Alan Clucas took 48 minutes off his 1995 time to move up one place from fifth to fourth.

Another veteran, Phil Readshaw of Douglas, walked the entire way in his collared shirt and white trousers to claim his second finish in seven years. Suffering with very sore feet, he was ready to pack-in on the Peel to Kirk Michael coast road, but he gritted his teeth and completed the second half of the event, passing Charlie Weston on the approach to Princes Motors at Laxey around daybreak. It was a lonely walk for Phil who saw no other competitors after Peel. Centurion, Mick Holgate, was in tandem with the Mylchreest Motors man through Peel, but stopped several times before claiming his seventh finish in ten years.

Jim Harvey was next to complete the gruelling course. Runner-up in the very first event of 1960 to older brother Henry, Jim removed his race number at the Town Hall having completed the veterans' course in eighth place. Revitalised by a sit-down and a cup of tea, he then decided to crack on and looked as fresh as paint at the halfway mark near Ballaugh.

Peter Kaneen of Union Mills was the first of several new names to complete the course. Impressive in this year's End to End, Peter walked the entire event at a steady sensible pace and always looked like making it back to Douglas in ninth place in a fraction under twenty and a half hours.

Kevin Tasker of Ballasalla walked much of the way with brother, David, but the latter quit at Andreas, the 55½-mile mark and was the last of the non-finishers.

David Radcliffe was also a first-time finisher in eleventh place, but that was not the case for the incredible David Collister who notched up his thirteenth consecutive finish, his first as a veteran.

After seven attempts, Manx Radio's John Moss finally made it to the finish for the first time, managing to conduct a live commentary along the route for the Saturday lunchtime sports programme.

Mark Bridson was another first-time finisher, as were Gary Poole, Winnie Callister and Geoffrey Barfoot, while last man home Kevin Martin made the finish with just 37 minutes to spare.

Dermot O'Toole, in fifteenth place, completed the course for the second time in a row. He was over 40 minutes quicker than last year when he was last of the 11 finishers.

In seventeenth spot, Winnie Callister of Kirk Michael was the only woman to go the full distance. She had walked all the way to Bride with husband, John, but then pressed on alone to finish in 22 hours 59 minutes 02 seconds.

1997

Although the Parish Walk is by far the Island's most physically demanding athletic event, many of those taking part lack the necessary willpower to go the full distance. Having gone against his better judgement and entered for the 1997, Lee Cain was adamant he was going no further than Peel. Twelve months before, the Foxdale footballer had uttered those now famous words, 'never again,' after winning the marathon walk for the first time in six attempts.

Another former winner threatening to call it quits at Peel was Charlie Weston. The Highgate Harrier, who took the second of his two wins in 1991, was desperate to win the veterans' race in what he claimed was his last Parish Walk. This left 64-year-old Brian Ashwell favourite as he was the only former winner from the biggest ever number of starters hoping to go the full distance.

Glen Vine's Peter Kaneen was another favourite having only taken up walking and fell-running a couple of years before, finishing ninth in last year's Parish and winning the End to End in fine style earlier this season.

The CMI sponsored event was a nightmare of epic proportion for race director, Raymond Cox. Commencing at the Villa Marina Gardens at 12 noon on Saturday 21st June, the record 410 walkers

The second of nineteen finishes in 1996 for Dermot O'Toole. Also in the picture are James O'Toole, Tony Barfoot and Brian Goldsmith.

1997

Left: Smiling faces on the way to Glen Vine.

Right: A first victory for Chris Flint.

Below: Twenty-five miles already done.

brought central Douglas to a standstill. Finch Road, Prospect Hill and Peel Road were totally clogged with the hardy walkers and their entourage of cars and helpers.

The lunchtime traffic came to a standstill too with the mayhem continuing out to Braddan and beyond to Marown where the annual foot-slog was already beginning to spread out.

As the stragglers were wending their way into Union Mills, the leaders were already on the approach to Braaid, four miles on where the mini-roundabout resembled something like Piccadilly Circus in a rush hour!

Allan Callow and Phil Ashworth of Manx Harriers were the early pacesetters, followed by last year's winner Lee Cain, Simon Cox and joint favourites, Peter Kaneen and Brian Ashwell. Ashworth was unable to maintain Callow's pace on the early climbs and fell behind on the approaches to Santon as conditions warmed up.

Heading south, many of the midfield walkers were caught by a short sharp shower of rain in the Blackboards area, which was a welcome refresher in humid temperatures reaching 11°centigrade. A ten-mile blanket of walkers covered the field with the front-runners nearing the Round Table while the back-markers were still approaching Ballasalla. The irrepressible Callow was leading by a margin of around three minutes from last year's winner Cain who was still insisting he was going no further than Peel.

Farther back, Brian Ashwell was still looking good and well clear of Peter Kaneen and Boyd Millen.

A staggering 395 made it to the southernmost church, including Ruth Whitaker, the winner of the ladies' under-21 event, who completed the 19½ miles to Rushen church in 4 hours 24 minutes, 7 minutes quicker than Roberta Kewley.

The junior men, led unofficially by an under 17-year-old, had another 13 miles to go to German. Stuart Christian, an 18-year-old first-timer from Ramsey, won this class, reaching Peel Town Hall in 6 hours 31 minutes 39 seconds, some 16 minutes in front of regular trials rider, Juan Readshaw.

First to Peel was veteran race winner Allan Callow in 5 hours 47 minutes 32 seconds. It was his sixth veterans' title in 12 years but the slowest winning time since 1992.

Lee Cain arrived just over 2½ minutes behind Allan. True to his word, he stopped and took off his number. A fine performance indeed from the farmer who never admits to training!

Next along was Brian Ashwell, but whereas he was expected to carry on, the veteran from Leicester also decided to call it a day. 'I slipped a disc some years ago and my back becomes very painful when I have to bend into the wind on steep hills,' explained the winner of two years past. Indeed, his 1995 victory was only his second race walk for 49 years!

Peter Kaneen was fourth to reach the eighth church and despite early suggestions that he too may stop, the garage mechanic casually took a sip of water and announced he was to crack on. 'It's a nice night for a walk,' he said wryly on what was the longest day of the year.

Kirk Michael FC player-manager, Les Brown, was next into Peel, officially third veteran home, followed one minute later by ex-Corinthians' man, Gordon Corran, who was more than pleased with his 6 hours 14 minutes 07 seconds performance.

The surprise result came from former Isle of Man Marathon champion, Robbie Callister, who was fifth veteran and seventh overall to Peel. Robbie was last out of the Villa Marina Gardens, passing no fewer than 404 walkers along the way and looking fresh as a daisy as he approached the Town Hall steps, having finally discarded his anorak windshield. Despite the persuasive efforts of many, Robbie decided against going on, preferring instead to wait for his mates and go for a pint. It was indeed a pity, as six miles further on he would have been leading the event overall.

Cumbrian, Boyd Millen was next into Peel, followed by Tromode's Jackie Bairstow. She deservedly took the ladies' honours after two second places behind Maureen Cox in 1995 and 1996, and was unaware how close she had come to being bridesmaid again. Jackie was passed by Jill Green on the Sloc and she remained a steady 50 yards or so behind until the approaches to Patrick. There she decided to put on a spurt and pass her just in case Jill failed to complete the full circuit as expected.

Bridget Kaneen was the third lady into Peel, completing her first Parish in a creditable 6 hours 34 minutes 56 seconds, some 20 minutes ahead of Donna Davies. Ballasalla's Anne Oates was fifth, Moira Hall sixth and Wendy Ross seventh – the Marks and Spencers sales assistant reaching the Town Hall as the clock struck seven.

Peter Kaneen reached the ninth church at 7:35pm however a lack of interest in continuing further forced the talented athlete to call it a day at the 39-mile mark.

Chris Flint now led the field out of Kirk Michael. However, the former Metropolitan policeman had never seen the Island's northern plains before and he required directions to get to Ballaugh. As darkness approached on the longest day of the year, Flint teamed up with Millen on the long lonely stretches through the Lhen and beyond to Bride. It wasn't until he was well through Ramsey and on the final leg south to Douglas that he slowly edged clear of his fellow Centurion to secure victory in a finishing time of 17 hours 36 minutes 40 seconds. It was certainly

A youthful Robbie Callister (No.164) before becoming famous!

1997

not the quickest Parish, but was a surprise result to say the least. 'The longest part of the entire course was the walk along the promenade to the finish,' said the well-spoken Englishman, commending the standard of organisation and the testing course.

Millen's wife, Lillian, a former world record holder for the women's 10-kilometre walk, followed her husband every inch of the way in their backup car. He crossed the finishing line at the Douglas War Memorial some 24 minutes after Flint, a few seconds past 6:00am followed by the first of the locals, Douglas postman, Ray Hughes.

Making his customary steady start, 'Rambling' Ray was going like a train after the midway point and was making up ground wholesale on those ahead on the lonely coast road to Jurby. He was tenth to Kirk Michael and sixth on the road at the Lhen following the retirements of Peter Kaneen, David Comish and Stephen Harvey.

After two attempts in three years, Jill Green completed the course for a second time in an impressive 18 hours 39 minutes 57 seconds, some 13 minutes in front of Tony Kneale who, like Ray Hughes, was completing the course for a twelfth time.

Sixth finisher was the redoubtable Jim Harvey. Now in his fourth decade of Parish Walking, the Abbeylands farmer, walked on well into the night wearing his statutory white bush hat and vest. He put in a brilliant performance to record his second sub-20-hour finish in succession, his fourth in all, having completed the early events of 1960 and 1961.

Mick Holgate, another well-seasoned campaigner, finished seventh for the second year in a row, some 24 minutes slower than last and notching his eighth finish in all.

Mylchreest Motor's workshop boss, Phil

1997-1998

Readshaw, struggled on through the Lhen to record his third finish in eighth spot, one place in front of Simon Cox who had never gone beyond the fortieth milestone.

Fellow all-rounder, Terry Bates, also completed the full distance for the first time while another school teacher, King William's College geography tutor, Bill Morton, proved he knew his way around, finishing in eleventh spot.

Former MGP and TT rider, John Crellin, completed his slowest-ever circuit in 20 hours 52 minutes 37 seconds while Dermot O'Toole and Ralph Martin crossed the line together in joint thirteenth place, Dermot scoring his third consecutive finish and Ralph his second in eight years. Together for eight hours, the two had walked in tandem from Andreas however Martin was lucky to reach the finish. In poor shape over the closing miles, he threatened to throw in the towel at the Liverpool Arms and it took great persuasion from the Steam Packet Captain to keep him moving.

Alistair Sutherland was the sixth new name to join the elite list of walkers to complete this gruelling event, finishing one place in front of the prolific David Collister who made it a fourteenth consecutive finish in 21 hours 25 minutes 34 seconds.

The second woman home was Angie Aire of Onchan, later followed by Kevin Skinner and the husband and wife team of Dave and Kate Cain.

First-time finishers Tony Blakeley, Phil Maltby, Irene Taggart and Wendy Watson were among the 24 walkers who completed the full distance.

Other performances worthy of mention were those of Martin Walters along with Highways, Ports and Property's Chief Executive, Roy Cooil, who both stopped at Lezayre after 62-miles. The furthest of the non-finishers was top local runner, Peter Costley, who made it to the 67-mile mark at Maughold before calling it a day.

1998

Under the auspices of the Race Walking Association, the Parish Walk of 1998 was lengthened by another 15 miles along Douglas Promenade for those wishing to achieve Centurion status.

The truly mammoth entry of 532 competitors attracted considerable interest from as far away as Australia, the UK and the continental countries of Belgium, Denmark and Holland. So huge was the entry that race organisers, Manx Harriers, along with the police, appealed to everyone to use discretion when following the event, which had in recent years, become a logistical nightmare for race director, Ray Cox.

It was expected that parts of Douglas town centre would be gridlocked while the Glen Darragh and Clannagh Roads had been granted closure orders to all bar a few official vehicles.

As expected, there were records all round in the thirty-seventh event, which started at 12 noon from the Villa Marina Gardens and held over the longest weekend of the year. From a best-ever entry, there were 498 starters of which 107 went beyond Peel. Of those, 35 made it all the way back to Douglas in the Clerical Medical International sponsored event. Furthermore, 11 brave, hardy souls continued for an extra 15 miles on Douglas Promenade to complete the first-ever 100-mile race to be staged on the Island, and the only event of its kind in Britain that year.

First past the post in the Parish and the Centurion events were the amazing husband and wife duo of Richard and Sandra Brown of the Surrey Race Walking Club. Richard produced the first sub-16-hour time since John Cannell in 1982, to win the traditional 85-mile Parish Walk at his first attempt in 15 hours 59 minutes 44 seconds, nearly 17 minutes in front of his wife with whom he'd walked for roughly half the distance. It was the quickest-ever female circuit of the 17 parishes. They went on to record times of 19 hours 22 minutes 26 seconds and 19 hours 32 minutes 26 seconds respectively for the 100 miles.

Immediately behind was Arie Boertjes of Holland in 19 hours 38 minutes 14 seconds, followed by Marleen Radder in 21 hours 16 minutes 56 seconds, and last year's Parish Walk winner Chris Flint of London in 21 hours 47 minutes 22 seconds.

The first local to complete the 100 miles was Douglas postman, Ray Hughes, in 22 hours 15 minutes 48 seconds. He was followed by great-grandmother, Jill Green, in 22 hours 22 minutes 30 seconds, second local, Tony Kneale of Douglas, in 22 hours 55 minutes 05 seconds, and the Dutch duo of Luc Nicque and Hans Van der Knaap in 23 hours 03 minutes 34 seconds. Ballasalla's Simon Cox was the other local to complete the 100 miles, making it to the finish with just 8½ minutes to spare before the 24-hour cut-off.

Dermot O'Toole trained hard for this event. He reached the Douglas War Memorial at 8:41am only to be told by former Commonwealth Games race-walker, Allan Callow, that there wasn't enough time to complete the extra 15 miles to achieve the Centurion status he so desired.

The best local in the 85-mile event was Peter Kaneen of Glen Vine who completed the course for the second time in three years, finishing fourth behind the Browns and Dutchman Boertjes in 17 hours 22 minutes 36 seconds but with no inclination to continue further.

Next to reach the Island's capital was Chris Flint, followed by Danish army mechanic, Karen Marie Brogger, who crossed the finishing line in sixth place in 18 hours 05 minutes 12 seconds. As she had just a few hours left before catching a plane home to rejoin the forces, she decided against going the extra distance.

Ray Hughes was the second local, in ninth place, with regular sparring partner, Tony Kneale, 40 minutes behind in twelfth spot. The near inseparable pair completed the Parish for their thirteenth time.

Above: Previous winner Brian Ashwell on the Sloc.

Right: There were 498 starters in 1998.

Below: Centurion Richard Brown was first home in the Parish Walk and then went on to complete another 15 miles on Douglas Promenade.

Bottom: Becky Sleight, Anthony Quayle, Les Brown and Philip Kenney at Glen Vine.

1998-1999

All-rounder, Willie Kneale, who had recently run the London Marathon, finished his second-ever Parish Walk, his first being way back in 1963 when he was one of the Island's leading walkers.

Mick Holgate completed his tenth Parish Walk, finishing in fourteenth place, followed by Simon Cox who then took almost four hours to complete the extra 15 miles in order to gain the much-coveted 100-mile status.

Well-known local hockey and squash player, Irene Taggart, finished the Parish for the second successive year, followed by first-timers, Dave Lockett and Gordon Corran, who recorded a joint time of 20 hours 35 minutes exactly.

Dermot O'Toole was twentieth, reaching the 85-mile finishing line in 20 hours 41 minutes 37 seconds. The disappointed Seacat skipper had lost valuable time on the Island's west coast, coming close to retirement at Jurby with his service provider missing since Peel.

Northern AC athletes, Mark Bridson and Stewart Sayle, walked together throughout, finishing joint twenty-first in 20 hours 48 minutes 18 seconds.

The remaining finishers were Susan Clements, Ramsey schoolteacher Mike Boulton, John Stubbs, Craig Phillips, John Fenton, David Collister, brothers, David and Kevin Tasker, Barbara Bagley, close friends Diane Turner and Sylvia Harrison, Kevin Martin and Julian Teare – the latter after having been on his badly blistered feet for 24 hours and 16 minutes.

The furthest non-finishers at Maughold were David Griffiths, Maureen Cox, Diane Corcoran, Mark Spiers, Tony Blakeley and John Corrin, the latter reaching the fifteenth church in 18 hours exactly and recorded as the final retirement of the day.

First to Peel and winning the official veterans' race was local primary school teacher, Terry Bates, in a time of 5 hours 39 minutes 10 seconds. He had a dice for much of the way with visiting walker, John Paddick. The pair was matching strides out of Douglas in blazing sunshine and joined for a short while on the flat section through Malew and Arbory by Peel's Robbie Lambie. The latter was forced to pull up at the 19½-mile mark with hip problems.

After going through his worst patch around Colby and in light rain, Bates really dug deep over his favourite stretch of the course, the Sloc. He had pulled back a two-minute deficit by the top, which was shrouded in thick mist and driving rain. Later he overtook Paddick on the descent to Dalby where the weather had begun to improve.

Not tempted to go on and complete the course for a second consecutive year, Terry joked: 'It was handy not being able to see the top of the Sloc for the mist.' It was his third time to Peel, having claimed the runner-up spot on his previous two attempts.

In her first attempt at the Parish, Jane Kennaugh won the 32½-mile ladies' race to Peel in what is thought to be only the second sub-six-hour time by a local woman in the 39-year history of the event. Some way short of Irene Corlett's amazing 5 hours 23 minutes 16 seconds record set in 1982, Jane's walk was nevertheless extremely meritorious for someone who can still be regarded as a relative newcomer to the sport. It was her furthest-ever race having previously contested a 50-kilometre race in Bradford on a flat course. She had to shelve plans for going the distance after struggling with a painful right knee for a good ten miles or more. She finished 14 minutes ahead of Bridget Kaneen, with third-placed Danish girl, Karen Marie Brogger, a further three minutes behind. The local trio of Karen Locking, Elaine Bawden and Marie Draper completed the top six.

Sandra Brown, runner-up in the main event, was the first veteran woman to Peel in a time of 5 hours 42 minutes 21 seconds, 10 minutes ahead of Jane Kennaugh. Fellow Centurions, Marleen Radder and Jill Green were next, with the veterans' prize going to fourth-placed Helen Renecle, ahead of leading locals, Donna Davies and Sue Partington.

A performance worthy of mention came from Sue Biggart of Glen Vine who reached the western capital at her first attempt in 7 hours 06 minutes 40 seconds.

Phil Readshaw made it to Kirk Michael in 9 hours 04 minutes while Ralph Martin continued on to the halfway mark at Ballaugh, arriving at the gate of St. Mary's Church in 9 hours 18 minutes.

Brian Brough and Angie Aire were two of 20 retirements at Jurby, with Gordon Corran and Allan Corrin stopping seven miles further on at Bride. David Boultbee from the Ronaldsway Meteorological Office reached Andreas at 2:30am however his parish debut ended here with badly blistered feet.

The Murray Lambden Trophy for the under-21 men's class went to Stuart Christian for the second year in a row. He reached Peel Town Hall 3½ minutes ahead of Juan Readshaw, while Claire Belcher made it to her home Parish of Rushen in exactly 4 hours 34 minutes to win the under-21 ladies' class.

1999

Throughout its long history, the Parish Walk has captured the public's imagination like no other. Interest from all sides of the community, young and old, rich and poor have made this the most eagerly awaited athletic event in the Manx sporting calendar. As expected, the final event of the twentieth century event attracted a record entry of 660, including 18 of the last year's 35 finishers, plus previous winners, Chris Flint, Lee Cain, Graham Young and Charlie Weston. Members of the Manx legislature were also entered, including Noel Cringle, David Cretney, Bill Henderson and Phil Braidwood. Eighty-four-year-old Island resident Norman Wisdom was also entered, the comedy celebrity hoping to improve on last year's performance when he was forced out at Braddan after completing just two miles.

In appalling weather conditions that would make this the wettest Parish Walk on record, the event got underway from the Villa Marina Gardens at 12 noon on the longest weekend of the year. Nevertheless, the

Left: Selwyn Callister failed to make it round on this occasion.

Right: Gavin Dean (No. 87) on the way to Glen Vine.

1999

light drizzle that marked the start of the race had turned to a downpour by the time the 580 starters had reached the first church at Braddan.

Even at this early stage, the front-runners were clocking less than ten-minute miles on the long trek south to Santon. But the pace was too hot for Terry Bates who surprised timekeepers by becoming the first of 15 to call time at the 12-mile mark.

The deteriorating weather conditions may have accounted for many of the 200 walkers who stopped at the southernmost church where waterproofs and umbrellas became the order of the day. The leading walkers reached this point in 3½ hours however, the slopes of Cronk ny Arrey Laa offered little protection from the strong head wind and heavy rain, which hampered progress on the long haul over the Sloc to the Round Table.

Jane Kennaugh was the first to reach Peel, arriving there in 5 hours 27 minutes exactly. Her time was the third quickest ever recorded to this point and less than four minutes down on Irene Corlett's record time set in 1982. Veterans, Allan Callow and Colin Halsall, were the next to arrive followed by Chris Flint and Karen Marie Brogger, the first two walkers to proceed beyond the western capital.

The four MHKs reached Peel safely. Douglas North member, Bill Henderson, who walked the 32½ miles for the Manx Foundation for the Physically Disabled in just under nine hours, said the thought of not letting down his sponsors drove him on.

Many fine performances came from the 263 who stopped at the most westerly church. Chris Keown and Jane Mooney managed sub-6½-hour times over the shorter distance, with Jackie Bairstow and Wendy Ross not far behind. Southerners, David Tasker, Mike and Val Kneale, recorded excellent times with Noel Cringle completing the 32½ miles in 7 hours 08

minutes 56 seconds. Lee Cain, winner in 1996, arrived at Peel in quite good shape and sixth on the road. He would have been third to go beyond but decided to quit there and then. 'The conditions are awful and I'd have kept drier doing the tin bath race,' said the Braddan farmer.

Next to head north out of Peel was Mark Stewart followed by Alan Clucas, Tony Kneale and Ray Hughes. The remaining 80 brave and hardy souls continued beyond the western capital with the unrelenting wind and driving rain hindering their progress northwards. Unsurprisingly, a further 12 retirements were posted at Kirk Michael, the 39-mile mark.

Chris Flint, leading on the road by three minutes, checked in at the midway point at 7:56pm followed by the Danish visitor, Karen Marie Brogger. Both were soaked to the skin but looking good as they headed out onto the lonely road to Bride.

A further 15 retirements were posted at Ballaugh while Bill Morton, Maureen Cox, Marie Latham, Rosemarie 'Roey' Crellin, John Lovelady and Leslie Christian all succumbed to the atrocious weather conditions at the 45½-mile mark.

Charlie Weston headed a group of seven to stop at St. Bridget's Church, Bride. The Highgate Harrier reached the northernmost parish six minutes short of 12 hours but still over 2½ hours ahead of fellow veteran, Frank Oates, the final retirement at this point.

The wind and driving rain began to ease at midnight however it came too late for David Griffiths and Doug Allan, both stopping with seven others at the thirteenth church at Andreas.

Two minutes apart at Lezayre, David Chambers and Alan Cowin were two of 12 to call time at the 62-mile mark. Errol Watson, a further hour behind, was the final retirement of the day having been on

1999

Top left: A wet day in Peel for Tony Kneale.

Top right: Robert Broughton and Nick Cain three miles into the race.

Bottom left:Chris Flint receiving the winner's trophy along with runner-up Tony Kneale and third placed Danish visitor, Karen Marie Brogger.

Bottom right: Charlie Weston was first of seven to stop at Bride.

Jane Kennaugh, Allan Callow (No.36) and Colin Halsall were the leaders into Peel.

his feet ten minutes short of 16 hours.

In driving rain, Chris Flint hurried on through the Bride hills to Andreas where he was now 17 miles ahead of the trailing stragglers still to reach Kirk Michael.

The path leading to the thirteenth church was waterlogged and unlit as the leader checked in, with day now turning to night. An exchange of words with timekeepers Ted and Barbara Hyde, and the Metropolitan policeman was gone, hurrying on through the night to record a second victory in three years. His winning time of 17 hours 07 minutes 46 seconds was almost 29 minutes quicker than in 1997 and quite astonishing considering the adverse weather conditions.

Runner-up in only her second-ever long-distance event was Karen Marie Brogger. The Danish army mechanic finished over half an hour behind but still 27 minutes quicker than last year when she was sixth.

Tony Kneale went through a bad patch during the early sections but managed to fight it off and finished third. 'I wouldn't have given tuppence for my chances of finishing when on the Sloc,' said Tony later. 'I had cramp in both legs and still felt pretty rough heading out of Peel.'

Rushen rambler, Alan Clucas, had said he wanted to do the Parish just one more time before the end of the century. 'Never again,' he shouted vehemently as he headed off into the fading light at the Cronk with 43 miles now behind him.

Ray Hughes had made his traditional steady start and was going along nicely at the Dollagh, as was Willy Kneale. From the quintessential village green marking the midway point, there was only one change in the top six with Ray Hughes overhauling Alan Clucas for fourth place.

The eleventh finisher to make it back to Douglas

was regular mountain marathon competitor, Tony Okell, from the North of England. He was followed by Western AC's, Allan Corran and David Collister, the latter completing the event for an incredible sixteenth consecutive time.

Angie Aire made it round for the second time in three years, while it was two in a row for Craig Phillips, John Stubbs and retired schoolteacher, Mike Boulton.

Staunch Parish supporter, Dermot O'Toole, made it to the finish for a fifth consecutive time, almost one hour ahead of Tony Blakeley and local motorcyclist, Adrian Smith, who finished for the first time.

Martina Preuss was twenty-first and the last of the hardy souls to go the full distance in what will probably be remembered as one the toughest Parish Walks ever.

2000

Manx Harriers organising committee had their work cut out in 2000 with a Parish Walk entry exceeding all expectation. Held over the weekend of 18th and 19th June the annual classic had grown to such proportions over the last decade that no-one in their wildest imagination could have forseen 667 walkers taking to the road in the first race of the new millennium. It must be rembered that the historic walks of John Cannell and Colonel Anderson during the late nineteenth century bear little resemblance to those of today. The motor car was still to be invented and the term 'health and safety' not even coined. Working tirelessly for ten years to improve road safety, race director, Ray Cox, was in no doubt that a similar incident to that in 1968 could spell the end for this popular happening, now entering a fifth decade.

This year, and liaising closely with the police for

Below: It was a second victory in two years for Chris Flint.

2000

Above: A fun day out for most.

Right: It was a first victory for Peter Kaneen in 2000.

Below: Fancy dress for some!

Bottom left: Derek Appleton at Ballaugh.

Bottom right: Brian Ashwell (No. 32) finished in eighth spot.

road safety purposes, the Glen Darragh Road to the Braaid crossroads was restricted to one-way traffic in the direction of the race. The Clannagh Road to the Castletown Road was closed to all traffic and the Oatlands Road to Santon church, leading to the Blackboards was designated one-way in the direction of the race.

Last year's winner, Chris Flint, was again favourite, but Denmark's Karen Marie Brogger was making a third visit to the Island and hoping to become the first-ever lady winner of the gruelling 85-mile event.

The shorter distance to Peel looked like a two-horse race between last year's winner, Jane Kennaugh, and runner-up, Allan Callow, with Terry Bates in reserve should either fail.

With a 12 noon start from the Villa Marina Gardens, the warm and dry conditions accounted for a record number of walkers proceeding beyond the southernmost church. Nevertheless, the back-breaking climb over the Sloc took its toll on those unprepared for the demanding task with Kevin Edge, Michael Clough and John Christian all calling time at Patrick. That said, 433 hardy souls made it to Peel, Julie Quine the last to check in at the Town Hall after being on her feet for 9 hours 36 minutes.

Jane Kennaugh made it a hat-trick of wins in the ladies' race, leading her class from start to finish in the shorter 32½-mile event and only three minutes down on her personal best time of 5 hours 27 minutes. She finished over half an hour in front of fellow Manx Harrier, Bridget Kaneen, with Denmark's Karen Marie Brogger third. Jane was accompanied most of the way by veteran men's winner Allan Callow who lost count on how many wins he had notched up. They walked more or less together until the Round Table, but Jane descended much quicker to arrive at Peel Town Hall some ten minutes in front.

Terry Bates was runner-up to Allan in the veteran men's race, while former marathon man, Robbie Callister, was third.

Helen Renecle, Wendy Ross and Marie Gilbertson took the honours in the ladies' veteran class, while Allan Thomson won the under-21 event for the second successive year in an excellent time of 6 hours 07 minutes 28 seconds.

By late afternoon, the fog patches and low cloud that had persisted for much of the day were now replaced with blazing sunshine, making conditions far from ideal for the 125 walkers who continued beyond Peel.

A total of 23 retirements were recorded at Kirk Michael including those of Mark Bridson, Kevin Tasker and Chris Lyon, all of whom had little enthusiasm to continue further.

Brenda Charlton and Frank Oates, along with brothers, Brian and David Goldsmith were four of 23 to call time at the halfway mark while husband and wife duo, Mike and Val Kneale, went that bit further, stopping at St. Patrick's Church, Jurby an hour before midnight.

The first of 12 retirements at the northernmost parish of Bride was that of recent Centurion, Simon Cox. Charlie Weston went no further than Andreas while Ray Pitts, Alan Clucas and Sue Biggart all waved the white flag after 62 miles.

A reduced field of 50 walkers went beyond Andreas, but it was disappointing for staunch Parish supporters Irene Taggart and David Tasker who came to within 18 miles of the finish before retiring.

Only 39 made it past Maughold where the stragglers at a nearby party offered sustenance and encouragement to those who continued.

All 36 who reached Lonan made it back to Douglas to register a finish, Leslie Christian the last and just 15 minutes inside the 24-hour cut-off point.

Peter Kaneen not only achieved a long-standing ambition in winning the gruelling event, but also completed a double after finishing in the recent London Marathon. Peter and his wife Bridget have now achieved a unique set of local race walking distance wins between them, from 1-, 2-, and 5-kilometre sprints to 10-kilometres, 20-kilometres, 50-kilometres and the End to End Walk, as well as every class in the TT Relay 'That's it, we've done the lot now,' said the Manx Harriers man as he crossed the finish line shortly before three o'clock on Sunday morning in a winning time of 16 hours 59 minutes 54 seconds.

Runner-up, some 34 minutes later, Doug Allan of Knocksharry registered his first-ever finish after 37 years of trying. After a 30-year break from the sport, he said he had never before set out to complete the Parish. Seventh at the midway point near Ballaugh Bridge, he had just one goal and that was to make it back to Douglas. He overhauled or outlasted all bar one of the six in front of him to beat twice former winner, Chris Flint of London, into the number two spot by just under seven minutes.

Often the most talked about topic for days, if not months later, it is worth remembering the quotes from those who went the distance:

Winner: Peter Kaneen. After completing a grand slam of victories in every local long-distance walking event, Peter said: 'That's it – I've done the lot now.' A finisher twice before in 1996 and 1998, he continued: 'That was a hard one because I didn't see anyone else for ages. I walked on my own all the way from Peel.'

Second: Doug Allan. 'I have never set out before to finish. The conditions were perfect really. The only place it was a bit warm was after Rushen and down towards Peel. Otherwise, it was ideal.'

Third: Chris Flint. Last year's winner needed all sorts of concoctions, such as banana milk and banana milk-shakes, to keep him going. 'An old hamstring injury gave me problems from the start, which prevented me stretching out over the Sloc. Once I got to Bride the hamstring was much better and I was able to get motoring, but I was too far behind to catch Doug.'

Fourth: Karen Marie Brogger. Sixth and second in the previous two events, the Danish Army tank driver

2000

was yet again the first woman to cross the finish line. 'My time was not as good as last year. I was very tired at half distance. Maybe I can improve next year. We'll see.'

Fifth: Derek Appleton. Supported throughout by former Olympic champion, Don Thompson, he quipped, 'Don's the star, you need to talk to him, not me.' Dover man, Derek, also completed the End to End walk in May, but this was his first Parish Walk. He finished in excellent condition.

Sixth: Robbie Callister. 'I was going pretty well around Andreas, but I found it difficult from Maughold walking in the dark on the narrow roads. My worst spell was around Laxey, but once I got there I knew I had done it – it was just a case of getting back to Douglas.'

Seventh: Boyd Millen. A long-distance fell walker from Kendal, Boyd was supported by his wife, Lilian, a former world ranked walker. It was his first finish in the Parish and one he thoroughly enjoyed.

Eighth: Brian Ashwell. Winner back in 1995, the Leicestershire veteran struggled with a bad toe, but was more comfortable after changing his shoes at Peel.

Ninth: Ray Hughes. After finishing the walk for the fifteenth time, Ray said, 'It was a hard one – in the early 90s I collapsed at the Dhoon.'

Tenth: Martin Walters. He recorded his second consecutive finish in the race, lopping some 72 minutes off his 1999 time.

Eleventh: John Tasker. 'My brothers all did it in the 80s. I never bothered, but I had my arm twisted this year. It was about time.'

Twelfth: Gordon Corran. 'Is that the first lap?' was Gordon's enquiry on finishing the event, before he went for a jog to loosen up. He then vowed, 'Never again – that's it. I'll do Peel again, but no more.'

Thirteenth: John Stubbs. The Port Erin man walked most of the way with his friend, Gordon Corran, and shares his never again sentiments. 'That's it – I'm happy.'

Fourteenth: Tony Kneale. A man of few words, Tony lets his feet do the talking. Like near neighbour, Ray Hughes, it was his fifteenth finish. 'My back's a bit sore,' he said at Bishopscourt.

Fifteenth: Gordon Corrin. Postal manager Gordon was delighted with his first finish. 'I've been training hard with Doug Allan over the past few months, though I lost a few weeks with an injury. It's a lifetime ambition – I first entered in the mid-80s.'

Sixteenth: Marie Latham. First local woman home, Marie had quite a trouble free and composed walk throughout. 'Very pleased,' she said.

Seventeenth: Mick Holgate. Clocking up his eleventh finish, Mick was lucky to be walking at all after falling off a roof during the previous winter and suffering horrific injuries.

Eighteenth: Moira Hall and David Chambers. Moira, who also finished this year's London Marathon said, 'We walked together from Bride. We were both going about the same speed so we decided to stay

together and encourage each other to each checkpoint.' David, blistered feet and all, added, 'There's no way we would have done it alone, especially during the dark when it was really tough going.'

Twentieth: Angie Aire and Dave Collister. It was Angie's third finish in four years, Dave's seventeenth in a row! They walked together from Maughold. Angie's husband, Ian, commented, 'I told her she's going to have to train for this some time. If she's done more than four miles a week in training I'd be surprised!'

Twenty-second: Peter Christian. Local man, Peter, finished the race for the first time.

Twenty-third: Dermot O'Toole. Following his sixth finish, Steam Packet skipper, Dermot, claimed he'd not be doing it again. He'd said that before!

Twenty-fourth: Roey Crellin and John Loveday. Champagne celebrations awaited these finishers who had a huge following, including children from Roey's child-minder groups.

Twenty-sixth: David Griffiths. A first-time finish for Douglas man Dave. 'Wonderful organisation,' he commented.

Twenty-seventh: Justin Meechan and Kevin Watterson. The two airport firemen walked together to finish the race and had the blisters to prove it!

Twenty-ninth: Ken Kewley. Ken was following in the footsteps of his father, Bob, a former MGP rider, who finished the Parish in 1962, shortly after breaking both his legs. Ken said, 'The word that comes to mind is ouch. In the last five miles the pain kicked in and my knees didn't like it anymore. Up to then it was all going well and I was in great form.'

Thirtieth: David Gelling. Harbours Department diver, David, achieved his first finish in three attempts, having stopped at Lezayre in '98 and Peel in '97. 'It was tough going after Bride, with blisters. But I knew I would make it once I got past Maughold.'

Thirty-first: Bob Noonan. Bob was followed throughout the night by his friend, John Shimmin, who had been invited with the immortal line: 'Fancy a night out?'

Thirty-second: Kevin Martin. Regular local athlete, Kevin moved over from the Lake District a couple of years before – he spent most of his time here anyway. It was his third finish.

Thirty-third: Haydn Kenna. Haydn was unavailable to comment, but he was another first-time finisher.

Thirty-fourth: Adrian Beale. Top local sidecar trials competitor, Adrian trained hard for the event. 'It was horrendous,' he said. 'I had a nightmare at Maughold – I couldn't walk. I sat down for half an hour to get my head together, but I couldn't eat or drink. It was a surreal experience. I didn't know whether to laugh or cry.'

Thirty-fifth: David Whorral. Yet another first-time finisher, David found it more difficult than expected. 'Willpower got me through, my backup team literally pushing me to the end. Coming up the promenade I could see the Villa Marina – it just didn't seem to get any closer. I will certainly not be doing this again.'

Thirty sixth: Lesley Christian. Manx woman, Lesley travelled to the Island for the event from her home in South Africa. After a steady walk, she reached the finish line just 15 minutes before the 24-hour cut-off point, supported throughout by her mum and dad, Sheila and David Christian.

2001

The continuing support of sponsors Clerical Medical International had made the Parish Walk easily the biggest participant event on the Manx sporting calendar. For many, the Manx Harriers organised event had become an almost compulsive challenge; for others a vehicle for raising charitable funds; but for the vast majority of individuals, it was a battle against the course and the elements with willpower always the winner.

A record entry, plus the refurbishment of the Villa Marina in 2001 gave the Parish Walk a new look with the event starting from the National Sports Centre for the very first time. Those registering for the event did so at the Manx Harriers' clubhouse between half past five and nine o'clock on the evening prior to the race. As well as being issued with a race number, the £20 entry fee also included a uniquely designed T-shirt by local Commonwealth walker, Steve Partington.

The new starting point required one complete lap of the 400-metre track then a lap and a half of the tarmac perimeter road before filtering out briefly on to the Castletown Road and along the TT access road to Braddan.

This new routing arrangement still maintained the 85-mile distance but avoided Douglas town centre and the traffic congestion so often met at Quarter Bridge where in previous years much policing and marshalling was required.

Father and son, Phil and Juan Readshaw finished together in 2001 in 26th spot.

Manx Harriers' organising committee, under the directorship of Raymond Cox, certainly had logistical problems with the new format while Chief Marshal, Winston Liu, performed a balancing act of the highest quality by moving his limited workforce from stage to stage as the event progressed.

Favourites for this year's event were previous winner, Lee Cain and veteran, Brian Ashwell. John Stubbs and ex-Isle of Man marathon champion, Robbie Callister, were expected to mount strong challenges, as was Doug Allan who had had an amazing walk last year to finish runner-up. Always a steady starter, Doug was unlikely to feature prominently before the hours of darkness but he was a tough campaigner with years of experience under his feet and undoubtedly the man to watch. In the wings, should the favourites fail, were 15-time

Left: Smiling faces at the Braaid.

Right: Weary legs near the top of the Sloc.

2001

finishers, Ray Hughes and Tony Kneale.

At the startline, 17-time finisher, David Collister, caused some stir when he discovered that he had been missed off the entry list and was assumed to be a non-starter.

The first woman to Peel was expected to be Bridget Kaneen of Glen Vine whose husband Peter had won the 85-mile event last year. He was having this year off after contesting a gruelling 50-kilometre event at the Dublin Grand Prix the preceding weekend.

Weather conditions for the fortieth event looked promising with the Ronaldsway Meteorological Office forecasting a fine day with light south-south-easterly winds and plenty of sunshine.

With a new start time of 10:00am, the 728 starters were sent on their way by race director, Raymond Cox. Soon, roads in the east and south of the Island were gridlocked as the vast army of walkers headed south and beyond.

Peter Marshall was the first retirement of the day, reaching Santon in 2 hours 42 minutes and calling time along with 36 others. Eight retirements were recorded at Malew, five at Arbory and 224 at Rushen.

The climb over Ballakillowey and the Sloc accounted for many more retirements, but well over half made it to Peel with 150 hoping to go that bit further.

First of the former winners to fall by the wayside was Leicester's Brian Ashwell who stopped at the Round Table with a recurrence of a back injury. 'I had a slipped disc a few years ago and I seem to get problems with my back each time I tackle the Parish,' said the 68-year-old former winner. 'If it's not right, it's just not worth struggling on.'

Londoner, Charlie Weston, winner in 1989 and 1991, made it as far as the veterans' finish in Peel before coming to a halt with 310 others.

Robbie Callister was the first to arrive in Michael Street, Peel, the church clock striking four as he made his way to the Town Hall steps. Bridget Kaneen was a further 41 seconds behind, closely followed by John Stubbs, Wendy Ross and Helen Renecle. It was Stubbs' fifth attempt but he decided to stop at the 32½-mile mark and claim the veterans' prize for a first time.

John paced himself well in the early stages, leaving behind early leaders Dave Griffiths, Brian Ashwell, Bridget Kaneen and Nigerian 20-km walker, Charles-Tunde Arosanyin. Also well placed in the early stages was Gordon Corran, husband of Liz, the race secretary. Nevertheless he went off too fast and paid the ultimate price later. 'I held the overall lead for about five minutes before Robbie Callister passed me towards the top of the climb,' he said later.

Second into Peel, Bridget Kaneen's time of 6 hours 03 minutes 12 seconds for the ladies' event easily secured first place and she was more than delighted with her first victory. Husband, Peter Kaneen, a winner of the overall event last year, acted as backup support on his mountain bike. He had urged his

better half to continue when at one point she had felt like throwing in the towel. 'Last year Peter was set to pack-in during the night-time, but I managed to talk him round. So he was just getting his own back,' said Bridget after a superb descent from the Round Table.

Seven days after competing in a 20-km race at the Dublin Grand Prix, Bridget, a Manx Harrier, had started steadily enough, only to hit a bad patch in the Ballabeg area. 'I struggled with a tight hamstring in the back of my leg on the way through Arbory, Rushen, and the climb to the Round Table. Then it eased off and I gained back the ground I'd lost on the climb. At one point, the Glen Vine woman dropped to third place in the ladies' race, behind Wendy Ross and Helen Renecle. She passed tall South African, Helen, on the relatively flat run towards the Round Table and overhauled Wendy close to the Eairy Cushlin turn-off. In the meantime, Bridget had also accounted for senior man Lee Cain, while veteran men's winner, John Stubbs, was sidelined at Glen Maye.

'It's about time I won,' smiled Bridget. 'I've been second twice to Jane Kennaugh and third at my first attempt, behind Jackie Bairstow and Jill Green. I may have stopped earlier only for Peter nagging me.'

Wendy Ross dropped some five minutes in eight miles to Bridget but still came home a clear second to take the veteran ladies prize in 6 hours 07 minutes 56 seconds, beating Helen Renecle, the class winner of the two previous years, by just over three minutes.

Robbie Callister was the first to reach the crossroads at the foot of South Barrule, some 1,100 feet above sea level. Here, at the 25-mile mark, the views were simply breath-taking but Callister was on a mission with no time to stop. In fact, he was moving so quickly that race director, Raymond Cox, was unable to stay ahead as he frantically marked out the course for the advancing pack.

Callister was the first to leave Peel, his ten-minute advantage over nearest challenger, 1996 winner Lee Cain steadily increasing on the road to Kirk Michael. But the pace was too hot for the Trollaby farmer who called time at Devil's Elbow. 'I felt fine one minute, then sick the next,' said Lee, somewhat disappointedly. 'To that point, I thought it would be between Robbie and me for the honours and I really felt on for it'. So, by the 36-mile mark, there were no previous winners left in the race and the pressure was off to a certain degree.

Having led from halfway up the Sloc, Callister touched the gates of St. Mary's Parish Church, Ballaugh at three minutes to six. Next to reach the midway point was Doug Allan, some 21 minutes later having stretched six minutes out of Nigerian student Charles-Tunde Arosanyin in as many miles.

Allan Thomson, winner of the under-21 race to Peel a year earlier, was looking good in fourth place, as was Jim Harvey's son, Mark, who went through at 6:41pm.

At Kirk Michael, 21 walkers called it a day and a

Top: Allan Stewart Thomson was very fortunate to reach the finish.

Below: Bridget Kaneen won the ladies race to Peel in a fraction over 6 hours 03 minutes.

Left: Marie Latham was one of twenty-three retirements at Jurby.

Right: First of five wins for Robbie Callister.

further 18 at Ballaugh including previous finisher, Martina Preuss who reached the midway point in a fraction over 12 hours.

Marie Latham and Sue Partington were two of 23 retirements at Jurby, timekeeper Mitch Joughin closing down the checkpoint with Guy Sutton the last to throw in the towel after 12 hours 20 minutes.

By now, Callister was moving so fast, that on reaching the 50-mile point at Smeale crossroads, he was 19 miles ahead of Violet Platt and Moira O'Connell, last of the finishers to check in at the western capital at 7:39pm.

Seven retirements were recorded at Bride while Wendy Thirkettle, from the Manx Museum, was the last of 15 to stop at Andreas, the 55½-mile mark. Exceeding the time limit to this point by 21 minutes, her near 15½-hour ordeal was finally over as she handed in her number to timekeepers, Ted and Barbara Hyde.

The long haul through the northern parishes took its toll on the many stragglers hoping to reach the finish. Neil Shimmin, James Kennish and Ian Ashcroft succumbed to the pain barrier at Lezayre. Cliffie Keyes struggled on along the dark, tree-lined road leading into Ramsey, desperate for paracetamol to numb his growing pain. In company with the trio of Dermot O'Toole, Graham Kelly and Richard Cooil since St Judes, the 24-year-old was moving at a funeral pace on the difficult climb to Maughold where his gallant effort expired. 'All the money in the world will not entice me to go further' he said.

The relatively short night soon turned to day as the last of the 45 checked in to and out of the fifteenth church with 18 miles to go.

But heartache was not far away for Dave Taylor who was the farthest non-finisher. Walking all the way with David Crowe in what was his first attempt, Dave reached Everlasting Bend on the approach to Laxey shortly after six o'clock on Sunday morning. There he collapsed at the roadside, just 8½ miles from the finish. 'The next thing I knew was waking up in Nobles Hospital,' said the Murray's Road man who was kept in for observation for three days.

Callister was never threatened over the closing miles and went on to complete his journey around the Island's 17 parishes in 16 hours 59 minutes 27 seconds, 27 seconds quicker than Peter Kaneen's time of a year ago.

The battle for second place went all the way to the wire, and while the tall Nigerian, Arosanyin appeared somewhat bewildered at the mileage and terrain of the event, he stuck at the task boldly, despite being warned by race judges for 'lifting' soon after the start – the rules of race walking clearly stating that a straight leg and unbroken contact with the ground to be maintained at all times.

The Nigerian walked in company with Allan Stuart Thomson for some time, but then the Nigerian eventually pulled away and set his eyes on veteran Doug Allan. In what was the closest finish for second place, Arosanyin, the 2002 Commonwealth Games hopeful, used his 20-kilometre track prowess to out-sprint the Knocksharry forester to the line, denying him a second consecutive runner-up result. The margin at the finish was just two seconds!

Ray Hughes walked much of the way with Ballasalla's Simon Cox, but went ahead to record his sixteenth finish in another sub-19-hour time.

The ever-consistent Willie Kneale notched up his fourth finish, some 38 years after his first, coming home six minutes ahead of Mark Harvey who picked up the prize for the fastest local first-time finisher in 19 hours 17 minutes 52 seconds.

John Lovelady of Glen Vine took some 90 minutes off his finishing time 12 months earlier to cross the line in joint eighth place with former Union Mills and Corinthians' footballer, David Cain. The pair walked every inch of the way together.

First-time finisher, Julian Thomas, slotted into tenth place ahead of three-time former finisher Allan Corran, while Ray Pitts and David Chambers walked more than half the way together to finish in joint twelfth spot.

David Collister, thought at one time to be a non-starter, again made it all the way to record his eighteenth consecutive finish. He was the last of the sub-20-hour men and in fourteenth spot.

First of the eight women to go the full distance was Roey Crellin of St. John's, who crossed the finish line at the Douglas War Memorial shortly after 6:00am in an excellent fifteenth position. It was her second successive finish.

Glen Vine's Sue Biggart came through strongly in the latter stages to record her first finish in eighteenth spot, behind Kevin Tasker and Bob Noonan, while Allan Thomson slotted in ahead of joint third place women, Angie Aire and Irene Taggart. Both were completing the full course for the fourth time in five years.

It was a lucky and perhaps fortunate ending for Thomson who came very close to not finishing. On course for a sub-19-hour circuit, last year's junior winner dehydrated so severely over the closing stages that he was forced to stop for over an hour at the White Bridge for medical attention.

The trio of Dermot O'Toole, Graham Kelly and Richard Cooil walked the final 27 miles together, finishing joint thirtieth several seconds inside 22 hours.

The last of the 44 finishers were close friends Stuart Counsell and Andrew Sewell of Peel, who crept in with less than 25 minutes to spare before the 24-hour cut-off.

Stephen Edwards reached Peel in 6 hours 47 minutes 35 seconds to win the under-21 men's event while Sara Nelson completed the shorter distance to Rushen to win the under-21 ladies' event.

The 'Time to Heel' trio of Ray Hughes, Mick Holgate and Dermot O'Toole won the team event on a combined aggregate of their finishing times after dead-heating with 'David's Angels.'

Ladies' race winner, Roey Crellin, second woman home, Sue Biggart, and local advocate, David Doyle, had a similar combined mileage of 255 miles but with a slower aggregate time.

Later in the year, the Island's sporting community was saddened to hear the news of the recent death of sporting stalwart, Arthur Jones.

Born in 1912, the year of the sinking of the Titanic, Arthur was involved in many sporting activities, some dating back to 1970 when he took part in the inaugural Manx Mountain Marathon.

Joining their organising committee in 1974 he later became the event's race secretary, a position he held for 20 years. Arthur was a regular competitor in the End to End race throughout the 1970s and completed the first of seven TT Course Walks in 1969. His best time for the 37¾ miles was 8 hours 17 minutes 32 seconds, recorded in 1973 when aged 61.

Arthur was also a regular competitor in the Parish Walk until the late 1980s and was still capable of reaching Peel in 7½ hours when nearly in his eightieth year!

A past president of the Isle of Man Badminton Association, Arthur will be remembered most for his dedicated involvement in the Parish Walk, which he almost single-handedly organised each year prior to walking the veterans' race to Peel in sandals!

After making sure the event was running smoothly, he would return home for a brief sleep before returning to All Saint's parish church, Lonan, to check in the remaining walkers. Here, he would hand-write certificates for those who had retired, before returning to Douglas to complete the task. He was undoubtedly a grand ambassador for Manx athletics and will be greatly missed.

2002

With a thousand walkers expected to take part in the 2002 Parish Walk and road safety a major concern, the temporary restrictions implemented in recent years to vehicular traffic were also extended to the south of the Island. For the first time since the inception of the event, the Sloc Road from above Ballakillowey to the Round Table was made one-way with emphasis put on vehicle support crews to seek alternative routes and to drive with due care and attention.

After an absence of some years, the two most successful competitors in the history of the Parish Walk came out of retirement to contest the event, held over the weekend of 22nd and 23rd June.

Derek Harrison and John Cannell, who between them had won no fewer than 11 Parish Walks, stressed they were only doing it for a bit of fun and wouldn't be going all out for a finish. 'Iron Man' Derek, was a phenomenal competitor in his day and still holds the absolute course record of 15 hours 20 minutes 51 seconds, set in 1979 during one of his five victories. John, who had one more win to his name, is one of only five men to have completed the full course in less than 16 hours.

A former Island footballer and marathon runner, Derek, scored back-to-back wins in 1972 and 1973 and again in 1979 and 1980, with a final success in 1984. Perhaps his greatest achievement was creating a world record for completing a distance of 136 miles and 735 yards in 24 hours on a short circuit in Rouen, France, in 1978.

At the age of 67, Derek suffered a stroke shortly after undergoing a hip operation and, on this occasion, he would be more than happy to reach the 19½-mile mark at Rushen. 'I'll see how I feel after that, but don't expect too much of me,' said the Island's only true world champion. Both ex-Commonwealth Games competitors were specialists at ultra-distance events, John in Edinburgh in 1970, and Derek four years later in Christchurch, New Zealand.

John completed his first Parish Walk in 1967, finishing runner-up to the legendary Albert Johnson. His first win was in 1976 and he went on to become the first to achieve a hat-trick of wins between 1981 and 1983. He was set to repeat that feat ten years later, when, after winning the 1993 and 1994 events, his career came to an end with stress fractures of both legs. 'I suppose it was a result of all the walking I'd done over a period of 30 years or so,' said the 56-year-old Douglas postman, whose hopes of an early return to the sport were put on hold again when he had suffered an angina attack two years previously.

'I've not really done any training for the Parish other than my day to day work and casual walking,' admits John. 'I'm aiming for Peel, but it won't be the end of the world if I don't make it to there.'

Favourite for the overall event was last year's winner, Robbie Callister, while veteran, Allan Callow, and previous three-time ladies' winner to Peel, Jane Gibson, née Kennaugh, were expected to go head-to-head over the shorter distance. Waiting in the wings should either slip up were Stephen Locking and Marie Latham. In the 85-mile event, Doug Allan looked the only candidate to challenge the previous winner.

The weather forecast was not good and this may have accounted for the unusually high number of non-starters who failed to make the start line. Setting off from the National Sports Centre at 10 o'clock on Saturday morning, the 838 starters soon had roads leading west and south gridlocked to London Marathon proportions with many hopefuls unprepared for the physical and mental nightmare that lay ahead.

The early leaders were through the southernmost parish in a little over three hours but the skies were darkening towards the south-west where a total of 264 walkers stopped at the 19½-mile mark. As expected, the poor weather made its appearance during late afternoon with katabatic winds and driving rain spilling down off the slopes of Cronk ny Arrey Laa, soaking all but the early leaders.

First to Peel for the third occasion was Jane Gibson, reaching the western capital in 5 hours 36 minutes 33 seconds, some ten minutes ahead of her nearest rival, Steve Locking. Eventual overall winner, Robbie Callister, was a further seven minutes in arrears. Allan Callow was the clear pre-race favourite and looked set to take the title yet again when a nagging back problem struck him on the descent from the Round Table. 'I was fine on the flat and on the climb, but once I started dropping towards Dalby

David and Kevin Tasker failed to reach the finish on this occasion.

the problems started,' revealed Allan later. He attempted to continue after a short respite at the Ballacallin but got no further than another three or four hundred yards before completely calling it a day.

Locking was not far behind and had been able to see Callow and ladies' race winner, Jane Gibson, on some of the longer stretches earlier. He had realised Allan was slowing but was surprised when he saw him at the side of the road. 'I've trained for the past six months for this event,' said the 40-year-old Edgewater mortgage consultant. 'I knew I would have a good chance in my first year as a veteran, even though Allan was the clear favourite.'

Marie Latham was next to reach Peel. Behind her came veteran, John Stubbs, in 6 hours 04 minutes 50 seconds with Doug Allan not far behind.

Callister was the first to head out of the quaint town, some 28 minutes ahead of Doug Allan – the 56-year-old forester who just got quicker with age. Next through the most westerly town was local advocate, David Doyle, who really was setting a storming pace after many winter months of intensive training. He'd set off in the early part with training partner and friend, Roey Crellin, but was over two minutes ahead at German and walked the rest of the way alone.

In all, 192 walkers made it to Kirk Michael. Terry Qualtrough, Graham Kelly and Chris Lyon were three of 16 to stop at the halfway mark where Callister had stretched his lead to 37 minutes and already half an hour up on his time to this point last year. Doug Allan touched the same church gate at precisely 6:17pm, by which time Callister was just four minutes short of the next parish church at Jurby.

David Doyle was going exceptionally well too, another 16 minutes down at Ballaugh, with Roey

2002

Top left: Vicki Rawlinson (No. 871) was the final retirement recorded at Maughold.

Top right: Mark Harvey was one of 775 competitors who failed to reach the finish.

Above: A second win for Robbie Callister in 16 hours 34 minutes 30 seconds.

Right: Jane Gibson was the first woman to reach Peel in 2002.

Crellin and Kendal milkman, Jim Bispham, close together at another five minutes.

By now, the heavy rain that had soaked the middle-to-late-comers on the approaches to Peel had caught up with the leaders. They received a good soaking on the Ballaugh to Lhen section, but were later treated to some welcome late-evening sunshine and a reduction in the wind strength that had hampered progress earlier. However, the improving weather conditions came too late for staunch Parish supporters Val Kneale, Brian R. Goldsmith and Guy Sutton, three of 31 retirements recorded at Jurby.

Callister reached the northernmost church at 7:54pm, probably the earliest anyone had ever reached St. Bridgets as a result of the earlier start time. He hurried on over the Bride hills, along the Burma Road and into Andreas, unchallenged and nearly an hour ahead of his nearest rival, Doug Allan.

Kevin Tasker, Mike Kneale and Maureen Cox were three of 25 to retire at the 52½-mile mark, while previous winner Charlie Weston, and Terry Bates continued another three miles before calling it a day at Andreas.

Callister was moving so fast that he had little time to take in the country smells of freshly cut silage and sweetly scented honeysuckle along the hedgerows of the northern plains. Still clocking 11-minute miles, he reached the fourteenth church shortly after 9:30pm, now a staggering 21 miles ahead of David Rads Quayle, last of the back-markers and still to reach Kirk Michael.

Ray Pitts made it to Lezayre in a little over 13½ hours but decided against going further and was one of a dozen to throw in the towel at the 62-mile mark.

Darkness was descending as the leaders made their way through Port Lewaigue and Port e Vullen – the short but steep climb to Maughold tiring and retirements for two posted.

Ray Hughes had been contesting fifth place for much of the late evening. However dehydration and fatigue took its toll on the Douglas postman who was barely moving on the punishing Ballajora climb, his journey ending 13 miles short of the finish.

A record 65 walkers made it to Maughold, Ramsey's Vicki Rawlinson the last to this point at 2:46am and the farthest non-finisher of the day. By this time, Callister had already finished by 11 minutes with many back-markers still to reach Lezayre. His time of 16 hours 34 minutes 30 seconds was 25 minutes quicker than last year making him the fourteenth quickest winner in the 42-year history of the event. He extended his winning margin over Doug Allan to just over an hour and looked capable of going quicker in future years.

Overtaken in the final two miles by Nigerian Charles-Tunde Arosanyin a year earlier, Doug was in no doubt about the number two spot this time. He was second on the road all the way from Peel and appeared to rattle up his third consecutive finish with consummate ease in a time just five seconds slower than his previous best.

However, the performance of the day had to be that of his near neighbour, David Doyle. Just dipping under 18 hours for the distance, his time was an amazing 3 hours 52 minutes 30 seconds quicker than his only finish 12 months earlier.

Ramsey's David 'Lon' Chambers produced a personal best by over 1½ hours to finish an excellent fourth, over 20 minutes clear of leading lady, Roey Crellin. She managed to break clear of Cumbrian long-distance fell walker, Jim Bispham, to finish in 18 hours 34 minutes 07 seconds, the sixth quickest woman in the history of the event and second fastest local only behind the 'queen' of them all, Irene Corlett. Roey, who had a great tussle with Ray Hughes earlier in the night, was in fact only 26 minutes in front of Sue Biggart who missed out on a sub-19-hour walk by just nine seconds.

Rushen United footballer, Neil Shimmin, won the prize for the highest-placed local first-time finisher in eighth spot, overtaking sixteen-time finisher, Tony Kneale, in the closing stages.

John Lovelady, David Cain and Julian Thomas walked much of the way together for the second year in succession. They finished tenth and joint twelfth, split by Parish first-timer, Michael Readshaw.

In spite of saying 'never again' on previous occasions, Onchan plasterer, Gordon Corran, made it round for the fourth time in five years, just 17 minutes in front of Juan Readshaw who made it two in a row, finishing fifteenth.

Regular finisher, Mick Holgate, completed his circuit of the 17 parishes in a shade over 20 hours with the much-talented Sean Hands a further 36 minutes back.

Centurion Simon Cox notched up his fourth finish, albeit his slowest, recording a time of 20 hours 46 minutes 10 seconds and just managing to stay ahead of David Comish and David Collister who rounded off the top 20.

Having surrendered at the fifteenth parish 12 months earlier, Cliffie Keyes made it to the finish for the first time, as did Dave Taylor who had come within nine miles of success the year before.

Police Assistant Chief Inspector, Dudley Butt, teamed up with a more than thankful Dermot O' Toole in Andreas village, the pair walking in tandem to finish joint twenty-seventh. Irene Taggart was a further four minutes in arrears, completing the full distance for a fifth time in six years and becoming the event's most successful-ever lady walker.

Veteran Frank Oates completed the 85 miles for a second time in 33 years, reaching the finishing line just 27 seconds in front of a tired but more than pleased, Wendy Thirkettle. Brenda Charlton also made it two in a row, improving on last year's time by a shade over 13 minutes.

However, there was disappointment for the sixty-third and final finisher, Paul Waters, who after a gallant performance, ran out of time midway along Douglas Promenade to finish in 24 hours 08 minutes 11 seconds.

2003

Legends of the past, Michael Gray (No. 419) and John Cannell.

Above: A sixth finish for Irene Taggart.

Below: Val and Michael kneale reached Andreas after ten attempts.

2003

In a bid to make the Island's biggest participant sporting event safer, organisers of the Clerical Medical International sponsored Parish Walk were forced to make major changes to its format in 2003. The start time was brought forward to 9:00am and traffic on the A27 road from the Round Table to Dalby routed one-way in the direction of the race.

With the earliest ever start to the event, race leaders were expected to reach Peel by mid-afternoon. In past years, most walkers only saw the Jurby to Bride coast road during the hours of darkness, however on this occasion the leaders were expected to be well through Ramsey as day turned to night.

After an absence of three years, Peter Kaneen made a welcome return to the Parish Walk in 2003 and was co-favourite for the overall honours along with winner of the event for the last two years, Robbie Callister.

Kaneen, a garage proprietor from Union Mills, admitted to having done no training whatsoever for this event and was in doubt that a sub-16-hour circuit was on the cards.

Meanwhile, Callister had been training hard throughout the winter and could be found on many a night pounding roads in the south of the Island from the Sloc to the Round Table. Eager to become only the third competitor in the history of the event to score a hat-trick of consecutive wins, the National Sports Centre swimming pool attendant was fully aware that this would be a fast, two-horse race, played out by the Island's very best.

Other previous hat-tricks in the event's 43-year history were those of John Cannell, who won three in a row between 1981 and 1983, and Willie Corkill's similar run of three straight wins in 1985, 1986 and 1987. Douglas postman, Cannell, who was again walking for fun, headed the list of overall wins with six to his credit.

Chris Flint and Charlie Weston, who had both won the event twice, were again making their annual pilgrimage to the Island, confident of victory should the gladiators fail.

Others in with a chance were three-time finishers Doug Allan who had been bridesmaid on two occasions, Ramsey's David Chambers and John Stubbs, with the latter expected to go well over the shorter distance.

Douglas advocate, David Doyle, sensation of last year's event, was hoping to achieve a hat-trick of finishes too, having worked overtime on the training circuit throughout the winter and hoping for a sub-17-hour time.

No strangers to this Herculean task, Ray Hughes, Tony Kneale, Mick Holgate and David Collister were all expected to make it round for the umpteenth time, the latter under immense pressure to record his twentieth consecutive finish.

Controversial 1968 winner, Ian Turnbull, and five-time finisher Chris Keown were two veterans on the comeback trail. Also making an appearance was Jim Harvey, the Abbeylands farmer and sensational runner-up in the inaugural event held back in 1960, who now sported an artificial hip.

Jane Gibson and Marie Latham were non-starters this year, leaving Roey Crellin from Peel as the pre-event favourite in the ladies' class both to Peel and the full distance. Daughter of the late Herbie Cannell, who came so close to winning the event in 1961, 48-year-old Roey had trained more than ever and still had an outside chance of becoming the first-ever lady winner, an achievement her father would have been proud of.

Sue Biggart and sparring partner, Ray Pitts, trained exceedingly hard throughout the year too with a punishing schedule boxer Mike Tyson would have been proud of. The 40-old staff nurse from Ontario, Canada, but now a Manx resident, was hoping to achieve a hat-trick of finishes, but well aware that there are no guarantees in the Island's most gruelling athletic event.

The veterans' 32½-mile race to Peel was without its defending champion, Steve Locking, leaving the class wide-open with previous winners Allan Callow and John Reynolds very much in contention.

Addressing the 939 starters assembled at the National Sports Centre on Saturday 21st June, Graham Young, chief judge and twice-winner, set out the rules of engagement. On this occasion, the organising committee was not going to enforce the straight leg rule. However, sitting in motor vehicles whether for rest or attention was prohibited and would lead to instant disqualification. The wearing of reflective clothing was also mandatory for those proceeding beyond Peel and non-compliance would also lead to disqualification.

Guest starter for the forty-second event was Eric Culpan, one of only four finishers in the 1960 inaugural event. Now approaching his ninetieth year and still in sound health, he sent off the record entry at 9:00am precisely.

Making the best of near-perfect weather conditions, Allan Callow and Les Brown led the procession of walkers out of the National Sports Centre and soon the long column of hopefuls stretched out as far as the eye could see.

Clocking near ten-minute miles, the two reached the second parish church at 9:43am, some 37 minutes ahead of Fiona Shaw who was the last of six retirements recorded here.

Behind the leading pair came David Griffiths, Peter Kaneen, John Reynolds, David Chambers and race favourite Robbie Callister. Even at this early stage, a considerable gap had opened with Roey Crellin and Sue Biggart managing to stay inside the first dozen.

Despite the earlier start, roads leading west and south were packed with spectators, awheel and afoot. Never in the history of the event had such scenes been witnessed, the fleet of service vehicles and roadside helpers disrupting normal weekend

2003

Above: A seventeenth finish for Tony Kneale.

Right: A second win for Peter Kaneen in 2003. Robbie Callister had to settle for the runner-up spot on this occasion.

Above: Early leaders on the TT Access Road.

Left: Ray Hughes on his way to a seventeenth finish.

Right: Roey Crellin and David Doyle were front runners for much of the journey south.

2003

Left: Sue Biggart on her way to seventh place.

Right: Maureen Cox at the Braaid crossroads.

traffic which at times was reduced to funeral pace.

At Malew, the race had settled into a steadying pattern with Roey Crellin and Sue Biggart the leading ladies, while juniors Philip Marshall and James O'Toole held their own with the 'grown-ups', both reaching the pelican crossing at Ballasalla in eighth and fifteenth spots respectively. Between the second and fifth churches, 33 retirements were registered, with David Cain and Chris Keown unexpected casualties among the 259 who stopped at Rushen.

Peter Kaneen was third on the road at Ballakillowey but drew level with David Griffiths and race leader, Allan Callow, on the summit of the Sloc where weather conditions were near perfect. Robbie Callister was fourth to climb the mountain, rapidly gaining on Kaneen, however the Glen Vine man had been saving himself for the descent and sprinted on to Peel. He arrived in 5 hours 34 minutes exactly, having increased his margin over last year's victor by nearly 16½ minutes in the 7½-mile descent to the most westerly town.

A full 200 reached Kirk Michael with Simon Cox the first of 33 to retire at the midway point, St. Mary's Parish Church, Ballaugh.

Nineteen-time finisher, David Collister, was struggling along the winding road to Jurby and was well aware that he must finish if he was to keep the consecutive 'run' intact.

Meanwhile, two-time finisher Bob Noonan, and brother and sister duo, Billy and Carol McCoubrey, all called it a day at St. Patrick's Church having been on their feet for 11½ hours exactly. The conspicuous white landmark of the lonely church was also the stopping place for a further 34 walkers including David Rads Quayle who went six miles further than last year.

The late evening sunshine brought out the masses.

A band was playing at Ballaghennie where children along the roadside offered the weary walkers lollipops and jelly babies before cheering them on to the most northerly church. Thirteen retirements were recorded at Bride and a further 26 at Andreas.

Three-time finisher, David Chambers, was the first casualty at St. Andrew's Parish Church where his 'front-running' campaign came to an end shortly after nine o'clock in the evening. Husband and wife duo, Mike and Val Kneale were past caring too, handing in their race-numbers to timekeepers Ted and Barbara Hyde, having reached their most distant point in ten attempts. Not yet a veteran, but reaching Andreas after 11 attempts, DHSS civil servant Chris Lyon was absolutely delighted with his longest distance ever.

The leading walkers reached the fourteenth church during early twilight. Moira Hall and Charlie Weston were early casualties at this point, and of the 82 who touched the church gates, only 74 ventured beyond.

Approaching darkness was of no concern to Kaneen on the longest day of the year. Still clocking 11-minute miles, he hurried on to Maughold, the fifteenth church, where he took a four-minute break for a snack and a change of shoes and socks. He was so far ahead at this time that back-marker Haydn Mark Kenna was only checking in at Ballaugh, the midway point.

Unchallenged with just 18 miles to go, Kaneen sprinted on through the fading hours of daylight touching the gates of St. Peter's parish church, Onchan, shortly after midnight, leaving himself about 20 minutes to make it down Royal Avenue via Port Jack and on to Douglas Promenade.

With the clock ticking away, he finally race walked across the finishing line in supreme fashion. It was the performance of a lifetime and came within five minutes of Derek Harrison's all-time record of 15 hours 20 minutes 51 seconds, set in the millennium year of 1979. Recording a time 93 minutes quicker than his previous best for the full 85-mile distance, the 41-year-old produced the second-fastest walk in the history of the event to finish nearly 39 minutes ahead of his nearest and arch-rival, Robbie Callister, winner of the previous two events. 'I realised once I got onto the promenade that the record was within my reach, but the last mile and a bit can be such a long way when you are against the clock like that,' said Peter. He dedicated the win to the memory of his late father John who was so supportive of him in his early years as a walker and who had provided the physical backup for him the last time he won the event in 2000. Not one to make excuses, it would be fair to say that Kaneen's progress had been handicapped slightly in the closing stages by a tightening hamstring in the right leg. He became only the sixth walker to go under 16 hours for the event, Derek Harrison having achieved this milestone on two previous occasions.

Joint favourite for the honours, Robbie Callister, could not have done more, taking almost half an hour off his winning time of last year and looking typically smooth throughout.

One man who was simply elated with his own personal performance was Ray Pitts. Forced out last year at the 62-mile mark, he was rewarded for months of intensive training with a marvellous third place and a new personal best time of 17 hours 04 minutes 19 seconds – roughly 2 hours 50 minutes quicker than before.

Undoubtedly, one of the walks of the day came from the first woman home, Roey Crellin, in fourth place. Roey had paced herself well and while she was the second woman to Peel behind her great rival, Sue Biggart, the pair was more or less level-pegging by St. Patrick's Parish Church, Jurby. Indeed, they did walk together for a brief while thereafter, but Roey gradually pulled clear. It was not long before she had ousted Londoner, Chris Flint, the overall winner in 1997, and 1999, and Doug Allan, who for so much of the way had looked a good bet for third. Roey had plenty left in the latter stages to stride home amidst a rainstorm at 2:12am, setting a time of 17 hours 12 minutes 19 seconds. This was the second quickest time ever by a woman in the history of the event, behind visitor, Sandra Brown, who recorded 16 hours 16 minutes 36 seconds in 1998 on her way to completing the full 100 miles in the extended Centurion event.

Seasoned campaigners, Doug Allan and Chris Flint, together in the early stages, came in just eight minutes apart in fifth and sixth places respectively, while Sue Biggart lopped over an 1½ hours off her 2002 time, once again finishing seventh and becoming the third quickest woman ever.

Sean Hands and the Island's leading short distance race-walker, Kevin Walmsley, completed the circuit together, crossing the finish line in joint eighth place. Kevin received the Ray Hughes award for the best first-time finisher having reached Jurby on his last serious assault on the full distance some ten years ago.

Mike Readshaw overcame tendonitis in his ankle to finish a very good tenth in only his second attempt. Parish regulars John Stubbs, Gordon Corran, Andrew Titley, Tony Kneale and John Shimmin filled the next five places, the latter recording a creditable time of 19 hours 23 minutes 06 seconds.

A controversial result in the men's veteran race to Peel resulted in Allan Callow taking the honours, although he was only fourth to check in at the Town

Peter Kaneen, exhausted at the finish but a worthy winner in 15 hours 26 minutes 07 seconds.

Hall. Such is the constitution of the Parish Walk, if the leading veterans go on to complete the full 85-mile distance they are then excluded from the results for the separate veterans' event over the shorter 32½-mile course so they do not effectively take all the major awards. It is certainly a topic for debate.

While in theory the idea of sharing the awards to a larger number of competitors is laudable, it does make a bit of a farce of the actual Peel race. As happened in this particular instance, the men and women who allegedly pace themselves for the full distance are denied a title, which should be theirs. Quite bizarrely, if Peter Kaneen or Robbie Callister had been unable to complete the full distance they would have automatically been declared the winner of the veterans' race to Peel.

It is a strange ruling and one that dates back to the years when veterans were very much in the minority, but these days more veteran men and women complete the full circuit than the youngsters aged under 40 and 35. Perhaps the way out for the organisers would be to have a straight race to Peel for whoever wished to enter, irrespective of age, and this is declared on the entry form before the event. People like David Griffiths, under 40 years of age and with no intention of going beyond Peel, would then get recognition. David was actually second to reach the western capital at 2:48pm, 14 minutes down on Peter Kaneen and two minutes ahead of Robbie Callister.

However, nothing should be taken away from Allan Callow who had won this event on many occasions in the past. He walked a well-gauged race to finish over ten minutes in front of former hockey player and runner-up, John Reynolds, the winner of the End to End Walk a few years earlier. 'The conditions were lovely,' admitted Allan. 'It was a little warm early on but the slight breeze on the Sloc will have helped a lot of people.' Fortunately, he had no re-occurrence of the back problems which had put him out of the event 12 months earlier at the Ballacallin, but he was well off the record pace he had achieved ten years ago, which saw him reaching Peel in a little over 5 hours 18 minutes. 'I've not trained for the mileage so I have to be happy with my time,' he concluded. Landscape gardener, Simon Capelen was the third veteran into Peel, Les Brown, joint-leader in the early stages, having paid the penalty for going off too quickly and dropping several places on the descent to Dalby.

Earlier in the year, Manx Athletics mourned the loss of its mentor, Dennis Lace.

Born in Douglas in 1922, Dennis was one of a family of five children and educated at Hanover Street School, Douglas. Later, he trained as a joiner and was employed by the Department of Local Government for many years until his retirement.

Dennis joined the Boundary Harriers during their early years and along with Kevin Madigan, he had helped to steer Manx Athletics through stormy waters during the early 1960s.

However, the Commonwealth Games was his real passion, taking up the post as athletics team manager at the Edinburgh Games in 1970, the Brisbane Games in 1982 and deputy team manager at the Aukland Games in 1992. He worked on the Commonwealth Games Council for many years and was well known by UK athletic officials in the race walking section where for some time he was a grade-one judge.

He leaves a wife Betty, and a son Peter and will be sadly missed.

2004

Although Ray Cox and his willing army of helpers deserve much praise for steering the Parish Walk in a safe and true direction over the past 13 years, we must never forget the invaluable contributions of the late Arthur Currie, Haydn Wood and Johnny Quine, instigators of the revived event who worked tirelessly to make all this possible.

With the last year's disappointment firmly behind him, Castletown's Robbie Callister was determined more than ever to win the 2004 Parish Walk, his rigorous on and off the Island training schedule securing him as favourite for the honours.

Last year's winner, Peter Kaneen, and twice runner-up, Doug Allan, were both non-starters, Peter due to race commitments elsewhere, while Doug was struck down by a serious bout of flu.

A 'dark horse,' Sean Hands was more than capable of pushing Callister to the limit. Others with an outside chance were training partners, Ray Pitts and Sue Biggart, both regular front-runners who had completed extensive training sessions throughout the winter months.

With ex-Common Wealth representative Allan Callow also a non-starter, the veteran men's race was expected to be a close call between Les Brown and visiting English race-walker, Mark Byrne. Marie Latham was expected to be the first woman to Peel in the veteran ladies' class while in the junior event Philip Marshall and James O'Toole were hoping to replicate their performances of last year.

But the main question on everyone's mind was could Robbie Callister improve on Peter Kaneen's near record time of last year and dislodge the all-time record of 15 hours 20 minutes 51 seconds, set by Derek Harrison a quarter of a century ago.

The Meteorological Office at Ronaldsway Airport predicted fine weather for the weekend of 19th and 20th June, however strong north-westerly winds in the early part of the day were expected to make the going difficult.

A new record entry of 1,234 walkers had registered with race secretary, Liz Corran, including stalwarts Noel Cringle and Jim Harvey. Icon of the past also making an appearance after many years of absence was Henry Harvey, albeit on this occasion as official race-starter. Winner of the event in 1961, 1962 and 1964, the Abbeylands farmer, now in his seventieth year, was the focus of media attention

2004

Above: Start 0f the 2004 Parish Walk.

Far left: Peter Wood, Marian Garvey and David Collister setting out on a journey that saw 100 finishers.

Left: Sixty-year-old Robert Brown exceeded the 24-hour time limit by four minutes.

Below left: Nobles Hospital consultant anaesthetist Keith Wilkinson finished for a first time.

Below right: Terry Moffet at the start of the 85 mile walk.

2004

Above: Marie Latham anxiously awaits starters orders.

Right: Karen Jones leads this group to the fourth church.

prior to setting off the 1,079 starters from the National Sports Centre at 9 o'clock on Saturday morning.

Les Brown, Marie Latham and Sheffield's Mark Byrne were the early leaders from the word go, interchanging the lead through the early miles to Marown until relieved of that heavy burden by Robbie Callister on the climb to the Braaid.

At the Stugadoo crossroads the gap was widening with John Stubbs, Kevin Marshall and Roey Crellin challenging for fifth spot, some distance ahead of Ian Callister, Ray Pitts, Sue Biggart and Sean Hands, all bunched together with seven miles already done.

Callister was 12 minutes ahead of his 5½ mph schedule at Santon where 19 early retirements were recorded. A further 25 stopped at Malew and Arbory with a whopping 346 retiring at Rushen, a point reached by Callister at 12:13pm having clocked ten-minute miles throughout in a time similar to Peter Kaneen's a year ago.

The trio of Brown, Latham and Byrne were the next to arrive at the southernmost church, just four minutes in arrears. However, the pace was too hot for Byrne and he was an early casualty on the Sloc

where a north-westerly gale was seriously hampering progress.

Despite the strong headwind, Callister continued to maintain a decent pace on the descent to Peel, arriving shortly after 2:38pm, some 12 minutes quicker than last year.

Arriving at the Town Hall steps 8½ minutes later, veteran Les Brown had a two-minute advantage over Sean Hands and Marie Latham, the 43-year-old mother of two achieving her ambition of dipping under six hours with a time of 5 hours 50 minutes 17 seconds and reclaiming her prize of two years past. 'It was particularly hard work on the Sloc,' she said. 'There were gusty crosswinds and one or two nearly blew me backwards. All things considered, I am delighted with my time.'

Parish regulars, Alison Brand, Linda Shimmin and Marie Gilbertson all stopped at the western capital as did veterans Chris Keown, David Tasker and Jim Harvey, the latter completing the 32½ miles in a shade over seven hours.

Wasting no time on the coast road to Kirk Michael, 11 minutes now separated Callister and Hands at Ballaugh, the halfway mark.

Left: Famous for 'never again' quotes, Gordon Corran sets out once again on the well-trodden route.

Right: Simone Thornton and Hannah Newton in no hurry to leave the Braaid.

2004

Ray Pitts was the third to leave Peel and was now walking a lonely race having left behind Simon Cox and training partner, Sue Biggart. By Kirk Michael he was a short distance in front of visiting first-timer Kevin Marshall with Cox and Biggart separated by similar intervals behind him. Cox began to overhaul Marshall at Ballaugh with Biggart dropping time after a short stop.

In superb shape after many months of intensive training, the 41-year-old staff nurse from Noble's Hospital was making race walking look easy as she sprinted northwards. Sue's nearest and arch-rival, Roey Crellin, was down on her amazing pace of 12 months earlier and by mid-distance she was trailing the leading woman by some 11 minutes and briefly enjoying the company of eventual sixth-place finisher, Mike Readshaw.

A total of 62 walkers called time at the seventh and eighth churches and a further 42 at Jurby. Callister reached this point at 4:59pm, some ten minutes in front of his nearest rival, with the bulk of the entry still to reach Peel and late stragglers as far back as Dalby.

The two-mile gap between Callister and Hands remained constant on the long stretch north. Shortly before 6:20pm the leader checked in at the northernmost church ahead of schedule, having completed the 52½ miles in just over nine hours. Here at the twelfth church, Brian Blair was the first of 16 to stop, while Maureen Cox and Mark Harvey were two of 22 early retirements registered further on at Andreas. Adrian Cowin of the Ronaldsway Meteorological Office, whose heavily strapped knees had come to the end of their journey, also retired at this point.

Stan Sille, John Lovelady and Steve Kelly were three of the 19 who struggled along the dark and

busy A3 road to Ramsey, finally calling it a day after 62 miles.

Two-time finisher Juan Readshaw was in poor shape both mentally and physically when he passed the Ramsey Grammar School, insisting to his accompanying father that he was going no further than Maughold. He was walking in tandem with Keith Wilkinson, author of the book *Manx Murders*. The two had walked together inch for inch since Devil's Elbow, however the climb out of Ramsey along the dark and twisting tree-lined road to Ballure took its toll on first-timer Wilkinson, who not feeling well, collapsed on the roadside. Nevertheless, the 48-year-old consultant anaesthetist from Noble's Hospital was not prepared to accept defeat, and with great tenacity, raised himself to his feet to continue alone from Maughold and record a well-deserved finish in 20 hours 42 minutes 10 seconds.

With Callister 21 minutes ahead at Maughold, the margin continued to grow and there was never any doubt from there on that he would gain his third title in four years. The question on everyone's mind was, could he get anywhere near to the outright record, or perhaps better the time of Peter Kaneen set 12 months earlier. 'My backup crew encouraged me to maintain the pace as they knew I was close to the all-time record,' said Callister. 'At Glen Mona I had 13 miles to go and 2 hours and 25 minutes to get to the Douglas War Memorial. Mentally I knew it was almost possible and I kept plugging away. With 6½ miles to go, I finally gave up on the record, but tried hard to equal Peter's winning time last year of 15 hours 26 minutes 07 seconds. Touching the gates of St. Peter's parish church just after midnight, I knew it would be tight so I gave it one last try down Summerhill and onto the promenade.'

The seconds ticked away with every aching yard

2004-2005

Left: A third victory for Robbie Callister.

Right: Hardly appropriate attire for such a demanding event.

of what was an epic walk. As he approached the finishing line with the clock clearly in view, Callister openly admitted that he could not remember the previous year's winning time. 'As I crossed the line, someone said I was six seconds slower than Peter but it was actually 24. I wasn't at all disappointed, just glad to be able to stop walking. To be honest, I was chuffed to get so close to the record.'

Sean Hands crossed the finishing line in second place some 36 minutes and 24 seconds later, completing the circuit of 17 parishes for the third consecutive time and more than pleased with his performance.

Sue Biggart's performance in finishing joint third with Ray Pitts was quite phenomenal. Lopping almost 45 minutes off her previous best time, she set the fastest-ever performance by a local woman and the second-fastest ever to visiting walker, Sandra Brown, who had set a time of 16 hours 16 minutes 36 seconds in 1998 en route to completing the extended 100-mile event.

Ray Pitts improved on his time too, walking a well-controlled race throughout.

Visitor, Kevin Marshall did well in what was his first attempt at the back-breaking event, while Simon Cox and Mike Readshaw came in joint sixth, ahead of second female, Roey Crellin.

Of the 110 who reached Maughold, 100 made it to the finish with Gary Allen and Paul Jempson agonisingly close, only to surrender at the penultimate church, 6½ miles from the finish.

Other performances worthy of mention came from youngsters, Philip Marshall and James O'Toole. Winner and runner-up respectively of the junior event last year, the pair raced each other to Peel, improving on their previous times to finish just 4½ minutes apart.

David Collister circulated the 17 parishes for a record twenty-first consecutive time, while Ray Hughes and Tony Kneale each made it for the eighteenth time. Mick Holgate improved his tally to 14 while Dermot O'Toole made it to double figures with consecutive finishes.

At her third attempt, and after major heart surgery earlier in the year, Monica George put in a courageous performance finishing in twenty-eighth place in a time of 20 hours 16 minutes 44 seconds.

Robert Brown fulfilled his ambition of completing the 85-mile distance, albeit 4 minutes and 3 seconds outside the 24-hour limit. The 60-year-old school crossing patrol officer from Douglas fittingly received a lollipop from Lieutenant-Governor, Air Marshall Ian MacFadyen, after completing a very courageous walk. Despite suffering from blisters and having had a brief spell in hospital after his epic walk, Robert was on duty at Fairfield School as usual on Monday morning.

2005

Overcast skies with cool conditions were the perfect ingredients for the 2005 Parish Walk. Held over the weekend of 25th and 26th June, the annual Manx Classic attracted a record entry of 1,330, including that of three-time winner, Robbie Callister.

Firm favourite for the gruelling 85-mile event, Callister had trained exceptionally hard, having spent much of the month of May trekking along the Camino de Santiago in Spain in preparation for an assault on the all-time record of 15 hours 20 minutes 51 seconds, set some 26 years ago by the iconic Derek Harrison.

Last year's runner-up, Sean Hands was expected to push Robbie to the limit in what was expected to be a fast and two-horse race. In the ladies' event to Peel, Sue Biggart was hoping to improve on her personal best time of last year. Months of intensive

Top left: Liz Corrin leads the way out from the National Sports Centre.

Middle top~: Past champion Lee Cain was walking for fun on this occasion.

Top right: Joe Brown, 1963 winner starts the 2005 Parish Walk.

Top right below: Scene on the TT Access Road.

Above: Allan Corran (No. 24), John Callister and Lynda Baker make a slow exit from the National Sports Centre.

Right: Sky Television covered the event for the first time in 2005.

Bottom right: A third finish for Chris Cale (No.85).

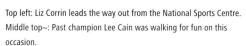

2005

Left: Maureen Cox is no stranger to the annual classic.

Right: Anne Oates finishing for a second time and relief that it is all over.

training with friend Ray Pitts were expected to yield dividends for the Nobles Hospital staff nurse who was attempting to break the all-time ladies' record of 16 hours 16 minutes 11 seconds, set by Sandra Brown in 1998.

James O'Toole of Union Mills was hoping to break records too. Runner-up in the junior race to Peel for the past two years, the 19-year-old Leeds University student certainly had the miles under his feet. Frequent 20-mile training sessions up and down the Sloc set the groundwork for his ambitious attempt to crack the junior record of 6 hours 07 minutes 05 seconds, set at the turn of the century by Allan Stuart Thompson.

Media attention focused more than ever on this year's event with Sky Television televising the entire race for the very first time. Dermot O'Toole's recent book tracing the history of the Parish Walk and titled *A Walk Through Time* received a good review, and with the Island awash with Parish Walk euphoria, the scene was set for a possible record-breaking race.

With celebrity starter Joe Brown, winner in 1963, sending off the 1,132 starters at 9 o'clock on Saturday morning, the huge field was soon spread far and wide along the A1 main road to Marown. Indeed, Callister was showing great composure at the second church and was already a considerable distance ahead of the chasing pack led by John Stubbs, Sean Hands, Sue Biggart and Ray Pitts. Only by looking at the calibre of the supporting cast could one make a judgement that the 85-mile race was not effectively done and dusted by the Stugadhoo crossroads. Here at the seven-mile mark, the three-time winner was slightly down on his own time schedule, however the relatively benign early morning conditions were favourable and by Rushen church in

the south of the Island, he had turned this deficit around and upped his pace considerably.

Up and over the infamous Sloc, Callister pressed on, eager to increase his three-minute lead over his main rival Sean Hands who was showing remarkable fortitude after only three years of serious race walking.

Relieved to get this section of the race behind him, Callister reached the eighth church at 2:35pm, some four minutes quicker than previously and a shade over three minutes ahead of Hands. It was a punishing pace over the 32½ miles but still 11½ minutes down on Irene Corlett's record time in 1982.

Julian Thomas was next to Peel, a further 21 minutes in arrears and followed by Andy Gosnell, Ray Pitts, Sue Biggart, Andrew Titley and veteran Doug Allan. John Stubbs fought off serious cramp at Juan ny Clarey's bridge to finish in eighth spot and claim the veterans' prize.

A superb performance from James O'Toole kept him in firm contention with the leading pack and he was tenth to Peel in 6 hours 09 minutes, fractionally off the all-time junior record but supreme enough to be the recipient of the junior prize.

Weather conditions remained as predicted through much of the day, however by early evening, clearing skies made the going uncomfortable for the 314 walkers who ventured beyond Peel. In fact, a staggering 700 walkers went no further than this point, Mike Krupp the last to check in at 7:15pm, but some 23 miles adrift of the leader, now approaching the most northerly church.

Callister maintained the pressure for he reached the halfway mark at 4:18pm, five minutes ahead of Hands. At St. Patrick's Parish Church, Jurby, his lead had increased to ten minutes with his nearest

Left: Journey's end and an eleventh finish for Dermot O'Toole.

Right: David Collister made it round for the twenty-second consecutive time.

2005

challenger losing ground after feeling quite ill.

But Hand's was no quitter for he made a remarkable recovery on the long haul to Bride, maintaining his ten-minute deficit but beginning to look the stronger of the two early leaders.

The relatively warm evening sunshine was of little concern to the 195 brave and hardy souls who proceeded beyond the lonely whitewashed church at Jurby, some only just ahead of the 9:45pm time limit which timekeepers were strictly adhering to. Here at the 45-mile mark, 1996 winner Lee Cain was maintaining a credible tenth spot. However continuing with severe cramp over the northern plain, his dream of re-writing the record books came to an end at the most northerly church where he was the first of 28 to call time.

With a welcoming party atmosphere along the roadside leading to Bride, Hands began to grind away at Callister's slender lead. He clawed back over one minute on the Burma Road and by Andeas, the thirteenth church, he had reduced the deficit to nine minutes, reducing this to 6½ minutes at Lezayre. The pace had been punishing with Callister admitting to the television crew at Church Town that he was extremely tired.

Crowds were gathered in Parliament Square, Ramsey where Hands had slashed Callister's lead to only five minutes. But Callister was not yet beaten, and fighting the inevitable depression, he increased his pace on the tough climb out of Port e Vullen, reaching the fifteenth church at 9:01pm, still maintaining his five-minute advantage.

Sensing victory was still possible Callister went into overdrive on the undulating, twisting and tiring road to Ballajora where he again began to pull away.

The two leading contenders had played their part

as long as possible. Throughout the late evening, spectators around the course had lived with a dream of a battle to the finish, but it was not to be. Callister had dug deep into his reserves and in an amazing turnaround of events he stopped teasing the gallant challenger by delivering a knock-out blow from which Hands never recovered. By the Glen Mona Hotel, the 72-mile mark, Callister had stretched his advantage to 6½ minutes and at the penultimate church his lead had increased to 11 minutes.

With midnight approaching, Callister was still on course to crack the record – but only just. Cheered on by crowds of well-wishers at the Liverpool Arms, and later on the approaches to Onchan, he checked in to the final church close on two minutes past midnight and 19 minutes away from making Parish Walk history.

With the clock ticking away at a seemingly alarming rate, the three-time winner knew deep down there was not enough time to cover the remaining two miles or so to the finish. Cheered on by the biggest-ever crowd of spectators along Douglas Promenade, he literally sprinted into the Island's capital before running out of time and just 600 yards short of making Parish Walk history.

It was indeed a superb victory but not enough to crack Derek Harrison's all-time record. Callister's time of 15 hours 24 minutes 24 seconds was the second fastest time ever recorded and some 12½ minutes ahead of Hands who came home to a similar ovation. It had been a blistering pace from the word go. In fact, on finishing, the two were so far ahead of the trailing field that back-markers Mark and Ilona Leadley were still negotiating the Burma Road, 31 miles further back.

But there was disappointment etched on the face

2005

of the champion when interviewed by the media later. Chased throughout by the courageous Sean Hands, Robbie had given his best performance ever but fallen short when it mattered most. The all-time record remained intact for another year and perhaps his best-ever opportunity to enter the Parish Walk Hall of Fame has been lost forever.

Others to suffer disappointment were Ray Pitts and Sue Biggart. They walked the entire way together to finish joint third for the second successive year. Their time of 16 hours 53 minutes 54 seconds was in fact more than five minutes slower than their time last year and a long way off the ladies' record, set seven years ago.

Roey Crellin was impressive as ever, recording a time of 17 hours 27 minutes 15 seconds to finish fifth in as many years.

Eamonn Harkin was over half an hour quicker than last year, while Simon Cox completed his fourth finish in eighth spot, ahead of David Cain, early front runner Julian Thomas, Derek Atkinson, John Shimmin and veteran campaigner Doug Allan.

Race secretary Liz Corran made a brilliant comeback after a 12-year absence to win the veteran ladies' race to Peel. It was her fourth win over the shorter course and her time of 6 hours 33 minutes 05 seconds was commendable considering she carried a knee injury into the event and came close to calling it a day at Rushen.

David Collister made it round for a new record of 22 times in succession. Anthony Kneale and Ray Hughes 19 times apiece, Mick Holgate 15 and Parish Walk author, Dermot O'Toole an 11th successive finish.

Of the 101 walkers who checked in at Maugold, 98 made it to the finish.

As always, the closing miles were difficult ones,

with 63-year-old Brenda Charlton, the final finisher and perilously close to the 24-hour deadline. Her time of 23 hours 56 minutes 22 seconds guaranteed a fourth finish and a place in the record books as the oldest-ever finisher.

The Norfolk 100-mile challenge

Walking 100 miles in 24 hours may seem a tall order for most, but spare a thought for that elite Manx group of six Parish Walkers who did exactly that in the Norfolk 100-mile Challenge just six weeks later.

Held over the weekend of 30th and 31st July, the two-mile Kings Lynn circuit was the venue for the annual Centurion 100-mile event, attracting an entry of 95 which included many of Europe's very best distance athletes.

Overseen by the Race Walking Association, the race began at 1:00pm with Manx competitors Robbie Callister and Sean Hands setting a blistering pace from the word go.

Callister very soon built up a lead, however about four hours into the race he was unfairly disqualified for stepping onto a grass verge, allegedly cutting a corner and gaining an advantage. Normally in such circumstances, a competitor would be warned of subsequent infringements before being excluded. However, on this occasion Callister had no option other than to accept the decision of the judges. As a consequence, the five-time Parish Walk winner had to sit out the event, resulting in much bad feeling among the Manx contingent for the rest of the day.

With Callister excluded, Hands went on to dominate the race, crossing the finish line in 19 hours 02 minutes 57 seconds, some 22 minutes ahead of Sandra Brown, who at the time, was the fastest women ever to complete the Parish Walk.

Roey Crellin and Eamonn Harkin walked together throughout to finish in 21 hours 33 minutes 59 seconds.

Keith Wilkinson, a Nobles Hospital consultant anaesthetist and twice finisher of the Parish Walk, completed the distance in 23 hours 02 minutes 32 seconds, some six minutes in front of close friend Dermot O'Toole who was more than happy with a finishing time of 23 hours 08 minutes 42 seconds.

Selwyn Collister was the last of the Manx contingent to cross the finish line – his time of 23 hours 18 minutes 09 seconds being commendable considering he was close to exhaustion and unable to stand upright at the conclusion.

Those unsuccessful at the full distance included John Stubbs, stopping after 76 miles, Alan Kinvig at 70 miles and 20-year-old James O'Toole at 36 miles.

2006

No one knows better than Robbie Callister the qualities for success in this Heculean event that has seen grown men reduced to tears. Although a past winner on no less than four occasions, the 52-year-old was not favourite for the 2006 event with attention instead focused on Sean Hands, runner-up

Above: Caroline Cain made it all the way on this occasion.

Below: The great Derek Harrison was at the finish to see the winner home.

2005

Top views from left to right: Steven Carridge (No.191) and David Cain above Union Mills; Sue Biggart and Michael George both made it to the finish; Vinny Lynch (No. 93) stopped at Rushen but Ray Pitts kept going to claim third place; David Cain (No. 13) and Mike Readshaw went all the way and it was a second finish for Selwyn Callister.

Left: Sean Hands (No.3) became the first man ever to go under fifteen hours. Robbie Callister (No.1) was runner-up and Eamonn Harkin, fifth.

Bottom left: Four minutes apart, Andrew Titley finished ninth and Roey Crellin tenth.

Below: Allan Callow knows the way to Peel better than most.

2006

Top views from left to right: A fun day out for John Qualtrough; Chris Cale and Maurice Bellando on the way to Newtown; Phil Colebourn was one of 163 finishers in 2006; previous finishers Teresa Gurney and George Blair fell short of the ultimate goal on this occasion and Sam Brennan (No.1530) was one of 1351 starters in 2006.

Left: A first-time finish for David Cretney, MHK.

Below left: Fiona Gill, (No.1252) in company with with Gill Edmonds and Angela Southern.

Below: Fintan Suddards was a finisher twenty years ago.

Bottom view: Brian Madrell (No.369) and Steve Cawley on the Clanna Road.

Left: Noel Cringle greets Stanley Cleator - official starter for the 2006 event.

Right: Lots of water and bananas to keep energy levels high.

in 2004 and 2005 plus victor of the 100-mile Norfolk Challenge held in Kings Lynn, Cambridgeshire later that year. His time of 19 hours 03 minutes for the coveted event was nothing less than outstanding and many now felt he was more than capable of eclipsing Derek Harrison's 27-year-old Parish Walk record time of 15 hours 20 minutes 51 seconds.

A grey and overcast sky greeted the 1,351 starters gathered at the National Sports Centre on Saturday morning, 24th June. As in previous years, race director Ray Cox addressed the record entry with emphasis on road closures and changes to the course around Ballasalla.

On the grounds of safety, the course above the Blackboards had been re-routed along the Orrisdale road to the St. Marks road thence to Ballasalla. Accordingly, the slightly increased mileage was adjusted at the start to maintain the 85-mile distance. The new start time of 8 o'clock in the morning also raised the possibility of the race being completed on the same day it started.

Stanley Cleator was the guest starter for the 45th event. Now in his 75th year and living in England, the former Douglas postman was a popular winner of the first modern-day Parish Walk held in 1960, in which only 35 entrants took part. Today, three of those stalwarts were hoping to retrace their steps, namely Noel Cringle, Jim Harvey and Michael Gray.

Excitement was high with the Island's three radio stations awash with talk of a new course record, while Sky Television was televising the event for a second year. As a result of this intense media coverage, both Callister and Hands were late appearing on the start line.

Wasting no time, Steve Carridge was an early leader on roads leading west and south – reaching the third church at 9:52am and already some considerable distance ahead of the chasing pack. Here at the 11½-mile mark, the former junior Parish Walk champion led Robbie Callister and Sean Hands by two minutes – both walking in tandem and happy for him to set the pace. Steve Partington was next to the whitewashed church, soon followed by Ray Pitts, Eamonn Harkin and leading lady Sue Biggart.

Callister and Hands regained the lead at Malew church, a point they reached at 10:32am and already 15 miles into the race. The pair was still together at Rushen, reaching the most southerly church in 3 hours 18 minutes and well ahead of schedule. Commonwealth Games specialist Steve Partington was looking comfortable in third spot with Glen Vine's Peter Kaneen in close proximity and fourth. Surprisingly, Ray Pitts was now separated from training partner Sue Biggart as Eamonn Harkin and Roey Crellin challenged for sixth spot.

As in previous years, the casualty rate was high. Five stopped at Marown, 15 at Santon, 15 at Malew, six at Arbory and a staggering 397 at Rushen.

For Dru Hamm, it was a proud moment when she finally touched the door of the second church after being on her feet for 4 hours 20 minutes. The 35-year-old accountant was born with cerebral palsy and told by doctors that she would never walk. After surgery and seven years of physiotherapy, she proved them wrong and was delighted to walk 4½ miles and raise money for the Green Third World Fund. Hers was an outstanding achievement for which she received considerable credit.

But failure was not an option for Callister and Hands, both of whom quickened their pace on the tortuous Sloc ascent. With no time to take in the breath-taking views across the south of the Island,

2006

'Larking about' on the Clanna Road.

the two hurried on to the Round Table, aware of foul weather approaching from the west.

Wasting no time on the descent to Dalby, Hands surged ahead of his rival to reach the western capital at 1:32pm – nearly two minutes ahead of Callister and seemingly on course for a record-breaking time.

Glen Vine's Peter Kaneen was next to into Peel, however by his standards, a time of 5 hours 46 minutes was poor and he promptly retired leaving Ray Pitts to occupy third spot, some 19 minutes behind the leader.

Maintaining his marginal lead over Callister on the coast road to Kirk Michael, Hands reached the ninth church at 2:39pm. Looking fresh, his average speed to this point was an impressive 5.85mph. Callister too was enjoying himself and appeared not concerned at his two-minute deficit.

Ray Pitts of St Johns was also having an uneventful walk. As always, he looked solid, in third place and eager for victory should the favourites falter.

With the race now progressing beyond the 40-mile mark, Steve Partington was beginning to tire. Even by his standards, this was an exceptionally fast pace for such distance and the former 50-kilometre Commonwealth Games representative would soon struggle to hold his fourth place.

From this point on, there was little change in position. Irishman Eamonn Harkin continued to walk the race of his life, maintaining fifth spot and ahead of the leading lady, Sue Biggart who was sixth.

But the clouds were gathering on the western horizon by early afternoon and what began as a shower soon turned into a downpour of biblical proportions. How could the Meteorological Office at Ronaldsway have got this one so badly wrong? Only hours earlier, forecaster Colin Gartshore had predicted fair weather for today's sporting events which also

included the golf championships at Peel and the power boat races in Douglas Bay. His prediction of only a ten per cent chance of rain was widely off the mark.

Indeed, the great majority of competitors were soaked to the skin on reaching the Round Table and this may have accounted for the 17 retirements at Patrick, followed by 493 at Peel.

Sean Hands extended his lead to three minutes at the halfway mark and was seven minutes up on Callister's schedule last year. Twenty miles further on, his advantage had increased to ten minutes as he advanced along the flat and seemingly endless road to Bride.

With an air of remarkable serenity, Hands reached Lezayre at 6:43pm, some 15 minutes inside the course record to that point and an amazing 22 miles ahead of back-markers at the rear of the field.

Callister was next to touch the gate of the fourteenth church but was now 19 minutes in arrears and experiencing severe pain from a swollen kneecap. As a result, he lost valuable time on the tiring road to Maughold but still managed to cover the five miles in 59 minutes, reaching the ancient church at one minute past eight and 24 minutes adrift.

Although his lead equated to two miles distance, Hands too, was struggling on the demanding Ballajora climb and well aware that Callister had the tenacity to haunt him at any time. He later admitted that the punishing climb out of Maughold to the Hibernia was undoubtedly the toughest part of the race.

Inspite of losing time between Andreas and Maughold, Callister regained his composure over the final miles, looking amazingly quick on the descent above Laxey. Here at the old mining town, the four-time champion was on schedule for a personal best

even if it was for the runner-up spot

On reaching the church above the hill at Lonan, Hands knew the race was all but won and history in the making. Cheered on by a large crowd of onlookers and friends at the Liverpool Arms, he upped his pace at the White Bridge before checking in to the final church at Onchan at 10:22pm with only 2½ miles separating him from success or failure.

Royal Avenue and Port Jack were a distant blur as the 43-year-old set his sights on the ultimate goal, now no more than a mile away. With day quickly turning to night and Douglas Promenade awash with spectators urging him on, Hands crossed the finish line to a tremendous reception. In a time of 14 hours 47 minutes 36 seconds, he had not just beaten the all-time record but he had also recorded the first-ever sub-15-hour time to become the first competor to complete the full 85 miles on the same day as he started.

Finishing a little over 28 minutes later to claim the runner-up spot for the second time in four years, Callister also improved on Harrison's outstanding record by the best part of five minutes.

Ray Pitts took the final podium place in a new personal best time of 16 hours 17 minutes, some six minutes in front of training partner Sue Biggart.

Eamonn Harkin finished inside 17 hours, while Alan Cowin, Mike Readshaw, Michael George, Andrew Titley and second woman home Roey Crellin rounded off the top ten.

A total of 162 walkers completed the distance within the 24-hour time limit – the legendary Derek Harrison completing the full 85 miles late on Sunday morning and achieving his own personal goal in a time of 26 hours 15 minutes 50 minutes.

100-MILE CENTURION WALK ON THE ISLAND

Fresh from his record-breaking Parish Walk victory Sean turned his attention to even greater distances eight weeks later and won the annual 100-mile Centurion Walk in a time of 19 hours 16 minutes 03 seconds, some 12 minutes off his winning pace at Kings Lynn 12 months earlier.

Held over the weekend of 19th and 20th August, the 24-hour event was making its second appearance on the Island, however on this occasion it was to be officiated by the Race Walking Association of Great Britain.

Organised by a sub-committee of the Isle of Man Veterans' Athletics Club, the JCK and Bradford and Bingley International, the event could not have enjoyed better conditions or indeed, a more suitable and above all safe venue, as although not initially first choice, the National Sports Centre turned out to be more than ideal.

With the start scheduled for 2:00pm, protagonists Sean Hands and Robbie Callister were soon early leaders of a race that required 131 circuits of the perimeter and athletic track.

Maintaining a speed in excess of 6 mph, Hands soon drew away from Callister, carving out a seven-minute lead in the first 20 miles. But it was a punishing pace by the Parish Walk record holder who came close to throwing in the towel after seven hours.

Outclassed and very much on the back foot, Callister soon found himself in the unusual position of having to dig deep to stay in contention. Although holding on to second spot, the 52-year-old finally admitted defeat after 60 miles when he stopped with

Welcome sustenance for the long haul to the Round Table.

2006-2007

an injured knee.

Tired and worn out, Hands lost his composure through the night and with it valuable time. Centurion status does not come easily and the 42-year-old was very fortunate to fend off a late challenge from the legendary Sandra Brown. Relaxed and confident throughout, the 1998 ladies' Parish Walk record holder chipped away at Hands' lead through the night to take the runner-up spot 12 minutes in arrears, and in doing so, completed her twenty-first 100-mile event!

Walking the race of her life, Glen Vine's Sue Biggart took third spot in 20 hours 08 minutes 10 seconds, eight minutes clear of Dutchman Marcelino Sobczak. Next to finish, Kevin Marshal completed the event for a third time in as many years, fractionally dipping under the 20½-hour mark.

Local hotelier Michael George secured sixth place in a thrilling finish which saw him edge out Irishman Eamonn Harkin by just ten seconds.

But time ran out for the youngest competitor, James O'Toole, who was attempting the distance for a second time in twelve months. Incredible pain and unable to continue one step further brought to an end the 21-year-old's dream of becoming the youngest-ever finisher of this demanding event. It was a courageous walk from the Leeds University student who made it to the 92-mile mark before admitting defeat.

Lesley Christian also failed to go full distance. Timed out after the 24-hour limit, the three-time Parish Walk finisher fell short of the ultimate goal by just four miles. As expected in a race of such distance, the casualty rate was high with only half the 80 starters completing the full distance, six of whom were women.

2007

Robbie Callister was in no doubt that the 2007 Parish Walk would probably be his toughest race ever. Convincingly beaten into second place last year, the 52-year-old veteran was under no illusion that this event would be any easier than his last.

As in previous years, a record entry had produced a quality field. In particular, Ray Pitts and Michael George had stepped up their winter training schedule and both were eager to steal the limelight should Callister fail.

Although not expected to improve on his record-breaking performance 12 months earlier, reigning champion Sean Hands was clear favourite for the classic 85-mile event held over the weekend of 23rd and 24th June.

Light winds and overcast skies were a blessing for the 1,127 competitors assembled at the National Sports Centre. They were in fact perfect conditions for the 8 o'clock start on Saturday morning, however rain was forecast later by which time the leaders were expected to be approaching the halfway mark.

For most, the occasion was very much a fun day out with varied expectations. Reaching the 32½-mile mark at Peel was the ultimate goal for many, however exceeding this distance would require high levels of stamina and mental discipline that only few possessed.

But these qualities were not an issue for Robbie Callister and Sean Hands, both no strangers to foot-slogging around the Island's 17 parishes. Gladiators of this Herculean event, Callister and Hands seized the lead from Sue Biggart shortly after Marown, and in tandem, reached Santon in 1 hour 56 minutes, easily outclassing the many pretenders on the long journey south.

Recording one of the fastest-ever times to Rushen, Callister and Hands reached the sixth church in 3 hours 20 minutes. They had averaged nearly 6 mph for the 19½ miles, however the pace was punishing for the reigning champion. A hamstring injury on the brutal Ballakillowey climb ended his defence of this prestigious event leaving Callister to continue the remainder of the race alone.

Recorded as the first retirement at Rushen, Hands was not alone in failing to ascend the infamous Sloc, a physically demanding five-mile haul to the lower summit of South Barrule. Indeed, a total of 323 walkers called time at the most southerly church with a further 52 failing to even reach that point.

Disappointment was clearly etched on the reigning champion's face, who later admitted that he had been lazy over the winter months and had not trained as hard as in recent years.

Ray Pitts, closely followed by Michael George, were next to check in at the whitewashed church with twice-Centurion Andrew Titley trailing in fifth spot.

Up and over the Sloc, Callister pressed on with great urgency, the steep, twisting road leading to the Round Table offering little resistance to a man well-practised over this difficult terrain. Such was his consistency that Callister had never lost a race when leading from this position.

Confident and supreme, Callister reached the western capital at 1:39pm, his time some six minutes slower than that of last year. Michael George arrived three minutes later followed by Ray Pitts a further four minutes adrift.

Although Hands was no longer a threat, the same could not be said for George and Pitts. They were both very experienced and more than capable of harassing Callister to the bitter end.

A popular venue for spectators, Peel Town Hall was the final destination for the many social walkers flowing through the bustling streets of the seaside town, some as many as three hours after the leading contenders had passed through.

Aware of deteriorating weather to the west, the leaders hurried along the coastal road to Kirk Michael, their placings unchanged.

Enjoying a six-minute comfort zone, Callister reached Ballaugh at 3:07pm, some nine minutes slower than his time last year.

2007

Top views from left to right: Peter Beighton (No.73) made it to Jurby - Mark Hempsall to the finish; Monica George made it to Peel in a little over 7 hours 19 minutes; a first-time finish for Billy Mc Coubrey and Jim O'Neill (No.640) and Michael Hayler head a group approaching Newtown.

Left: Stella Corlett made it round for a fourth time in 2007.

Bottom left: The legendary Jim Harvey was one of 323 to call time at Rushen.

Below: Eleanor Bingham (No. 996) leads this group of happy walkers to Newtown.

Bottom view: Robbie Callister won the event for a fifth time in 2007.

2007

Left: Eamonn Harkin taking time out for a drink on the Clanna Road.

Right: James O'Toole was the first of thirty-eight to retire at Kirk Michael.

Still short of the halfway mark at Ballaugh, a point midway between the new church and the old, Callister quickened his pace on the tiring road to Bride. Here at the 52½-mile mark, his lead had extended to seven minutes over George with Pitts a further eight minutes back in third spot.

Cheering crowds welcomed the leader into Andreas. However a mile or so further on George was looking uncomfortable on passing Kerrowgarrow chapel and visibly slower at St. Judes where he relinquished his advantage to the advancing Pitts.

By 6 o'clock in the evening, heavy rain was falling across the northern plain making life difficult for the 727 who continued beyond Peel. Even at this early stage, Callister held a 20-mile advantage over back-markers – many still to reach Kirk Michael.

In preparation for a wet night ahead, Callister changed into a waterproof jacket before crossing the famous TT course and turning left for Ramsey, arriving in Parliament Square as the 7:40pm bus departed for Laxey.

Ballure, Port Lewaigue and Port e Vullen were passed with effortless ease as Callister negotiated the undulating road to Maughold. A large crowd had gathered in the picturesque village square to applaud the past champion, who had by now extended his lead over Pitts by 17 minutes. George followed three minutes later, however the Douglas hotelier looked in no state to mount a late challenge with only 18 miles to go.

Torrential rain throughout the night accounted for premature retirements of biblical proportions. Thirty-eight were recorded at the halfway mark, 42 at Jurby and a further 30 at the northernmost church. Andreas was the stopping point for a further 27 with another 16 failing at Lezayre. One hundred and sixty four

braved the harsh weather conditions beyond Lezayre while at Maughold George Blair headed a list of 11 calling time.

But failure was not an option for the 153 who passed through the Island's most historic parish, all of whom went on to the finish. For many, the long slog through the hours of darkness had been a punishing experience and one not to be repeated.

Michael George was fading fast on the tortuous climb to the Hibernia. The 42-year-old appeared unsteady on his feet at Glen Mona, at times resembling that of a dead man walking. Behind, Eamonn Harkin, Thomas Melvin and Jock Waddington were separated by less than ten minutes but managing to hold off a late challenge from Sue Biggart, still looking strong at the Dhoon.

Spared the downpour which came later, Callister reached the old mining town of Laxey as day was turning to night. Extending his lead over Pitts to 14 minutes, the four-time champion charged to the finish to record a well-deserved victory in 15 hours 36 minutes 47 seconds – the fourth fastest time to date.

Pitts was delighted with his runner-up spot, shaving 25 minutes off his personal best and joining the elite sub-16-hour club.

In an amazing change of fortune, Michael George dug deep over the finishing miles to come within two minutes of the runner-up spot. He later admitted that dehydration followed by spells of dizziness hampered his progress and brought him close to retiring at the 52½-mile mark.

There were many worthy performances on a day of high drama. In particular, David Collister made it round for the twenty-fourth consecutive time.

Meanwhile, Michael Gray became the oldest-ever finisher. At 72 years of age, the retired harbour

2007

Top views from left to right: Carol and Lynn McCoubrey both called time at Maughold; Sue Chapman (No. 745) and Emma Metcalfe put on a brave smile for photographer Bill Dale; Bethany Clague well kitted out for the daunting task ahead; In tenth place was Jane Mooney with a time of 17 hours 26 minutes 36 seconds, she was the second woman home in 2007 and Jane Kennaugh is still the second fastest woman to Peel.

Left: Vinny Lynch was the first of thirty-eight to throw in the towel at the halfway mark.

Bottom left: An exhausted David Cain at the finish.

Below: Past finisher John Ryder on the Clanna Road.

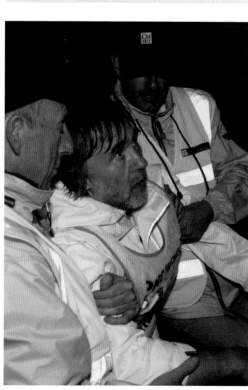

2008

policeman completed the course for the second time and 47 years after making his debut.

2008

It was a walk just too far for Castletown's Robbie Callister – his dream of equalling John Cannell's six Parish Walk titles laid to waste by the genius of the relatively unknown Jock Waddington.

In a dazzling display of race walking technique not seen for many years, 42-year-old Waddington was a surprise winner of the 2008 event, finishing ahead of a record entry that saw 121 complete the course. His time of 15 hours 44 minutes 33 seconds was some 24 minutes up on race legend Callister with Maurice Bellando edging out Michael George for the final podium position.

Manx Canadian Sue Biggart of Glen Vine took the honours in the ladies' section, securing fifth place overall but outside Sandra Brown's record time of 16 hours 16 minutes 36 seconds set in 1998. Leading throughout, her time of 16 hours 42 minutes 09 seconds was only fractionally outside her personal best.

Age and experience by far played a major role in the day's event that accounted for all but one of the top 20 finishers aged 35 or more.

Unseasonal weather on the longest day of the year accounted for the event being the wettest in living memory. It was the second wettest June day since records began with forecasters at Ronaldsway airport issuing a severe weather warning for later in the day. With the Steam Packet's fastcraft sailing severely disrupted, prospects looked daunting for the 1,311 starters assembled at the National Sports Centre for a Saturday morning 8 o'clock start.

No longer required to touch the church door at Braddan, David Griffiths led a seemingly endless procession of walkers along the busy main road to Marown where threatening skies were gathering to the west.

Despite the rapidly deteriorating weather at the Braaid, the leading contenders pressed on at a blistering pace with Griffiths the first to reach the 9½-mile mark at Oatlands in a little over an hour and a half. The normally quiet road was today packed solid with service vehicles and their attendants. With rain falling heavily, the tree-lined road linking the new road to the old offered little refuge to those changing into more suitable attire for the punishing task ahead.

As expected, the casualty rate was high on the rain-sodden route south with 42 calling time at Santon, 18 at Malew and nine at Arbory.

Holding on to his slender lead, Griffiths was the first to reach Rushen in a phenomenal time of 3 hours 14 minutes 04 seconds. With no intention to progress further, he promptly retired to head a list of 440 stopping at this point

Separated by less than two minutes, sparring partners Hands and Callister were the first to depart from the whitewashed church. Jock Waddington, Michael George, Maurice Bellando were next to head north with Sue Biggart in hot pursuit.

Making light work of the notoriously difficult climb to Ballakillowey, Hands was well aware that it was at this point last year when he retired having shared much of the lead.

Gale force winds and torrential rain made life unbearable for those ascending to the highest point of the course, 1,175 feet above sea level. Here at the 24-mile mark, headway was a feat in itself, the television crew struggling to maintain station as the weary walkers trudged by.

Despite the appalling conditions, a total of 790

Left: Alex Wijsman entering Peel in 2008 - the wettest Parish Walk in living memory.

Right: The author, well kitted out for a miserable and long night ahead.

Top left: Scene at Oatlands - the new Castletown Road soon to be replaced by the old.

Top right: Sean Hands was the first of twenty-four to call time at Andreas.

Top right below: James Betteridge finally called it a day at Ballaugh.

Above: Robbie Callister splashing his way through Michael Street, Peel.

Right: Moira Hall (No. 65) stopped at Bride.

2008

hardy souls made it to Peel, Hands was the first to the steps of the Town Hall where he recorded an incredible time of 5 hours 26 minutes 12 seconds. Already 1½ miles ahead of Callister and quicker than his record best of two years past, the twice Centurion resisted the temptation for a brief stop, favouring instead to press on to Kirk Michael, his lead now extended to 17 minutes over Waddington with Callister slipping to third having stopped for some considerable time at the eighth church.

Simon Cox was an early and surprise retirement at Kirk Michael. Although 313 made it to this point, only 274 reached the halfway mark at Ballaugh with a further 36 throwing in the towel at Jurby.

Succumbing to the elements at the 45½-mile mark, seasoned veterans Stan Sille and David Cretney were reluctant names added to a growing list of retirements, the likes of which had not been seen for many years.

Unrewarded for her commendable near 11-hour journey to Bride, Jane Moody was the first of 27 to call time at the northernmost church, a point reached by the race leader some two hours earlier. However, the former champion and race record holder was far from comfortable on the windswept, soaking wet Burma Road leading to Andreas. Six minutes down on his time to this point two years ago, he splashed his way along the tree-lined track leading to St Andrew's Parish Church to check in at 5:46pm.

Not quite what it was designed for in 1936, the public telephone box in Andreas village was a welcome place of refuge for Steam Packet captain, Dermot O'Toole. Soaked to the skin and frozen to the core, the thirteen-time finisher made use of the Edwardian relic of the past to change into dry clothes for the long night ahead.

Visibly tired and in some form of distress at St. Judes crossroads, Hands eased his relentless pace on the never ending road to Sulby, his lead over Waddington now cut to 15 minutes. Hampered by a groin injury at Ginger Hall, he limped on another two miles to head a list of 24 calling time at Lezayre.

Meanwhile, after a lengthy stop at Peel, Callister seemed to inherit a new lease of life on the long haul north. Driven by the dramatic news of Hands' retirement, he slashed Waddington's lead to 16 minutes at Maughold, leaving Sue Biggart clinging on to third spot, her lead over Michael George cut to one minute at the 67½-mile mark.

Even at this late stage of the race, torrential rain failed to deter the rapid progress of Maurice Bellando. Putting in a strong surge at the Hibernia, he had caught and passed both George and Biggart by the Dhoon and from this point on was never challenged.

His lead extended to more than two miles at the White Bridge, Waddington made easy work of the remaining miles to Douglas, crossing the finishing line shortly before midnight on the same day that he started. Delighted with his time of 15 hours 44 minutes 33 seconds, Waddington had nothing other than praise for Hands and Callister, both of whom

pushed him to the limit. It was a well-deserved victory for the 43-year-old Douglas civil servant who later admitted to suffering from severe cramp on the killer climb to the Round Table.

Somewhat disappointed with the runner-up spot, Callister later admitted it was his toughest race ever and one that may have had a more favourable outcome had he not stopped so many times.

Further back, the now decimated field was spread far and wide between Andreas and Onchan with conditions not seen in the history of the event. At midnight, driving rain turned into fog, reducing visibility to near zero at Maughold. Of the 124 who ventured beyond this point all but three made it to the finish, Edward Cleator, Michael Farnworth and Ben Coates being reluctant casualties at the penultimate church.

In the junior events to Peel, Breeshey Harkin took the honours in the ladies' class after walking every bit of the way with her father, five-time finisher Eamonn Harkin. Her feet badly blistered, the 18-year-old's time of 6 hours 48 minutes 05 seconds was four minutes quicker than James Moore of Douglas who comfortably secured the men's junior title.

There were many fine performances throughout the day including that from Martyn Biesmans. Despite his not-to-be recommended diet of a homemade pub lunch served with all the trimmings, the Dutchman completed the distance in a shade under 18 hours to secure twelfth place.

In fifteenth spot, seven-time finisher Gordan Corran came close to a personal best, falling short of the 18-hour barrier by 26 minutes.

However it was a walk too far for the Island's bishop, Robert Patterson. Raising money to help teenagers improve their quality of life, the leader of the Anglican community called time at Arbory after just 17 miles.

For Chris Moon, completing the Parish Walk in 23 hours 21 minutes complemented his already impressive list of sporting achievements few would have thought possible. The army veteran who lost an arm and a leg some years ago was no stranger to foot-slogging having completed many of the world's toughest marathons to raise funds for charities assisting the disabled.

2009

With the Island bathed in glorious sunshine through much of the month of June, meteorologists at Ronaldsway airport were cautiously optimistic that unsettled but dry conditions would prevail for the most eagerly awaited occasion in the 2009 Manx sporting calendar.

Heavy overnight rain cleared by dawn giving way to overcast skies with a cool south-westerly breeze, certainly an improvement on 12 months earlier when monsoon-type conditions accounted for the event being the wettest in living memory.

In a year marking the fortieth anniversary of the

2009

first moon landing, the question being asked was could Robbie Callister overturn last year's surprise result and seal his place in history by equalling John Cannell's impressive tally of six wins?

At 55-years of age and his best work probably done, Callister continued to be a man of boundless energy, motivation and the will to succeed. His staying power is second to none, however the road to victory is never short and he would have to be at his very best to fend off expected challengers from last year's winner, Jock Waddington, twice runner-up Ray Pitts and in-form physical education instructor, Mark Hempsall.

For veteran John Cannell, the longest weekend of the year was momentous in more ways than one. Guest starter for the forty-eighth event, the three-time Centurion and multiple Parish Walk winner sent off the record entry at 8 o'clock on Saturday morning before taking his place at the rear of the field with high expectations for another finish.

Confirmation of an accurate number of starters is never easy to establish. Many of those registering fail to turn up at the start line. Others quickly realise that they have bitten off more than they can chew and fail to make it to the first check point at Santon so their retirement goes unrecorded.

But failure was not an option for Jock Waddington, the first of 1,396 to check in at the third church shortly before 10 o'clock. Nevertheless, the 44-year-old Douglas civil servant relinquished his marginal lead to stalwarts Robbie Callister and Ray Pitts on the journey south. In hot pursuit, Janice Quirk and Sue Biggart were next to the southernmost church, with Mark Hempsall two minutes down in sixth. Even at this early stage, retirements were high with no less than 382 falling by the wayside between the start and the 19½-mile mark.

Ray Pitts was the first to tackle the most demanding section of the course with Callister close on his heels. The two were side by side at Tom the Dipper's corner with Waddington some distance in arrears and looking tired and uncomfortable. Suffering from cramp, and at times feeling queasy, he was eventually overhauled by Janice Quirk who appeared to make light work of this unforgiving five-mile uphill slog that continues to break the hearts of many. At over 1,100 feet above sea level the views were simply breath-taking, a far cry from last year when near arctic conditions reduced progress to a funeral pace.

Having eased ahead of Pitts, Callister was the first into Peel however his time of 5 hours 53 minutes was poor by even his standards and some 25 minutes down on Allan Callow's 1993 record time.

Four minutes separated the leading trio on their way out from the western capital. Waddington seemed to find a new lease of life on the picturesque road to Kirk Michael. Well into his stride, he overhauled Pitts and Janice Quirk at Devil's Elbow and was literally breathing down Callister's neck as he exited the dip at Glenwyllin.

Overhauled by Waddington on the outskirts of

Kirk Michael, Callister was now relentlessly pursued by Ray Pitts and Janice Quirk, both of whom appeared supremely confident as they checked in at the halfway mark.

By late afternoon, the casualty rate was rising alarmingly. Forty-two retirements were posted at Kirk Michael and 48 at Ballaugh. James O'Toole reached Jurby in ten hours exactly to head a list of 58 calling time after 45 miles.

Leader on the road by four minutes, Waddington touched the gate of the most northerly church at 5:49pm unaware that his nearest two challengers were close to quitting.

Losing valuable time at Jurby to change his footwear, Callister was finally caught and passed by Pitts above the golf course at Glen Truan. But his surge was short-lived for a mile further on he retired with a recurring back problem that had plagued him for years.

Callister covered the three-mile section of the Burma Road in 39 minutes but was still unable to make any impression on Waddington. Tired, weary and walking on willpower alone, he threw in the towel at Andreas much to the surprise of Ted and Barbara Hyde, timekeepers at this church for the past 25 years.

Admitting he had not put in enough time training, Callister later said: 'It was a bit of a bluff early on. I thought I would test the water and see how the others reacted. I didn't have the miles in my legs to be a serious challenger at the finish.'

Stalwarts David and Kate Cain were next to call time at the 55½-mile mark, their heavily bandaged and taped feet of no advantage on this occasion.

With Pitts and Callister no longer a threat, Janice Quirk rose to the occasion, managing to cut Waddington's advantage to 18 minutes at Maughold. In third spot, Glen Vine's Sue Biggart was a further six minutes back, followed by Mark Hempsall, Mike Readshaw, Eamonn Harkin, Martyn Beismans, Alan Cowin and Vinny Lynch, each more than capable of taking the honours should Waddington falter.

Seasoned veterans George Blair and Ray Hughes were two of 12 to go no further than Maughold where day was quickly turning to night. Nevertheless, 189 continued beyond this point with Quirk noticeably quicker, rising to the challenge of possibly becoming the first ever woman to win this historic event. She had cut Waddington's lead to 15 minutes at Glen Mona and 13 by the Dhoon. Hempsall too was looking strong at this stage. Easing past Sue Biggart above Laxey, he began distancing himself from the chasing pack and from that point on was never seriously challenged.

Pursued relentlessly by Janice Quirk over the closing miles, Waddington left nothing to chance, crossing the finishing line at 14 minutes to midnight. It was his second victory in as many years but also one that so easily could have slipped from his grasp.

A fighter to the finish, Quirk took the runner-up

Walkers on the Sloc in the mist during 2009.

2009

Top views from left to right: A seventh finish for Chris Cale; a first finish for Irishman Vinny Lynch who made it round in 17 hours 05 minutes 08 seconds; Dave and Kate Cain were two of forty-four to throw in the towel at Andreas; three seconds short of ten hours, James O'Toole headed a list of fifty-eight retirements at Jurby and reigning champion Jock Waddington claimed a second victory in 2009.

Left: Glen Vine's Sue Biggart was fourth home in 16 hours 28 minutes 41 seconds.

Bottom left: No stopping on the TT access road.

Below: Two-time champion Chris Flint brought his tally of finishes to eight in 2009.

Left: Susan Moore at the Round Table. She went on to finish in a fraction over 20 hours 15 minutes.

Right: Sarah Thornhill taking time out at the Round Table.

spot some 12½ minutes later and in doing so, bettered the ladies' record that had stood since 1998.

Hempsall's late dash to the finish was enough to secure third place in front of Sue Biggart who completed the course for an eighth time.

Delighted with a near flawless performance, Eamonn Harkin finished fifth, his time of 16 hours 35 minutes 44 seconds good enough to edge out the talented but tiring Readshaw by five minutes.

Although the front-runners were home in bed soon after midnight, many of the 200 still out on the course had not reached Lezayre.

Full of drama and never short of surprises, the Parish Walk shows no mercy to those unprepared. Terri Sammon's failure to wash and break in her new 100-mile socks before the event cost her dearly. Her feet were so badly blistered at Lezayre that she was functioning on willpower alone. Barely moving at times, the 47-year-old veteran from Onchan stubbornly carried on through the night in the belief she could make it to the finish for a ninth time. But time finally caught up with the Douglas florist, who unable to descend the unforgiving hill leading to Onchan, admitted defeat just three miles short of her

Left: Which way do we go from here?

Right: Janice Quirk on her way to becoming the first woman to break the sixteen-hour barrier.

2010

ultimate destination.

A record 185 walkers made it back to Douglas inside the 24-hour limit. But there was disappointment for Ian Craig and Amanda Dougherty, both failing to beat the clock and crossing the finishing line shortly after 8 o'clock in the morning. Never mind, there's always next year to do it all over again!

2010

Unlike the weather of two years past, blazing hot sunshine accounted for the 2010 Parish Walk being one of the toughest ever. Not since 1977 had temperatures soared so high. Then, severe exhaustion and dehydration played a key role in decimating a field that produced only one finisher – a record itself and one that will never be repeated.

Billed as the Jubilee event but really only celebrating its past 50 years, the forty-ninth event saw 1,498 starters come to the start line, of which 133 finished.

Held over the weekend of 26th and 27th June, the annual foot-slog to the Island's 17 parish churches had a slightly different look to it this year with the main road between Union Mills and Glen Vine closed to vehicular traffic between 8:30am and 9:30am.

With race record holder Sean Hands a non-starter and five-time champion Robbie Callister struggling to maintain form, the question asked was could Jock Waddington win for a third consecutive time and join an elite pair to have completed such a feat. At 45 years of age, the Douglas civil servant and father of two would have to produce a performance of outstanding quality, both physically and mentally, for seasoned campaigners, Ray Pitts, Mark Hempsall and Michael George were each capable of victory should he falter.

With the National Sports Centre packed to capacity for an 8 o'clock Saturday morning start, the race was only seconds old when it nearly claimed its first casualty. Tripped from behind and both shoes torn off, sixteen-time finisher Dermot O'Toole was fortunate to gain his composure and continue. Why there is such a stampede at the start line remains a mystery for most taking part in this Herculean task have as much chance of completing the course as they would climbing Mount Everest in a pair of carpet slippers!

Unique as the only parish not sharing a boundary with the sea, Marown was reached in a little under 50 minutes. Michael George and Mark Hempsall were the early pacesetters, 80 yards or so in front of Jock Waddington and Vinny Lynch, both of whom would later stamp their authority on this show-piece event.

The warm sunshine and a near cloudless sky quickly took a toll on those unprepared for such conditions. Olympic Games silver medallist and 400-metre runner Roger Black, who officially started the race for new sponsor Scottish Widows, was one of 40 to call time at Santon, the first official check point. Seventeen stopped at Malew and eight at Arbory.

Inspite of sharing the lead from the start, Hempsall's bid for glory failed at Ballabeg where he was disqualified for ungainly technique despite being warned by race officials on several occasions.

Elevated into second spot, Waddington looked confident on the flat but twisting main road to Rushen, now in sight of the race leader and soon to commence the back-breaking climb to Ballakillowey.

Irishman Vinny Lynch was the next to turn north for Peel, some five minutes ahead of Callister who in turn was pursued relentlessly by course record-holder to Peel, Allan Callow, Ray Pitts, Richard Gerrard, Stephen Harvey and Eamonn Harkin.

Ben O'Hare (No. 138), Jane Foster and Chris Flint finished together in fifty-first position.

Even at this early stage, the intense midday sun was having a devastating effect and timekeepers at Rushen were overwhelmed with retirements that numbered 382 at this point, a figure greater than the entire entry in 1996!

Having overhauled George on the lower reaches of the Sloc, Waddington pressed on alone, reaching Peel in 5½ hours and the third fastest over this distance but falling short of Allan Callow's 1993 record time by 12 minutes.

By mid-afternoon, the party atmosphere at Peel Town Hall was in full swing. The band was playing and the flags were flying as Saturday afternoon shoppers stood aside for the advancing army of walkers, many just glad to finish at this point and put aside their thoughts for another year.

Many gutsy performances ended at the 32½-mile mark. Surprisingly, only three of the top 20 reaching this point could lay claim to being under the age of 40! Vickie Rawlinson was the first woman there however her time of 6 hours 19 minutes was nearly an hour adrift of the ladies' all-time record set in 1982 by Irene Corlett.

Charlie Doyle was a popular winner of the junior event for men under the age of 21. Other worthy performances to Peel came from David Doyle, David Cain and James O'Toole, names added to an ever growing list of retirements at this point that numbered 571 by the official cut-off time of 9:30pm.

Surprisingly, a total of 465 continued beyond Peel with George and Lynch exchanging blow for blow and separated by only yards at the halfway mark. Nevertheless, at Jurby, the relatively inexperienced Lynch had opened a two-minute advantage and now set his sights on the leader.

In an event that he had dominated for many years, Robbie Callister's appetite for success remained voracious as ever. However on this occasion the 56-year-old found himself continually under pressure in order to contain fourth place.

Ten minutes behind the iconic legend Alan Cowin, Richard Spenceley and Richard Gerrard were in bitter conflict with each other for fifth spot, separated by only 24 seconds.

With no time for cigarettes, Terry Moffat worked exceedingly hard to fend off a serious challenge from veterans Ray Pitts, Stephen Harvey, Michael Readshaw and Eamonn Harkin. The chasing pack was separated by less than eight minutes, however the latter man's time of eight hours to the halfway mark was of little consequence for he was the first of 62 calling time here, leaving 339 to continue.

Although sick on several occasions, Waddington never faltered on the long tiring road to Bride. Extending his advantage over Lynch to 17 minutes, he looked supremely confident on the climb out of the quintessential village with 32½ miles to go.

Having given a good account during the early stages, Callister's quest for further limelight eventually faltered for a second consecutive year. Shadowing George for most of the day, he looked tired and

No stranger to foot-slogging, Terri Salmon finished for a fourth time in 2010.

2010

weary and never really looked in contention during the long haul north. Forfeiting fourth place to Richard Gerrard soon after St. Judes, the five-time winner was the first of 43 to call time at Lezayre.

Desirous to put further distance between himself and Lynch, Waddington pressed on with boundless energy through the seaside hamlets of Port Lewague and Port e Vullen, Maughold his ultimate destination before turning for home.

Extending his lead to 33½ minutes, Waddington checked in to the fifteenth church at 7:47pm but too early to witness the International Space Station passing overhead shortly before midnight.

Never an easy section to negotiate, the tough climb out of Maughold to the Hibernia left its mark on two of the 135 who continued beyond this point.

Approaching the finish line, Anne Dooley (No.1322), Carol and Billy McCoubrey.

2010

Top left: Lynne McMenemy checking in at Santon.

Top right: Journey's end for John Callow.

Top right below: Satisfaction for Andy Green who finished in ninth place.

Middle left: A total of 1498 competitors checked in with Manx Telecom at Santon.

Middle right: A well deserved hat trick of wins for Jock Waddington.

Above: Finishing in tenth spot, Ray Pitts is congratulated by his wife, Glynn, Leslie Christian and Sue Biggart.

Right: Brenda Stoffberg was delighted with forty-eighth position.

Desperately short of time and in no fit state to continue, veterans Jill Hamlin and Samantha McLean were bitterly disappointed to end their ordeal at Lonan with only six miles to go.

For Susan Moore, in only her third Parish Walk, the lonely church high on the hill was the penultimate stepping stone in her bid for Parish fame. Holding her nerve on the difficult descent into Onchan, the mother of two held off a late challenge from Chris Cale to claim twelfth spot and victory in the ladies' event.

Inspite of losing precious time over the closing stages, Waddington kept up the pressure by completing the final 18 miles in a shade over 3½ hours. Nothing short of phenomenal, his overall time of 15 hours 18 minutes 09 seconds was over 2½ minutes inside Derek Harrison's all-time record that has stood for 27 years. By securing his third victory in as many years, the Douglas civil servant can now lay claim to being the third quickest around the 17 parishes.

2011

Intensive training and mental discipline of the highest calibre were the key elements to Jock Waddington's electrifying performance in the 2011 Parish Walk.

Although forced to concede centre stage after many years at the top, former champion Robbie Callister and 2007 runner-up Michael George were equally determined to stamp their authority on this show-piece event, first held in 1913 when a dozen starters set off into the unknown.

With a record number of 1,505 competitors assembled at the National Sports Centre on Saturday morning 25th June, the fiftieth event since 1960 promised to be the best yet. Although weather conditions were ideal, nothing can be taken for granted in this race of endurance that break the hearts of many.

With Waddington a clear favourite to win a fourth consecutive title, it came as no surprise that his superb time of 3 hours 06 minutes to Rushen was one of the quickest ever recorded. Nevertheless, 399 walkers failed to make it past this point leaving Waddington, Michael George and Richard Gerrard first to tackle the long haul to the top of the Sloc.

First to the Round Table crossroads, Waddington steadily increased his lead on the fast descent to Peel where he arrived at the Town Hall steps at 1:23pm, a time only bettered by Allan Callow and Irene Corlett many years ago.

Having caught and overtaken George by the Round Table, Gerrard was next into Peel, eight minutes adrift of the leader with Vinny Lynch a further 3½ minutes back.

Richard Spenceley, Michael George and veteran Robbie Callister were next to negotiate the town's busy high street however it was unlikely that their sub-six-hour times to this point would make any impression on Waddington, by now well advanced on the coast road to Kirk Michael.

Also reaching the most westerly church in less than six hours, Stephen Harvey, Tufty Nash and Maurice Bellando were next to the Town Hall where hundreds had already gathered to soak up the atmosphere and mid-afternoon sunshine.

In the men's under 21 event, Liam Park exceeded all expectations by recording a superb winning time of 6 hours 17 minutes, one of the quickest junior times ever to this point. Jenny Newberry was the first woman there, her time of 6 hours 37 minutes enough to claim the junior ladies' title for a second consecutive year.

By 2010, Tony Kneale and David Collister had a combined total of 48 finishes.

2011

Top left: Sarah Leece made it to Maughold.

Above: Beverly Loughran and Sharon O'Neill contemplating whether or not to continue.

Left: Angie Astley leaving Malew church.

Below left: Anne Dudley made it as far as Lezayre.

Below: Frank Koske leaving for Arbory.

2011

Top views from left to right: Mike Readshaw was the second of 567 to call time at Peel; Michelle Turner was the second of 351 to stop at the most southerly church; James Betteridge (No. 61) finished for a second time while Andreas was the stopping point for Michael Farnworth; Carolyne Gelling (No. 1069) and Christie Morgan soon to tackle the Sloc; Moira Hall (No. 105) stopped at the halfway mark and Monica George at Peel.

Left: Chantal Johnson (No. 1099) made it to the halfway mark.

Bottom left: A personal message to one of the 1505 starters.

Below: Jock Waddington on his way to a fourth consecutive win.

SCOTTISH WIDOWS
PARISH WALK
60
manxtelecomtiming

SCOTTISH WIDOWS
PARISH WALK
118
manxtelecomtiming

Angie Aire made it round for a
third time in 2011.

A top-ten finisher for many years, Michael Readshaw was a surprise retirement at Peel where 1,106 walkers checked in before the 5pm deadline.

There was disappointment too for veteran Michael Gray, who in company with his daughter, suffered severe cramp on the Sloc, effectively ending his dream of completing the full distance for a fourth time, the first way back in 1961 when he was one of nine finishers.

In glorious late afternoon sunshine, the party atmosphere at Kirk Michael was well established with standing room only outside the public house where hundreds had gather to cheer on the 531 that ventured this far.

Waddington's relentless pace to Ballaugh saw him reaching the halfway mark under 7½ hours and well ahead of Sean Hands' record time here five years earlier. Gerrard was still holding second place but losing ground rapidly to Lynch and it was only a matter of time until he was overhauled. Spenceley remained in fourth spot with Callister now elevated to fifth having overtaken George who stopped at Kirk Michael for the best part of two hours and then continued with his wife to Maughold and alone to the finish.

Making light work of the tiring twisting road to Bride, Waddington reached the most northerly church in a fraction over nine hours – some four minutes inside the all-time record to this point. Although he mentally viewed this as the halfway mark, there were indeed still 32½ miles between here and the finish.

On the climb out of Bride to West Kimmeragh, Gerrard looked visibly tired as Lynch continued to erode his advantage, now less than a minute. Four minutes apart, Spenceley and Callister were next onto the Burma Road, the five-time champion desperately trying to make up lost time but unlikely to do so at this late stage.

Cheered on by a rapturous crowd at Andreas, popular local resident Terry Moffat had cut Callister's lead to eight minutes. He reduced this even further by Sulby Bridge where the past champion was now firmly in his sights. At Maughold, the deficit was down to less than four minutes with the two side by side on the punishing uphill climb to Ballajora.

But the pace proved too much for Moffat and his challenge slowly faded from this point on. Callister meanwhile, dug into his deepest reserves and much credit must given to the 57-year-old for his sheer tenacity in producing a near vintage performance that secured fifth spot, albeit in a time greater than desired.

Having overhauled a weary Gerrard at Sulby Bridge, Lynch was beginning to show signs of a late resurgence and was now only 16 minutes off the lead at the 67½-mile mark. Waddington's early arrival at Maughold saw him still in with a chance of shattering the all- time record of 14 hours 47 minutes 36 seconds, however in doing so, he would have to complete the remaining 18 miles in no more than 3

Six-time winner John Cannell approaching the Blackboards.

2011

hours 10 minutes – a tall order considering his present level of fatigue and the weather soon to deteriorate. That said his incredible pace to this point had opened a gap of 26 miles over those at the rear of the field, many still to reach the halfway mark and certain to be timed out at the next church.

Even at this late stage, quality was in abundance from those in pursuit. Contesting seventh spot, Maurice Bellando and Stephen Harvey were only three minutes apart at Glen Mona, both having drawn ahead of Michael Bonney and Tony Okell at the Hibernia where visibility was down to a few yards.

A mile or so back, Chris Cale in ninth spot was managing to hold on to a four-minute advantage over Michael Shipsides despite spells of sickness at Port e Vullen. No stranger to this neck of the woods, the 39-year-old Douglas sports shop proprietor made light work of the tiring road to Ballajora, his unique and effortless style the envy of many.

With no change in the leader board from this point on, and determined that Waddington not be allowed to plough a lone furrow over the closing miles, Lynch pressed on along the endless road to Laxey in the faint hope that there was still time to mount a late challenge.

At the old mining town, he had cut Waddington's lead to less than 15 minutes, however time was running out for the plucky Irishman and from here on his challenge faded allowing his friend and training partner to march on to the finish and claim a fourth victory in as many years.

To rapturous applause from a huge crowd of well-wishers gathered on Harris Promenade, Lynch crossed the finish line some 15 minutes later to secure the runner-up spot for a second consecutive year. His time of 15 hours 15 minutes 44 seconds was a

2011

Top views from left to right: Dave Mackey reached the eighth church in 6 hours 19 minutes 19 seconds; Jenny Newbery won the junior ladies race to Peel; David Chambers nearing Peel; Maurice Billando approaching the Blackboards and Sammy White leaving Patrick church.

Left: Angela Martin finished for a third time in a fraction over 19 hours 50 minutes.

Bottom left: Marie Gilbertson, (No.77) comfortably cracked nineteen hours to finish for a seventh time.

Below: Marie Gilbertson and Samantha Draper approaching the Blackboards.

personal best and the third fastest-ever recorded.

As day turned to night and with the bullk of walkers still to reach Maughold, the quintessential village was passed unnoticed as thick fog descended across the parish making life even more difficult for the 163 soon to tackle the punishing four-mile journey through Ballajora to the Hibernia. Never an easy section to negotiate, it was indeed a walk too far for Brenda Stofberg, Robbie Stockton, Mark Armstrong and Hadyn Kenna, all calling time at Lonan, six miles short of their ultimate goal.

Full of drama from start to finish, there has never been a Parish Walk encounter quite like this one, and run over a few miles more, the outcome may have been much different. To quote the Duke of Wellington after his great victory at Waterloo in 1815: 'It was a close-run thing and could have gone either way!'

2012

In a race of high drama from start to finish, Michael George's bid to win the 2012 Parish Walk was dealt a severe blow during the latter stages when the combined resources of Vinny Lynch and Richard Gerrard denied him victory in a race he had dominated for the best part of 60 miles.

Although setting a relentless pace throughout and improving on Sean Hands' all-time record set in 2006, it was a bitterly disappointing finish for the 47-year-old Douglas hotelier who produced a masterclass in race walking intelligence but came up short when it mattered most.

Held over the weekend following the summer solstice, the Manx Telecom sponsored event will go down in history as the fastest and most exciting of all time. Not since 1971 had this gruelling 85-mile classic produced a head-to-head encounter of such quality. It was a scene reminiscent to that played out 40 years ago when Graham Young and Derek Harrison fought out a bitter dual on Douglas Promenade with the Douglas postman claiming victory by the narrowest of margins.

With last year's champion Jock Waddington a non-starter and five-time winner Robbie Callister walking for fun, attention was focused on Michael George, Vinny Lynch and Richard Gerrard, no strangers to foot-slogging and each intent on adding a new name to the trophy for the first time in four years.

Making a welcome return after an absence of three years, Nobles Hospital staff nurse Sue Biggart was firm favourite to produce another class-winning performance in the ladies' event however it was unlikely she would improve on Janice Quirk's record time of 15 hours 58 minutes 35 seconds set in 2009. On this occasion the nine-time finisher was supported by training partner Ray Pitts, himself a past runner-up but taking time out having recently returned from completing Wainwright's Coast to Coast Walk across England.

With an identical number of starters as last year, most came prepared expecting the worst, however the heavy overnight rain cleared just before the 8 o'clock start leaving no time to change into clothing more appropriate.

Manx Telecom entered several teams for the 2012 event.

Start of the 2012 Parish Walk with little room for manoeuvre.

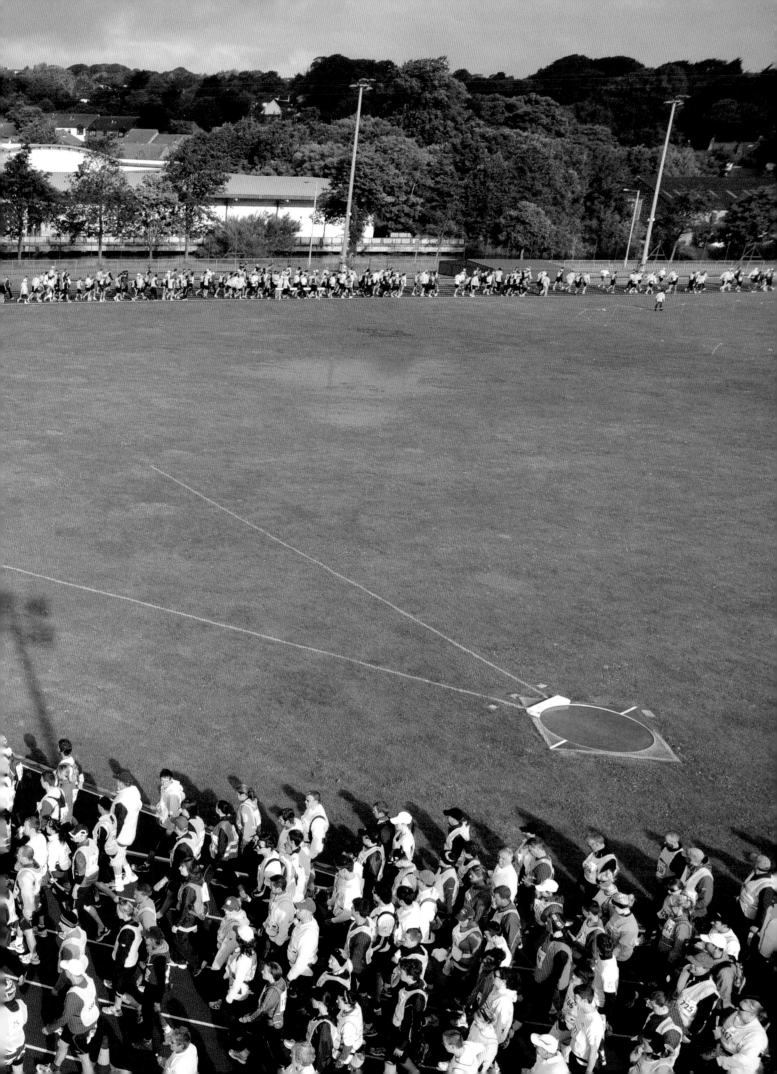

2012

Top views from left to right: Fifth place and a second finish for Phil Marshal; a fine sixth place for Mike Readshaw; a tenth finish for Chris Cale in 2012; Sarah Leece was the second of thirty-one to call time at Lezayre and Alexandra Valentine at Glen Vine.

Left: From left to right: Andy Green, Simon Briggs, Sue Biggart and Eamonn Harkin.

Left below: Eamonn McGee was the second of 379 to throw in the towel at Rushen.

Below right: David Walker (No 19) stopped at Andreas but Vinny Lynch and Richard Spenceley (No 5) both reached the finish.

Another view of the start in 2012.

Now that it was no longer a requirement to touch the church doors at Braddan and Marown, the leading pack wasted little time in reaching Santon, the first of Manx Telecom's 16 electronic checkpoints. Richard Spenceley was the first here in a fraction over an hour and three-quarters, however his lead was slender with only 25 seconds separating the top four. Nevertheless, Richard's early arrival at Rushen was of little consequence for his ten-second lead over Vinny Lynch and Richard Gerrard was soon erased on the punishing climb to Ballakillowey. Such was the pace to this point that fifth-placed Callister had already stretched his advantage to 25 minutes over Sue Biggart, the leading lady and holding twelfth spot.

Wasting no time descending from the Round Table, Michael George was first to reach Peel, his time of 5 hours 17 minutes 24 seconds the fastest time ever to this point and eclipsing Allan Callow's long-standing record time set in 1993 by the best part of a minute. His time was so fast that race officials were caught napping setting up their reception apparatus at the Town Hall steps. To rapturous applause from the large crowd gathered, Spenceley and Gerrard were next to this point, already 6½ minutes in arrears and having to work overtime to fend off Irishman Lynch, a minute further back.

Making his appearance into Michael Street some 25 minutes later, fifth-placed Robbie Callister was quickly followed by Phil Marshall and Mike Readshaw, all of whom cracked the six-hour barrier to this point.

With Spenceley relegated to fourth spot on leaving Peel, attention turned to Lynch and Gerrard, both arriving together at Kirk Michael but unable to make any impression on George's eight-minute advantage. The gap continued to grow on the long haul to Bride where George's relentless pace saw him arrive at 4:43pm, well inside the all-time record to this point and a lead now extended to 12 minutes.

Like any marathon of this magnitude, the pressure of leading is its own challenge and sometimes it is easier to hunt than be hunted. In George's case, isolation at the head of the leader board for such an extended period was bound to produce adverse effects, both mentally and physically. Those requiring a lesson in race tactics need look no further than Mo Farah's outstanding performances in the 2012 London Olympic Games.

Unable to hold down food or fluid of any description, George was violently sick at the most northerly church and later stopped on the Burma Road for massage to his legs. Wasting valuable time, he stopped again at Andreas to take on vital sustenance, without which he was doomed to failure. News of his extraordinary and unscheduled six-minute delay quickly spread with local radio stations reporting the drama as it unfolded.

With the race soon to enter its tenth hour, Lynch and Gerrard had cut the deficit to less than five minutes at Sulby Bridge and it was now only a matter of time before George came into view. Incredible as it may seem, the pace had been so extreme to that point, that the leading trio had gained 27 miles over back-marker Kelly Lemon, still short of her goal and the last of 1057 that reached Peel.

In atrocious weather conditions reminiscent to those in 2008, the relentless hunt continued through Lezayre and Maughold with the dynamic duo grinding down a lead once thought impenetrable.

Functioning on reserves close to depletion, George commenced the back-breaking climb to Ballajora with the knowledge his immediate pursuers would soon

2012

Above: Jane Farquhar and David Collister setting out for the Braaid.

Below: Michael George led the race for nearly sixty miles but came up short when it mattered most.

Right: Vinny Lynch and Richard Gerrard approaching the most northerly church.

Below left: Amanda Butler (No. 123), Sam Looker and Karen Lawrie.

Below right: Tony Ruddick's attire attracted considerable attention.

Various views from the 2012 event including a happy smile from Jayne Harrison above.

2012

2012

Lucy Veale made it to Peel in a fraction under 8 hours 18 minutes.

be in sight. Turning for home at the Hibernia, it was soon apparent that his four-minute lead would be insufficient to achieve the victory he so richly deserved.

Sick once again on the rain-sodden road above Laxey, George had to dig into his deepest reserves to climb the notoriously difficult hill leading to the penultimate church with Lynch and Gerrard hot on his heels.

But time was running out for the near-exhausted Douglas hotelier, his 25-second lead finally surrendered shortly after crossing the tram tracks above Baldrine. Like passing ships in the night and few words exchanged, Lynch and Gerrard disappeared into the distant twilight, marching on to a joint victory in a new race record time of 14 hours

42 minutes 32 seconds.

A forlorn figure, humiliated and beyond redemption, George battled on against all odds, arriving in the capital less than five minutes later. Completing his seventh Parish Walk but physically and mentally wrecked, George was understandably in no frame of mind to address the media, or indeed participate in celebratory proceedings. Shell-shocked and at times resembling that of a lost soldier on the Western Front, he was so exhausted and emotionally drained that at times he seemed unaware of his surroundings. In producing a class performance that ranks above all others, the Douglas hotelier will be remembered for his pluck and consistency for many years to come. Not only did he raise the bar above all expectation, he proved that total commitment and

m:

This is to certify that

Richard Gerrard

competed in the

Manx Telecom Parish Walk

on Saturday 23rd June 2012 and walked to
Finish Church, a distance of 85.0 miles
in a time of 14 hours, 42 minutes, 32 seconds.

Organiser - For Manx Harriers

manx telecom

sheer tenacity remain the driving forces to success.

With the euphoria of this extraordinary finish reverberating into the early hours, most of the 200 walkers still to finish were scattered far and wide with back-markers as far as Andreas!

A little over an hour off the final podium place, Richard Spenceley produced his best finish to claim fourth spot in 15 hours 50 minutes 20 seconds, some 42 minutes ahead of 28-year-old rising star Phil Marshall who was fifth. The ever dependable Mike Readshaw made it round in 16 hours 43 minutes 23 seconds, edging out Simon Briggs by 10½ minutes for sixth spot.

In eighth place and the first woman home in 17 hours 03 minutes 53 seconds, 49-year-old Sue Biggart made it round for the tenth time and unaware that she had overtaken Robbie Callister somewhere in the Dhoon area.

Nevertheless, unused to being outmanoeuvred by the fairer sex at this late stage, credit most be given to the iconic five-time champion for remaining focused to the end to edge out Jonathan Wild who was tenth.

As night wore on, weather conditions went from bad to worse with heavy rain and casual water a serious hazard between Glen Mona and Laxey. That said, of the 204 who went beyond Maughold, all but one made it back to Douglas – Jack Walton unlucky to call time at Lonan, six miles from the finish.

In the ladies' under-21 race to Peel, Jenny Newberry was a convincing winner in a time of 6 hours 37 minutes 12 seconds – nearly 21 minutes ahead of 20-year-old Sam Looker who claimed the men's junior title at the first attempt.

Mark Boyd, the last official finisher, had to plead with race officials at the penultimate church to let him continue. Twenty minutes outside the time limit, he went flat out over the final miles to arrive at the finish with four minutes to spare. But Sarah Callin, the last and unofficial finisher was not so lucky. Her race effectively came to an end on Queens Promenade as the 24-hour time limit ran out. Nevermind Sarah – there's always next year!

Whether you took part or just looked on for fun, memories of this great occasion will linger for years to come. Controversial as it may seem, the collaboration of Vinny Lynch and Richard Gerrard at such an early stage was undoubtedly the key to their success.

Nevertheless, the final word must go to Michael George, by far the hero of the day. Brave, courageous and now more determined than ever to set the record straight. Next year's race may have seemed a long way off but it's certainly an occasion he'd not miss!

2013

The burden Michael George has had to carry as a serious contender for Parish Walk glory was finally lifted in 2013 when he reached the pantheon of true greatness few do. His long wait to win this show-

A seventh finish for Stella Corlett.

2013

piece event is over and those fortunate enough to witness it don't know how privileged they are.

After last year's disappointment when the iron-hard disciplinarian was denied victory by the closest of margins, many at the time wondered whether he would ever be able to bounce back and win this extraordinary event that has captured the imagination like no other. But incredibly he did it at the very next attempt. What an extraordinary example of how to improve yourself and get better and better at something. What a champion and what mental and physical powers. What reward for all those lung-busting hours spent on the track in all kinds of weather when most of us would rather stay indoors doing nothing.

The realisation of an ambition that he tenaciously pursued for many years, his was a masterclass in perseverance, an occasion when he had to dig deep, as deep as he has ever done, when he had to grit his teeth and just get on with it. No heroics or collapsing at the final hurdle – just a belief in himself.

Although entry numbers were significantly down on previous years, the 2013 Parish Walk will go down in history as the second fastest and most exciting race of all time. From a field of 1,321 starters, a record 215 went full distance, 12 more than the previous best with 89 completing the testing 85-mile course for the first time.

Held over the weekend of 22nd and 23rd June, the much awaited centenary event was quite literally a battle of the titans with no less than four previous winners plus last year's runner-up slugging it out for the top spot.

Tantalisingly close to achieving his dream of winning the biggest prize in Manx athletics a year ago, but falling short when it mattered most, the big

2013

question was could the Douglas hotelier overcome his past disappointments and secure the victory he so richly deserved?

When it comes to mental strength and physical ability, some would say Michael is head and shoulders above the rest. Undoubtedly the man in form and one to beat, his punishing training programme bordering on 100 miles per week would put many a work-horse to shame. Nevertheless, last year's joint winners Vinny Lynch and Richard Gerrard also trained exceptionally hard, each determined on this occasion to claim the title outright.

In spite of adding a third ladies' title to her tally last year, Sue Biggart was aware that this occasion would probably be her last at bidding for further glory. Not one to rest on her laurels or say 'never again,' the 51-year-old ten-time finisher was up against 2009 ladies' race record-holder Janice Quirk, who after an absence of three years, was favourite for the title.

Packed to capacity for an early morning 8 o'clock start, many of those taking part had no idea what they were about to undertake. Just to complete this Herculean event is an achievement itself, for the Parish Walk is as much a test of mental strength as it is of physical endurance and sometimes that is not fully understood. It takes so much hard work and discipline to keep going when the going gets tough, so failure is often an easy option.

Making the best of the sunny but cool conditions that later turned to persistent rain, the four pre-favourites reached the most southerly church two minutes down on last year's time. Unusual for the leaders to be together at this point, Richard Gerrard, Vinny Lynch, Jock Waddington and Michael George were first to tackle the tortuous five-mile climb to the Round Table where the views take your breath away. Although determined to win a fifth title, Waddington suffered severe cramp on this most difficult section, forcing him to ease off and lose sight of the leaders.

In only his second Parish, 27-year-old Dave Mapp received a tumultuous welcome from the huge crowd of spectators gathered outside Rushen church. Adrift of the leaders by five minutes and carrying a backpack as far as Peel, the Onchan Silver Band conductor was amazed to find himself in fifth spot and one place ahead of Island running champion Tony Okell.

Brian Wade, Chris Cale and Dave Walker were next to the whitewashed church with leading ladies Janice Quirk and Sue Biggart in hot pursuit.

Unlike last year when he led from the front for the best part of 60 miles, George bided his time on the punishing climb to Ballakillowey, walking at a more leisurely pace in the company of last year's joint winners. As expected, he was strongest over the mountain and soon developed a 45-second lead. But Gerrard and Lynch were having none of it, and piling on the pressure to stop this turning into a one-horse race, they cut the deficit to 11 seconds at Patrick.

Cheered on by a boisterous crowd gathered at Peel, the leading trio of George, Gerrard and Lynch reached the Town Hall shortly after 1:30pm – some four minutes down on last year's time. Six minutes back and still suffering from the effects of cramp, four-time champion Waddington was next to register with the timekeepers, however leg cramps on the Rushen to Patrick section had seriously hampered his progress leaving the chasing pack of Tony Okell, Dave Mapp, Brian Wade, Chris Cale and Dave Walker a serious target to aim for. In tenth spot, Janice Quirk was living up to expectations with a three-minute lead over fellow veteran Sue Biggart – a figure that would grow to 36 by the end of the day.

Although Ray Pitts was only going to Peel on this occasion, his time of 6 hours 04 minutes 30 seconds was disappointing in view of the punishing training programme he had undertaken throughout the winter with training partner Sue Biggart. A seasoned veteran and runner-up to Robbie Callister in 2007, the 61-year-old headed a field of 433 who stopped at this point.

Other regular campaigners to fall short at the eighth church included Doug Allan, Mick Holgate and Dudley Butt – the former Police Assistant Chief Inspector disheartened with the deteriorating weather and plagued by back problems since his last finish six years ago.

In the male under-21 race to Peel, 20-year-old William Brown from Foxdale fought off a serious challenge from former Queen Elizabeth II school mate Sean Unsworth to claim the junior title. Although weather conditions were ideal at this stage, William's time of 6 hours 41 minutes 58 seconds was well outside the junior record set by Allan Thomson some years ago.

In the same race for women under-21, Caitriona Dooley and Gemma Cairney walked every step of the way together to jointly claim the honours in a time of 7 hours 23 minutes 08 seconds. It was an emotional occasion for the two girls who took part as a tribute to Gareth Cowin who died in South Korea some months before while representing the Isle of Man at the Special Olympics

Although cheered on by a huge crowd of well-wishers gathered outside the Mitre Hotel, six-time winner John Cannell and 22-time finisher Anthony Kneale were unable to muster further enthusiasm for this Herculean task and were two of 62 retirements posted at the 39-mile mark.

Still locked together as one at the halfway stage, a point midway between Ballaugh's old church and new, George, Gerrard and Lynch were like boxers exchanging blows but no one taking the initiative to take a bigger step forward.

By reducing the deficit to eight minutes at Jurby, Waddington appeared to have overcome his bouts of cramp for he was still holding on to fourth spot as he briefly glimpsed the leading trio heading off towards the prison. Here at the lonely church, David Lon Chambers was the first of 85 to call time – the experienced veteran on his feet for nine and a half hours through unseasonal weather with heavy rain

Top views from left to right: Kellie Hands (No.70) and Angela Martin approaching the Braaid; Maureen Moffatt (No.19) and Sue Biggart lead the ladies on the journey south; Robbie Callister and Andrew Titley finished five minutes apart and Paul Kennish and Matt Cannell enjoying a fun day out.

Left: David Cretney was one of 433 to call time at Peel.

Below: Walkers offered food at the Braaid.

2013

Top views from left to right: Robert Corkish and Angie Aire on the way to Santon: Dave Horisk collecting for his chosen charity; Kenny Valerga made it round for a second time and Steven Downward and Shaun Nesbitt leaving Rushen church.

Below: Enjoying a 'sweet' break at Rushen church.

Above: Electronic timing by SPORTident has been in use since 2007.

Right: Walkers at Rushen church on a fine sunny day, the stopping point for 273 walkers.

Below: Thirty-two miles already completed for this group of walkers.

Below left: Maureen Moffatt and Samanth Bowden both finshed in 2013.

Below right: Not the best footware for Marcie Brabbs.

2013

making life unbearable for competitors and organisers alike.

A race official for 48 years and timekeeper at Jurby for half that time, Mitch Joughin was soaked through to the skin at the church gates where 355 wet and weary souls reluctantly trudged on into the night.

Featureless, and for the most part boring, the seven-mile journey to Bride was not made easy by the abundance of service vehicles blighting the area. With the race entering its twelfth hour and the leaders already approaching Laxey, the road through the Lhen to Blue Point was totally gridlocked on both sides leaving competitors little room to manoeuvre.

After failing to eat and drink sufficiently last year, George revised his strategy by taking nothing for granted on this occasion. Under the watchful eye of coach and two-time winner Graham Young, the 49-year-old meticulously controlled his food and drink intake with absolute precision in anticipation of ploughing a lone furrow from this point on.

Although the pace was slightly down on last year, the leading trio reached the most northerly church at 5:07pm having averaged five and three quarter miles an hour for 52½ miles. Considered to be the turning point for home, the quintessential village at Bride accounted for a whopping 44 retirements including that of Ray Hughes – a 22-time finisher and runner-up on no less than three occasions many years ago.

The party atmosphere was well established at Andreas where George finally signalled his intent. Putting his best foot forward, he began distancing himself from his pals and by Lezayre he had carved out a two-minute lead over Gerrard with Lynch a further three minutes back in third.

Waddington wasn't hanging about either. Sensing there was still sufficient time to mount a late challenge on the lead, the Douglas civil servant increased his stride along the Burma Road to once again catch sight of the leaders as they made their way out of Andreas village.

Although attention was focused on the pre-race favourites for much of the day, many close encounters were also taking place further down the leader board. The sudden exit of Tony Okell at Andreas elevated David Mapp into fifth spot with Janice Quirk the first woman there and in sixth spot.

With little separating them at Lezayre, Parish regulars Terry Moffat, Michael Bonney and Simon Briggs headed off into Ramsey with the knowledge they were being closely monitored by Douglas sports shop proprietor Chris Cale and five-time winner Robbie Callister – both matching each other step-for-step and five minutes ahead of Andrew Titley in twelfth spot.

The heavy rain that caught up with the many back-markers leaving Peel was now making its presence known to those at the top of the leader board. Cheered on by a huge crowd of well-wishers gathered in Maughold village square, George wasted no time on the back-breaking four-mile climb to the Hibernia, his lead over Gerrard now extended to three

minutes with Lynch a further eight minutes adrift and soon to relinquish third spot to a resurgent Waddington who appeared to have sufficient fire left in his belly to mount a late challenge.

Easily the most tiring part of the course for those fortunate enough to have made it this far, Ballajora was the spot where Waddington finally edged out the Irishman for the final podium spot and from this point on there was no change to the leader board .

With his nose well in front and victory in sight, George piled on the pressure above Laxey, determined not to let this soon-to-be victorious occasion slip from his grasp. At the old mining town, his advantage stood at six minutes and although he and Gerrard passed each other like ships in the night on the climb to the penultimate church, there was no way that last year's joint winner could make any impression with only six and a half miles remaining.

This was a race only George could win – and win he most certainly did. Conscious that it was at this point last year that he collapsed like a condemned block of flats, leaving Gerrard and Lynch to emerge from the rubble with a hero's swagger, he hurried on to the finish without the slightest glance over his shoulders.

Cheered on by hundreds of well-wishers lining the route through Onchan and the walkway leading to the Douglas War Memorial, he crossed the finish line to claim a richly-deserved victory and silence those doubters who questioned his ability to claim the richest reward in Manx athletics. Nearly two minutes quicker than his previous best a year ago, his time of 14 hours 44 minutes 49 seconds was the third fastest-ever recorded.

Delighted with the result and understandably overcome with emotion on the finish line, Michael later said: 'I was beginning to wonder if I'd ever do it. It's been a monkey on my back for some time now and each year it gets harder. Richard has come a long way in a short time and is extremely experienced and talented now. He's also a lot younger and I am aware that time stops for no one.'

Incredible as it may seem, over nine hours elapsed between the first and last competitor home. Although a near full moon briefly made an appearance through a watery sky during the early hours, the night was long, wet and miserable for most of the 220 who continued beyond Maughold.

For Gary Deuchar, Andrew Howard, Maryja Judkowska, Ralph Peake and Ian Harrison, it was a journey just too far with the penultimate church their final stopping point.

Nevertheless, these were worthy performances that did them all proud – in particular that of American and four-time finisher Deuchar, who unable to stand upright after walking many hours with an injured back, struggled on to the Liverpool Arms before admitting defeat just three and a half miles from the finish.

Other fine performances worthy of mention included that from 79-year-old Michael Gray who

Above: Gordon Corran finished for a ninth time.

Right: Roberta Convery and Claire Jackson at Ballaugh.

Below: Paul Morgans, Anthea Sharpe, Wynand Bezuidenhout and Tim Crookall in Michael Street, Peel.

Below left: Busy scene on the way to Peel Town Hall.

Below right: All starters received the Manx Telecom medal in 2013.

2013

walked all the way to Lezayre in company with his daughter Stephanie before parting company so she could continue alone to the finish. A Parish Walk debutant in 1960 and fifth place the following year, Michael still holds the record as the oldest finisher.

Also making history by becoming the oldest-ever competitor to take part in the annual classic, Robert Corkish walked to Santon with his daughter Angie Aire to raise money for Manx Blind Welfare, his chosen charity. The partially sighted 86-year-old completed the 11-mile distance in a fraction over three and a quarter hours.

Yet another veteran proving that age is no barrier to success, 62-year-old Gordan Corran added another finish to his tally of ten with a near flawless performance that saw him claim 30th spot in 18 hours 33 minutes 55 seconds – one of his quickest-ever circuits. Like a maturing red wine, the Onchan plasterer, famous for 'never again' quotes, seems to get better with age.

No strangers to foot-slogging, with seven finishes between them, sisters Lynn and Carol McCoubrey walked every step of the 85 miles together – surprising themselves in the process with joint 100th place and a superb best time ever of 20 hours 47 minutes 24 seconds.

For nineteen-time finisher Dermot O'Toole, the 2013 event was his toughest for many years. 'I didn't have a good day and mentally couldn't come to terms with the heartache that is never far away,' he later said. 'I walked a hundred miles in 23 hours not so many years ago so I don't have a physical problem at getting round. Remaining focused after Peel has always been my Achilles heel and it doesn't get any easier. Luckily on this occasion I teamed up with Selwyn Callister over the closing miles and that helped me to restore some sanity. Ironically, the event has turned into a love-hate relationship for me in recent years and just gets harder and harder with the passing of time.'

So, on a day of drama and excitement in equal measures, and one that will be remembered for many years to come, the final word must surely go to David Collister, who annually since 1984, has taken part in every Parish Walk and finished! Never away on holiday, never injured or ill, the landscape gardener from Archallagan has literally been to hell and back in his quest to accomplish 30 consecutive finishes – a record in itself and one unlikely to be repeated.

Although David didn't set out all those years ago to break any records, the annual pilgrimage around the 17 parishes has become a big part of his life with expectations high but failure never an option. Completing the holy grail of Manx athletics for a twentieth time was something special, but to follow that up a decade later and make it 30 just beggars belief!

Time stands still for no one, and at 59 years of age this was the toughest race David could ever remember. It was also his second-slowest and he was fortunate not to be timed out at the penultimate

church where he arrived just one minute inside the cut-off time. 'I was under pressure throughout to keep going and sick on several occasions during the latter stages,' he later said. 'The eight or so miles from Laxey to the finish were probably the most difficult I've ever undertaken. I was functioning on reserves alone and have nothing but praise for my support team who stubbornly willed me on to the finish with just 22 minutes to spare!'

So, with very little separating the Island's current top four distance walkers, what makes these men so special and rank in a league of their own? What drives them to such levels of athleticism and what strategy did each adopt to make this the second most exciting race of all time?

MICHAEL GEORGE:

It took a few days to regain a healthy perspective immediately following the 2012 race and in all honesty, the constant sympathy I was awarded for weeks after left me close to tears on many occasions. Immense doubts remained in my mind about both whether I would ever be able to circulate the course without suffering the debilitating sickness and if I could rediscover the will to put in such a high volume of training once again. However, it wasn't long before 'never again' became 'probably.'

A successful autumn saw me regain my Guernsey Church to Church title that I won in 2010. I also took the honours in Holland at the 50-kilometre Championship with a new personal best time. It wasn't until after an extended injury-motivation break that I began to train again for the Parish Walk in the New Year. It really surprised me how quickly my appetite for the road and my pace returned and it wasn't long before I was recording times that began to excite me.

The Manx Open 20-kilometre was held at the beginning of March and I finally managed to cross the line in under the 1 hour 40 minutes 45 seconds which I had set five years previously with a superb time of 97 minutes 33 seconds. Nevertheless, injury problems prevented me using the hills to practice, as well as severely curtailing the time spent walking with my friends and rivals during March and April.

The next big event was the Sara Killey, a 50-kilometre race which is run along the Parish Walk route from Peel to Ramsey. I started tired, not confident that I was fit enough and I had been overruled about tactics by my coaches. I set out to stretch the field, almost succeeding in breaking them but once again, it was Richard Gerrard who just refused to capitulate. Despite his pressure, I clung on for my third win, though by less than a minute.

It was a conversation I had later with Dave Mackey that probably directly led to my Parish victory a couple of months later. He was adamant that I just hadn't consumed enough liquids and though I dismissed it at the time, I investigated further and found that the stomach shuts down if it becomes dehydrated. All my years of failure, basically caused very simply, by not drinking enough.

RICHARD GERRARD:

The Parish Walk of 2007 was my first attempt and I got as far as Andreas. The following year, which was the wettest in living memory, I finished for the first time in just over 21 hours. Since then I have had five further finishes with my times steadily improving.

In terms of my training for the 2013 walk I didn't really stop over the winter, as I would still go out on Tuesday and Thursday evenings plus a longer session on most Saturday mornings.

Although an active footballer in the Veterans' League, my appearances were fairly limited during the 2012-2013 season as I was focusing on the Roubaix 28-hour walk in September 2012 followed by the Big Walk in Cape Town, South Africa two months later.

In the build-up to the Centenary Parish Walk, I achieved personal best times for 5 kilometres, 10 kilometres, 20 kilometres and 50 kilometres, so fitness and endurance was not an issue. As the event neared, I was training five or six days a week, building up to a peak weekly mileage of 50 miles walking and 15 miles running.

Unlike last year when I was uneasy about being favourite, I was much more relaxed on this occasion despite injuring my back two days earlier which required an emergency visit to the physio.

Only when I arrived at the NSC at half past seven on the morning of the walk was I reminded what a great event it is. Exchanging pleasantries and chatting to people I hadn't seen for a while provided me with greater encouragement and helped to relieve the pressure that is always present when one is favourite.

The race didn't start as quickly as I had expected, so I was quite happy to take things easily for the first few miles. Only after Santon did the pace start to pick up – the leading group whittled down to Michael, Vinny, Jock and myself. At that point we were all probably sizing each other up, looking for any sign of weakness and waiting to see if anyone would make a move. With the four of us training together on a regular basis, we know each other well and so chattered for much of the way round. Unfortunately, Jock suffered from cramp on the Ballakillowey climb, so although down to three, we fully expected him to make a recovery and catch us up.

Vinny, Michael and I continued together until just before Bride where we heard that Jock had reduced our lead from seven minutes to five. To be honest, we could have pushed it harder on this stretch and that seemed to be Michael's prompt to make a break and go on alone. I followed closely for a couple of hundred yards, but he was too quick for me, so I backed off a little in the hope of catching him on the more demanding section still to come.

I didn't feel great to Lezayre, but after checking in had I a good walk to Maughold, and feeling revitalised, joined the main road at the Hibernia in

excellent spirits. Here at the 71-mile mark, I heard the news that Michael was nearly six minutes ahead, so it was now or never to try and catch him.

Despite a concerted effort and closing the gap to three minutes at Glen Mona, Michael was a different man to the one I had met the previous year, when heading up to Lonan church and unsteady on his feet, he relinquished the lead soon after. This year the Douglas hotelier said a cheery hello as he sped past and I knew then I wouldn't catch him. Nevertheles, I was more than delighted with the runner-up spot and once again managed to break the 15-hour barrier. To my surprise, the final 18 miles were covered quicker than last year so breaking last year's all-time record is certainly a future possibility.

JOCK WADDINGTON:

Friends and rivals for many years, Vinny Lynch, Richard Gerrard and Michael George have raced against me on numerous occasions in recent years and we have all experienced success and failure at some stage. We know each other well, train together and can sometimes be found in a well-known upper Douglas public house discussing why the wheels fell off in a particular race. We also know each other's strengths and weaknesses. It is this friendship and competiveness which has seen the Parish Walk winning times plummet over the last five years.

In 2006, Sean Hands broke Derek Harrison's 27-year record by over 30 minutes and it was thought then that his new record time would remain intact for decades, so impressive was his time. Nevertheless, the winning times have been steadily coming down until last year when Sean's record was broken in some style by no less than three athletes in the same race.

Also worth noting is that although Derek's record stood firm for 27 years until 2006, it has been beaten ten times in the last four years so there was an expectation that the record could well be broken yet again this year

On the morning of the race, with around ten minutes until the start, the main protagonists ducked under the rope and made their way to the very front. Eager to get going, the countdown to the start is always a fractious time which ironically seems to fly and drag at the same time. Within the last ten seconds, the whole group of well over 13 hundred competitors counts the time down to zero and we're off.

The first few miles were at a steady but quick pace with the leading group consisting of Chris Cale, Brian Wade, David Mapp and Tony Okell as well as Richard, Vinny, Michael and myself. As with our regular training walks, we chatted inanely about nothing in particular, but unlike those sessions, there was an underlying tension which was almost palpable as each of us wrestled with our own curiosity of how each of the others was planning to tackle the race.

Although out of the limelight for the past two years, my plan was fairly simple in that I expected

2013

Michael to take to the front early on and gradually try to increase his lead as the race wore on. This was his tactic in 2012 and it almost paid off for him but for the tenacity of Richard and Vinny who wound him in towards the latter stages of that race.

With Michael taking the initiative, I expected Richard to go with him and for Vinny to either go with Richard or to up his pace and follow the other two at a manageable distance. I, on the other hand, was going to let them go as I had set myself the target of slightly over ten-minute miles and I knew that the others would be going quicker than that judging by the previous two years' statistics.

We walked together as a group of eight for about 12 miles before starting to fragment and by the time the leaders arrived at Rushen church, the group of eight was down to four. It was at this point that I started to go through a rough patch. I had felt fine until perhaps after Arbory church when my legs began to feel heavy and it was becoming more of an effort to keep up with Michael, Vinny and Richard. Of all the places to have a bad patch, heading to Ballakillowey and the Sloc has to be the worst place to have one.

As we left Rushen and headed north, I started to fall behind the others but I wasn't too concerned as I was about one minute ahead of my own time target at this point. My plan was to let them go and to reel them in later when they started to tire. I suffered leg cramps on a number of occasions which slowed me down even more. This was probably due to the very hot and sunny spell we were going through at that time and I may well have been a bit dehydrated.

On approaching the Round Table, I briefly saw Richard about 500 metres ahead of me. By the time I reached Peel the leading trio were over six minutes ahead of me. Again, I wasn't concerned as I was now two minutes ahead of my own schedule.

Six minutes doesn't sound too much, however, in real terms, it is well over half a mile on the road. As the route north from Peel to Kirk Michael is fairly straight, I thought I would see them at some point through the hedgerows but I never did.

At Kirk Michael, they had increased their lead by over a minute – the gap at the halfway mark now at nine minutes but feeling quite good having got over the earlier bad patch.

Approaching Jurby, I half expected to see them retracing their steps to the main road however they were already well on their way towards the prison which deflated me somewhat.

Still feeling good at this point, I continued on towards Bride. It is a journey of seven or so miles but feels twice that on a road that seems never ending. Once again, I had hoped to see what I was chasing. Seeing your target lifts your spirits and encourages you to try even harder. In reality though, I never saw them. I wasn't too bothered as I felt good and was coming to my favourite part of the course from Andreas to Maughold.

At Bride, I had reduced the deficit to six minutes. Again, I expected to see them on the long Burma Road leading to Andreas village, but I didn't. This began to play on my mind somewhat as I was working hard but not seemingly closing the gap as quickly as I had hoped. As I approached the village clock, I saw Michael heading out of Andreas closely followed by Richard with Vinny about 15 metres behind. Seeing them buoyed my mental strength for I now had a target to aim for.

At Andreas church, the gap had reduced to five and a half minutes. Everything seemed to be falling into place with the leading protagonists appearing to tire and the gap becoming smaller.

The biggest problem when catching the leaders in an event such as this is that it is now virtually impossible to 'sneak up' on them without them becoming aware of what is happening behind. The live radio coverage in conjunction with tracking systems and mobile phones makes it impossible to remain 'under the radar' so to speak. I was very aware that the gap was now down to a little over five minutes and it soon became obvious that the same information had filtered through to the leaders too as it was at this point that Michael upped his pace. Richard went with him but Vinny was struggling and losing touch – a situation I was unaware of as I rejoined the TT course at Sulby Bridge.

At Lezayre, I was five minutes behind what I presumed was the group of three. I had no idea that Vinny was now over two and a half minutes adrift of the leaders.

On the way to Ramsey, I started to feel rough again and was convinced that I was slowing down. I was but at the same time, my backup was telling me that Vinny was not far ahead so I kept on plugging away despite aching all over.

Approaching Maughold, I overheard Manx Radio's commentary announcing that Vinny had arrived at the church. So, although I couldn't see him, I knew he was only a few hundred metres ahead and would soon come into view.

I also knew at this point that my chances of winning this year had gone. Michael and Richard had

1974 finisher, Ron Ronan on point duty at Ballabeg corner.

just too much of a lead so I resigned to settling for the final podium spot.

Vinny has the remarkable ability to pace a race impeccably. In the last two 50-kilometre races we have competed in, I have shot off with child-like enthusiasm only to have Vinny wind me in and pass me with ten kilometres to go. It was therefore a nice change for me to catch him up on the punishing climb to Ballajora. He was suffering and had no energy at that point. Bearing in mind I last saw him at Andreas, it had taken me approximately 13 miles to overhaul him.

Tactically, the thing to do when you catch someone up is to shoot straight past, otherwise, if you slow down to chat, the chances are that the person being caught will start to mentally feel better because you are talking to them and they will also eat and drink and then, when they are feeling physically better, speed up. This is a bad thing and negates all the hard work previously done to reel them in in the first place.

Slowing to talk to Vinny who was more than glad of the company, we walked together for a mile or so chatting but as I was not feeling too bad at this point, I upped the pace slightly and Vinny started to drop back. I didn't think I would see him again.

I was now aware that Michael had pulled ten minutes ahead of us at this point with Richard three minutes behind him.

Elated at passing the Hibernia with just 14 miles to go, the route to Glen Mona is all downhill and perhaps my favourite section. Nevertheless, I was tiring on the approach to Laxey and could see Vinny about 200 metres behind me and appearing to close the gap.

At the old mining town, I discovered that Richard, who was in second place, was eight minutes ahead of me and that unless he got lost, there was no way I would even see him let alone catch him up. I resigned myself to third place providing I could fend off Vinny with a pointy stick as he was obviously feeling much better now and was gaining on me and less than a minute behind. It was now a case of gritted teeth and determination for the remaining seven miles to the finish.

At Onchan, Vinny and I passed in the dip on Church Road which meant I had 200 metres on him – a gap he was more than capable of closing in the remaining two miles.

The final mile or so along Douglas Promenade seems to go on forever. Walking within the cycle way I had a few glances over my shoulder to keep a wary eye on Vinny who was closing rapidly. Or was it my imagination? A young boy shouted to me at one point 'Don't let him catch you, Mister.' I had no intentions of letting that happen and crossed the finish line in third place with Vinny right on my tail and only 30 seconds behind.

As is now customary, we all met up the following day at the pub to discuss the previous day's events and to establish where things went wrong, but also to congratulate Michael on his richly-deserved and definitely overdue win.

VINNY LYNCH

One of only two people to have jointly won the Parish Walk, Irishman Vinny Lynch had great difficulty in getting motivated for the centenary event in 2013.

Without making excuses, my performance this year was a little disappointing and probably due to a lack of fitness inspite of intense training from February onwards. I use several training routes including a loop from Douglas to Glen Roy of approximately 20 miles. A shorter loop of ten miles around the Groudle area is ideal on winter days when daylight is at a minimum.

Teaming up with Jock and Richard on most weekends, Vinny tries to walk the entire course in set stages throughout the winter.

If the weather is half-decent, I sometimes walk to work – a distance of seven miles from Douglas to the airport so its all good training for an event I would dearly love to win outright.

Whatever people may think, those at the sharp end of race walking suffer just as much, if not more, than those walking just for fun. When Michael made the break at Bride I had nothing left. My reserves were just about depleted making the final 15 miles the most difficult in my life. Nevertheless, my advice to any budding finisher is to remain focused, mentally strong and you will achieve the ultimate dream.

A well deserved victory for Michael George.

Fact File Parish Walk

ALL THE WINNERS

The *Isle of Man Times* promoted the first Parish Walk in 1913 which produced 12 starters. Harry Bridson led five finishers home in a time of 18 hours 56 minutes for the estimated 80-mile circuit.

There were only two competitors in the next event, held in 1923 and won by Gerald Bridson in 20 hours 23 minutes.

In 1924, again only two starters came to the line with Gerald successfully defending his title against 15-year-old schoolboy, Marshall Braide in 20 hours exactly.

Now in its sixth decade, the revived Parish Walk is undoubtedly the Island's most prestigious race walking meeting. Over the years, it has produced some outstanding performances in 52 events. No one in 1960 could have foreseen over two hundred finishers in the year 2013 and the question now asked by many is how much more can it grow?

There were five events held over the 85-mile course during the period 1960 to 1964 and organised by the Manx Amateur Athletics Association. The leading competitor in those races was Henry Harvey, a farmer from Abbeylands who won the event in 1961, 1962 and again in 1964, his last victory being his fastest in a superb time of 16 hours 21 minutes 06 seconds.

Another fine walker was Onchan postman Stanley Cleator. He won the very first race in 1960 in 19 hours 50 minutes 30 seconds – the slowest time ever recorded. The following two years he had to settle for the runner-up spot to Henry Harvey.

The 1963 event was won by Joe Brown of Laxey in a fine time of 17 hours 04 minutes 09 seconds. Willie Kneale claimed the runner-up with Douglas Corkill third. It was a race that saw two ladies finish for the very first time – Eunice Davies claiming fifth spot in 20 hours 51 minutes 24 seconds but over two hours ahead of Irene Cottier who was sixth.

With no events in 1965 or 1966, it was in 1967 that British International Albert Johnson cracked the Parish Walk sixteen-hour barrier for the very first time, taking nearly half an hour off Henry Harvey's record with a time of 15 hours 54 minutes 51 seconds.

There was controversy in 1968 with two winners claiming the title. Leece Kneale was first to cross the finish line in 16 hours 05 minutes 52 seconds. However, the Laxey walker was entered in the non-athletic section so the winning trophy was awarded to 29-year-old Ian Turnbull, the next to finish but nearly one and a half hours later.

Twenty-one-year-old Ian Hodgkinson made history in 1969 by becoming the youngest-ever winner in a time of 17 hours 11 minutes 25 seconds.

The new decade saw an English visitor Dudley Seddon claim the title in 17 hours 21 minutes 49 seconds.

In 1971, we were entertained by the closest finish ever with just 54 seconds separating Graham Young and Derek Harrison. With the gap down to 300 yards

on Central Promenade, spectators were treated to a nail-biting finish that saw the Douglas postman claim the first of his two victories in a new record time of 15 hours 43 minutes 12 seconds.

A year later, Derek went one step better, winning in 16 hours 19 minutes 15 seconds – his second best time for the course.

Derek won again in 1973, his time of 16 hours 36 minutes 04 seconds nearly two and a half hours ahead of runner-up Steve Gardner who completed the course for a third time in as many years. Only six of the 46 starters reached the finish.

A large contingent of walkers from Ireland made a big impression in 1974 with Irish International John (Paddy) Dowling taking the honours in an excellent time of 16 hours 40 minutes 07 seconds. Ian Turnbull claimed the runner-up spot 27 minutes later, some three and a half hours ahead of Ron Ronan, the third and final finisher from a field of 94.

English walkers stamped their authority on the 1975 event with Ted Warner taking the title in 18 hours 49 minutes 52 seconds. His Leicester team mate Bill Roe took the runner-up spot in the third slowest race ever.

Commonwealth Games walker John Cannell, a postman from Douglas, won the first of his six races in 1976 in a time of 17 hours 28 minutes 12 seconds having finished second nine years earlier.

1977 was the year the elements claimed all but one of the 90 starters. The scorching temperatures that day saw the field reduced to 23 by Kirk Michael. At daybreak, only seven were left on the road. Three made it to Maughold but Simon Capelen and Jeff Clayton called time there leaving Castletown's Steve Gardener as the sole finisher in 19 hours 11 minutes 01 second.

Murray Lambden was a popular winner in 1978. His time of 16 hours 19 minutes 37 seconds was the fifth fastest time ever recorded in a race which produced only eight finishers.

Millennium year in 1979 saw Derek Harrison quite literally sprinting around the 17 parishes in 15 hours 20 minutes 51 seconds – a record time never thought possible and one that stood for the following 27 years.

Derek won the race again in 1980, albeit at a more subdued pace of 16 hours 13 minutes 10 seconds. Irene Corlett was a popular runner-up in a race that produced only seven finishers.

John Cannell recorded a fast time of 16 hours 15 minutes 11 seconds in 1981 to win the event for a second time and finish nearly two and a half hours ahead of runner-up, Frank Dolan. The following year, John won in convincing style, becoming the fourth walker to record a sub-16-hour time. In the same race, Irene Corlett set the fastest-ever time to Peel in the ladies' class by recording a superb time of 5 hours 23 minutes 16 seconds.

The first hat-trick of consecutive wins came in 1983 when John Cannell won the event in a slightly slower time of 16 hours 31 minutes 38 seconds.

Approaching his fiftieth birthday in 1984, Derek Harrison won the event for a fifth time in 16 hours 10 minutes 17 seconds. Twelve months later, Colby's Willie Corkill was first across the line in 16 hours 29 minutes 31 seconds.

Willie again won the events of 1986 and 1987 in times of 17 hours 03 minutes 45 seconds and 16 hours 58 minutes 33 seconds respectively to become only the second competitor in the history of the event to record a hat-trick of wins.

Martin Lambden was a surprise but popular winner in 1988, out-sprinting Charlie Weston at Laxey to record a time of 17 hours 12 minutes 01 seconds.

Nevertheless, Charlie made up for his disappointment the following year in by winning the event in 18 hours 17 minutes 55 seconds. It was a wonderful achievement for the veteran who had been runner-up on three previous occasions.

Making his Parish Walk debut in 1990, Foxdale schoolteacher Gordon Vale won the first CMI sponsored event in 17 hours 55 minutes 10 seconds. Only six of the 154 starters finished.

Charlie Weston was again victor in 1991, the 57-year-old Londoner completing the 85 miles in 17 hours 46 minutes 58 seconds – some 18 minutes in front of Chris Keown.

Graham Young made a welcome return in 1992 and repeated his victory of 21 years past in a fine 16 hours 38 minutes 27 seconds.

Another on the comeback trail in 1993 and 1994 was John Cannell. He won both events comfortably from twice runner-up Lee Cain in times of 16 hours 11 minutes 11 seconds and 16 hours 13 minutes 46 seconds respectively.

In 1995, 62-year-old Centurion Brian Ashwell became the oldest-ever winner of the Manx Harriers classic with a world-class performance of 16 hours 37 hours 47 seconds.

After many attempts, and at least once getting lost, Trollaby farmer Lee Cain earned a well-deserved victory in 1996 with a time of 17 hours 26 minutes 29 seconds.

Former Metropolitan policeman Chris Flint won the 1997 event at his very first attempt in 17 hours 36 minutes 40 seconds. A year later, fellow Centurion and visitor to the Island Richard Brown produced the first sub-16-hour time since John Cannell's epic walk in 1982. After completing the 85 miles in 15 hours 59 minutes 44 seconds at his very first attempt, Brown continued for an extra 15 miles on Douglas Promenade to win the first-ever 100-mile race held on the Island, and the only event of its kind staged in Britain that year.

Chris Flint won the event for a second time in 1999 with a much improved time of 17 hours 07 minutes 46 seconds in a race that only 21 finished.

Glen Vine's Peter Kaneen won the first event of the new millennium just six seconds inside 17 hours. Arch-rival Robbie Callister convincingly won the next two events in creditable times of 16 hours 59 minutes 27 seconds and 16 hours 34 minutes 30 seconds respectively.

However, the Island's marathon champion failed to make it a hat-trick of wins in 2003 when he was convincingly beaten into second place by Peter Kaneen. It was the second fastest Parish Walk ever with Kaneen coming to within five minutes of the all-time record set by Derek Harrison nearly a quarter of a century earlier.

Nevertheless, quick to shake off disappointment, Callister trained exceptionally hard for the 2004 event, and after leading through the early stages, extended his lead considerably to record the third fastest-ever time through the 17 parishes. His superb time of 15 hours 26 minutes 31 seconds was only 24 seconds outside Peter Kaneen's time 12 months earlier.

Increasing his tally of wins to four in 2005, Callister's superb time of 15 hours 24 minutes 24 seconds was overshadowed by his failure to improve on Derek Harrison's all-time record set in 1979. There were 63 finishers in this race which was televised for the very first time.

Twice runner-up, but never far from Callister's shadow, 44-year-old Sean Hands produced a masterclass in race walking intelligence in 2006 to bring to an end Derek Harrison's incredible long-standing record and enter the record books as the first person to walk the course in under 15 hours.

Style may not be Robbie Callister's forte but he was still sharp enough to win in 2007 and silence those critics who maintained his best days were behind him. Dominating the race from Ballakillowcy onwards, the 52-year-old went on to increased his tally of wins to five and now remains one short of John Cannell's all-time record of six wins.

The Parish Walk of 2008 will be remembered as the wettest and arguably the toughest of all. From start to finish, the wind and rain never stopped, making life difficult for the record entry who took part. Having taken command of the lead on the lower slopes of the Sloc, favourite Sean Hands came to a grinding halt at Sulby Bridge leaving the relatively unknown Jock Waddington to soldier on and become only one of 121 finishers to complete the arduous journey on the same day it started. Robbie Callister once again claimed a runner-up spot with Maurice Bellando third.

In spite of more favourable weather, Jock Waddington's victory in 2009 was still a minute shy on his time 12 months earlier. Securing the lead from arch-rival Robbie Callister at Kirk Michael, the quietly spoken, but cheerful 46-year-old had to dig into his deepest reserves over the final miles to hold off Janice Quirk who fell short by 12 minutes of becoming the event's first ever female champion.

With Sean Hand's suffering from long-term injury and Robbie Callister approaching his twilight years, the 2010 event turned into a one-horse race soon after the 20-mile mark with Jock Waddington beating off a strong challenge to claim a hat-trick of wins from one of the toughest fields the competition has ever seen.

Fact File Parish Walk

Life in the fast lane got really serious in 2011. In Parish Walk history, few men have announced their greatness like Jock Waddington. But even fewer men have defended this great title, and no man has won the event more than three times consecutively. When the Douglas civil servant crossed the finish line on Douglas Promenade to win the event for a fourth time, he not only became one of the greatest walkers the Island had ever seen – he also became a legend. There seems no limit to what this man can do – five, six, even seven titles are possible thus putting his outstanding record number of wins out of reach forever!

Every great story needs a great ending and this was the year to tell it. Collaborating in the fastest and probably the most exciting race of all time, Irishman Vinny Lynch and Manxman Richard Gerrard, quite simply tore up the record books in 2012 to become the first-ever joint winners in a new record time of 14 hours 42 minutes 03 seconds. Although the Island was buzzing with excitement throughout this momentous day, the real hero was perhaps 47-year-old Douglas hotelier Michael George who led the race for the best part of 60 miles only to come up short when it mattered most.

Redeeming himself after last year's bitterly disappointing result, Michael George won the 2013 centenary event in the third fastest time ever recorded. Unusual for the leading trio to stay together for the best part of 50 miles, the Douglas hotelier took the initiative soon after Bride and from that point was never seriously challenged. Although the entry was significantly down on previous years, a record 215 walkers made it back to Douglas.

THE ORGANISATION

The Parish Walk was revived in 1960 under the auspices of the Manx Amateur Athletic Association, later renamed the Manx Athletic Club.

Haydn Wood, Arthur Currie and John Quine were the men behind the event and it is thanks to their foresight that we now have the modern multi-participant Parish Walk. Following two absentee years, 1965 and 1966, the Boundary Harriers took over the organisation of the race in 1967.

In 1991 the Boundary Harriers merged with the Manx Athletic Club to form the Manx Harriers, the club that continues to organise the Parish Walk to the present.

During the late 1970s and 80s interest in the Parish Walk ebbed and flowed, but it was one man, Arthur Jones, who by his enthusiasm and hard work kept the race going.

Not only was Arthur the race secretary but he also took part in the race, walking to Peel on many occasions wearing a pair of sandals. Following a brief rest at his home in Ballasalla he would be telephoned when the first walker reached Maughold so that he could man the check-in point at Lonan. Here, while waiting for the last walkers to pass through, he would write out the certificates for the finishers.

Arthur was a great man for recycling and he was ingenious in hand-making the numbers, reflective bibs, scorecards and checkers' boards. When he retired as race secretary in 1994, he handed over one box with all the parish walk equipment. In 2013, paraphernalia required to stage the event filled a whole barn!

Since 1995, an extended committee under the chairmanship of Raymond Cox has organised the race on behalf of the Manx Harriers, during which time actual starters have grown from 269 to a record 1505 in 2012. The event originally was targeted at long-distance walkers who wished to take up the 85-mile challenge. During the late 90s and well into the new millennium, the event attracted a much broader entry with the race becoming a national event with over two per cent of the population taking part, many raising thousands of pounds for their chosen charities.

The bringing on board of corporate sponsorship, first done in 1990, has provided the resources to upgrade the infrastructure and improve the Parish Walk experience to a high level. CMI were the first main sponsor and they supported the event until 2011 under the guises of Clerical Medical and Scottish Widows. In 2012, Manx Telecom who had been the results and timing sponsor since 2007 took over as headline sponsor of the race.

Planning and organising for the forthcoming Parish Walk starts in the July of the previous year when the nine-person committee meet to review the recently held event and record the suggestions for future changes and improvements. Each of the committee has his or her own role as, with the massive growth in entry numbers, it now requires a huge amount of effort to co-ordinate a vast number of agencies ranging from the police, civil defence and first aiders, to private companies who supply the feed stations along the course.

Raymond Cox, a finisher in his one and only attempt at the Parish in 1994, is the current race director. He oversees all aspects of the organisation and liaises closely with main sponsors Manx Telecom and all the other companies that supply goods and services for the event. Over the winter months new improvements to the set-up are discussed during the monthly meetings and put into action during the spring in readiness for the big day in mid-summer. Race day is usually the Saturday closest to the longest day to ensure maximum daylight for the competitors.

The Race secretary is Liz Corran, another very experienced race-walker. Her very demanding role in dealing with the huge number of entrants has been vastly aided by technology. The old days of paper-based entries have given way to all online entries being made via the excellent website www..parishwalk.com. Murray Lambden, winner in 1978, maintains this site and while not on the organising committee he spends considerable time providing backup to the organisers and maintains a steady flow of information to perspective walkers via the website. Murray is also the official statistician of the Parish Walk and has created a mind boggling array of stats on the race over the years.

Kevin Walmsley has been associated with the organisation since the early 1990s and now assumes the role of Course Director and also acts as a race referee. Kevin oversees the placing of safety notices around the course and the smooth running of the feed stations during the early part of the route. He follows the last walkers during the night and closes the check-in points once the last walker has passed through. Ensuring walker safety during the hours of darkness around the narrow roads in the north of the island is one of his responsibilities as well as checking that the rules are obeyed, both by the walkers and their support crew. Even when the last walker has reached Douglas Promenade, by Sunday morning Kevin still has tasks to carry out as he co-ordinates the prize presentation evening which, given the large number of finishers over the last decade, has become a very big affair. He receives help from both his sister Debbie Surgeon and father Geoff Walmsley, who are Assistant Course Directors.

Chief Marshal is Winston Liu who, with some 150 volunteers, maintains the highest level of safety for the walkers. With upwards of 1,500 walkers in close proximity over the first part of the course, he and his team have important responsibilities in keeping the race flowing and also in dealing with the traffic problems that accompany the walk.

With the rise in race numbers over the years, increasing pressure was brought to bear on those charged with checking in each walker at the churches. Long gone was the system whereby the vicars of each church stayed up during the night to mark the walkers' cards. For many years teams of people manually checked in the walkers, passing the completed sheets to the results team of Karen Kneale and Martin Lambden, himself a Parish Walk winner in 1988. Dealing with the results improved with the advent of computers during the 1980s and 90s. However the biggest advance came in 2007, when courtesy of Manx Telecom and Sport Ident, the entire timing and results system became electronic. By using state of the art electronic equipment every walker could check in at the various churches and not only have their time recorded automatically but also have this information relayed instantly to the results website allowing the rest of the world to follow on their computers or mobile phones.

Allan Callow, the second fastest man ever to Peel, is in charge of marking the course. This is particularly important on the latter part of the course when walkers must find their way on unfamiliar roads – many of them in darkness. Mile markers, lights and directional arrows are now the norm. However in the early decades of the race, walkers had to find their own way, which led to many incidences of them going astray. In order to help walkers find the correct route, a pillion passenger on a scooter ahead of the leaders would sprinkle white chalk dust on the road

at various junctions indicating the way ahead. It was certainly effective providing it remained dry and the wind did not blow! A trophy called the Scooter Man Cup was once presented in memory of this service.

Allan can't remember when he first started marking out the course – but it was a long time ago. 'The Parish Walk has been a big part of my life since my teenage years,' he recently said. 'I watched those early pioneers of this great event wending their way through the streets of Douglas, some looking far from athletic in their attempt to take on what appeared to me to be an impossible task.'

It requires a huge number of people to ensure that the Parish Walk goes ahead without mishap. Many officials have carried out the same role for many years, turning out at all hours often in bad weather. These people are not paid for their efforts but they give time freely because they all have one thing in common, a love for this unique challenge that is known as the Parish Walk. Everyone connected to the walk enjoys the agony and the ecstasy of each individual's adventure whether that be to walk to Santon or complete the full 85 miles back to Douglas Promenade.

Since Allan's involvement, the event has grown in stature and is now considered to be the most eagerly awaited athletic feature on the Manx sporting calendar. The event has changed considerably since 1960 with four different starting points and nine different starting times. It has also become hugely popular in recent years with an entry exceeding 700 in 2001 that required the traditional starting point at the Villa Marina Gardens to be abandoned in favour of the National Sports Centre.

Safety concerns and road traffic congestion in recent years have seen road closures and traffic restricted to one-way in the direction of the race. A major change to the course was introduced in 2006 with the route above the Blackboards diverted at Orrisdale to avoid the centre of Ballasalla. The resultant change in distance was then adjusted at the start to retain the overall distance of 85 miles.

A temporary change to the routing of the course occurred in 1984 when a rock slide on the coast road at Bulgan necessitated a diversion over Ballaragh. A decade later Peel town centre was closed due to cart racing, requiring the course to be diverted at Patrick. It also added an extra mile to the overall distance making it the longest Parish Walk ever.

There is no doubt that road surfaces are a vast improvement on those of yesteryear. Nevertheless, road camber still presents a challenge with one leg often having to work harder than the other. In the Andreas area, pavements are so poorly maintained that walking on the road and facing oncoming traffic is recommended as a safer option. Although Roman soldiers probably marched on the left because the sword was on the left side and drawn by the right hand, it was not until the late eighteenth century and during the French Revolution that Napoleon ordered all traffic including his troops to march on the right.

Fact File Parish Walk

Irrespective of whatever side of the road we walk on, one obstacle today's competitors no longer confront are the railway crossings at Marown, White Strand, Ballaugh and Sulby, all sadly confined to history with the closure of the Douglas to Ramsey railway in 1968.

Throughout its long history the Parish Walk has constantly adapted to ever-changing health and safety requirements. Other than the tragic death of a 17-year-old pacer during the 1968 relay race, the event has had an exemplary safety record second to none. The modern-day format may bare little resemblance to that held in 1913 however the course remains largely unchanged and is one those early pioneers would still recognise.

CHANGES TO THE ROUTE

Over the years, the Parish Walk has seen many start times and changes to its defined route. The first race in 1913 started outside the Palace gates on Douglas Promenade. Competitors initially headed west before turning up Broadway, following York and Stoney roads to the Quarter Bridge and then on to Braddan. Here at the first church, competitors could take any route of their choice – through country lanes, farmyards, over the fields, in fact whatever way they wished, providing each parish church was reached in the correct order.

Beyond Jurby, the route differed considerably from that of today. Leaving the whitewashed church overlooking the sea, competitors had a choice of route to Andreas, entering the village at the same point that today's walkers depart.

With the Burma Road a quarter of a century away from construction, Bride was reached by following the old loop road through the now decommissioned Andreas airfield to its junction at Thurot Cottage. It is uncertain which direction the route took from this point on but more than likely it followed the Kimmeragh road to Bride and thence to Glascoe and Regaby. From here on, it's probable that walkers took a direct course across open fields to the Garey before crossing the TT course at Lezayre. This would certainly account for the course at that time being considerably shorter.

The first of the present day races took place in 1960 and was organised by the Manx Amateur Athletics Association. At a hastily convened meeting on 10th March 1960, the committee announced plans to reintroduce the event following the route of the ancient 17 parish churches in a southerly and clockwise direction. Unlike earlier events, competitors leaving Jurby headed to Bride and then Andreas before turning south to Lezayre. They were required to touch the front door of each parish church to complete an overall distance of 85 miles before the race closed at midnight on the second day.

The starting place was somewhat different to that of today with the race beginning on Upper Church Street at the junction of Hope Street and Myrtle Street, close to the site of the now demolished Athol Garage.

Competitors taking part in this revived Parish Walk were unaware of the demanding physical and mental requirements and for some, their training and preparation was limited. No one had attempted a walk of this magnitude and no advice was readily available. There were no performance-enhancing shoes or modern-day energy drinks, yet their times recorded were comparable with, if not better than, those of today.

The race started in Douglas at 7:00pm on Friday 13th April with most of the competitors going straight from work to the start line. Considerable media attention focused on the 35 starters, however the daunting 85-mile task was too much for many and only four made it back to the war memorial on Douglas Promenade.

The event continued in this format the following year, however in 1962 and 1963 the ladies started at 6:30pm followed by the men an hour and a half later.

Upper Church Street continued to be the preferred starting venue for the 1964 event which saw the ladies setting off at 7:00pm followed by the men an hour later.

No races were held in 1965 or 1966. However Boundary Harriers took over the organisation of the event in 1967 and have been associated with it ever since. That year the start was moved to the Villa Marina Arcade with a start time of 6:55pm for the ladies and 7:00pm for the men. The course still measured 85 miles because competitors were no longer required to touch the door of each church and thus the effective distance was comparable to the 1960 to 1964 events. Unlike previous years, mid-May was now the preferred month with longer daylight and more favourable weather. The event continued in this format until 1973 when the race started an hour later at 8:00pm.

There was a new afternoon starting time in 1974 with the ladies setting off at 2:55pm and the men five minutes later.

Between 1975 and 1978, the ladies started at 2:30pm with the men half an hour later.

Mylchreest Motors began its eleven-year sponsorship of the event in 1979 which coincided with the F.A. Cup Final between Arsenal and Manchester United. Consequently, the event on Saturday 12th May saw the ladies starting at 5:30pm followed by the men half an hour later.

In 1980, the entry exceeded 100 for the very first time. The race retained its Saturday 3:00pm start time but moved to mid-June to coincide with the longest day of the year. It remained in this format until 1986, retaining its venue at the Villa Marina Arcade but moving to an earlier start time of 11:30am for the ladies and 12 noon for the men.

With ever-increasing entry numbers, the start moved to the Villa Marina Gardens in 1987. Starting times were retained, however competitors were no longer required to check in at the first church at

Braddan. The format lasted until 1991 and, with the leading lady walkers now capable of reaching Peel under six hours, a joint start time of 11:30am was introduced the following year and changed again in 1995 to 12 noon.

Clerical Medical International were the new sponsors in 1990 and with their involvement, the event grew steadily with entry numbers close to the six hundred-mark by the end of the decade.

With safety awareness becoming more important than ever by the turn of the century, race organisers in consultation with the police, introduced restrictions to motor vehicles accessing those parts of the course deemed to be unsafe. The Glen Darragh Road to the Braaid crossroads was restricted to one-way vehicular traffic in the direction of the race. The Clannagh Road to the Castletown Road was closed and the Oatlands Road to Santon, leading to the Blackboards, was also one-way in the direction of the race.

The closure of the Villa Marina for refurbishment forced Manx Harriers to look for an alternative start venue in 2001. The huge increase in entry numbers, plus concern for road safety seemed the perfect opportunity to make use of the new National Sports Centre just a mile away.

With the new venue came a new and earlier start time of 10:00am which greatly alleviated many of the logistical problems faced by the organising committee. To maintain the historic distance and retain Braddan Bridge as the two-mile mark, competitors first completed a lap of the inner and outer track of the NSC before proceeding along the TT access road to the River Walk housing estate. From this point, steps were then retraced to the Jubilee oak tree on the Douglas to Peel road before continuing to Marown.

There were several advantages for the early start. Mid-morning rush hour was now avoided which in recent years had been a major concern for the police. The earlier finish was also beneficial to race officials and competitors, who after a long and tiring day, could get to bed at a more civilised hour.

Nevertheless, perhaps one point overlooked by the organisers was the public viewing aspect of the event, which until 2001 benefited only spectators living in the south and west of the Island. Now for the very first time, those living in the northern parishes could view the event in daylight hours.

With over 800 walkers taking to the road in 2002, the temporary one-way road system for vehicular traffic introduced in recent years was now extended to the south of the Island. The Sloc Road leading from Ballakillowey to the Round Table and Dalby was also one-way, again in the direction of the race.

But cars are very much part of the Parish Walk.

The Manx Harriers Committee 2013.

Fact File Parish Walk

Love or hate them – they just won't go away! With so many service vehicles parked on the road above Ballasalla in 2006, organisers the following year had no option other than to re-route the course more safely via the Orrisdale and St. Marks roads. The slight difference in distance was again adjusted at the NSC with competitors completing only one lap of the inner track before departing for Quarter Bridge.

Nevertheless, the measures introduced did little to alleviate the problem. As entry numbers increased, so too did the number of vehicles servicing them. In 2008, a traffic jam between Ballasalla and Rushen nearly four miles long left many competitors at the rear of the field unable to maintain pace with their support crews which were advancing little better than funeral pace. In the wettest Parish Walk ever, 31-year-old Anne Dudley lost all touch with her support crew on leaving the Braaid. Unsuitably attired, without food or water and soaked to the skin, the Steam Packet stewardess walked all the way to Rushen protected by an improvised bin bag generously donated by a concerned onlooker.

There is no doubt that race organisers in the future will have to consider adopting more draconian measures to avoid the event becoming a victim of its own success. Support crews are not utilised when training through the winter months so why should race day be any different? There are plenty of drink stations en route and the majority of competitors are more than capable of walking the first 20 miles or so without backup.

Since 1960, the Island's population has nearly doubled while vehicle ownership during the same period has quadrupled. Today's car is so sophisticated that some motorists feel they are a better and safer driver when surrounded by distractions such as mobile phone texting and in-car entertainment systems – both of which contribute to a lowering of driving standards thus making pedestrians more vulnerable. That said, the event's safety record is second to none with only one serious incident noted in the history of the event.

Nevertheless, compliance with ever-changing health and safety requirements is paramount to the continuing safe-running and success of this long-established event. For those with short memories, recently introduced safety requirements have seen the demise of the TT Walk, TT Relay Walk, Douglas to Castletown Run, Boundary Stroll, Millennium Way Relay and the Peel to Douglas Run, the latter celebrating its golden jubilee in 2000 but now relegated to a cross-country run along the dismantled Peel to Douglas railway.

HIGHWAYS OF THE ISLAND

What of the roads over which this extraordinary event has been staged over the last one hundred years?

Until the motor car first appeared on the Island at the turn of the nineteenth century, roads were little more than dirt tracks that turned to mud in the winter

and baked rock hard during the summer. Movement along them was often difficult, and at certain times of the year, practically impossible. Nevertheless, improvements made to roads throughout the twentieth century have resulted in them being surfaced with smooth tarmacadam laid by machine or surfaced with chippings. It is easy to walk on them and even the minor roads carry less camber than previously, all of which is conducive to race walking techniques.

As we have seen this has not always been the case and roads were very different in 1913 when Harry Bridson won the first Parish Walk. He and his fellow competitors wore no special clothing, walked in their normal footwear and were oblivious to the task in hand.

Barely recognisable as a roadway, the 'Baare-ny-Ree' runs through the centre of the Island from Skyhill in the north to Castletown Rushen in the south. Almost certainly the oldest highway on the Isle of Man, the ancient track of approximately 28 miles is well worn having been neglected and badly damaged by numerous motorcycles over the years.

Also known as the 'Road of the King,' the Baare-ny-Ree was quite literally the road along which the king would travel to his dwelling places in the south and west after landing at the preferred northern port of Ramsey. In the fourteenth century, the monks of Rushen Abbey wrote about it in the 'Chronicle of Man' and it is quite probable that the road existed in a more primitive form long before then.

Prior to 1690, roads in the Island were no more than rough tracks wide enough to allow a horse with two creels to pass and generally used by people on foot to get to school or church. They were often muddy in winter and dusty in summer. Repair of these roads was the responsibility of the Captains of the Parishes and they used the local militia to carry out any repair.

After 1690, Tynwald, the Island's parliament, passed legislation transferring responsibility for maintenance to the Parish Overseer. He was given statutory powers to instruct adjoining landowners and occupiers to provide labour and tools to carry out such repair as he instructed. It should be remembered that at this time there was no formal drainage and water ran in open ditches which also had to be maintained.

The first Act of Tynwald to specifically address highways was the Highway Act of 1713 which gave the Parish Overseer more powers to fine those who failed to provide the necessary labour to maintain the roads. Subsequent legislation gave power to levy taxes but retained the statutory requirement for landowners to provide labour and materials and even stated 'repair of roads to be by the publick (sic) labour of the parish as required.' To ensure that the Parish Overseer discharged his duties a General Supervisor was appointed.

A good indication of the state of the highways was illustrated in the report of a disastrous fire which occurred at King William's College in Castletown in 1844. Castletown was the Island's capital and although the garrison had turned out to fight the fire, it was clear that help was needed. A rider on horseback was dispatched to Douglas for the only fire engine on the Island and five hours later it reached the College! It had been stuck in ruts and mud on the way. Clearly something more needed to be done.

Following the Highway Act of 1776, James Hamilton was appointed as the first Surveyor General and given authority to improve highways. He reported to the Committee of Highways which became the forerunner of the Highway and Transport Board. Not surprisingly, they instructed that the first highway to be improved should be the Douglas to Castletown highway. It was also the first mention of the width of such highways which were to be constructed eight yards wide (7.4 metres). By the end of the century, improved roads brought about the start of the coaching age, the first four-wheeled carriage arriving on the Island about 1780.

Stage coaches started to operate from 1805, the first was named 'Speculation Diligence' and was scheduled to take six hours for the journey from Ramsey to Douglas so clearly more improvements were needed.

At the height of the coaching era in the mid-nineteenth century, it was reckoned that Douglas had 45 livery stables, Ramsey 12 and Castletown 11 which gives some idea of the extent of this form of transport. Departing at 8 o'clock each morning, the Island's three coaching companies offered a round trip service to the four towns with fares starting at four shillings (20p) for a single journey from Douglas to Ramsey via Peel.

Coach journeys in England took even longer. Seven days were required to travel from London to York and 14 to Edinburgh. Nevertheless, the golden age of coaching lasted less than 40 years – its demise brought about by the rapid development of the railways.

Motor vehicles first came to the Island in 1899 – George Gilmore, telegraph engineer and pioneer of the Manx telephone system, was one of only three owners at the turn of the century. In fact only 23 cars were registered on the Island in 1903 – a figure that had grown to 331 by 1913.

These were soon followed by charabanc and by buses in Douglas from 1914. Nevertheless, the motor bus didn't appear on country roads until 1927 with introduction of the Manxland Bus Service.

Gradually, the provision of labour passed to the Committee of Highways and the network of roads that we have today came into being. Not all roads were surfaced in 1913, many were just bound with inferior macadam. In some town areas, the roads were bound together by tar from local gasworks.

In 1923, following a report to government on the condition of the Island's roads, it was resolved that all of the Island's roads were to be constructed with a proper foundation of crushed stone and finished with tarred chippings and then rolled. Steam rollers were introduced and stone crushing plant installed at the largest of the old parish quarries throughout the Island.

When Harry Bridson completed his walk in 1913, he would have not have encountered much traffic and most definitely would have needed to wear his boots because roads such as the Sloc were still not completely surfaced as many were in the north. Even up until 1960, walking on the roads was not without difficulty. Many had extreme cambers leading to problems with hips and ankles and foot blisters.

After the mid-1950s, a stone-coating plant installed at Poortown Quarry ensured that all future roads on the Island would have a machine-laid macadam surface and a programme of major reconstruction and widening of the Island's main roads followed. At that time no one could have envisaged the dramatic increase in vehicular traffic that we have today on the Island's 500 miles of roads.

COURAGEOUSNESS

In addition to having grown into the largest social competitive event in the island, the Parish Walk has possibly also become the biggest event drawing sponsorship for charities. Of recent times it has also produced instances of courage and determination that should be an example to us all.

At the age of twenty, Ed Kelly of Onchan entered the 2002 Parish Walk with a group of friends from work "for the fun of it", but surpassed himself by being one of the first of the under 21's to arrive at Rushen. Four months later, this perfectly healthy young man suffered a brain stem stroke, just three days after his 21st birthday. Very few people survive a stroke of this nature, and he was flown by air

Ed Kelly meets the vicar of Braddan Church.

Fact File Parish Walk

ambulance to Liverpool. Quadraplegic, he spent six weeks on life support and a total of eight months at the Walton Neurological Centre, followed by a further two months at Newlands.

Unable at first to even sit up by himself, he had to learn to both walk and speak again, as well as coping with other simple daily tasks - setting himself targets all the time. Upon his return home he was determined to enter the Parish Walk, setting Braddan as his target. Two miles may not seem a great distance, but it represented a huge step in his battle as a stroke survivor. It was the 2005 Parish Walk that he entered, with full coverage of his ordeal, virtually step by step, by the local newspapers. They told of the cars 'tooting' support, and of tearful strangers approaching and handing over donations for the Manx Stroke Foundation. One young mother brought her children "to show what grit and determination is" she told the reporter, as Ed slowly passed along the TT Access Road.

At the end of his two and a half hour battle to cover the two miles to Braddan Church, Ed was personally welcomed by the vicar, Rev. Canon Philip Frear. In the weeks that ensued, sponsorship came in from all over the island, resulting in £14,000 being raised for the local charity and the Walton Neurological Rehab Centre patients fund. At the prize presentation held in the Villa Marina, Ed received a standing ovation and a special certificate for reaching Braddan. Robbie Collister, first across the line that year, when receiving his certificate said he felt that "the true winner of the 2005 Parish Walk was Ed Kelly".

Romanticised, even sanitised at times over the course of its long history, the Parish Walk has witnessed some amazing displays of personal fortitude and courage that has often gone unreported. Walking all day and all night only to fall short of the ultimate goal must be the most soul-destroying moment an athlete could experience.

But this is exactly what happened to Brian McGovern in 2006. Entering the event for the first time with the intention of only going to Peel, the 26-year-old plumber from Douglas walked alone and unsupported throughout the night, losing his way at Bride where he added another two miles to an already painful journey.

Stopping to bandage a dislocated kneecap at Lonan, he hobbled on to Onchan with only 15 minutes to beat the 24-hour time limit. But his task was impossible, and unable to put one foot in front of another at the top of Royal Avenue, he became the farthest non-finisher in the history of the event.

In the same event a woman, told by doctors that she would never walk, surprised everyone including herself when she walked 4½ miles to Marown church.

Dru Hamm, a 35-year-old an accountant from Douglas was born with cerebral palsy which affected her lower limbs. Doctors said she would never walk, however after surgery and seven years of physiotherapy she proved them wrong.

Until the event, Dru had never walked more than three miles, however, supported all the way by friends Vicky McManus and Adam Douglas, she made it to the second church in 4½ hours, raising a considerable amount of money for the Grace Third World Fund, a charity funding surgery for orphans.

Another courageous walk that nearly ended in tragedy was that from two-time junior winner Allan Stewart Thomson during the 2001 Parish Walk. On course for a sub-19 hour time, the 22-year-old collapsed above the White Bridge within three miles of the finish and unaware that dehydration had got the better of him.

Attended to by paramedics for over an hour, and against all sound advice, he stubbornly rose to his feet and struggled on at funeral pace to Onchan with the intention of going no further. But chief timekeeper Peter Kaneen was having none of it, and reluctant to record his retirement, nursed him down to Port Jack leaving Gordon Corran to coax him safely on to the finish. His was undoubtedly a heroic achievement but also one that could so easily have had a less favourable outcome.

Although the Parish Walk is routed over 85-miles, there are others who have gone even further in this great event. Unable to secure a suitable venue for their show-piece event in 1998, the Race Walking Association in England combined the National 100-mile race with the Parish Walk by extending the Manx Classic another 15 miles along Douglas Promenade. The 11 hardy souls who took on the challenge all went on to achieve Centurion status including Manx Parish Walk legends Ray Hughes, Anthony Kneale and Simon Cox.

Nevertheless, the greatest distance ever walked in a Parish Walk far exceeds 100 miles.

After completing the 2008 event some three minutes short of 21 hours, 36-year-old Bethany Clague set off for the second time in less than 24 hours to fulfil her ambition of being the first person to complete two laps of the tortuous circuit inside 48 hours.

Anyone who has completed the Parish Walk will know that an undertaking of such magnitude is beyond the realms of possibility for most. To walk all day and all night and then retrace the best part of 150,000 steps all over again just beggars belief!

Encouraged by a dedicated support team including Sean Hands and Robbie Collister, both of whom took part earlier, Bethany resisted all temptation to stop for a rest, for had she done so, it is unlikely she would have had the willpower to continue.

Tired, disorientated and moving at less than a funeral pace on the back-breaking climb to Ballajora, undoubtedly the most tiring section of the circuit, she walked several miles supported and held upright by her concerned parents trying desperately to coax her on to the finish.

Cheered on by anxious spectators lining the walkway on Douglas Promenade, the Onchan gym teacher reached the war memorial at 20 minutes past seven on Monday morning to record the first-ever two lap Parish Walk finish and one unlikely to be repeated.

At the same time that Bethany was setting off on the second stage of her heroic journey, 40-year-old Chris Moon was nearing Laxey and would soon become the first person ever to complete the course with only one arm and one leg.

The army veteran who lost both limbs in a landmine explosion was raising money for the Crossroads for Carers charity after hearing about the Parish Walk while on a visit to the Island some years before.

Chris was severely injured while working for a charity clearing landmines in Mozambique in 1995. He stepped on a live mine and the blast tore off his lower right arm and leg. Doctors said he survived against the odds due to his determination and fitness.

Within a year of leaving hospital he successfully completed the London Marathon and has since gone on to complete many of the world's toughest marathons including the Great Sahara Run and running the length of Cambodia to raise funds for charities assisting the disabled.

After completing the course in 23 hours 21 minutes 29 seconds, Chris said maintaining a minimum speed was the most difficult part of the walk for him. 'I can walk all day but staying up to speed was difficult as it can cause my stump to swell up. Walking through the night was not pleasant but the atmosphere and encouragement from cheering spectators around the course really kept me going.'

INGREDIENTS FOR SUCCESS

So what are the vital ingredients necessary to complete this arduous journey of great distance? We could say train, train and train some more, however there is much more to this daunting task than first meets the eye. Fitness, total commitment and serious planning are certainly the building blocks to success. So too is motivation, the driving force to keep going when the going gets tough.

TRAINING

In general, younger people have better physique and stamina for events of this nature, yet they lack the mental capability so often found in middle-aged walkers. This is borne out by statistics of the 2013 Parish Walk in which all but one of the top 20 finishers were veterans aged 35 or over.

Preparation for the Parish Walk should start as early as September with consistent training sessions, if only over a short distance. Build up from a short comfortable level and only gradually extend the duration of your walk. Don't be too adventurous.

Long hard walks aren't necessarily good preparation as they take a long time to recover from. A good basic principle is to train every other day when starting out. Practice pace and rhythm that can be maintained for a long period to enable you to get the feel of what you will do on the big day. It is good practice to vary gradients once you have progressed from the flat. Hill or even mountain walking helps to strengthen leg muscles but remember the ground is always uneven and invariably leads to sprains and strains.

By January, ten-mile sessions twice a week should be encouraged to build up stamina for more intensive training later. If you look forward to your training sessions and believe that the goals you have set yourself are worthwhile, then your chances of success are much greater. It is pointless setting unattainable goals or ones that are easily attained. If you are inexperienced at distance events, have a plan, train accordingly and complete a reasonably long section of the course well in advance.

April is a good time to increase mileage. In addition, the weekly schedule should now include a walk of up to four hours. During this session, the emphasis should not be on speed or distance, but time spent on foot at the pace at which you intend to compete.

With about four weeks to the event and no less, a longer eight-hour walk should be attempted as this will prepare the body for the exceptional physical demands that lie ahead. Frequent ten-mile walks help keep the stamina levels high, but it is the 30-mile or more sessions that are most beneficial. Stalwarts such as Sue Biggart and training partner Ray Pitts are firm believers in this, as is nineteen-time finisher Dermot O'Toole, who once-annually, walks from Glen Vine to the Point of Ayre lighthouse to acquaint himself with the levels of physical and mental pain guaranteed to come.

The 'Parish' is above all a battle within one's self. It is so easy to give in when your body is tired and aching all over, hence the proverb 'mind over matter.' If you are reasonably fit it will be your motivation and willpower that ensures you achieve your target. Don't waste vital mental energy on the early part of the race but instead save it for a strong finish. In your build-up, mental rehearsal will organise your mindset for the task in hand. Be realistic and set a plan that fits your capabilities and then put it into place. Expect to have highs and lows but be determined to get through them. Most importantly remember that each step forward is one nearer to your individual target.

The last few weeks of preparation are vital, so under no circumstances over-train and tire yourself out. Concentrate on getting organised and do nothing, or indeed very little in the final week. Under no circumstances be tempted into one final training session that could so easily overturn all the good work done so far.

Huge mileage during training is not essential for novices. Nevertheless, previous winners Jock Waddington and Vinny Lynch can be found on many a winter's evening pounding the streets of Douglas hour upon hour. There are, however, exceptions to this rule and many have completed the 85-mile circuit with no form of training whatsoever. Fifty-seven-year-old David Collister never admits to training. The landscape gardener from Archallegan continues to defy the law of averages with his tally of consecutive finishes now numbering 30.

EQUIPMENT

This is also the time to assess footwear, clothing and use of anti-blistering agents. The human body does not take kindly to pain. Blistered feet may heal quickly but left unattended, pain will soon lead to loss of willpower culminating in mental shutdown. It is well known that pain induced by toothache, tonsillitis or just a simple in-growing toenail is more than enough to reduce some people to tears.

Environmental influences are also important but often the most neglected. You cannot change the weather or the road surface, but you can change what you wear. Choice of footwear may be personal but does not need to be expensive. The early pioneers in this great event had little, or indeed, no choice in footwear and yet were quite capable of recording sub-17-hour times. A good example of this was from three-time winner Henry Harvey who won the 1962 and 1964 events in under 16½ hours in shoes that would be laughed at by today's standards.

Shoes can be your best friend, or indeed, your worst enemy depending on choice, so it is paramount to get this right. Choose shoes half a size too large to allow expansion of the feet as they warm up. They should be flexible and comfortable with a motion control that suits the foot. Remember, it is advisable to have shoes worn in but not worn out. Take at least two pairs with you and change during the race if required. This prevents overstraining injuries because no two pairs of shoes put exactly the same stresses on your feet and legs. A quality pair of shoes should last three hundred miles before signs of deterioration appear. Just like electrical goods that are discontinued after six months, shoes too suffer the same fate, so consider purchasing a second and identical pair before stocks run out. Sound advice indeed, but not one the author adhered to during his long Parish apprenticeship. It took ten Parish Walks, three End to End Walks and two TT Course Walks for him to finally see sense and retire those well worn shoes to a darkened drawer from where they are unlikely to re-appear.

Even with the best footwear in the world, blisters will begin to make their mark at 30 miles or so. Prevention is better than cure, so apply Compeeds to sensitive areas before setting off. Bandaging both feet with surgical tape the night before also slows the blistering process, which if left unattended, will almost certainly lead to failure. Regular finisher David Cain, a firm believer in this method of damage limitation, has convinced the author of its merits to the extent that

he too has adopted this novice route to foot protection which certainly seems to work.

Nevertheless, padding, insoles, bandages or just plain sticking plasters all need to be applied correctly or they will create even further long-term damage. Socks too need to be carefully chosen. Ideally, they should be of suitable texture, cotton or lambs-wool and free from any creases that will inevitably lead to blistering. In an event alien to most, each foot can be expected to make ground contact in excess of 75,000 times so good foot protection may be the difference between success and failure.

Even the most intimate parts of the body can be affected on a warm day. Excessive pubic hair or recently grown stubble when in contact with perspiration are the perfect ingredients for blistering, so use of vaseline is highly recommended.

NUTRITION

Now that we are physically and mentally prepared for this great undertaking, we need to understand how our body and organs function and the fuel required to power it. Firstly, you've got a motor – your muscles, secondly an onboard computer – your brain and thirdly you've got fuel. All three of these need consideration when tackling ultra-endurance events.

Unlike a car engine that can run on a single type of fuel, our muscles are a multi-fuel engine that can run on carbohydrates, fat and at a push, even protein. Not only that, our muscles can even use some fuel with or without oxygen. The relevance of this becomes clear later.

'Hitting the Wall' is basically about running out of fuel. Ultimately, all fuels are used to provide chemical energy stored in the form of Adenosine Triphosphate (ATP) and it is this chemical energy release when ATP changes to Adenosine Diphosphate(ADP) that enables our muscles to contract.

The endurance athlete's primary source of fuel is carbohydrates in the form of blood glucose and glycogen (the polymer of glucose stored in muscles and liver) and also fats.

1 gram of carbohydrate = 4 calories (Kcal) of energy.

1 gram of fat = 9 calories of energy.

Surprisingly, the thinnest individual has enough fat stored in his body to fuel a 600 mile walk. While the typical untrained individual can store about 380 grams of glycogen or 1500 calories, intensive training and carbohydrate loading can raise these reserves as high as 880 grams or 3500 calories. Intense exercise, cycling, marathon running and elite Parish Walking will consume about 700 calories per hour. So it's a no brainer is it not? Fat is the obvious fuel, however it's not quite that simple. While fat can supply generous quantities of energy it's a slow and complex business as anyone who had dieted to lose weight will attest to. Also, the release of energy from fat requires a high supply of oxygen-rich blood, a precious commodity when walking as far and as fast as you can.

So its back to carbohydrates as the fuel of choice and it is now obvious that the tank is going to need refuelling several times during the course of the walk.

So what does this mean for the enthusiastic Parish Walker? The day has finally arrived, over a thousand people line up and there's lots of pre-race excitement. Typically you start out too fast and soon your heart cannot pump enough blood to your muscles to meet demands so your muscles start to metabolise glucose anaerobically. This is much less efficient than aerobic metabolism, about five per cent, and to make matters worse there is an accumulation of lactic acid and hydrogen ions. Not only do these make your muscles feel on fire, they also wreck havoc with normal control of glucose metabolism. You are well on your way to failure at this stage.

Start the walk at a pace you are comfortable with. At this pace you should supply your fuel 75% from carbohydrate and 25% from fats. If you fail to refuel the carbohydrates adequately while walking as the supply of carbohydrate dwindles, so the body will rely more on fats. As already mentioned the burning of fat requires lots of oxygen-rich blood. The heart therefore must work harder to supply this to the muscles and the likely result is that it becomes impossible to maintain your pace.

Here is a classic scenario. It's the middle of the night and you are in the last quarter of the Parish from Ramsey to home. At this point there is a real struggle to keep the carb tank topped up and the fat metabolism contribution goes up and as you slow down that PB (personal best time) starts to slip away. If you don't remedy the situation fast there is a distinct possibility of failing to finish. Run out of carbs completely and you inevitably hit the wall.

MENTAL AGILITY

It's the turn of the onboard computer. The brain makes a massive contribution to success or failure in the Parish Walk, so it comes as no surprise that it too can become fatigued as well as the muscles.

As already stated the brain can only use glucose as its fuel and it has no local glycogen store so relies entirely on glycogen released from the liver to maintain the correct level of glucose in the blood and hence fuel for the brain. Deplete the liver completely of its glycogen store and there may suddenly be no fuel for the brain. Brain fatigue probably causes far more people to give up than specific muscle fatigue. Apart from the very highly motivated competitor most do not push themselves to complete muscle fatigue.

Fat metabolism also contributes significantly to brain fatigue. During the course of the walk this can lead to an increased delivery of tryptophan to the brain and a rise in serotonin levels. Serotonin is an acknowledged central nervous system depressant.

So while fat metabolism helps keep the muscles working it is causing the brain to fade at the same time – a doubled edged sword so to speak. To make matters worse, at the time this is all taking place, the athlete's feel-good hormone dopamine is diminishing at the same time. A double whammy you could say. You've reached the stage when the brain says I cannot go on, but the muscles actually can. Correct this and you may well finish on a flourish rather than flounder in the gutter.

Training is very important to not only improve endurance and fitness but also can also be used as experimental sessions to try out the various food and drink supplements that are available on the market – remember, not all of them will suit everyone. It is essential that what we eat and drink on the day will be well tolerated and not lead to abdominal cramping, nausea, vomiting or even diarrhoea. Also use even short training sessions to get used to drinking while walking quickly.

Even mild dehydration on the day will negatively affect your performance dramatically, so it is important to keep hydrated at all times. As the body heats up, it begins to lose increasing amounts of fluid through the process of sweating. At that point even mildly dehydrated people, no matter how fit, become prone to making irrational decisions.

Indeed, under the extreme time pressure of the walk, a competitor suffering mild dehydration may start to believe they cannot afford to stop even to drink. A vicious cycle ensues, where the victim finds it harder to make life-saving rational choices.

Mild dehydration – between one and two per cent loss of normal water volume in the body – can significantly deplete a walker's thinking ability. Even then, people start to become confused. At two per cent dehydration, focus and short-term memory start to go. More importantly, a person's ability to understand how they feel also starts to fade.

Athletes desperate to prove themselves in the toughest conditions may convince themselves they don't need water and carry on. Worse still, such levels of dehydration creep up on people completely unawares. It is well known that our thirst sensation doesn't really appear until we are one or two per cent dehydrated. By then dehydration is well advanced and impacting how the mind and body perform. Beyond that point, the worse the dehydration, the more irrational the sufferer becomes.

To avoid early symptoms of this 'silent killer,' it is vital to be well disciplined and take on fluids on frequent basis. Attention needs also to be given to replacing electrolytes lost in perspiration. Some people prefer an all-in-one sports drink to do the job – others will do it differently by replacing individual components at different times. It doesn't really matter, what is important is to have thought about what is needed. Have a plan based on scientific principles and stick to it.

In summing up, what should the athlete do to minimise the risk of hitting the wall? Firstly the bulk of endurance sports nutritional research is based around marathon running, triathlons and endurance cycling and while it seems reasonable to make comparisons, the Parish Walk is quite unique in the super endurance field. That said the following is one approach that can help all Parish Walk competitors.

As mentioned earlier, begin winding down on physical activity in the week prior to the walk. Instead, take only gentle exercise and carb load to optimise muscle and liver glycogen storage. Take on low glycaemic index carbohydrates such as pasta and potatoes. On the morning of the walk try to eat about two hours before the start and eat a low glycaemic index meal such as porridge. Ensure you are well hydrated before the start and drink about 150 ml of sports drink every 20 minutes. Replenish carbohydrates as often as you can reasonably tolerate during the walk. A mixture of low and high glycaemic index carbs should be available for the duration of the walk. Growing evidence is emerging that the addition of a small amount of protein can enhance carbohydrate absorption and uptake, and carb protein drinks in the ration 4:1 are available commercially. Interestingly, semi-skimmed milk provides carbohydrate and protein in roughly the 4:1 proportion.

So there you have it, a brief overview of nutrition for the Parish Walk which may help you finish, may help improve your performance, but more importantly, may help to avoid the wall!

Now that we have an understanding of how our body and its organs function, we need to formulate a sensible training schedule applicable to our individual requirements.

In summing up the requirements necessary for a successful and pain-free assault on the 17 parishes, preparation, mental strength and physical ability, plus sound tactics are by far the key elements to success. Anyone doubting this fact should look no further than Jock Waddington and heed his expert tips on damage limitation. The first man to win the Manx Telecom Parish Walk four years in succession, Jock's sound advice for the big day is as follows:

'The most important thing is to set a target and stick to it. The Parish Walk is as much a test of mental strength as it is of physical endurance. Whether it's getting to Rushen, Peel or any other of the Parish checkpoints, it's essential to make a commitment to achieving that goal. If you go into the event saying "I'll try and get to Peel, and then carry on if I feel good," then chances are that you will stop when you get to Peel. No matter what your goal is – or the level of experience in this or other walking events – there will be times when you feel tired or hungry, or suffer blisters or other aches and pains. When this happens it makes it too easy to give in and stop if you adopt the "I'll see how I feel" attitude. It's much better to set a target according to your level of fitness and experience and focus on achieving that goal. Then, if you reach your target and feel good, you can always carry on.'

Pacing is also critical no matter how far you intend to walk, says Jock.

'It's easy for people to get carried away at the start and go off too fast. The excitement of the start, and the fact that everyone is full of energy, means that some walkers – particularly those who are new to the event or inexperienced – can go off much too fast. It's important to set a realistic pace right from the start based on the kind of speed you can maintain in training. Don't be tempted to keep up with those around you – remember they may be going faster because they don't intend to walk as far as you, or they may be much more experienced in the event. Stick to your own schedule and in the final miles to your target distance you can always pick up the pace a little if you feel confident. Above all, it's important for walkers of all levels not to get stressed with targets and times.'

Summing up, Jock says: 'The Parish Walk is a great community event as well as a sporting challenge. Enjoy the occasion, soak up the atmosphere and every mile will pass much more quickly.'

END TO END WALK

Although the Parish Walk is by far the most popular and eagerly awaited race walking event in the Manx sporting calendar, its younger sibling, the End to End Walk, is equally demanding but over a considerably shorter distance.

First held in on 1st October 1961, the 40-mile route beginning at the Point of Ayre lighthouse followed the Island's east coast through Ramsey, Laxey and Onchan to Quarter Bridge from where it followed the New Castletown Road to Ballasalla, Castletown, Port St Mary and on to the finish at the Sound.

There were 21 finishers in this inaugural race, Onchan postman Stanley Cleator being the first home in 7 hours 19 minutes 18 seconds. Ironically, another postman by the name of John Cannell was last over the finish line some two hours later. Nevertheless, John would have the last laugh 33 years on by winning the Parish Walk for a sixth time to become the most successful competitor in the events 100-year history.

Producing 20 different winners during the 40 years it was held on the east coast, the End to End Walk was won a record 11 times by Derek Harrison between 1970 and 1986.

Entry numbers regularly exceeded 100 during the latter years of the 20th century, however in 2001 concerns over road safety forced organisers to re-route the shortened course along the Island's west coast utilising much of the Parish Walk route in reverse from Bride to Rushen.

HISTORY OF THE CENTURIONS

With so many Manx walkers in recent years achieving Centurion status, it is worth detailing here a brief history of this unique brotherhood that celebrated its centenary two years ago.

A Centurion is one who, as an amateur, has walked 100 miles in 24 hours in a recognised competition. This definition describes the members of a very special brotherhood that was founded in 1911. Each member has a unique number, John Edwin Fowler-Dixon being given the number one in recognition of his having walked 100 miles in 20 hours 36 minutes 08 seconds in a race at Lillie Bridge, Fulham, London in 1877.

Centurion numbers come from many countries around the world. The numerous Dutch members of the Centurions 1911 have their own active organisation, and each year the English and Dutch Centurions compete for a special trophy. Some other countries organise Centurion races and make their own awards. The other five Centurion organisations worldwide are the Continental Centurions who are based in Holland and those of Australia, New Zealand, the USA and Malaysia.

A fascination with long-distance walking in the late nineteenth and early twentieth centuries contributed directly to the formation of the Centurions in 1911. At the inaugural meeting of the UK Centurions, held on 11th May 1911 at the Ship and Turtle Inn, Leadenhall Street, London, it was decided to form a brotherhood of those who had walked 100 miles within 24 hours under race walking rules. Fowler-Dixon, having the longest-standing qualifying performance, was given the distinction of becoming Centurion number one and being appointed the first President. The founding Centurions were in part the same small group of walkers – including Hammond Neville, and Barnes-Moss, who in 1907, founded the Southern Counties Race Walking Association.

Between 1877 and 2013, 90 Centurion qualifying events have been held in the UK. The 2013 event held on the Isle of Man for a third occasion saw local residents Richard Gerrard, Vinny Lynch and Robbie Callister claim the podium places.

Other than the two world wars when competition was suspended, Centurion qualifying events have been held annually and have come to incorporate the RWA long-distance Championship. The great majority of Centurion qualifying events have been road races, with 16 of the 90 events held to date taking place entirely on the track.

Occasionally, the 100-mile event has incorporated the RWA National 50-kilometre race. In 1998, the event was staged on the Isle of Man in conjunction with their annual Parish Walk – an occasion again repeated in 2006 but this time at the National Sports Centre in Douglas when over 100 competitors took part.

From the early years of Centurion qualifying events, some excellent times were achieved. Tommy Hammond's 1907 time of 18 hours 13 minutes 37 seconds was for the full 104 miles Brighton double journey. The event was organised by Surrey Walking Club 17 times between 1902 and 1967. Other point-to-point events took place between Bath and London in 1952 and Birmingham to London the following year. There was a race from Blackpool to Manchester and back in 1954 and Sheffield to Harrogate and back in 1956.

Between 1958 and 1978, Leicester Walking Club organised the Leicester to Skegness race 11 times while in 1998, the annual 85-mile Isle of Man Parish Walk was utilised by adding another 15 miles along Douglas Promenade.

Events on shorter courses during the 1960s, 70s and 80s included those at Chigwell, Bristol, Ewhurst, Leicester Congerstone and Hungarton courses, and in more recent times, public parks have been used at Hendon, Battersea Park, Colchester, Newmarket and Kings Lynn.

The 1993 Battersea Park event, organised by Surrey Walking Club and the Metropolitan Police WC, was the only British event to host a 200-kilometre qualifying race for the Paris-Colmar classic. Various tracks have provided venues for the 100-mile race from Lillie Bridge in 1877 onwards. They include the tracks at White City and Woodford Green, London, Walton and Motspur Park, Surrey, plus tracks in Bradford, Brighton, Leicester, Colchester, Blackpool and Milton Keynes.

Perhaps the most notable track event took place in 1960 at Walton where Hew Neilson (C145) set a new world record for distance walked in 24 hours of 133 miles 21 yards. Hew completed 20 Centurion events, a feat only equalled by Sandra Brown (C735) in 2005. Since then, Martin Fisher (C788) and Chris Flint (C849) have also completed 20 100s.

Richard Brown has won a record ten Centurion events (one jointly with his wife Sandra) while Dave Boxhall has six wins to his credit. The incredible Sandra Brown has completed 26 UK 100-mile events and has won the UK Ladies' 100-mile event 25 times. Sandra became the first person to achieve all six worldwide Centurion awards, a feat also achieved by Jill Green who finished seventh in her Parish Walk debut in 1995.

Further notable achievements include the first Centurion qualification by a woman, Ann Sayer (C599) in 1977, the completion of ten Centurion events between the ages of 65 and 75 by Eddie McNeir (C375) and the fastest Centurion qualifying time of 16 hours 55 minutes 44 seconds by John Moulin in 1971. Holland's Jan de Jonge holds the world record for 100 miles with a time of 16 hours 31 minutes 38 seconds set in Norway in 1982.

Olympians who have been Centurions include Tommy Hammond (C10), Frank O'Reilly (C276) who competed for Eire, Len Mathews (C316), Don Thompson (C631) and Dominic King (C1098) who qualified in 2012 alongside his twin brother Dan.

The Centurions, open to all walkers from all backgrounds and countries, have inspired many with the vision that 'long-distance walking is not only the most natural and beneficial of exercises but also leads to the health and happiness of mankind.'

MORE DISTANCE EVENTS

Other distance events worthy of mention include the

Fact File Parish Walk

Michael Readshaw 'checking in' at Santon.

Hastings to Brighton Walk which commenced in 1930 and was won by Tommy Green of the Belgrave Harriers in 6 hours and 35 seconds. Two years later, Tommy won an Olympic gold medal over 50 kilometres at Los Angeles!

Hastings to Brighton was a distance of 37 miles, though this was later extended to 38 miles with many great walkers taking the honours. It was deemed by many to be harder than the much longer London to Brighton race owing to the nature of the course.

Commencing on Hastings seafront and ending at Brighton Aquarium, the course took a testing route via Lewis. Britain's other Olympic 50-kilometre gold medallists, Harold Whitlock MBE (1936 Berlin) and Don Thompson MBE (1960 Rome) appear on the winner's list. Nevertheless, increasing traffic levels and concern over health and safety issues ended this event in the 1980s when it became a 50-kilometre race in Hove Park, near Brighton.

The Manchester to Blackpool Walk was a 48¼-mile race commencing outside Manchester Town Hall at 6:15am. Competitors were routed through Bolton and Preston before finishing on Blackpool's famous 'Golden Mile'. First held in 1909 with 22 entries, the race was won by T. Payne in 7 hours 43 minutes 53 seconds. Over the coming years, distances varied between 50 and 52 miles. There were no contests between 1935 and 1949 however, increasing traffic, falling numbers and dwindling numbers of officials brought about its demise in the 1990s. It was later replaced by a 50-mile race in a Blackpool park however this too has been confined to the history books.

Another popular race falling foul of health and safety requirements was the Leicester to Skegness 100-Mile Walk, promoted by the Leicester Walking Club.

First held in 1958, the race was won by Wilf Smith in a time of 18 hours 02 minutes 37 seconds with 25 of the 41 starters finishing. The route commenced in central Leicester's Victoria Park and finished on Skegness seafront by the clock tower, having gone through Peterborough, Spalding, Boston and Wainfleet on 'A class roads.' Many great walkers contested this event which was held bi-annually until its last staging in 1978 when increasing traffic levels and concern over safety issues brough about its demise. Don Thompson MBE, an Olympic gold medallist 18 years earlier, was one of 41 finishers in that final event. The race continued on a multi-lap format around the outskirts of Leicester, firstly at Congerstone then Hungarton before folding for good.

In the 1960s, a popular point-to-point event was the Colchester to Ipswich race which took competitors through delightful 'Constable Country.' It was 17½ picturesque miles through quiet villages but also required stretches of the busy A12 truck road to be negotiated. The last event was held in 1969 after which it folded when organiser and Ipswich resident Barry Ingarfield moved residence and nobody came forward to take over. In any case it would have ended by now as the A12 is now too unsafe to set foot upon.

With a distance of 103½ miles, the Birmingham to London Walk in 1953 was by far Britain's longest race.

In the year of Queen Elizabeth's Coronation, the race from Britain's second city to her capital, started at Yardley on Birmingham's Ring Road and ended at Wembley Stadium. There were 29 finishers from a start list of 53. A retirement option was offered at 100 miles for those seeking only Centurions' membership qualification, but none took it. The race winner was the famous Tom Richardson in 18 hours 56 minutes 36 seconds (18 hours 18 minutes 07 seconds for 100 miles). Any route between Britain's two largest cities was bound to be busy and a constant stream of traffic, including all-night truck movements ensured this event was never staged again.

Bath to London was another eagerly awaited 100-mile event on the sporting calendar. The 1952 event was won by Olympic 50-kilometre walker Rex Whitlock in 17 hours 44 minutes 40 seconds. Considerable crowds gathered for the start of this race which ended in Chiswick. A non-finisher was the 1936 Olympic 50-kilometre gold medallist Harold Whitlock MBE.

The 1957 race saw 61 competitors start but only 18 made it to the finish. The early leader at the 19-mile, mark was Hew Neilson who then fell ill after being given a drink of sour milk causing him to drop back before retiring after 50 miles – his first failure in eight ultra-distance outings. The winner was John Ridley of Queen's Park Harriers in 18 hours 12 minutes 04 seconds. High temperatures in the early stages, followed by a night of thunder, lightning and ferocious storms caused many to pull out of this event prematurely.

ROUBAIX 28 HOURS

For those seeking even greater distance, the Roubaix 28-Hour and Paris to Colmar ultra-distance events are considered to be the most demanding in the European race walking calendar.

Celebrating its 60th anniversary in 2013, the classic Roubaix 28-hour event was the brainchild of local walker Louis Bourgois. Over the years it has gone through many changes – from the original committee l'Academie des Sports de Roubaix to the present day Club des Marcheurs Roubaisiens. The course too has undergone many changes. Starting in the Rue d'epaule quarter, the race has a history of a large first lap followed by one shorter. Originally only 11 kilometres in length, the course grew in size to a grand first lap of 42 kilometres encompassing the surrounding area to as far as the Belgium border. The subsequent route has travelled down many local streets, often changing from year to year as well as the distance itself.

Unusual in being a race of 28 hours, the start and finish has historically started in the same street as the local cinema so the finish was timed to fit in between performances, thus capitalising on the maximum number of townsfolk out and about in the Rue d'epaule.

With a few exceptions the event has always been held over the third weekend in September and is one of the many qualifying races for the prestigious Paris to Colmar race.

Parish Walk legends John (Paddy) Dowling and Derek Harrison led the British invasion during the 1970s – the Irishman a finisher 21 times.

In 1978, Dutch walker Adrie Dirven became the first female to complete the course followed by Annie der Meer in 1980. The following year Britain's Ann

Sayer was sixth overall with a distance walked of 217 kilometres.

Sandra Brown was the first lady home in 1990, however numbers have dwindled in recent years as they did in many race walking events no matter the distance or the location.

In 2012, a number of Manx athletes took part with Vinny Lynch and Richard Gerrard astounding everyone by finishing second and third respectively.

THE PARIS-STRASBOURG/COLMAR RACE WALK

Undoubtedly the Olympics of ultra-distance race walking, the Paris-Colmar event is by far the ultimate challenge and one that very few can claim to have taken part in.

It was first held in 1929 as a race between Paris and Strasbourg and apart from interruptions during the World War II and again in the 1960s, it has been held every year since. With the increase of traffic in recent years, the course has been re-routed south to Colmar on the Swiss, German border.

Until recent years it was an event for men only, a gruelling near continuous walk of 540 kilometres. But as the traffic made even the Colmar route dangerous in places, so it has taken more to the byways and the hills. The men's event is now around 430 kilometres with the women racing some 290 kilometres (down from around 360 kilometres) in stages where the walkers are regrouped before setting off on each stage. This approach is better for the public who now get to see groups of walkers and the atmosphere of a race rather than seeing the odd lone individual.

Only two English men and two English women have ever completed the original classic Paris-Strasbourg or Paris-Colmar. Colin Young completed the former a number of times in the 1970s and Richard Brown completed the latter twice in the early 1990s. Richard's wife Sandra Brown completed three times also in the early 1990s and Jill Green completed the race a few years later. In 2013 Karen Davies successfully completed the new formula race. Over the years, several other British walkers have started the event.

Entrants must qualify at various 200 kilometre/24-hour races held mostly in France, and those selected number around 20 men and ten women. The completion rate for the Paris-Colmar can be as low as a third as each walker has to keep up a set pace or they are pulled out at a checkpoint. Each walker will have at least one van and accompanying crew, and the distance and time can take its toll of the supporters too.

Although the Paris-Colmar is not for the faint hearted, UK walkers are well capable of completing this challenge and it should be our collective aim to ensure that we are represented as often as possible in this pinnacle of athletics.

Where are they now?

WHERE ARE THEY NOW?

Colonel William Anderson

Born in Douglas in 1831, William James Anderson is one of only two men to have completed the Parish Walk twice during the nineteenth century. His first successful attempt in 1880 went unrecorded however a decade later when, aged 60, he set off from Patrick and walking northward, completed the journey in 19 hours 39 minutes.

Joining the British army as a subaltern in a marching regiment at the age of 17, he served with the 1st Battalion Duke of Cornwall's Light Infantry for nearly 30 years, gradually rising to the rank of Lieutenant Colonel until his retirement in 1880.

He saw action in India and Burma during the 1860s and came close to receiving the Victoria Cross for acts of bravery during the Indian Mutiny of 1857.

After being discharged from the army, Anderson returned to the Island where he was elected to the House of Keys as a representative of Glenfaba sheading – a post he held until 1886 when appointed Receiver-General of the Isle of Man. The position carried with it a seat on the Island's Legislatative Council and for 23 years he was chairman of the Highway Board and responsible for overseeing the construction of the new mountain roads from Creg-ne-Baa to Laxey and from Snaefell to Ramsey.

He sat on many special committees of Tynwald and was a member of the Asylums and Assessment Boards – his suggestions and his wide experience in many parts of the world being always most helpful to his colleagues.

During his term as Receiver-General, he was for 18 years secretary to the Harbour Board and associated with the construction of many harbour works of considerable importance to the Island, such as the extension of the Victoria Pier, the erection of the Queen's Pier at Ramsey, the building of the Alfred Pier at Port Erin and the construction of Peel breakwater.

Although beyond the Psalmist's span of life – three score years and ten, he maintained extraordinary vigour. His tall and somewhat stooped form was tough as steel, and when on in years he had the powers of endurance which were the envy of men in the prime of life. As a pedestrian he was simply marvellous. With him a walk of 50 miles without stopping was a mere nothing and it was probably this that contributed to his good fortune in circuiting the 17 parishes in 1890.

At a ripe old age of 81, Colonel Anderson passed away in September 1912, his internment at the family vault in Kirk Michael attended by the Lieutenant-Governor, the Lord Bishop and the Speaker of the House of Keys.

Stanley Cleator

Every picture tells a story and this one certainly did. Capturing the atmosphere of a Parish Walk like no other, the photograph of Stanley Cleator approaching the finish line on Douglas Promenade in 1960 is probably the most famous ever taken. There were no radio stations or mobile phones in those days, nevertheless, news of his pending victory spread like wildfire and huge crowds turned out to cheer him on to the finish at the Villa Marina gates.

Taken by the legendary press photographer Bill Peters, the photograph shows the victorious Onchan postman dressed in a woollen pullover, neatly pressed trousers, polished shoes and looking fresh as paint accompanied by work colleagues riding in a cavalcade of Post Office motorcycles, it is a classic scene of times past and one never to be repeated.

Runner-up to Henry Harvey in 1961, Stanley made history later that year by winning the first-ever End to End Walk in 7 hours 19 minutes 18 seconds. Promoted by Onchan United Harriers and held on 1st October, the 40-mile event starting at the Point of Ayre and finishing at the Sound attracted an entry of 65, many with distance experience, including John Tasker and Brian Shooter who finished second and third respectively.

For his outstanding achievements and contributions to Manx athletics, Stanley was later named Sports Personality of The Year, an award he was most proud of.

Recalling his great Parish victory when officiating as starter to the 2006 event, Stanley said, 'We started off in the dark in those days and straight from work after a busy shift at the Post Office. Our clothing was basic, just a jumper, trousers, work boots and a packed lunch my mother had made for the long night ahead.'

Now aged 82 and living in Hampshire, Stanley will all always be remembered for his great contribution to an event that has grown in stature from humble beginnings to a first-class race-walking meeting the envy of many.

Henry Harvey

By far the Island's most outstanding athlete during the early 1960s, the farmer from Abbeylands won the Parish Walk three times between 1961 and 1964.

Born in 1933, Henry's first walk was as a nine-year-old when in company with his father, he escorted a herd of cattle along the TT course from Ballaugh to Abbeylands, a journey of 16 miles that took over nine hours to complete.

As a young man, prize money was always high on Henry's agenda and he contested many Island events including the Peel Hill Race, La Columb Killey and the Peel to Douglas Road Walk, a race he won convincingly. He pocketed the first prize of £5 which at that time was nearly equivalent to a farm labourer's weekly wage.

Henry also took part in the 1962 Northern Cross-Country Championships held at Stanley Park, Blackpool where he was the first Manx finisher out of 1,500 starters. In the Parish Walk of that year Henry was awarded the recently introduced prize for the first man to overtake the leading lady. Although he had started from Upper Church Street, Douglas an hour

Above: Murray Lambden.
Right: Henry Harvey
Below: Albert Johnson.
Bottom left: Stanley Cleator.
Bottom left: Paddy Dowling.

Where are they now?

and a half after the women, he soon led the field, overhauling Irene Cottier on the descent to Dalby.

Now aged 80, Henry remains in good health and will talk to anyone willing to listen about the 'good old days' when he was always the man to beat. His outstanding sporting achievements are known to all and the likeable farmer was delighted to be chosen as starter for the 2004 event.

Joe Brown

Sadly no longer with us, the quietly spoken 32-year-old painter and decorator from Menorca Laxey, was a popular winner of the 1963 Parish Walk in which only six of the 66 starters completed the course.

Joe's victory was exceptional as atrocious weather conditions decimated the field early on, leaving him unchallenged from Kirk Michael onwards.

Nevertheless, his credible time of 17 hours 04 minutes 09 seconds was overshadowed by superb performances from Eunice Davies and Irene Cottier, also making history that day by becoming the first ladies ever to complete the full 85-mile distance.

Albert Johnson

A legend who set standards for others to follow, Albert Johnson was probably the greatest-ever overseas athlete to visit the Island.

Born with a diseased hip and deformed foot in Sheffield, Yorkshire in 1931, Albert was a late developer and unable to walk until he was six years of age.

Introduced to race walking at an early age, his first race was the local 12-mile Star event held annually in Sheffield. Although he was not expected to finish, his fine performance prompted him to enter the event in 1949 when he finished in a commendable third place.

Although still a novice, he won the Bradford 50-kilometre race in 1954 in a new record time of 4 hours 36 minutes 36 seconds. In total, he won this prestigious event on six successive occasions out of nine and still holds the record time for the original course. Later that year, he finished second in the UK 50-kilometre Championships and was chosen for the British team for the European Games in Switzerland.

In 1955, Albert dominated almost all amateur race walking events in Britain, however his main focus of attention was the Olympic Games held in Melbourne, Australia, finishing in eighth place in 5 hours 02 minutes 19 seconds. This was well below his best time for 50 kilometres – probably as a result of the intense heat which took its toll on many competitors. He was also chosen to represent Britain at the 1960 Olympic Games in Rome but was disappointed at his disqualification.

Relocating to the Isle of Man in 1965, he was soon involved in coaching young Manx hopefuls to a high standard. In fact, two of his pupils, Hadyn Gawne and Phillip Bannan, became household names and competed with him at the 1966 Jamaica Commonwealth Games. His influence inspired many Manx walkers, including Graham Young and Allan Callow, both of whom looked upon him as the ultimate mentor.

During his stay on the Isle of Man, Albert achieved considerable success with winning performances in the TT Course and End to End Walks. However his finest moment came in 1967 when he became the first-ever competitor to complete the Parish Walk in under 16 hours inspite of taking a wrong turning at Jurby and adding an extra mile.

Before leaving England to settle in Australia, Albert coached John Warhurst and Roy Thorpe to Gold and silver in the 1974 Commonwealth Games held in Christchurch, New Zealand.

Although Albert continued to coach in the warmer climate of the southern hemisphere, age and ill health prevented him from further competition. Sadly, he is no longer with us, passing away in 2009 but a shining example for others to follow.

Ian Turnbull

Another icon of bygone years but sadly no longer with us, Ian's athletic exploits both on and off the track are well known.

A student at Liverpool University during the early 1960s, his first venture into race walking was during the summer of 1961 when he took part in two TT Course Walks organised by the Young Farmers.

Hooked on the walking epidemic sweeping the Island, Ian took part in the inaugural End to End Walk that year and the Parish Walk in 1962 when he reached Lezayre at his first attempt. Ballasalla was his stopping point the following year and in 1964, he managed to get to Kirk Michael before throwing in the towel.

One of two winners in the controversial Parish Walk of 1968, Ian next turned his skills to administrative duties with the recently formed Boundary Harriers, taking on the roles of treasurer and auditor for many years.

He achieved a long held ambition in 1972 to better seven miles in less than an hour. In the 1974 Parish Walk, Ian was runner-up to Paddy Dowling, record holder of the John O'Groats to Lands End race. Later that year, he won the 40-mile End to End Walk in 7 hours 08 minutes 30 seconds before turning his attention to running.

The Manx Mountain Marathon became a priority between 1979 and 1984 and Ian completed the gruelling 32-mile slog over the Island's most inhospitable terrain on no less than five occasions. He also took part in the London Marathon in 1988.

Turning his attention to cycling during the early 1980s, Ian was a regular competitor in time trials and road races, however a serious accident in 1984 persuaded him to return to a slower pace and race walking was flavour of the month once again.

A civil servant for 25 years, his sporting credentials speak for themselves with finishes in 16 TT Walks, four End to End Walks and three Parish Walks

Ian Hodgkinson

Ian took part in several Parish Walks during the late 1960s and made history in 1969, when at the age of 21, he became the youngest-ever winner of the 85-mile event, a record that still stands today.

He represented Australia in the 1974 Commonwealth Games, and although a resident of Perth, Australia, he remains a frequent visitor to our shores.

Dudley Seddon

Although no longer with us, Dudley is recorded in the Centurions handbook as having completed six 100-mile events during a long and successful race walking career.

A member of Royal Sutton Coldfield Walking Club for many years, he qualified as a Centurion in the Leicester to Skegness 100 in 1966 in a time of 22 hours 35 minutes 24 seconds.

Competing against the brilliance of Albert Johnson and Derek Harrison, Dudley won the Parish Walk at his first attempt in 1970 with a convincing time 17 hours 21 minutes 49 seconds. followed by third spot the following two years. Although he had twice competed in the TT Course Walk, this was his first major win and he took great pleasure in his triumph.

Graham Young

Undoubtedly one of the finest athletes to have graced our shores, Graham's sporting achievements spanning nearly half a century speak for themselves.

Pictured in the first-ever photograph of a Parish Walk start in 1960, Graham was just a boy in a man's race and still to reach his fifteenth birthday. As the youngest-ever starter, the courageous 14-year-old reached Peel that year and Jurby in 1961. He finished second to Henry Harvey in 1964 and went on to win the classic event in 1971 and 1992.

It was soon apparent that the likeable Douglas postman was a distance man. In 1965 he was selected for the British Post Office team and their visit to Munich, Germany for the International Postman's Walk. His time of 84 minutes for the ten-mile event was more than credible considering it was achieved in full Post Office kit and carrying a mailbag! The old blue uniform was never designed for distance race walking and for him it was an outstanding result and one he is most proud of to this day.

In 1966, a year that saw English football triumph in the World Cup, Graham became the 383rd member of the exclusive Centurion Club, completing the 100-mile Leicester to Skegness course in 18 hours 54 minutes 05 seconds. The year also saw one of his finest performances with a fourth place in the Northern Counties championships.

A winner of the 1967 End to End Walk, Graham went on to complete a hat-trick of wins in the annual 40-mile event from the Point of Ayre to the Sound. A year later, he was stamping his authority on just about every event he entered. He took fourth place in the 15-kilometre Post Office Walking Championships at Swakleys, Middlesex as well as achieving a victory in the Open TT Course Walk.

By winning the Open TT Course Walk in 1969 for a third consecutive year, Graham indisputably placed himself top of the Manx walking elite, this latest achievement one of his proudest.

With Albert Johnson his greatest mentor, Graham trained six days a week with a punishing schedule second to none.

The 1971 Parish Walk was his next major triumph with just 54 seconds between him and arch-rival Derek Harrison at the finish. It was the closest ever finish in the history of the event and one that may have had a different outcome had the course been longer!

Quiet and unassuming, Graham was selected for the 1974, 1978 and 1982 Commonwealth Games. In 1986, he took on the role as athletics manager for the Manx team in Edinburgh. Perhaps Graham's greatest achievement came in 1981 at Stoke Mandeville when he recorded the fastest-ever time of 9 hours 36 minutes 23 seconds in the 100-kilometre British All Comer's Championship organised by the Race Walking Association.

A list of sporting achievements the envy of most, Graham has been without doubt an exceptional ambassador for Manx athletics and will be a difficult act to follow.

A postman for nearly half a century, 68-year-old Graham is now retired from competitive race walking, preferring instead to officiate at the Island's major events as a fully qualified judge. A father, grandfather and married to Marion, Graham spends much of the year in the warmer climate of Bulgaria where he owns a second home.

John Dowling

In a race walking career spanning over half a century, Irishman John Dowling has won just about everything there is worth winning.

His debut in the Sheffield 'Star Walk' in 1956 set the scene for an incredible list of race walking achievements far too numerous to list here.

In 1962, he completed his first of three Leicester to Skegness 100-mile races, earning coveted Centurion status which was a precursor to a wonderful future ahead.

Invited to take part in the Paris to Colmar ultra-distance event in 1970, John caused consternation at the start when he turned up without support. Although French officials provided him with two helpers, his journey came to an end after 150 miles when his customised leather shoes, borrowed from legend Albert Johnson, tore his feet to shreds.

Although runner-up on seven successive occasions over 100 miles, John's favourite venue was the Roubaix 28-hour race which he completed 21 times, finishing third on three occasions and fourth twice. For his consistency in this event he was presented with an individual award as the first man to complete the race 10, 15 and 20 times.

Where are they now?

On three occasions in the mid-1970s, John set new Irish records for 200 kilometres. In one of those races, his time taken at 100 miles confirmed that he had broken the 17-hour barrier by two minutes!

Although competing in half a dozen 24-hour or 200-kilometre races a year, John still found time to contest the Parish Walk in 1974, a race he won in 16 hours 40 minutes 07 seconds which was quick enough for him to collect the winning trophy, change his clothing and catch the morning boat to Liverpool before third-placed man Ron Ronan had finished!

Second on two occasions at the 24-hour Rouen event in France, John was comfortably leading the 1978 event from Derek Harrison when his French support team disappeared during the early hours of the morning. With no food left at the feeding stations, he quickly became weak and dehydrated leaving Derek to claim victory by several kilometres. Nevertheless, Derek's wife Sylvia came to the rescue over the closing stages and John's third place was good enough to secure a new Irish 24-hour record with a distance of 207 kilometres.

In 1983, he was invited to take part in the Nottingham six-day race. Walking at a constant 5½ mph for 18 hours a day he managed to cover 401 miles in the first five days, a distance that had taken six days in previous years. On the sixth and final day, he covered only 60 miles but it was still good enough to claim the runner-up spot with an overall distance of 462½ miles.

Although he won the National 100-mile events in 1986 and 1987, John by now had begun turning his attention to even greater distances. In a challenge race in Hull in 1986, he set a new 1,000 mile record of 14 days 23 hours 43 minutes. Later that year, he set a new Land's End to John O'Groats walking record of 12 days, 09 hours 41 minutes for the 840 miles, just missing out on the overall running record by seven hours.

There seems no end to what this man can do. At the age of 65 he walked from Malin Head to Mizzen Head in Ireland in under seven days, slightly slower than first attempt in 1982. His finally challenge before putting his trainers away forever came in 2006, when aged 76, he walked the breadth of Ireland from County Wicklow to County Kerry in six days.

Ted Warner

A member of the Leicester Walking Club, Ted won the 1975 Parish Walk in the third slowest time ever recorded. Taking over the lead from Stan Sille after Peel, Warner was caught and passed by Murray Lambden on the long haul to Bride and looked set to claim the runner-up spot. Nevertheless, Lambden surprised everyone at the most northerly church by announcing his retirement leaving the visitor to claim victory in a time of 18 hours 49 minutes 52 seconds – over three hours outside Graham Young's 1971 record time.

A notable absentee on the start line was John 'Paddy' Dowling of Sheffield United Harriers – last year's outright winner and hoping to compete in the veterans' race to Peel. He was held up on the inbound Manx steamer in Douglas Bay and started nearly 1½ hours later to begin a lone journey to Peel, making contact with the tail-enders by Rushen church. His actual time to Peel was well inside six hours however he had to be content with fifth and last place in a time of 7 hours 21 minutes. Nevertheless, the Irishman was awarded the Jimmy Quinney Cup for the most meritorious performance in this class.

John Cannell

Reaching the pinnacle of his race walking career at a very early age, 68-year-old John Cannell is by far the most successful competitor in the history of the Parish Walk.

One of only three men to record a hat-trick of wins, the ex-Douglas postman has won the coveted title no less than six times during an athletic career spanning five decades. His quickest time in 1982 saw him join an elite group of just five men to have completed the gruelling course in less than 16 hours.

John's first distance event was the 40-mile End to End Walk, first held in October 1961 and won by Stanley Cleator. There were 65 starters in this inaugural race with John recording a time of 9 hours 29 minutes 22 seconds and the last of 21 finishers. Two months later he took part in the very first Peel to Douglas Walk organised by the newly formed Boundary Harriers.

John also represented the Laxey Heralds in the Harvest Moon Relay in October 1963. This was a race of approximately 80 miles along the Island's coastline with his team of five taking second place.

Credited with Centurion status on five occasions, his first success at this prestigious 100-mile event came in 1966 when he recorded a time of 21 hours 45 minutes in a race from Leicester to Skegness. Twenty-two years later, John was runner-up to Richard Brown, recording an incredible time of 17 hours 10 minutes.

By 1967, John had matured into a top-class race-walker. Making his Parish debut that year, the 21-year-old walked a superb race to finish runner-up to the legendary Albert Johnson.

He represented Great Britain in Germany at the 1968 Bremen Postman's Walk and again in 1970 at the Crystal Palace where the BBC televised the event for a *Blue Peter* programme.

However John's greatest achievement was in Surrey in 1987 when, competing against the very best, he won the Race Walking Association's National 100-mile event, securing the team prize along with fellow Boundary Harriers Chris Keown and Willy Corkill.

Competitive to the highest standard, John has triumphed in all the Island's race walking events and remains an inspiration for others to follow.

Retired from the Post Office four years ago and now approaching his 69th birthday, John continues to participate in the winter league programme plus the annual well-trodden route albeit at a more sedate pace.

Reminiscing on past achievements prior to his last

victory in 1994, John added: 'When I was at school, race walking hadn't developed into what it is today. Instead, cross-country was flavour of the month and it was not until 1960 with the revival of the Parish Walk that the sport really took off.'

In 1961, long before his race walking success, John took to winning prizes in 880 yard and one-mile races. 'I had two good teachers, George Southern and Orry Teare. The Firemen's races were good fun and I was in these for about three or four years but never actually won anything. They were over six miles, attracting an entry of 100 or more.'

But it is the Parish Walk for which John has become particularly well known:

'The second time I entered was in 1967 when I did the full 85 miles and came second. I had Eddie Corlett with me and we got lost a few times having never been past Jurby in the dark before. I hadn't done the same amount of training then as I do now. We know a lot more about walking 85 miles now and Albert Johnson has been the inspiration behind it.

Before my first Parish Walk, I had already done a 100-mile race from Leicester to Skegness however it wasn't until 1976 that I first won the event. For me, this is the ultimate test. Even though I've done five 100 mile races, the Parish is still the toughest. There are some stretches which are very hilly and there are times when you think you will never make it'.

Victory in 1981, 1982 and 1983 secured the first-ever hat-trick of wins and John was absolutely delighted with an achievement many thought impossible. 'Every finisher is a winner in this great event.' he later said 'After a win and 16 hours of continuous walking, you're on a "high" so I like to go to the finish and see who's coming in next – my legs are still going so I always try to keep moving.'

The Parish Walk is not an event to go off on your own. John has two 'minders' as far as Peel then another for the remainder of the walk. Plasters, spare shirts and shorts, isotonic drinks and the odd banana are the necessary requisites to keep him going. 'I don't really eat during a race preferring instead to have a good meal beforehand.'

A good judge of the merits of different brands of trainers, John goes shopping in new footwear just to break them in for the many miles ahead With so much success over the years, he reckons £50 for new trainers is well spent. 'When I first started in the 60s, footwear was poor and blisters difficult to avoid. I bought my last pair over a year ago and they have now done well over 1,000 miles!

A postman since he left school all those years ago, John's job helped to keep him fit. Nevertheless, the workload at Christmas was such that his proper training regime had to stop. 'It is very hard to get back into routine,' he added, 'but the job did help after a long race to get rid of any stiffness.'

John is extremely disciplined when it comes to his training. 'I used to train on Monday nights with Liz Corran – even on the wettest occasions she would drag me out when I would rather have stayed at home!

Nearly all of John's training is done on the perimeter road at the Sports Centre where he reckons to have done more than 4,000 laps over the years, varying from just an hour's training but up to 10 miles a night if a big event is forthcoming.

All events before the Parish Walk are good training for him:

'The Bradford Whit Monday Walk was good fun – I even noticed Harry Ramsden's fish and chip shop on the way round! Everyone knows each other, it is a great atmosphere and in the past I've done the Post Office Walk in uniform as well.

Sponsor, Clerical Medical International, has been very generous over the years and my workmates all show a keen interest but of course you're always remembered for your last event which isn't always the most memorable. In a 124-mile race in Battersea Park many years ago, I did less than 20 miles after taking four days off work to go there'.

When he's not working or training John likes to relax by playing snooker and enjoying the occasional pint. Being a non-driver, he doesn't have to worry about drink driving – his trusty footwear seeing seen him home on many a night.

Derek Harrison

A legend from a bygone era and one who held the outright Parish Walk record for 27 years, 79-year-old Derek Harrison is one of only three men to have won the event five times.

Excelling at football, running and swimming at an early age, Derek turned his attention to race walking relatively late in life but soon made an impact. Runner-up to Graham Young in the closest-ever Parish Walk finish in 1971, Derek won the following two events, however he missed out in 1974, when suffering the after affects of a bout of flu, he was forced to retire when leading at Kirk Michael thus effectively ending his ambition of a consecutive hat- trick of wins. Nevertheless, his Parish success continued for another decade and he was again a worthy champion in 1979, 1980 and 1984.

Undoubtedly the most outstanding race-walker of the 1970s, Derek was probably at his peak in 1975 when he recorded considerable success both on and off the Island. That year in his first race for seven weeks following injury and illness, he won the Manx 20-mile Championship on the Southern 100 course. Forfeiting the Parish Walk for commitments in England towards the end of May, Derek recorded a time of 4 hours 50 minutes 28 seconds to claim sixth spot in the annual spring bank holiday Bradford Walk which incorporated the Northern Area 50-kilometre Championship – considered by many to be the 'Blue Ribband' of race walking.

Three weeks later, Boundary Harriers staged the National 20-mile road walking championships at Billown on the Southern 100 course. It was the first time that this prestigious event had been held outside England and as expected, Derek was the first Manx

Walker home in an excellent time of 2 hours 53 minutes 12 seconds to secure twentieth place.

Never one to rest on his laurels, Derek was again in action on the longest day of the year when he convincingly won the Boundary Harriers' annual classic over the TT course in a fraction under 6 hours 20 minutes. The event was again run in August however on this occasion Derek was up against some of the very best from England including John Eddershaw who set the early pace to the 20-mile mark. Judging things just right on his climb up the mountain, Derek strode on to a well-deserved victory in a time of 6 hours 01 minute 20 seconds, less than two minutes outside his best-ever.

Although many consider Derek's greatest achievement to be the 1979 Parish Walk in which his winning time of 15 hours 20 minutes 21 seconds was not bettered until 2006, many would argue that his best-ever outing was in France in 1978 when he set a world walking record of 136½ miles in 24 hours.

Undoubtedly a 'one-off' with a list of sporting achievements too numerous to mention here, Derek remains the most successful competitor ever in the End to End race – winning the 40-mile east coast event on no less than 11 occasions between 1970 and 1986.

Ironically, Derek's competitive career was cut short by a hip complaint that required him to wait the best part of 15 years for a full replacement operation in 2001. While undergoing the operation he suffered a serious stroke which affected his right-hand side. It also affected his speech, together with ability to read and write. But the former Manx marathon champion and Island international footballer has an extremely high pain threshold and he stubbornly battled back to make the 19½ mile mark at Rushen the following year.

Determined to have one final attempt at the gruelling event in 2006, Derek made it to Peel in 8 hours 26 minutes and then pressed on – arriving at the halfway point shortly after 7 o'clock in the evening and just inside the time limit. But 20 miles on at Lezayre he was visibly slowing. Checking in just before the time limit at 1:25am – some two and a half hours after Sean Hands had completed the full course – it looked highly unlikely he would make it back to Douglas inside 24-hour time limit.

As expected, Derek was late checking in at Maughold, however Course Director Kevin Walmsley kindly allowed him to continue with the support of his own family. Radio reports throughout the night had the seven-time finisher as going off the radar between Maughold and Lonan. But Derek was never a quitter and stubbornly battled on. He didn't stop to rest, or to change his trainers, though his pace was slowing all the time. He was fine in himself, no aches or pains, no blisters – but his legs had seized up and wouldn't go any faster.

Derek finally made it to the penultimate church shortly after 8 o'clock in the morning – two hours outside the cut-off time. A number of friends and supporters came out to support him over the final stages of an epic walk against all adversity.

The final mile is never easy, and cheered on by a large crowd eager to witness the unique occasion, Derek crossed the finish line shortly after 10:15am. Although over two hours outside the 24-hour time limit and therefore not eligible for a finisher's certificate, Derek's achievement was duly recognised by the organisers via a special award given at the prize presentation at the Villa Marina two days later.

In summing up Derek Harrison, it's fair to say: 'What he's done is unbelievable. You'll never see anyone of his kind again.' He set the bar for others to follow and with it athletic achievements probably never to be eclipsed. Derek was without doubt a unique athlete, reaching levels many considered unobtainable. His was a class act to follow and one unlikely to be repeated.

Steve Gardner

In an extraordinary sequence of events that led to just one finisher in the 1977 Parish Walk, 28-year-old Steve Gardner's triumphant victory will go down in history as a result never again to be repeated.

Blistering hot conditions throughout the afternoon decimated the field of 90 and by dawn he was the only one left in the race. Unchallenged from Maughold, the 18 lonely miles to Douglas were the most difficult in his life. Nevertheless, Steve kept on going in the knowledge his well-deserved win in 19 hours 11 minutes 01 second would be forever recorded in the Parish Walk Hall of Fame.

The best-placed local competitor and one of only five finishers from a field of 72 men and 18 women in the 1975 event, Steve's time of 19 hours 38 minutes 47 seconds earned him third spot in a race that was dominated by members of the Leicester Walking Club.

A man of few words and married to Gill with four children, Steve is a past chairman of the 'Castletown Ale Drinkers Society', promoters of the World Tin Bath Championships. His walking credentials are up with the very best and include ten Parish Walk finishes between 1971 and 1983 plus coveted Centurion status achieved in Gloucester in 1978.

Murray Lambden

A corner stone of the Manx Harriers for over a quarter of a century, Murray's skills both on and off the track helped gain him much respect. It was thanks to him that Clerical Medical International took up sponsorship of the Parish Walk between 1990 and 2011 raising the event to a level never thought possible.

A participant in Manx athletics at an early age, Murray's sporting achievements are known to all. His first of six attempts at the Parish Walk came in 1975 when, as a teenager, he reached Kirk Michael before succumbing to the pain barrier. The following year he was runner-up to John Cannell while in 1978 he tasted victory as one of only eight finishers in a creditable time of 16 hours, 19 minutes 37 seconds. Six days later, he took part in a 100-kilometre walk in Sutton Coldfield. Held on the partially constructed M42 motorway, the race was a complete disappointment for him as he failed to go beyond the 70-kilometre mark.

A convincing winner of the 1980 End to End Walk, Murray made history that year by becoming the first man to crack the six-hour barrier between the Point of Ayre and the Sound. His time of 5 hours 50 minutes 49 seconds on the old course has never been beaten.

Out manoeuvring Graham Young by the narrowest of margins in the 1981 TT Course Walk, Murray's record time of 5 hours 28 minutes 43 seconds still stands to this day. Unfortunately, the route over 37¾ miles was considered too dangerous and became a casualty of stringent health and safety requirements in 2000.

A former Commonwealth Games representative, Murray put his administrative skills to good use in 1994 when he took up the challenge as manager for the Isle of Man athletics team.

Although a keen runner and regular participant in the London Marathon, past sporting injuries have finally caught up with the 57-year-old who now devotes considerable time to updating Parish Walk statistics on his informative website.

Willy Corkill

Yet another legend from the Parish Walk Hall of Fame, Willy Corkill is one of only three men to have scored a hat-trick of wins in this demanding event.

A resident of Colby, Willie's first encounter with the Island's premier athletic event came in 1962 when as a 14-year-old schoolboy, he took part in the Parish Walk Relay, a junior event established the previous year and open to youth club teams of four.

Turning his attention to motocross during the 1970s, Willie enjoyed considerable success on two wheels before joining Boundary Harriers in 1979 with the intention of taking part in the Parish Walk.

However, the athletics club's shorter distance events were more appealing to Willy and it was not until 1983 that he seriously contested the annual 85-mile classic by claiming the runner-up spot to John Cannell.

Training in excess of 100 miles per week for the 1984 event, Willie was greatly disappointed when he was forced to retire during the early stages. Nevertheless, he bounced back in 1985 to win the event convincingly, again taking the honours in 1886 and 1987.

Martin Lambden

One of only two brothers to have won the richest prize in Manx athletics, 35-year-old Martin Lambden was the unlikely winner of the 1988 Parish Walk having failed to finish on two previous attempts. Pacing himself for a late challenge on race leader Charlie Weston, the dairyman from Braddan made his move soon after Laxey and went on to win by 15 minutes in a time of 17 hours 12 minutes 01 seconds.

Yet another member of the Parish Walk organising committee who contributes much time to the smooth running of the event, Martin, now 60 years of age, is one of the many judges overseeing the race. He is also one of the many timekeepers around the course and can be found in the loneliest of places, his station always open until the final stragglers have passed through.

Charlie Weston

A frequent visitor to our shores and a nine-time Parish Walk finisher, 55-year-old Charlie Weston achieved a well-deserved victory in 1989 when he became the oldest winner of the event, finishing some 45 minutes ahead of his nearest rival. It was a wonderful experience for the Highgate Harrier who rated this win on a par with his Centurion status achieved in the Leicester to Skegness race of 1976 when he recorded a time of 18½ hours for the 100-mile event.

Born in London in 1934, Charlie served two years of National Service before taking up a post as a bus driver in the nation's capital. His brief spell in the army set the corner stone for an athletic career spanning six decades.

A member of the bus company's athletic team in 1959, he soon developed a passion for race walking and joined the Highgate Harriers the following year.

By 1967, Charlie was making a name for himself by completing the first of eight Hastings to Brighton walks – a distance of 38 miles and finishing in 6 hours 49 minutes. Weeks later, he completed the first of 12 London to Brighton Walks, covering the 53 miles in 9 hours 13 minutes 47 seconds, a time he bettered by 23 minutes two years later. Other walking success was to follow including the 52-mile Manchester to Blackpool race, an event he completed ten times. Running too was high on Charlie's agenda, completing 28 marathons, 13 of which were in London with a best time of 3 hours 14 minutes in 1985.

Charlie's first visit to the Isle of Man was in 1975 when he took part in the National 20-mile Walk. His love for the Island blossomed and in 1985, he returned to take part in the first of his 23 Parish Walk starts, finishing second to Willy Corkill in a best time of 16 hours 57 minutes 47 seconds. A third place in the 1986 veterans' race to Peel and the runner-up spot the following two years sowed the seeds for further success, with Charlie winning the 1989 Parish Walk in 18 hours 17 minutes 55 seconds.

Runner-up to Gordon Vale in the 1990 Parish Walk, Charlie returned to his beloved island in 1991, winning the event for a second occasion, while a year later he took third spot behind Graham Young.

Not one to rest on his laurels, Charlie secured a fine sixth placing in 1996 plus another superb finish in 2004, his time of 21 hours 35 minutes 13 seconds his slowest-ever and the last of his nine finishes.

These are indeed impressive statistics from the Island's most popular visitor who continues to participate in the annual classic but at a more sedate pace and happy just to get to Peel.

Where are they now?

Above: Willy Corkill.
Right: Michael George.
Below: Robbie Callister and Sean Hands.
From left to right: Vinny Lynch, Jock Waddington and Martin Lambden.

Gordon Vale

Adding his name to an impressive list of record holders, 28-year-old Gordon Vale, a teacher from St. Mary's Primary School in Douglas, made history in 1990 when he won the Parish Walk at his very first attempt.

The former Great Britain junior race walking champion who held 20 and 50 kilometre track records in England and Austria in 1981, completed the punishing 85-mile course in 17 hours 55 minutes 10 seconds, the fourth slowest and over two and a half hours outside Derek Harrison's 1979 record time.

Although an unlikely contender and one of only six to finish, Gordon paced himself well throughout, taking control at the Dhoon and edging out Charlie Weston by 55 minutes.

Now 51 years of age and no longer participating in a sport that gave him much success, Gordon cut his ties with the Isle of Man in 2010, preferring instead to live in Moscow where he has resumed his profession as a primary school teacher.

Brian Ashwell

There is just not enough time or space here to list the incredible athletic achievements of super-fit veteran Brian Ashwell in a career spanning seven decades.

A man of boundless energy and obsessed with breaking records, the octogenarian from the Leicester Walking Club won the 1995 Parish Walk in a truly amazing performance to become the oldest-ever winner of the Manx annual classic – a record that will almost certainly stand the test of time for years to come.

Although Brian has been involved in local athletics since the 1940s, his enthusiasm for glory shows no sign of waning.

Born in 1932, he took up cross county running aged 12 after being inspired by Wilson the Wonder Athlete, a fictitious character from the comic book Wizard who joined a race from the crowd and run a three-minute mile!

As a teenager, Brian would run after dogs and rabbits and even claimed he could run a third of a mile in 80 seconds. During his National Service in the army, he was capable of long-jumping almost 19 feet, fully attired with backpack and boots. He could also run a mile in just over 4 minutes and 100 yards in 11 seconds!

During an attempt on the 42-mile world record in 1955, Brian was third to world record holder Tom Richards – an event for which he did no training. In fact, most of his training in those days was done in heavy boots!

Reminiscing on his younger days, Brian explained: 'In 1956, I went to a fast 30-miler and said to 1960 Rome Olympics marathon runner Arthur Kiely: "You are going to have to break the world record to beat me today."' Brian was in front for some time but then got severe stomach pains and was forced to stop leaving Keily unchallenged to secure the record.

Taking a break from athletics between 1965 and 1978, Brian met a friend who suggested he take up veteran running. This soon led to the 50-year-old running a world indoor best of 4 minutes 33 seconds over 1500 metres.

Turning his attention to race walking when he was 60, Brian set a world age-best for a 65-year-old in 1998 when he clocked 5 hours 31 minutes 31 seconds for 50 kilometres.

The records continued to tumble and in 2001 he walked the fastest time in the world for his age to clock 55 minutes 40 seconds for 10 kilometres. Walking a marathon in Leicester some months later, he clocked 4 hours 33 minutes for 26 miles 385 yards – quite an achievement for a man aged 69!

The records kept on coming, and in 2005, Brian set another world age-best for one-hour track running by covering 14,644 metres.

Ten days after celebrating his 75th birthday, the remarkable athlete reduced the British and European marks in the 1,500 metres with a 5 minute 29.94 seconds clocking. The following day, Brian, who regularly runs 70 miles a week in training, showed no ill effects as he carved 17 seconds off the British M75 best for 10,000 metres by crossing the line in 41 minutes 30.32 seconds.

Brian holds the British age-group one-hour track records for men aged 70, 72 to 75, 78 to 79 and now 80. In 2012 he took the honours in the annual Leamington one-hour track race by completing 12,872 metres.

Approaching his 81st birthday, Brian's ambition is to run a mile in under six minutes. Having been in athletics for nearly 70 years, Brian says he's perfected his training techniques. 'I've not got a naturally straight leg so I get pulled a few times. I was the Leicester junior walking champion at 17 and came second in the British 100-mile Championship when I was 60. My twice a day training schedule involves a five-kilometre session alternating between fast and slow bursts in the morning and 100 repetition runs of 100 metres, each of 22 seconds with a 25-yard walk recovery in the afternoon.'

Brian maintains that training with people who are 30 or 40 years younger gives him a great deal of confidence. 'I don't do distance, only quality,' says the octogenarian. 'To be honest, I don't really like racing in competitions. I just enjoy the freedom of running and I think that's the key to my success. I am not after any glory or pats on the back, I usually just go home after a race.'

The super-fit pensioner has never smoked, never drank alcohol and does not eat junk food. However, he also claims not to drink water either, opting instead for 15 cups of tea a day.

He is years ahead of his time when it comes to training techniques. 'I did altitude training in my back bedroom years ago,' he recently said. 'I used to go on my treadmill, shut the windows and doors and put on a gas mask.'

Age seems no Barrier for Brian Ashwell, his appetite for world age-best records showing no signs of waning. Presently suffering from a hamstring injury, Brian has had to give the Centenary Parish Walk a miss. Nevertheless, he remains confident at completing the gruelling event in 2014, and if successful, will be by far the oldest-ever finisher.

Lee Cain

Fifth in the 1991 Parish Walk and runner-up in 1993 and 1994, Lee Cain was a worthy winner in 1996. His time of 17 hours 26 minutes 29 seconds was slightly slower than in recent years but still nearly half an hour quicker than his nearest rival Tony Kneale.

After several failed attempts and getting lost on many occasions, the farmer from Braddan who never admits to training took the lead soon after leaving Peel and from that point on was never challenged. Only 17 of the 304 starters completed the gruelling 85-mile course – a statistic that bears out just how difficult this event is.

A past Foxdale FC player and staunch member of the Central Young Farmer's Club, 43-year-old Lee has retired from the sport that once gave him much pleasure. Married to Sarah with two children, he now resides at his new home in Crosby – a project that took several years to complete.

Chris Flint

A popular and regular visitor to Manx shores and one who has enjoyed considerable success in the Parish Walk, Chris Flint's athletic career began on a wet and cold January afternoon in 1962 when, with 60 fellow police cadets, he was told to circumnavigate the old Hendon aerodrome in race walking mode under the direction of Inspector Tom Edwards, a great enthusiast for the sport.

Reflecting on those days long past Chris said: 'Surprisingly, around four or five of us grasped the principles fairly quickly and on being dispersed around London we joined local clubs. I joined the London Vidarians' Walking Club and it was my club until it disbanded in 2007, some 104 years after its formation. I now walk for the Surrey Walking Club.'

As a club walker Chris participated in the traditional 7, 10 and 15 miles races, which included the classic races such as London to Brighton and Hastings to Brighton. Representing the Metropolitan Police in its matches against clubs, Chris was awarded his MP Colours in 1982. 'I would have remained an average club walker had it not been for the Watts brothers who were ultra-distance eventers and encouraged me to enter the 100 miles in 24 hours race in 1989 hosted by the Metropolitan Police. I successfully completed the 100 miles in just over 20 hours, and qualified to be Centurion 849.' This started Chris's participation in long-distance races and between 1989 and the present, he achieved the following success:

  21 successful 100 miles in 24 hours completions in the UK.

  National UK distance champion in 1997 and 2003.

  Twice-winner of Isle of Man Parish Walk, finishing no less than six times.

  Successful completions of the Roubaix 28-hour race, the latest in 2013.

  Participation in 24-hour races on the Continent, particularly at Bar le Duc, Dijon, Chateau Thierry and the Netherlands where he became Continental Centurion 333.

On the administrative side of race walking, Chris is the secretary of the Centurions 1911 as well as the secretary of the Race Walking Association (Southern Area). He is also an active member of the RWA committee and until recently, was the walking secretary of the Veterans' Athletic Club of which he is now Vice President.

Chris says:

'The success of recent 100 miles races at the NSC in 2006 and 2013 plus the 1998 event which was incorporated in the Parish Walk represents the best of our sport as the numbers of entrants from the Isle of Man reflect a desire and interest in achieving the status of becoming a Centurion. This goes to enhancing the reputation of Manxmen and women as sports people, many of whom have reached a high standard in race walking. It is hoped that they will continue to support and motivate people to take part in these hard, mentally and physically demanding events. The rewards are great, especially that feeling of achievement and I am proud to have been a winner on a couple of occasions of the Parish Walk'.

Richard and Sandra Brown

By far Britain's most successful distance athletes, the husband and wife team from England have dominated race walking throughout Britain for the best part of 30 years.

A Parish Walk winner in 1998 at the very first attempt, Richard has for many years been one of Britain's greatest ultra-distance walkers and runners.

He has won the Centurions 100-mile annual classic a record ten times and is the UK record holder over 100 miles with a time of 17 hours 01 minutes and 200 kilometres in 21 hours 42 minutes. He is only one of two Englishmen (the other being Colin Young) to have successfully completed the gruelling Paris to Colmar multi-day race.

Richard also holds a range of UK running records which have been built off his race walking speed, including indoor 48 hours (357 kilometres) outdoor track 48 hours (401 kilometres), six days (835 kilometres), Irish End to End and Land's End to John O'Groats (835 miles) in 10 days 02 hours.

Still very much competitive, Richard holds world age-group records at various levels. He also manages and coaches Team GB's 24-hour running squads and so aims to pass on to a younger generation some of the experience and pleasure he has been fortunate enough to have acquired over some 30 years of competitive racing.

The Captain of Centurions 1911, Sandra Brown has

completed a record number of Centurion events in Britain and around the world since she qualified as Centurion 735 in 1982.

She has completed 27 British Centurion events, up to and including the IOM 100 in 2013, winning the ladies' race 26 times. Sandra was the first person to hold all six Centurion awards worldwide: GB, Continental, USA, New Zealand, Australia and Malaysia. To date, she has completed 42 Centurion events around the world.

A prolific ultra-distance walker and runner, Sandra has completed over 150 events of between 100 miles and 1,000 miles. A past President of Surrey Walking Club, she is the author of the club's 1999 centenary history *Unbroken Contact.*

Peter Kaneen

Born in 1961 and a garage proprietor from Union Mills, Peter Kaneen only took up race walking as a health kick after giving up smoking in a bid to improve his lifestyle.

Inspired by Derek Harrison and John Cannell – probably the best distance walkers the Island has ever produced, Peter took part in his first Parish Walk in 1995, later turning his attention to the winter walking league in a bid to improve his technique.

A late beginner to race walking, he soon made up for lost time, enjoying considerable success both on and off the Island. He is a twice Parish Walk champion and three-time finisher out of ten attempts.

Although a superb athlete over the shorter distance, Peter is equally impressive on more demanding circuits and is a past winner of the End to End Walk. His demolition of all opposition in the first Parish Walk of the new millennium paved the way for an outstanding performance two years later when he came within six minutes of the all-time record.

Having proved to be a man of distance, Peter began concentrating on shorter distances in the hope of qualifying for the Commonwealth Games. He now had a preference for 20- and 50-kilometre walks and often competed against the Island's very best such as Steve Partington, Steve Taylor and Kevin Walmsley. 'I came into the sport late at around 36 years of age and felt that time was limited to achieve my goal of trying to make the Commonwealth Games,' he said. 'I also decided that I wanted to compete in the best International walks, however due to my age, I found that National quads did not want to know. Just the honour of racing against some of the best athletes in my sport was something I will always be proud of. Intense competition took my fitness to a level above that I thought possible when I walked my first Parish.'

Peter considers winning the UKA team gold at the 20-kilometre National Road Championship to be one of his best achievements. His two 50-kilometre races in 2005, when aiming for qualifying time for Melbourne, were also impressive. 'I did 4 hours 31 minutes 43 seconds in Slovakia and 4 hours 30 minutes 26 seconds in Denmark,' he said.

Another record he is most proud of is a personal best time of 93 minutes 47 seconds over 20 kilometres at Dublin in 2005.

Although approaching his 54th year and with his best days behind him, Peter remains athletically active, albeit at a much reduced pace. Married to Bridgit with three daughters, he still finds time between work and family life at Glen Vine to train on the well-trodden route that has given him immense pleasure over the years.

Robbie Callister

Although semi-retired from front-line race walking, 59-year-old Robbie Callister took the Parish Walk to a new level during the first decade of the new millennium by scoring five victories during the first eight events.

A resident of Castletown and educated at Castle Rushen High School, Robbie was greatly influenced by Steve Gardner, winner of the 1977 Parish Walk and a ten-time finisher.

As a teenager, Robbie took part in the 1973 Parish Walk, reaching Kirk Michael at his first attempt. Throughout the decade, race walking continued to be flavour of the month for him, however by 1980 he had begun to show interest in motorcycling

Trials, motocross and endurance racing were soon high on Robbie's agenda, and he took part in the 1983 International Six Day Enduro event held in Wales.

But the slower pace of life seemed to suit the promising athlete better. Running was now flavour of the month and in 1985, he completed the Dublin Marathon in a credible time of 3 hours 11 minutes. Further success followed in 1889 when he was chosen to represent the Isle of Man at the Island Games held in the Faero Islands. This prestigious event hosted a 26-mile marathon in which Robbie finished fourth, thus enabling the Manx team to win the gold medal.

Employed for many years in the operations room at Manx Airlines, he began dominating the athletic scene in 1990, winning everything in sight including the marathon of that year. He was again chosen to represent the Isle of Man at the 1991 Island Games held in Aland where he finished fifth in the half marathon. Victory came his way later that year when he convincingly won the 26-mile marathon held on the Ramsey course. His success continued in 1992 when he recorded the first Manx win in the TT 40 running race, a 40-mile event held over an extended TT course. His victory was quickly followed by yet another marathon win, an event he continued to dominate throughout until 1994. In fact, Robbie participated in a total of 25 marathons, six of which were in London.

Perhaps his greatest achievements were reserved for the dawn of the new millennium. In an awesome demonstration of race walking intelligence, Robbie quite effortlessly crushed all opposition to win the 2000 British Veterans' Marathon Championship, held for the first time on the Isle of Man.

Victory in the 2001 Parish Walk paved the way for

Where are they now?

further success in the recently revived End to End Walk. The 40-mile route along the Island's picturesque west coast was a new challenge and he dominated the event with victories in 2002, 2003, and 2004.

A popular winner of the 2002 Parish Walk, Robbie was now on course to join that elite pair of race-walkers who have completed a hat-trick of wins, John Cannell in 1983 and Willie Corkill in 1987. Nevertheless, the showdown between the Island's very best in 2003 saw the event won for a second time by Peter Kaneen, thus denying Robbie any hope of the hat-trick he so longed for.

His back-to-back wins in 2004 and 2005 were overshadowed the following year when he was convincingly beaten by Sean Hands in the fastest and first-ever sub-15-hour circuit of the seventeen parishes.

Impressive credentials as they are however, acquiring Centurion status in 2006 remained elusive when he was unfairly disqualified at the Norfolk Challenge for allegedly cutting a corner while comfortably leading.

Putting that disappointment behind him, Robbie went on to win the 2007 Parish Walk in 15 hours 36 minutes 52 seconds. He was runner-up to Jock Waddington the following year, fifth in 2011, ninth in 2012 and eleventh in 2013. In the same year at the National Sports Centre, Robbie finally gained recognition as a Centurion by completing 100 miles and finishing third in 19 hours 19 minutes 45 seconds.

Approaching his 59th birthday and still very much competitive, the likeable all-rounder continues to support the event he has dominated for the best part of a decade. His best years behind him, Robbie will always be remembered for being 'the man to beat.'

Sean Hands

Making his Parish Walk debut in 2001, 49-year-old Sean Hands is yet another man who has come a long way in a short time.

Runner-up to Robbie Callister in the 2004 and 2005 events, Sean achieved even greater success later in 2005 when he convincingly won the Norfolk 100-Mile Challenge at Kings Lynn to qualify for coveted Centurion status, an event he again won on home ground a year later.

A man of few words, Sean's greatest sporting achievement was undoubtedly the 2006 Parish Walk when he quite simply swept aside all opposition to break Derek Harrison's long-standing record and become the first-ever man to break the 15-hour barrier.

Although it was expected that Harrison's record would eventually go, not even Sean could have envisaged it happening in such a dramatic fashion. His time of 14 hours 47 minutes 36 seconds was simply outstanding and 33 minutes inside a record time that had stood for 27 years.

Nevertheless, three years of tough competition have taken its toll on the past Parish Walk and twice Centurion champion. A re-occurring hamstring injury suffered some years ago continues to aggravate Sean to such an extent that he no longer competes at distance events, preferring instead to officiate at most of the Island's major race walking events..

Jock Waddington

A man who has come a long way in a very short time, four-time champion Jock Waddington is the only quadruple winner of the Parish Walk having scored consecutive victories between 2008 and 2011.

With no interest in sporting activities until he was 40, Jock was quite content to be an armchair sports fan and couldn't understand why anyone would want to walk for 85 miles non-stop.

In fact, it was only in 2004 that he first toed the line in a walking race and what a baptism by fire! On the day of the race, after three months' worth of questionable training, Jock felt he had done enough miles and was mentally convinced that he would finish. But he soon found out that there is more to a Parish Walk than first meets the eye. Blisters at Malew took the wind out of his sails and by Kirk Michael he was a broken man and extremely disappointed at being unable to go any further. Nevertheless, he bounced back quickly and three months later completed the White and Healthy End to End Walk three months later in 9 hours 25 minutes 21 seconds.

Hooked on race walking after just two events, Jock joined Allan Callow's training sessions at the National Sports Centre in Douglas and listened carefully to his coaching advice before he developed too many bad habits.

He soon became a regular competitor at most of the local events, the coaching and training sessions in 2005 helping him achieve his first Parish Walk finish in a commendable time of 21 hours 43 minutes 59 seconds. Although absolutely exhausted both mentally and physically, Jock was ecstatic with his performance. 'Your first Parish finish is a fantastic feeling and nothing can compare,' he said later.

Finishing twentieth in the 2006 Parish Walk, Jock surprised even himself two months later by achieving Centurion status at the National Sports Centre in Douglas. Slipping from sixth to ninth spot over the final ten miles, he completed the gruelling 100 miles two and a half minutes inside 21 hours.

Jock's sub-17-hour circuit of the 17 parishes in 2007 was just enough to claim sixth spot, edging out first woman home, Sue Biggart, by less than two minutes.

The incessant and unrelenting rain in 2008 failed to dampen Jock's spirits for he caught and passed second-placed Robbie Callister at the Iron Bridge between Peel and Kirk Michael. Although race leader Sean Hands had a comfortable 21-minute lead, he later retired at Ginger Hall with a hamstring injury leaving Jock to control the race from that point on and claim his first victory in 15 hours 44 minutes 33 seconds.

Overwhelmed with emotion, Jock later said: 'I had inherited the lead and then started to panic. For years,

I had stood in awe and admiration of Robbie, Sean and other Parish Walk regulars, who year after year, would make the top six. Now, I found myself in the lead of the biggest race on the Manx athletics calendar and I wasn't really sure what I was supposed to do next.'

Jock went on: 'After my initial panic, I dug in and carried on, continually looking over my shoulder to see where Robbie was because I was expecting him to chip away at my ten-minute lead as the race progressed into the latter stages of Maughold, Lonan and Onchan.'

By 2009, people were asking Jock if he was confident enough to defend the title and win for a second time. A natural enough question, but although he trained exceptionally hard, and was fairly confident of doing well, the Parish Walk is a test of mental strength, physical ability and endurance. Regardless of how much training one does, the race is punishing throughout and anything can happen on race day.

Maintaining fourth place up until Peel, Jock passed Ray Pitts and Janice Quirk and by Kirk Michael, he had caught Robbie Callister to take the lead.

As the race progressed to Ramsey Janice Quirk pushed hard and was only 19 minutes behind on the twisting road through Port e Vullen. Nevertheless, Jock kept his nerve to win by 13 minutes in a race that saw 18 minutes taken off the ladies' record.

When asked by Olympic athlete Roger Black if a hat-trick of wins was possible in 2010 Jock replied: 'I will certainly give it my best shot – it all depends on how it pans out on the day.'

Race day was incredibly hot which caught out a lot of competitors who quickly became dehydrated in the intense heat. Michael George was the first to leave Rushen however he was overhauled by Jock on the climb to Ballakillowey and from that point on was never seriously challenged. Establishing an eight-minute lead at Peel and feeling comfortable, he pushed on, half expecting the heat to punish him on the long haul to Bride.

Keeping well hydrated and covered in sunscreen, Jock survived fairly intact to cross the finish line on Douglas Promenade for a third time in as many years and join John Cannell and Willie Corkill to become only the third person to achieve a hat-trick of wins.

Determined to win again and become the first person ever to win four races back-to-back, Jock knew the 2011 event would be his toughest yet.

Setting off at a steady pace on the longest day of the year, he soon moved to the front of the field. He had fully expected Michael George, Vinny Lynch and Richard Gerrard to make a challenge however it never came and by the halfway mark his lead had extended to ten minutes.

At Bride, some ten miles on, the gap had increased by another minute to 11. By the time he reached the penultimate church with darkness well advanced, his lead over Vinny Lynch had grown to 14 minutes, more than enough to secure victory for a fourth consecutive time and secure a place in the Parish Walk Hall of Fame.

Jock gave the 2012 Parish Walk a miss but returned for the centenary event the following year, finishing third in 15 hours 12 minutes 39 seconds – his second fastest time ever. Not one to rest on his laurels, he took to the NSC track once again in August and achieved Centurion status for the very first time, finishing fourth in 19 hours 34 minutes 01 seconds.

Vinny Lynch

A man of many words, there is a lot more to Vinny Lynch than first meets the eye. Turning his attention to race walking relatively late in life the likeable Irishman made Parish Walk history in 2012 by becoming the first-ever joint winner in a new record time of 14 hours 42 minutes 03 seconds.

Born in Sligo in February, 1961 and one of eight children, Vinny left school in 1978 and like most youngsters in Ireland at that time, had three choices – America, England or the army. Choosing the latter, he crossed the border and signed up for the Royal Irish Regiment and so began a two-year army apprenticeship as a toolmaker.

Athletically motivated at an early age, Vinny quickly developed a passion for middle-distance running, soccer and Gaelic football. On leaving the army his fitness levels had improved to such an extent that he made a one-off appearance in the 1981 Dublin Marathon, recording an impressive time of 2 hours 26 minutes! There was no payment for this performance but there was when he played in the League of Ireland for Sligo Town. 'We weren't paid enough to give up our full time jobs but it was still nice to receive a fee of some sort.'

During his time overseas, Vinny spent several years in Australia and New Zealand before moving to the Isle of Man in 1996. 'I came to the Island for a Paddy's weekend, fell in love with the place and have been here ever since,' he said.

Vinny's first appearance in the 2005 Parish Walk was the result of a work-mate talking him into walking to Peel. 'I didn't know at the time that it was a 33-mile walk so I left him at Santon and got to Peel in 6 hours 49 minutes – not bad for a first time effort,' he later recalled.

Determined to go the full distance the following year, Vinny trained hard throughout the winter only to fall short at Rushen after been dragged along too quickly by Ray Pitts, Sue Biggart and Michael George.

Intensive training through the winter of 2007 failed to produce that elusive finish he so much desired. 'You must get yourself training with other walkers faster than you,' he said. 'Do everything you can to to stay close and find out why they are faster, what they are eating and how much training they are doing.'

Although training in excess of 70 miles a week and often walking from Douglas to his place of work at Ronaldsway, Vinny failed to go beyond Bride in 2008, the wettest Parish Walk in living memory. Nevertheless, he set his sights on winning the trophy for the fastest first-time finisher in 2009 and to his surprise, reached the finish line on Douglas

Where are they now?

Promenade in 17 hours 05 minutes 08 seconds.

Runner-up to Jock Waddington in 2010 and 2011, Vinny achieved his ultimate goal the following year, when in collaboration with Richard Gerrard, he stormed around the well-trodden route to become the first-ever joint winner in a new record time of 14 hours 42 minutes 32 seconds.

At the Roubaix 28-hour race in France ten weeks later, Vinny was delighted to claim the runner-up spot by walking 145 miles, some four miles greater than friend Richard Gerrard.

Although Vinny trained exceptionally hard for the 2013 Parish Walk with high hopes of an outright win, he was somewhat disappointed to finish fourth and down 31 minutes on his best time 12 months earlier.

Not one to sulk on his past performances, Vinny took to the NSC track six weeks later and was runner-up to Richard Gerrard in the RWA 100-Mile Championship, completing 206 laps of the perimeter road in a fraction over 19 hours to claim much-coveted Centurion status for the very first time.

Richard Gerrard

Inducted into the Parish Walk Hall of Fame in 2012 as one of only two people to have jointly won the annual classic, 41-year-old Richard Gerrard is yet another example of age being no barrier in this Herculean event.

Married to New Zealander Kyley with children Tom and Hannah, Richard made his Parish debut in 2007, reaching Andreas before succumbing to the pain barrier. At the time, he was considerably overweight and the occasion provided him with the incentive to live a healthier lifestyle. Later in the year he tackled the End to End Walk, completing the 40-mile course for the first time.

Despite falling into a ditch at Ballajora during the 2008 Parish Walk – the wettest and most difficult event in living memory, Richard's determination and sheer tenacity undoubtedly paved the way for his first-ever finish in 21 hours 12 minutes 38 seconds.

Four hours quicker and a credible eleventh spot the following year, Richard surprised even himself in 2010 by finishing fourth in 16 hours 13 minutes 22seconds.

Intense training during the build-up to the 2011 Parish Walk saw Richard shattering his best time by over 50 minutes to secure the final podium spot. In the End to End Walk three months later, he quite literally swept all opposition aside to win the 40-mile event in 6 hours 48 minutes, an achievement he was most proud of.

But it was in 2012 that Richard really made a name for himself. Collaborating with Vinny Lynch during the second half of the race, he outmanoeuvred race leader Michael George at the penultimate church to jointly claim a well-deserved victory in the quickest race of all time.

Not content to put away his shoes for another year, Richard finished third in the Roubaix 28-hour classic in France ten weeks later, completing 141 miles within the requisite time period.

With his race walking apprenticeship now complete, Richard turned his attention in 2013 to defending last year's hard-won Parish Walk and, like friend Vinny Lynch, he trained exceptionally hard throughout the winter months in the knowledge that the centenary event would be a far different proposition to the one 12 months earlier.

Unusual for the leading trio to stay together as far as Bride, Michael George took the initiative thereafter, carving out a six-minute lead and marching on to the finish to reap the rewards for his labour. Although Richard was nine minutes outside his best time, he was more than pleased with the runner-up spot and gracious in defeat.

Nevertheless, Richard made up for his disappointment six weeks later when he won the RWA 100-Mile Race Walking Championship held at the NSC in Douglas for the second time in seven years. Taking the lead early on, he completed the compulsory 206 circuits of the perimeter track to claim Centurion status for the first time in a fraction under eighteen and a half hours.

Michael George

A Manx resident since 1978 and no stranger to media attention, 47-year-old Michael George is best remembered for his heroic effort in the 2012 Parish Walk when he led for the best part of 60 miles only to come up short when it mattered most.

With a punishing training programme, at times in excess of 100 miles per week, Michael's preparation both mentally and physically makes him a difficult act to follow and always the man to beat. He is by far the Island's quickest middle-distance walker having recently recorded a personal best of 97 minutes 31 seconds to place him high on the all-time list of local walkers over 20 kilometres and the fourth fastest age-best time in the world for 45 to 49-year-olds.

Like many of those before him, Michael was a late entrant into race walking, his first appearance in the Parish Walk being in 2003 when he and his wife Irene walked to Peel in 8 hours 51 minutes 03 seconds. This spurred him on to join the Manx Harriers later in the year when he firmly established himself as a midfield runner.

Although he completed his first Parish Walk in 2004 in a commendable time of 22 hours 25 minutes 55 seconds, the occasion was not without drama. While negotiating the northern plain in the black of night, Michael fell two feet into a ditch when answering a call of nature. It required the effort of his support team to pull him clear. Nevertheless, he struggled on, eventually regaining his composure to finish in a time of 22 hours 25 minutes 55 seconds.

Due to an Achilles injury that wouldn't go away, Michael missed the 2005 event, however he returned in 2006 to post the biggest improvement in the history of the event by holding off strong finishing Andrew Titley on Douglas Promenade to claim eighth spot in 17 hours 12 minutes 31 seconds.

Several months later at the National Sports Centre, Michael achieved even greater distance by finishing sixth in the Centurion 100-mile classic with a superb time of 21 hours 34 minutes 01 seconds.

Third in the 2007 Parish Walk and cracking the 16-hour barrier by three minutes in the process, Michael had to settle for fourth place in 2008 with a slightly slower time of 16 hours 40 minutes 53 seconds. Although this was the wettest event in living memory, a surprising 121 hardy souls made it to the finish

A non-starter in 2009, he claimed third spot in 2010 with a time of 16 hours 04 minutes 07 seconds, some 6½ minutes behind runner-up Vinny Lynch.

The record books tell us that Michael's slowest circuit of the 17 parishes was in 2011 when he took 22 hours 38 minutes 58 seconds, finishing in 125th place! The reason for his extended journey was that he walked with his wife to Kirk Michael, stopped there for two hours and then continued on alone to the finish.

Although too numerous to mention in detail, Michael's impressive list of athletic achievements certainly makes good reading. In 2012, he became the eighth fastest age-best in the world over 10 kilometres and the fourth fastest age-best in the world over 20 kilometres.

Although the 2012 Parish Walk is one Michael may wish to forget, history will tell us that this race was lost not through his wrong doing but more importantly, it was won by the combined resources of Vinny Lynch and Richard Gerrard, who over the closing stages, went on to produce an unexpected result.

But not one to be outdone, Michael's obsessive training in the build-up to the centenary event was rewarded with a well-deserved victory in 14 hours 44 minutes 49 seconds thus silencing those who doubted his ability to claim the richest prize in Manx athletics.

Taking little time off from his punishing training schedule, Michael enjoyed further success 13 weeks later when he won the End to End race in a record-breaking time of 6 hours 24 minutes 32 seconds, finishing some seven minutes ahead of arch-rival and runner-up, Richard Gerrard.

Allan Callow

Over five decades of competitive race walking have established Allan Callow as on of the finest, if not the best-ever short distance race-walker the Island has ever produced.

Athletically active from an early age, Allan was placed fourth in the 1966 National Junior championships and just missed out on team selection for the Commonwealth Games in Jamaica that year.

Selected for the Commonwealth Games in 1970, 1974, and 1978, he achieved a superb eighth place in 1974 over the 20-mile course.

A resident of New Zealand between 1974 and 1980, Allan returned to the Isle of Man to resume his profession as an architect, a vocation he actively pursues when not officiating at the numerous events on the race walking calendar both on and off the Island.

Influenced by the late Albert Johnson, Allan took to coaching juniors and seniors, something he continues to do on a twice-weekly basis at the NSC in Douglas. It is probably fair to say that over the years, many of the Island's top race-walkers have benefited from his tuition by developing a style and technique that has led many to greater things.

Although not a natural distance walker, Allan competed in the 1982 Parish Walk, finishing fourth in 19 hours 40 minutes 13 seconds – an event he says he'll not be competing in again!

Aged 68 and his best days behind him, Allan will probably be best remembered as a regular winner of the veterans' shorter race to Peel, in particular, the 1993 event when he quite literally sprinted to Peel in a little over five and a quarter hours – a record that was not broken for another 19 years.

Steve Taylor

Born in 1966, Steve Taylor is one of very few Manx race-walkers to have taken up the sport at early age and scored considerable success. His first flirtation with race walking was in 1982 when asked to make up a team for the Merseyside Schools. Although he received praise for his efforts in the 5-kilometre event, finishing faster than any other competitor, Steve didn't make the team participating in the English Schools event. Nevertheless, he had caught the bug and thereafter started walking with Mike Karran and Andrew Garrett under the watchful eye of Allan Callow.

As a 20-year-old junior, Steve was selected to represent Great Britain over 20 kilometres in Madrid, Spain. Winner that day was Daniel Plaza of the host nation who went on to become Olympic champion in 1992. Steve also represented Great Britain as a senior however the highlight of his athletic career was competing for the Isle of Man at the 1994 Commonwealth Games in Victoria, Canada when he produced probably his best performance ever.

Turning his attention to race walking judging in 1997, Steve gained considerable experience while standing alongside senior judges at many mainland events. He was also fortunate enough to be able to 'shadow' some of the best judges in Europe, and having passed the UK's written examination, he was placed on a fast-track programme to become qualified at European level. His target was to achieve the necessary pass mark never thinking he would be good enough to be elected to the European panel and so it was an enormous surprise when the results of the examination were announced that he was top of the class! This led to him being selected by the European Athletic Association for the next IAAF examination in Paris and again his aim was to achieve the pass mark. Up against judges from all corners of the world, Steve was more than delighted to hear that not only did he pass, but in finishing third overall, he was elected to the international panel of race walking judges.

Although he has travelled much of the world both as a competitor and officiator, it is nearer to home that Steve received the greatest accolade when he was

Where are they now?

appointed chief judge for the 2012 London Olympics. This was undoubtedly the highlight of his career but let us not forget that he was also instrumental in getting race walking included in the programme for the Commonwealth Youth Games held on the Isle of Man in September, 2011.

Actively involved in Manx athletics at grass-roots level, Steve is a judge, organiser and statistician. Although his best days are behind him, he remains competitive, day-dreaming at times that he himself is competing in the Olympics or World Championships!

Although the Parish Walk has grown in stature over the years, the event still has to be judged to a high standard and race walking rules adhered to. IAAF Rule 230 states that race walking is a progression of steps so taken that the walker makes contact with the ground, so that no visible (to the human eye) loss of contact occurs. The advancing leg shall be straightened (i.e., not bent at the knee) from the moment of first contact with the ground until the vertical upright position. International rules require at least three judges present and each walker is only disqualified if three red cards are received from all judges. Domestic rules require only one or two judges, either of whom can disqualify an athlete on the spot – 'one shout and you're out' is the graphic phrase.

In summing up these sometimes confusing rules, the Parish Walk, due to its nature and logistics, is judged as a category B event and therefore under domestic ruling. Any judge can disqualify a competitor without prior warning if it is felt the athlete is not complying with these rules.

Mick Holgate

Now aged 68, Sheffield-born bricklayer Mick Holgate is lucky to be alive after falling from the roof of a house that he was building for himself in 1999.

Although he was fortunate to avoid brain damage, Mick's injuries were so severe that surgeons had to pin both his arms and neck which incapacitated him for many months. Nevertheless, he exercised tirelessly over the following winter and to the surprise of everyone, took part in the first Parish Walk of the new millennium finishing in 20 hours 12 minutes 16 seconds.

Reaching Rushen at his first attempt in 1984, and Jurby the following year, Mick made it to the finish in 1986 thus setting the scene for a glorious career that would see him complete the well-trodden route no less than 17 times.

Ultra-distance events during the late 1980s, and early 1990s saw Mick achieve Centurion status on three occasions, Ewhurst, Hendon and Battersea, the latter in 1993 when he took the Northern 100-Mile title covering 107 miles in 24 hours.

Exhibiting great determination, mental discipline and undoubtedly a shining light for others to follow, Mick has never considered failure during a Parish Walk. Proud of the fact that he has completed this Herculean task during his 40s, 50s and now 60s, Mick is more determined than ever to achieve one more finish in four decades of trying.

Chris Cale

Although short in height and of slight build, the sports shop proprietor from Douglas punches well above his weight having completed the Parish Walk on ten occasions not to mention the Ramsey Bakery End to End Walk in which he has clocked up nine.

Chris first entered the Parish Walk in 1997. Intending to walk to Peel but feeling good and looking fresh as paint, he continued to Bride. However, on that occasion he lost his confidence after leaving Jurby and like so many others, found the road to the most northerly church exceedingly difficult.

Chris made it to Andreas in 1998, Jurby in 1999 and Andreas again in 2002. He missed the first two events of the new millennium but has consistently finished the gruelling event every year since.

A first Parish Walk finish is always special, however Chris was lucky not to be timed out in 2003 when he reached the finish line on Douglas Promenade with only 16½ minutes to spare.

Training hard through the long months of winter, Chris improved on his 2004 time by nearly an hour. His work colleague Lisa Motley walked with him for much of the night, pushing each other through difficult times to finish together in 22 hours 45 minutes 26 seconds.

Robbie Callister may have provided Chris's motivation to improve his time by two hours in 2005 – a year that saw him finish ahead of training partner and quadruple champion Jock Waddington. In 2006, Chris went one better by completing the Parish Walk in less than 19 hours. Two months later he achieved Centurion status at the National Sports Centre in Douglas by completing 100 miles in 23 hours 22 minutes – a time he improved on by two and a half hours at the same venue in 2013.

Over the years, Chris's ability to improve on his times has been quite extraordinary. Back problems in 2007 and the worst weather on record in 2008 failed to dampen his spirits and in 2009 he went under 18 hours for the very first time. A finisher in the next three Parish Walks, Chris went even faster in 2013, finishing tenth in a best time of 16 hours 43 minutes 22 seconds.

Although comfortable with distance, Chris surprised even himself in 2012 by completing over 114 miles in the Roubaix 28-hour race in France – an event that has guaranteed the likeable 41-year-old a well-deserved place in Manx athletic history.

Gordon Corran

More famous for his 'never again' quotes than actual Parish Walk finishes, 62-year-old Gordan Corran's exemplary race walking record speaks for itself with eight finishes out of 16 starts.

A man of many words, Gordon made his Parish debut in 1994, a year that saw the event diverted from Patrick, adding another mile to an already painful journey that for him, ended at St Johns.

Persuaded by Mick Holgate to prove it was no fluke, Gordon not only made it to Peel in 1995 but

1924

Above: Richard Gerrard.
Right: Peter Kaneen.
Below: Steve Gardner.
From left to right: Lee Cain, Charlie Weston and John Cannell, and Chris Flint.

Where are they now?

also did for the next three years. He improved every year with a best time in 1997 of 6 hours 14 minutes 07 seconds.

In 1998, Gordon took the plunge and decided to walk the whole course with his friend Dave Lockett. 'It was the year that the Centurion's 100-mile event was incorporated in the Parish Walk, but if you wanted to walk the extra 15 miles up and down Douglas Promenade you had to pay an additional entry fee.' Gordon didn't think that he would make it back in Douglas in time so he missed his opportunity to walk 100 miles in 24 hours, a feat considered by many to be the ultimate challenge.

The following year he broke the twenty-hour barrier by two and a half minutes, a time he improved on by 38 minutes in 2000.

Taking a break from full distance in 2001 when he only went as far as Peel, Gordon came back with a vengeance in 2002, finishing fourteenth in 19 hours 31 minutes 02 seconds. The following year he improved his time by half an hour, finishing twelfth.

So, after an 'easy' year to Peel in 2004, he made what he thought would be his last chance at full distance in 2005, missing out by nine minutes on a personal best.

Taking time out, Gordon returned in 2008 and despite the wettest weather in living memory, he smashed his best time by nearly 45 minutes to finish in 18 hours 16 minutes 10 seconds – an achievement he was most proud of.

After years of pounding the well-trodden route, Gordon now realises the value of technique and isn't too concerned at what time he reaches Peel. Afterall, 32½ miles is fairly insignificant in an 85-mile walk, recommending instead that those desirous of a good time should enter shorter races in a bid to improve their speed.

A plasterer by trade and married to race secretary Liz Corran, Gordon's impeccable athletic achievements are perhaps overshadowed by his failure to obtain Centurion status when the opportunity arose in Douglas in 2006. That said, there is still life left in the soon-to-be pensioner who is bound to say 'never again' at least one more time before bowing out from an event that has given him much pleasure and satisfaction over the past 20 or so years.

Irene Corlett

A legend from the past and one who dominated ladies' race walking for over two decades, 70-year-old Irene Corlett has the distinction of being the first Manx women to complete the Parish Walk.

Her first serious venture into race walking was in 1961, when as an 18-year-old, she jointly won the ladies' section of the first End to End Walk, completing the 40 miles from the Point of Ayre lighthouse to the Sound in 8 hours 28 minutes 56 seconds.

Her picture rarely missing from the sporting columns, Irene dominated women's athletics throughout the 1960s an 1970s, her finishing time of 22 hours 51 minutes 19 seconds in the 1963 Parish Walk an achievement she considers to be one of her best.

Rarely beaten in whatever event she turned her attention to, Irene set a ladies' Parish Walk course record of 17 hours 41 minutes 40 seconds in 1980, a time not bettered until Sandra Brown's phenomenal near 16¼-hour circuit 18 years later.

A regular winner of the ladies' race to Peel, Irene set the fastest time ever in 1982 when she reached the western capital in 5 hours 23 minutes 16 seconds. It was a phenomenally quick pace and to date, only Michael George and Allan Callow have covered the distance quicker.

One of the fastest-ever women to complete 100 miles, Irene gained Centurion status at Leicester in 1982 with an incredible time of 18 hours 54 minutes 05 seconds. A month later she made history by becoming the only woman ever to win the End to End Walk outright in a time of 6 hours 58 minutes 32 seconds. Only six of the 14 starters finished.

Sue Biggart

An eleven-time Parish Walk finisher from 14 starts, 50-year-old Sue Biggart is by far the most successful woman to have completed the Parish Walk with no less than seven ladies' victories to her credit

A Canadian citizen and resident of Glen Vine, Sue is married to Mathew, a consultant anaesthetist at Nobles Hospital whom she met in Toronto while working together at a children's hospital.

One of five children, Sue's first encounter with the Island's most physically demanding athletic event came in 1998 when she reached Peel in a little over seven hours. Her parents, who have both since passed away, witnessed her achievement, the only time they saw her race. She made it to Peel in 7 hours 20 minutes in 1999 and Lezayre the following year.

Training exceptionally hard and putting times out of her mind, Sue completed her first finish in 2001 in 20 hours 41minutes 39 seconds. She was only nine seconds over 19 hours the following year, and in 2003, she cruised around in 17 hours 33 minutes 16 seconds. It still wasn't fast enough to win though as it was the year that Roey Crellin set a Manx ladies' record time of 17 hours 12 minutes 19 seconds – the second fastest at the time but 54 minutes short of Sandra Brown's phenomenal time set five years earlier.

That year, Sue had made her debut in the winter league walks, the Peel to Douglas Walk, and perhaps uniquely, competed in the last ever TT Course Walk and the final End to End Walk along the now defunct east coast route.

Determined to improve her race walking technique and go even faster, Sue teamed up with Ray Pitts in 2004, their frequent early Sunday morning training sessions around St Johns and the Switchback, along with sound coaching from veteran Allan Callow, certainly paying dividends. That year she was the first lady home in a time of 16 hours 48 minutes 32 seconds and third overall with Ray Pitts.

The event was televised for the first time in 2005

with much attention focused on Sue who went on to claim a second victory albeit five minutes slower than her last outing. Her hat-trick in 2006 remains her fastest in 16 hours 23 minutes 14 seconds and she blames herself for not going even faster by being too casual with her service stop at Andreas.

The wins kept on coming and by 2008, the wettest Parish Walk ever, she made it five wins in a row. Later in the year, Sue set a women's best time in the End to End Walk, an event she has participated in many times.

But records are only made to be broken. In 2009 the relatively unknown Janice Quirk made sporting headlines by lowering the ladies' Parish Walking record by 18 minutes. Sue and Janice walked together during the early stages but she was unable to maintain Janice's pace. Although it was her first defeat in six years, it removed a huge burden from her shoulders as she was now no longer expected to win each year.

Over the years, Sue has managed to combine her Parish Walk training with a career in nursing as well as raising three children with her husband Mathew. Nevertheless, she says that the event can be ideal for anyone with a busy lifestyle as it's possible to fit in training around other family commitments. When she first heard about the 'Parish' it motivated her to train for more challenging goals and now she's often asked for advice on how to prepare for the event.

'For beginners, training for the Parish Walk is really about getting out and walking as often as you can and building up to a weekly distance that you aim to walk in the event itself. If possible complete one long walk every week in the build-up to the event. It's not necessary to achieve distances, it's easier to think in terms of time spent on your feet' she says.

After a glittering race walking career spanning 15 years, the smiling girl from Canada has finally accepted that there is more to life than a demanding training programme that constantly interferes with her family life.

After taking two years out to spend more time with her husband and three children, Sue made a welcome return to the Parish Walk in 2012 and as expected, she was the first woman home in 17 hours 03 minutes 53 seconds. In finishing eighth, she not only achieved a well-deserved victory, but also managed to finish one place ahead of five-time champion Robbie Callister – and that can't be bad can it?

Although Sue has said 'never again' on many occasions, 2013 was probably her last outing when she finished equal thirteenth in 16 hours 52minutes 25 seconds.

Elizabeth Corran

Born in Glasgow in 1955, married to Gordon and a mother of two, Elizabeth took up race walking during her early thirties as a way of keeping fit. Nevertheless, her natural style soon caught the attention of Common Wealth Games representative Allan Callow and over a few short years, Elizabeth developed a technique that took her to a competitive level both on

and off the Island.

A top ten place in the ladies' UK rankings for a number of years, Elizabeth set British and Manx records at three, five and 10 kilometres. She has clocked 1 hour 27 minutes 22 seconds over ten miles, while at Bruges in 1996 she set a Veterans' British world record time of 1 hour 47 minutes 10 seconds over 20 kilometres.

Elizabeth has also represented the North of England on several occasions with podium places in the senior ladies' age group.

Equally impressive over greater distances, Elizabeth has featured prominently in the Parish Walk and won the ladies' race to Peel on three consecutive occasions.

Prior to celebrating her 51st birthday in 2006, Elizabeth, with friend and training partner Bridget Kaneen, took on the daunting task of completing the Parish Walk for the one and only time. Although both women were apprehensive at continuing beyond Peel, they soldiered on together to finish in 20 hours 48 minutes 37 seconds.

No longer competitive, much of Elizabeth's spare time is taken up by coaching the Island's juniors' to a high standard. She is also heavily involved in administrative work for the Manx Harriers.

Secretary of the Parish Walk organising committee for the past 19 years, Elizabeth works tirelessly throughout the year to ensure the Island's most prestigious athletic event functions like clockwork. It is a very time-consuming chore however her husband Gordon, himself an eight-time Parish Walk finisher, is supportive by sharing much of the workload.

Jane Kennaugh

Yet another late entrant to a sport growing in popularity, Jane Kennaugh's first attempt at serious race walking was back in the 1990s when she completed two legs of the TT Relay Walk for the Central YFC ladies' team.

Building up stamina by walking home from work, a distance of eight miles, Jane was soon on Allan Callow's radar and began serious training twice a week at the National Sports Centre under the watchful eyes of Allan, Elizabeth Corran and Maureen Cox. She also trained most other days using either cycling, swimming or running as a means of improving physique.

A keen participant in the winter league programme during the mid-1990s, Jane enjoyed considerable success both on and off the Island at distances of five, ten and 20 kilometres.

Although of slight build, she appeared more comfortable at extended distance, experiencing considerable success at the Bradford 50-kilometre Walk, the End to End Walk and Parish Walk – the latter an event she has completed twice with a best time of 17 hours 31 minutes.

Ladies' champion to Peel on no less than four occasions, Jane's superb time of 5 hours 24 minutes to the western capital some years ago is the third quickest ever recorded.

Where are they now?

Marie Jackson

A legend herself 53-year-old Marie Jackson dominated women's middle-distance race walking throughout the first decade of the twenty-first century.

Like so many before her, Marie took up race walking relatively late in life and was 38 years of age when she took part in her first competitive event – the 1998 TT Relay Walk. Two years later she recorded the first of her two consecutive ladies' titles in the End to End Walk, a precursor to the 2000 Parish Walk when she was the second lady home in 20 hours 06 minutes 55 seconds.

But it was over middle distances that Marie excelled best. Achieving a host of Manx titles and age-group records over distances of three, five, ten twenty and 50 kilometres, Marie was always notoriously difficult to beat.

Training hard for the 2004 Parish Walk, she convincingly won the ladies' race to Peel in a superb time of 5 hours 50 minutes 17 seconds beating, her 2002 best time by over 11 minutes. In the wet event of 2008, Marie was the third lady home, recording a personal best time of 18 hours 20 minutes 22 seconds.

Considerable success off the Island saw Marie claim a bronze medal in the UK National 20-kilometre Championships in 2004 – an achievement she repeated fours years later over 50 kilometres.

However, her greatest athletic highlight was undoubtedly representing Great Britain in the World Veteran Athletics Championships in Italy in 2007 when she won an individual age-group silver medal leading the Great Britain team to victory in extremely hot conditions.

Marie's success off Island continued through 2010 and 2011 when she won the ladies' title in the classic Guernsey Church to Church 19.4-mile race walk, recording the second fastest time by a lady in its 75 year history.

Although her best days are now behind her, Marie continues to support the events that have given her considerable success and much pleasure over the past 15 years.

Roey Crellin

Making her Parish Walk debut in 1996 and going as far as Peel, Rosemarie (Roey) Crellin is no stranger to foot-slogging having completed the gruelling 85-mile circuit on ten consecutive occasions since 2000, as well as being the first lady home on three occasions.

Daughter of the late Herbie Cannell, founder member of the Boundary Harriers, Roey was born in 1956, educated at Braddan primary school and spent her early years at the family home in Trollaby Lane, Union Mills.

Like so many before her, she took up race walking late in life, wasted little time in making sporting headlines and proved that age is no barrier to her sporting achievements which are plentiful.

One of six Manx walkers to gain Centurion status at Kings Lynn, Norfolk in 2005, Roey completed the two-mile circuit 50 times and was runner-up to Sandra Brown in the ladies' section in a superb time of 21 hours 33 minutes. In France the following year, she represented Great Britain in a team event that saw her completing a remarkable 108 miles in 22½ hours

Although Roey has completed the End to End Walk on three occasions, the TT Walk, Mountain Marathon and Millennium Way once each, success came her way off Island in 2000 with a superb 4 hours 42 minutes performance at the New York Marathon.

In more recent years, but at a considerably slower pace, Roey has undertaken several expeditions across the lower Himalayas as well as a successful ascent of Mount Kilimanjaro, Africa's highest mountain 19,341 feet above sea level.

Now a resident of Peel and employed by Isle of Man Post, Roey is married to Kenneth with grown up children John and Rachael. She no longer participates in the Island's most physically demanding athletic event, preferring instead to maintain her level of fitness by delivering the mail to the remotest of places.

Anne Oates

Fifty-seven-year-old Anne Oates from Ballasalla is no stranger to foot-slogging having scored four Parish Walk finishes out of 16 starts.

Although her style in recent years has deteriorated due to injury, it is results that matter most and over a near 30-year period, Anne has been the recipient of many.

Born in Ronague in 1956, Anne became interested in race walking after watching Parish legend John Curphey train around the country lanes close to her home. She was also inspired by Irene Corlett, another legend from a bygone era who dominated women's athletics in the Isle of Man throughout the 1960s, 1970s and early 1980s.

Although Anne was nearly 30 years of age before she took part in her first Parish Walk, she was a regular competitor between 1985 and 2003, completing the ladies' race to Peel on no less than 11 occasions with an average time fractionally over seven hours.

Encouragement was plentiful too with Roey Crellin, Maureen Cox Mick Holgate, Charlie Weston and Jean Oldroyd all offering words of wisdom – but more importantly, sound advice on how to keep going when the going gets tough.

After completing her first Parish Walk in 2004, Anne immediately set her sights on improving her time the following year. With a one hour improvement at her second attempt and more than half an hour taken off that with her third finish, she went through the inevitable setback phase by taking nearly 21 hours to complete the 85 miles in 2008 – the wettest race in living memory.

Perhaps her toughest encounter with the elements, both physically and mentally was that in 2006, when at the National Sports Centre in Douglas, she achieved Centurion recognition by completing 100 miles inside 24 hours. However it was by no means easy, her leg seizing up and forcing her to walk for many miles leaning to one side and in great discomfort.

In recent years, Anne has been plagued with back-pain requiring intensive physiotherapy. As a consequence she has temporarily withdrawn from race walking, preferring instead to offer encouragement to Danielle, her 17-year-old granddaughter who seems to have all the ingredients for a successful race walking future.

David Collister

No one person in the history of the Parish Walk has walked a greater distance than David Collister. By covering 2,730 miles in 34 events, the 59-year-old landscape gardener from Archallagan lays claim to a record of 30 consecutive Parish Walk finishes since 1984.

David's first attempt at the Parish Walk was in 1975 when he made it to Peel in a fraction under eight hours. He bettered that by 8 minutes in 1977, while the following year he made it to Bride in 14 hours 57 minutes.

Residing in Ireland for some years, he returned in time for the 1983 event but retired at Lezayre, the last time that he has stopped anywhere other than the finish.

His first Parish Walk finish came in 1984 but it was also his most painful. The normally strictly controlled deadline was extended by race secretary Arthur Jones on the understanding that he would finish a few minutes outside the 24-hour time limit. However, after taking the best part of an hour to negotiate Douglas Promenade, David finally made it to his ultimate goal in a time of 25 hours 08 minutes 26 seconds. The 'never again' quote hadn't been coined in those days but it must have crossed his mind!

In spite of finishing more times than anyone else, completing the gruelling 85-mile walk year after year does not get any easier. For David, it is not a case of how high up the leader board he finishes, but more a case of grinding out another finish no matter how long it takes. He thought about calling it a day after reaching his twentieth finish in 2003 however he stubbornly carried on to record his thirtieth consecutive finish in the same year the event celebrated its centenary.

Although David's times have been relatively consistent over the past two decades, his 2013 finishing time was his second slowest ever and he was extremely lucky to make it back to Douglas inside the 24-hour time limit.

Good health and a sound mind have undoubtedly contributed to David's extraordinary finishing streak. Nevertheless, let us not forget those loyal people behind the scenes who kept him going through good times and bad. Triana, his wife, plus mum and dad — both no longer with us but remembered for their loyal support in making all this possible.

Anthony Kneale

Parish Walk records make fascinating reading and its interesting to note that only two men in the long history of the event have completed the course 34 times apiece. Although David Collister holds the record 30 consecutive finishes from 34 events, 62-year-old Tony Kneale holds the unique record of having started in every race since 1980. Of his 22 finishes, all but two have been under 20 hours.

And what a year he chose to make his debut. Until the atrocious weather conditions experienced by competitors in 2008, the 1980 event was arguably the wettest ever. He changed his clothing three times on the journey to Peel, reaching that point in 7 hours 42 minutes and has never stopped trying since.

Although he said 'never again' on that occasion, Tony decided to improve his technique and enrolled in the 'Murray Lambden Six-Week Training Programme,' He made it to Jurby the following year, Bride in 1982 and was delighted with his first finish in 1983.

Winner of the winter league in 1980 and the team award with Frank Huntley and Ian Corlett in 1985, it is probably safe to say that Tony has walked more miles than anyone else in an athletic career spanning 33 years. He has finished third in the Parish Walk on four occasions and was runner-up in the 1989 and 1996 events.

Perhaps his greatest achievement was that in 1998 when he finished the Parish Walk and continued along Douglas Promenade to claim Centurion status in a time of 22 hours 55 minutes 05 seconds.

Tony has also finished the Peel to Douglas Walk and the TT Relay

Walk on seven successive occasions and is a four-time finisher of the TT Course Walk, finishing ninth in 1983 in a best time of 6 hours 53 minutes 09 seconds.

Twice runner-up in the End to End Walk, Tony's best time was in 1985 when he completed the east coast route in 6 hours 58 minutes 10 seconds. He has also finished the Millennium Way Walk on four occasions, his best time in 1994 when he covered the 29 miles in 6 hours 23 minutes 55 seconds.

Over the shorter distance, Tony has been equally impressive with a fourth and seventh position in the Boundary Stroll's of 1982 and 1984. He has also completed the Castle to Castle Walk three times, the first in 1982 in a time of 7 hours 43 minutes.

Nevertheless, over the years, Tony has had more than his fair share of experiences, some good and some bad. On one occasion in 1993, he was attacked by a pole cat in the Bride area and had to make a hasty retreat which cost him time and distance on an already painful journey.

Having finished 22 times, Tony is full of praise for the support he receives from the public even in the most remote of places. At Smeale, there is a lady who never misses the occasion to wave and say hello from her window. Year in year out she is in the same spot, at the same time, offering words of encouragement which helps to numb the pain which is never far away. He has vowed that one day he will knock on her door and give thanks for all the support she has given in making his journey over the years that much easier.

A trade mark left over from his early days of competition, Tony's string vest has for many years been a topic of much debate. When asked why he favoured such a relic from the past he replied: 'It came in handy for pinning on race-numbers and was easy to fit over existing clothing. I've been using it since 1984 but it has a few extra holes in it now.'

Although his best days are well behind him, Tony continues to take part in the event that has given him considerable success for over half his lifetime. Asked recently if it was now time to throw in the towel, he replied: 'I will think about that when David Collister does – and that could be a long way off yet!'

Ray Hughes

An icon from the past and one of three postmen to stamp his authority with regularity in the annual classic, Ray has an impressive list of Parish Walk achievements, as good as it gets.

A finisher 22 times from 30 starts and rarely off the leader board , Ray has enjoyed considerable success since his first outing in 1984 when he reached Peel with no training whatsoever. Fifth in his first finish in 1985, Ray has been fourth on five occasions, third on five occasions and a runner-up three times.

Training hard for the 1989 event, he fell down a staircase three weeks before the event and ended up in plaster for the next three months. Nevertheless, with the aid of crutches, he walked to Santon raising considerable money for charity. As a gesture of goodwill, race organisers later refunded his entry fee!

One of two men that dominated Manx race walking during the 1990s, Ray's many contests with arch-rival Tony Kneale saw him gain podium place on seven occasions between 1991 and 1997.

Equally impressive over the shorter distance, Ray enjoyed considerable success in the End to End Walks during the 1990s. Third on several occasions with a best time of 7 hours 25 minutes, he took great delight in 1990 when he was first to Ballasalla in the 50-kilometre section.

Nevertheless, Ray's greatest achievement was probably that in 1998, when after finishing the Parish Walk in ninth place, he continued for another 15 miles along Douglas Promenade to become the first Manxman to gain Centurion status on home soil.

When asked what factors contributed to his remarkable success, Ray replied: 'I try to set aside time for two 20-mile training sessions through the week. Douglas to Port Soderick via the Marine Drive is a favourite route of mine. So too is Ballanard Road through to the Baldwins, however in recent years I've come close to being knocked down several times and have since gone elsewhere.'

Ray also has a terrific support team both day and night. He wears three pairs of thin cotton sock and shoes one size too big. He is also a firm believer in 'greasing up' the most intimate parts to avoid perspiration rash which inevitably sets in during the later stages leading to excruciating pain.

Injuries, blisters cramp and pulled muscles are all part of the Parish Walk and Ray has had many. To help him recover more quickly at the finish, Ray would often make his way onto Douglas foreshore, and to the disbelief of many, briefly immerse himself in the freezing seawater!

Time stands still for no one and by 2002 Ray's best days were well and truly behind him. After climbing out of a roadside ditch on the punishing climb to the Hibernia, he all but collapsed on the roadside thus bringing an end to an incredible run of 18 consecutive finishes.

Age being no barrier, Ray returned the following year only to spend the latter part of the race assisting a Bulgarian competitor to the finish. Lost in Andreas, without food or water and unsure of the way home, Ray generously shared his rations with the visitor, the pair making it to the Douglas War Memorial in 19 hours 09 minutes 19 seconds – his slowest circuit since 1990.

Not one to give in easily, Ray has struggled to complete the course in recent years – his last finish in 2008 the second slowest ever.

Dermot O'Toole

Other than fourth on the all-time finishers list, the Steam Packet skipper is probably more famous for 'never again' quotes than his 19 consecutive finishes from 21 starts.

Andrew Titley

No stranger to foot-slogging home or away, Andrew is up there with the very best when it comes to ultra-distance race walking.

Born in the year the Rolling Stones were top of the charts with 'I can't get no satisfaction', Andrew could never have imagined that nearly half a century later he would have accumulated 12 Parish Walk finishes, End to End finishes plus achieving Centurion status on no 6 less than occasions as well as covering 120 miles at the Roubaix 28-hour event in France in 2012.

Married to Rachel with daughters Emma and Lucy, Andrew played football for Colby and Rushen in his younger days and, like so many of his contemporaries, turned his attention to race walking relatively late in life.

His first attempt at the Parish in 2001 was easier than he'd imagined, completing the 85 miles in a little over 23 hours. 'I was only planning to go to Peel but felt so good that it seemed pointless to stop' he later said. 'The response to my finish was overwhelming. I have never experienced recognition like that before. Although I had done some jogging in the past, I really thought that the Parish Walk was for serious athletes only. It was a good learning curve for me as I now realise that practically anyone can do the event if they are positive and apply their mind sensibly.'

Not that he intended to do it again. 'Never again' are the words spoken by most first-timers and Andrew was no exception. Nevertheless, he did come back the following year, and other than missing the 2011 event due to race commitments overseas, he has finished the gruelling 85-mile event ever since.

On five of those occasions Andrew went under 18 hours, the quickest being in 2013 when he made it round in 16 hours 50 minutes 51 seconds to claim twelfth spot. In his early days, he trained with Eamonn Harkin and many of the Island's top distance walkers, all of which helped to develop him into the talented walker he is today. Turning his attention to even greater distances in 2005, Andrew completed his first 100-mile race in the Netherlands in a commendable time of 22 hours 55 minutes. The following year he repeated this feat at the National Sports Centre improving his time by 36 minutes.

Eamonn Harkin

A qualified accountant and resident of the Isle of Man since 1977, 53-year-old Irishman Eamonn Harkin has risen to the pinnacle of his chosen career in recent years and is now a managing director for a Swiss trust company based in Douglas. He resides in a beautiful home at the Howe, Port St Mary, and is married to wife Jan with two daughters Breeshey and Catreeney.

Flown off the Island by air ambulance in 1999 and lucky to be alive after suffering a life threatening brain haemorrhage, Eamonn was introduced into race walking by work colleague Murray Lambden who considered exercise to be a good form of therapy.

His first venture into serious race walking was in 2002 when both he and his wife Jan took part in the Parish Walk and managed to go as far as Rushen.

Completing the End to End Walk later that year, Eamonn set his sights on going full distance in the 2003 Parish Walk, and although Jan made it to Peel, Eamonn kept on going to record his first finish in a time of 21 hours 43 minutes 33 seconds.

Over the next three years, his times improved dramatically, setting a personal best time in 2006 of 16 hours 31 minutes 48 seconds.

Comfortable at even greater distance, Eamonn was one of six Manx athletes to achieve Centurion status at Kings Lynn, Norfolk in 2005 – a feat he again accomplished 12 months later at the National Sports Centre when he finished seventh in 21 hours 34 minutes 11 seconds.

He recorded a time of 16 hours 40 minutes 24 seconds in 2007 however after a well-deserved massage in the back of a horse box on Douglas Promenade, he lost his footing in damp conditions and ended up in Nobles Hospital with two broken ribs and in considerable pain for many months later.

With his sights set only on Peel, Eamonn and his daughter walked together in 2008, their time of 6 hours 48 minutes 30 seconds good enough for Breeshey to claim the overall under-21 prize. Later in the year, he experienced a severe angina attack which required him to undergo an emergency coronary artery stent implant.

Nevertheless, he bounced back in 2009 to record a superb finishing time of 16 hours 35 minutes.

Severe sickness between Glen Wylinn and Kirk Michael got the better of Eamonn in 2010 and although not one for quitting lightly, he quite sensibly retired at Ballaugh after being on his feet just seconds short of eight hours.

Taking a year out to spend more time with his family, Eamonn trained exceptionally hard in 2012 with training sessions of 12 miles or more often taking him over the infamous Sloc to the Round Table and back. However a heavy cold and not feeling well throughout the day contributed to a disappointing time of 17 hours 55 minutes 25 seconds – his second slowest ever.

Mike Readshaw

Born in 1957 and educated at Ballakermeen and St. Ninians High School, Mike played hockey for the best part of a quarter of a century before turning his attention to race walking relatively late in life.

With seven Parish Walk finishes from nine starts, the 55-year-old employee of Manx Telecom is always a safe bet for a top ten finish in the annual classic. Indeed, his Parish debut in 2002 saw him complete the full distance in 19 hours 09 minutes 41 seconds – not bad for a first time effort that comprised of just three seven-mile sessions during a five week period!

Mike's best time of 16 hours 40 minutes 36 seconds in 2009 earned him sixth spot for a second occasion. He has also been placed seventh on two occasions, eighth once and tenth twice.

Reflecting on his inaugural attempt Mike said:

I hadn't prepared to go beyond Peel – infact I now know I hadn't prepared at all! At Patrick, I said to my wife that I wanted to try to go beyond Peel however I would need more food and drinks. She left me with a temporary bum bag and limited provisions in order for her to purchase more food and water at the nearest shop. On opening the bag a mile or so further on, I was surprised to find it contained not essential sustenance for a weary walker, but a hairbrush and a single pain killer which I gratefully took to combat my blistered feet. It was only an hour later when Jackie returned that she informed me she hadn't provided any painkillers and so I must have taken one of her blood pressure tablets by default. Fortunately, I probably needed it at that point!

On another occasion in 2005, Mike remembers being violently sick at Knocksharry where Sky Sports were filming the event for the first time. 'I had seen their vehicle parked on the coast road and spotted the crew on the hedge. Although I was out of sight but doubled over, I could hear them discussing my predicament. I didn't want my first TV appearance to be seen throwing up on the roadside so I got it over and done with before proceeding to their vantage point.'

Nevertheless, Mike's stomach problems returned several hours later, forcing him to retire at Jurby – the only occasion he has never finished.

Equally impressive in the End to End Walk in which he participated on many occasions, Mike secured a well-deserved victory in the 2012 event with a time of 6 hours 57 minutes 24 seconds.

Where are they now?

Ray Pitts

Remarkably fit and agile for his 61 years, Ray Pitts still remains a force to be reckoned with having finished the Parish Walk on seven occasions.

Securing third spot four times between 2003 and 2006, Ray went one better in 2007 when he was runner-up in a best-ever time of 15 hours 51 minutes 42 seconds.

Educated at St Johns School, Ballakermeen and St Ninians, Ray has been for married to Glyn for 40 years with children Adrian and Neil.

Although his first venture into race walking was in 1968, when he took part in the Parish Walk Relay, Ray's interest in the full 85 miles came about from frequent conversation with work colleague Doug Allan, himself no stranger to foot-slogging and a Parish Walk legend from bygone years.

Ray's first attempt in 2000 ended disappointingly at Lezayre after hitting the 'wall' and mentally being unable to continue. Realising that it was over for another year, Ray took the incentive to train harder, and in 2001, he completed the course for the first time with David Lon Chambers in 19 hours 54 minutes 49 seconds.

But it was over mid-distance events that Ray excelled best. He was always a safe bet in the End to End Walks having finished each time between 2002 and 2007 and being runner-up twice with a best time of 7 hours 11 minutes.

Also successful off the Island, Ray took eighth place in the National 100-mile Walk at Colchester in 2004, gaining Centurion recognition in a time of 21 hours 53 minutes. The following year at Kings Lynn, he won the Twilight Twenty Walk, an event that later in the day saw six Manx competitors achieve Centurion status.

Returning to the mainland in 2008, Ray took the honours in the Blackpool 50-Mile Race with a time two minutes short of eight hours. At the same event over 50 kilometres, he was second-placed in 5 hours 26 minutes.

Although Ray was tenth in the 2010 Parish Walk, just six weeks after a serious accident at work, his time of 17 hours 16 minutes 51 seconds was nothing short of phenomenal. He later admitted it was the toughest walk he'd ever done. As a consequence he was off work for the best part of a year and missed the 2011 event.

Turning his attention to walking at a more leisurely pace, Ray took on the challenge of Wainwright's Coast to Coast Walk in 2012, completing the 190-mile journey in 16 days with good friends John Tarrant and Lesley Christian.

Now recovered from his injury, Ray once again took to serious training for the centenary event in 2013. On this occasion he was hoping to crack the six-hour barrier to Peel but missed out by 4 minutes to head a list of 433 who stopped at this point.

Maureen and Simon Cox

During the past 20 years, the married couple from Ballasalla have achieved considerable race walking success both on and off the Island.

Taking up the challenge to compete in the Island's most demanding athletic event in 1991, Maureen remembers the occasion well.

In those days the walk started at noon from the Villa Marina and all I wanted to do was walk round and finish back in Douglas within the 24-hour time limit. During the night section I took a wrong turning towards Maughold thus adding an extra couple of miles to an already tiring journey. Rescued and put back on the correct road by Steve Brennan, the weather then deteriorated with wind and rain seriously hampering my progress during the hours of darkness that seemed to have no end.

Determined to finish and prove the doubters wrong, I put on a spurt towards Laxey and thankfully made it back to Douglas with a little over an hour to spare so becoming the eleventh woman to complete this extraordinary and demanding journey.

Elated with such an achievement, I started training more seriously and for the next five years I walked to Peel only, finishing third female in 1992, second female in 1993 and in 1994, 1995 and 1996 first female.

In August 1995, Maureen attained Centurion status after walking 100 miles in under 24 hours around Battersea Park in London. The following year she took part in the Roubaix 28-Hour Walk in Northern France walking a distance of approximately 112 miles. She didn't complete the Parish Walk again until 2005 when she finished in 20 hours 22 minutes 39 seconds which was her quickest time to date. Many times Maureen tried to finish the Parish but always seemed to end up in the gutter being violently sick! Her third finish was in 2007 when she walked with her husband Simon in 20 hours 56 minutes 46 seconds. With a hat-trick of finishes behind her, Maureen has now turned her attention to encouraging and helping others to conquer this demanding course.

A fell runner, marathon runner and now race-walker, Simon Cox took part in his first Parish Walk in 1993 when he got as far as Peel in 6 hours 02 minutes 08 seconds. The following year the course was diverted at Patrick with Simon winning the veterans' class to St Johns in a time of 5 hours 55 minutes 54 seconds with his wife Maureen not far behind.

Completing the full distance for the first time in 1997 with a time of 19 hours 45 minutes, Simon went one better in 1998 when the Parish Walk was incorporated into the Race Walking Association's annual Centurion 100-mile event.

Reminiscing on that tiring day, Simon added: 'After finishing the Parish Walk in 20 hours 06 minutes 23 seconds, we had to walk up and down Douglas Promenade for another 15 miles to achieve the prestigious Centurion status. I didn't think it was possible to beat the 24-hour time limit however Graham Young gave me great encouragement, and by digging in to my deepest reserves and cheered on by crowds of well-wishers, I made it to the finish line with 20 minutes to spare.'

A non-starter in the 1999 Parish Walk so that he could take care of Maureen in her failed attempt to complete the course for the first time, Simon went on to record a further eight finishes between the new millennium and 2013 – his best time being 17 hours 14 minutes 03 seconds in 2004.

Michael Gray

Born in 1934 and a Parish Walk finisher on four occasions, Michael Gray has the distinction of being the oldest-ever finisher of the annual classic. One of 35 starters in the inaugural 1960 event, the 26-year-old Douglas Corporation gardener left work with just enough time for a bite to eat and a change of clothing before making his way to Upper Church Street, Douglas for the evening 7 o'clock start.

Taking the lead from Noel Cringle between Kirk Michael and Ballaugh, Michael looked like a possible winner until foot blisters, brought about by inappropriate footwear, necessitated an emergency visit to Ramsey Cottage Hospital.

Nevertheless, he quickly got over his disappointment, returning the following year with a vengeance and completing the 85 miles in 21 hours 43 minutes 50 seconds. Although he made several further attempts to finish during the 1960s, all were unsuccessful so he turned to fell-running instead.

As a veteran, Michael made a comeback in 1987 and 1988, making it to Peel on both occasions. However, it was his walk over the same distance in 2003 that started the modern involvement of the Gray family. Following in her father's footsteps, daughter Stephanie made it to Andreas at her very first attempt in 2005 while the following year she completed the course while dad walked as far as Lezayre at the age of 71.

Until 1990, the over-60s were not allowed to walk beyond Peel so with the rules now relaxed, Michael set two records in 2006. Firstly he became the oldest-ever finisher and secondly, he had the greatest gap between finishes of 46 years.

Despite the wettest event in living memory, Michael and Stephanie repeated their team effort in 2008 albeit at his slowest time ever. He made it to the finish the following year but was unable to compete in 2010 due to undergoing a routine operation at Nobles Hospital. Fully recovered and more determined than ever to get around one last time, Michael bravely walked as far as the Round Table in 2011 while the following year he went that bit further to the White Strand.

Michael's athletic achievements spanning six decades are nothing short of phenomenal. Sadly, his parents were not alive to witness them. In fact, Michael doesn't remember them for his mother passed away with meningitis when he was 18 months old leaving his maternal grandmother, Mrs. Daugherty to bring him up.

Michael's father served in the British army, however after the fall of Singapore in 1942, he was shipped out to the Solomon Islands as a Japanese prisoner of war and was later executed along with many other British troops. Many years later their bodies were exhumed and in 2008 both Michael and his brother travelled to Papua New Guinea where they saw their father's grave for the first time.

Michael's passion for horticulture led him to take up a post as school gardener at Ballakermeen in 1966 where for two years he worked closely with rural science teacher Gerry O'Toole. He joined the Harbour Police in 1967 and rose through the ranks of Sergeant and Inspector until his retirement in 1994.

Married for 56 years, Michael's wife Olga is well-known for her charity work. She is a sister to the late Dennis Lace, the former Isle of Man Athletics Association and Boundary Harriers' chairman who helped to make the Parish Walk the event it is today.

In 2005, the family were drawn into even further charity work after the death in New Zealand of their oldest daughter Michele. Since then, the family have worked tirelessly for the charity Breakthrough Breast Cancer, raising awareness and much-needed funds for research into a disease which claims the lives of so many women.

Approaching his eightieth year, Michael maintains his fitness with a daily four-mile walk around the Marine Drive plus a weekly visit to the swimming baths at the National Sports Centre. His clean living has certainly contributed to his longevity and, along with 1,320 other competitors, he once again took his place on the start line for the centenary event, on this occasion walking as far as the 61½-mile mark.

Allan Corlett

Like the Harvey boys from Abbeylands, the Corlett brothers from Crosby, Allan, Roy and Dickie, plus wives Irene and Stella, have been involved with the Boundary Harriers since its formation in 1961.

Allan got involved in race walking through the Manx Gym Club where he trained with weights under the supervision of Phil Boyd. This later led to him taking part in country sports events and winter league cross-country races organised by the Manx Amateur Athletics Association.

Missing out on the inaugural Parish Walk in 1960, Allan made up for his disappointment the following year by walking the full distance in 21 hours 55 minutes 48 seconds to claim sixth spot. He also won the team prize with fellow walkers Herbie Cannell, Terry Crellin and Michael Gray.

Reflecting on his Parish Walk achievement all those years ago Allan said: 'It was a tough outing and much harder than I expected. There were only eight finishers from a field of 84 which in those days was a massive entry.'

Setting off at 7 o'clock on the evening of 28th April 1961, Allan's team of helpers included his brother Dickie, Olga Gray and John Christian, the verger of Braddan church. 'Some of us stopped at Rushen church where fish and chips were plentiful. Mrs.

Clauge's house on the corner at Patrick was the next stop where a delicious buffet was enjoyed by all. Nevertheless, it was a bit of a struggle to reach Peel on a full stomach with daylight an hour away and still nowhere near the half way mark! Later, a hearty breakfast awaited me outside Ballaugh new church where Olga had managed to cook our food on a primus stove.'

Allan remembers well the clear morning and waiting for the sun to climb the eastern sky and warm him up for the long day ahead. 'We drank fresh milk at East Kimmerick Farm, however the journey through the northern plain was not easy and a good massage was required at Ballacannell to relieve the pain and give me strength for the remaining haul to Douglas.'

Back at the finish, Allan's support car was still well stocked with sustenance just in case he felt up for another lap! There was also a boot last for minor repairs plus a freshly pressed suit in case of a late finish and a dash to the presentation!

Roy Corlett

Although retired from race walking for a number of years, 64-year-old Roy Corlett made quite an impression in the Parish Walk during the early 1980s with podium positions on four occasions out of eight attempts.

Born in Douglas in 1949, Roy's earliest memory of the Parish Walk goes back to 1961 when he acted as family support for older brother Allan, one of nine finishers that year.

Reminiscing recently about that momentous day Roy said: 'My first and lasting impression was approaching St Judes crossroads and coming across Darryl Gribbin rolling around in agony in the middle of the road with badly blistered feet. Albert Road in Ramsey was the next "hot spot" with most walkers taking time out for a massage from Leslie Norton. As a 12-year-old, I thought they were all nuts!'

But over time the Parish Walk bug begins to bite and in 1980, along with sister-in-law Irene Corlett, cousin Tony Kneale and a few others, Roy decided to have a serious attempt at walking the 85 miles.

The weather was appalling that year and although Derek Harrison and Irene Corlett finished in exceptionally quick times, Roy called it a day at Bride with back and ankle problems.

Roy's first finish in 1981 nearly ended in tears on the top of the Sloc where he spent considerable time in a hedge contemplating whether or not to continue. The thought of all that winter training being wasted prompted him to get up and crack on for Peel, where fortunately, he met up with Roy Cooil with whom he walked to the finish. The elation of walking onto Douglas Promenade in the early hours of that June morning was certainly one of the highlights of his life.

Roy's other finishes were more routine however he has been plagued for years with back problems. For some reason he remembers 1983, not because it was the only time he completed all four local long-distance events in one year, but the fact that he was chairman of the Boundary Harriers. 'I always remember Murray Lambden coming up to me at Jurby that year and telling me 25 walkers had gone through Peel' to which I responded: 'Jesus Christ, we'll be bankrupt if they all finish – we don't have prizes for that number of finishers!'

Equally impressive over greater distance, Roy achieved Centurion status at Leicester in 1982 when he finished equal 18th in 22 hours 54 minutes 43 seconds – some four hours behind sister-in-law Irene who was also competing that year.

Although the End to End Walk from the Point of Ayre lighthouse to the Sound was never high on Roy's agenda, he finished third in 1983 in a time of 7 hours 36 minutes 05 seconds.

After retiring from race walking, Roy and his wife Stella marshalled as timekeepers at Kirk Michael Church for 15 years. Then in 2002 Stella shocked everyone by announcing her intention to walk to Peel, a feat she accomplished quite easily in a respectable time of 8 hours 18 minutes 42 seconds.

The following year Stella went that bit further to Jurby while in 2004 with minimal training she made it all the way round in 23 hours 43 minutes 43 seconds – the first of eight finishes, the last in 2013 when she only made the 24-hour deadline by 21 minutes.

Ron Ronan

There are not many sporting activities that Ron Ronan has turned his attention to and been unsuccessful.

Born in Castletown in 1942, Ron attended Victoria Primary School and then Castle Rushen School, where for six years he was a member of the school football and cricket teams.

A keen footballer from an early age, Ron joined Castletown Football Club in 1957, playing in almost five hundred matches until injury got the better of him in 1976. There were successes in the Association Cup, Railway Cup, Hospital Cup and Woods Cup finals plus the Combination Division One title. He also made 11 appearances in the Island Team, four as a junior and seven a senior.

Although Ron was unsuccessful with a trial for Manchester City in 1963, he was undoubtedly one of the Island's best footballers of his era. He has continued to maintain a close affinity with the club that gave him much pleasure during his youth and has been a President of Castletown Football Club since 2003.

Although a keen badminton player for the best part of 50 years, it is tennis that Ron has excelled in. A member of Castletown Tennis Club for over 40 years, he won the Isle of Man singles title in 1965 at his very first attempt and over the years has appeared in 40 finals, both singles and doubles. He has won a total of 19 Championship titles, five singles, five men's doubles and nine mixed doubles.

Extremely fit for his 71 years, Ron continues to play his beloved sport at least once a week in Castletown where he is the captain of the over 65s team.

Ron was introduced to race walking in 1971 when

Statistics and the future

good friend Derek Harrison organised a team of Castle Rushen Old Scholars to take part in the TT Relay Walk of that year. The team consisting of Derek, Ron, Dave Wilkinson and John Corrin finished second in the non-athletic club selection. Over the years, he took part in this popular event on 30 consecutive occasions until it was abandoned in 2000 on the grounds of safety.

The Peel to Douglas Walk attracted Ron's attention in 1972, finishing this well contested event no less than 32 times until its demise in 2010 – yet another victim of health and safety measures that have in recent years robbed the Island of many of its sporting attractions.

By now, Ron was addicted to race walking and he joined the Winter Handicap League in 1973, an event he hasn't missed in 40 years. The End to End Walk was another of his favourites, managing to complete his thirtieth outing in 2012 albeit slightly slower than his best time of 7 hours 25 minutes 11 seconds in 1974.

But the ultimate test for Ron came in 1974 when he decided to enter the Parish Walk for the very first time. There were only three finishers out of an entry of 84, Ron grabbing the final podium position behind John 'Paddy' Dowling and Ian Turnbull in 20 hours 40 minutes 34 seconds.

He took part again in 1975 and 1976 however blisters at Andreas and Bride brought an end to any ideas of emulating his only finish. By the late seventies the event had moved to the end of June however it clashed with the start of the tennis season so he no longer took part. Nevertheless, Ron continues to stay in touch with the Parish Walk and he is one of dozens of marshals overseeing its safety.

Also a keen runner with 16 marathons and ten Great North Runs to his credit, Ron has proved that age is no barrier and in 2009 he received a Lifetime Achievement Award for services to Manx sports.

STATISTICS

Statistics always impress and the Parish Walk has no shortage of them. Since 1960, 52 events have produced 21,754 starters, 2,113 finishers and 28 individual winners. However, not all those making it back to Douglas have done so in the 24-hour time limit. The slowest-ever circuit of the 17 parishes was that by 17-year-old Eddie Christian, who in 1967, took 28 hours to complete the course only to find everyone had gone home in preparation for the presentation later.

On 23rd July 1852, John Cannell of Douglas became the first person to visit all the Island's parish churches within a 24-hour period.

Setting off from Douglas at 7 o'clock in the morning on horseback, he called at Onchan, Lonan, Maughold, Lezayre, Bride, Andreas, Jurby, Ballaugh, Michael, German, Patrick, Rushen, Arbory, Malew, Santon, Marown, and Braddan thus accomplishing an estimated distance of 77 miles in 15 hours.

Wishing to emulate this great feat the following year, John left Douglas just before midnight on 17th September, and proceeding northward on foot, he visited the 17 parishes and four towns of the Island in 23 hours 45 minutes.

In 1881, 50-year-old James William Anderson, a retired Lieutenant Colonel in the British army and eminent member of the Manx legislature also accomplished a similar feat however his time went unrecorded.

Ten years later and determined to improve on his previous attempt, the colonel set off from Patrick just before 3 o'clock in the morning. Proceeding northward on foot he visited all 17 parish churches in 19 hours 39 minutes.

The first official Parish Walk in 1913 started and finished outside the Palace gates on Douglas Promenade. Setting off at ten o'clock in the evening of 28th May the 12 competitors made their way to Quarter Bridge via Broadway, York Road and Stoney Road. After reaching Braddan, competitors could choose any route they wished as long as each church was passed in sequential order. While taking a short cut between the top of the Sloc and Dalby, several lost their way in poor visibility resulting in only five making it back to Douglas, two of whom were well outside the 24-hour time limit.

An unofficial starter, 62-year-old Douglas chemist John Young also completed a circuit of the 17 parishes in 23 hours however his was a journey on four legs rather than two. Not wishing to bring his horse to the crowded start on Douglas Promenade, John set off from Quarter Bridge shortly after the walkers had passed through. Conversing with farmers and village folk along the way, he stopped at Kirk Michael to shod and feed the thoroughbred before continuing to the finish. Taking several short cuts along the way John's equestrian journey of 80 miles was a magnificent achievement and given better conditions, he felt he could have completed the course in 16 hours.

The intervention of the Great War prevented any immediate repetition of the 1913 event. However in 1923 and 1924, two challenge matches were held, each with only two competitors and both won by Gerald Bridson, a prominent member of the Manx Legislature.

There was an unsuccessful attempt to lower the Parish Walk record in 1933 when the intrepid New Zealander Harry Coulston underestimated the daunting task ahead. Setting off from Douglas Promenade at 6'oclock on an August evening, atrocious weather on the Sloc forced him to take refuge at a residence in Kirk Michael. His overall time of 36 hours is the slowest ever recorded.

Onchan postman Stanley Cleator won the inaugural 1960 Parish Walk in a time of 19 hours 50 minutes 30 seconds – the slowest winning time ever officially recorded. As there was no age limit, Graham Young, still to reach his fifteenth birthday, has the distinction of being the youngest-ever competitor. In the same race, runner-up Jim Harvey became the youngest-ever finisher at 16 years of age.

In 1963, Eunice Davies of RAF Jurby became the

first-ever woman to finish the Parish Walk in a time of 20 hours 51 minutes 24 seconds. Two hours later Irene Corlett from Crosby became the first-ever Manx woman to complete the course. Of the 74 starters, only six made it back to Douglas.

There were no races in 1965 or 1966 due to disagreement within the organising committee as to how the event should be managed.

The legendary Albert Johnson won the 1967 Parish Walk and in doing so, became the first person ever to go under 16 hours.

There was controversy in the 1968 event when the first man over the finish line was denied the winner's trophy. Because Leece Kneale was not in a recognised athletic club, the trophy was awarded to runner-up Ian Turnbull who actually finished two hours later. It was a situation never envisaged and forced race organisers, Boundary Harriers, to review entry procedures the following year.

In its long history the Parish Walk has continued to maintain an exemplary safety record. Nevertheless, 1968 was marred by the tragic death of a 17-year-old youth in the Parish Walk Relay, held a week before the main event. The deceased was acting as a pacer when he was struck by a passing car while walking alongside a competitor on the Peel to Kirk Michael coast road. The incident brought to an end a popular event first held in 1961.

On the hottest Parish Walk day in living memory, Castletown's Steve Gardner made history in 1977 as the only finisher in 19 hours 11 minutes 01 second. It was the second slowest-ever circuit with only three from a field of 90 reaching Maughold.

It was not until 1980 that an entry exceeded 100. In the same year Mylchreest Motors sponsored the event for the first time. Three years later, John Cannell made Parish Walk history when he became one of only three men to record a hat-trick of wins.

In 1990, Clerical Medical International began a 22-year sposorship of the event.

A frequent champion of the veterans' shorter race to Peel, Commonwealth Games representative Allan Callow set the fastest-ever time to Peel in 1993 – a record that stood the test of time for another 19 years.

At his very first attempt in 1995, 62-year-old Brian Ashwell from Leicester became the oldest winner in a time of 16 hours 37 minutes 47 seconds.

Although there is no maximum age limit, a publicity stunt in 1998 saw 84-year-old comedian celebrity Norman Wisdom become the second oldest starter, reaching the two-mile mark at Braddan in 50 minutes

History was made in 2004 with over 1,000 starters taking to the roads. There were 100 finishers in this race with 60-year-old Robert Brown the last home but exceeding the 24-hour time limit by four minutes.

Suffering from cerebral palsy and told by doctors that she would never walk, Dru Hamm proved them wrong in 2006 when she walked from the start to Marown in 4½ hours. On the same day, Sean Hands broke Derek Harrison's long-standing record to become the first person to complete the course in less than 15 hours.

Keith Wilkinson forgot to submit his entry in 2006 so rather than waste three months of intensive training the 48-year-old unofficially walked the old course backwards in a time of 22 hours 24 minutes. Setting off from the war memorial on Douglas Promenade at precisely the same time that the event got under way from the National Sports Centre, the Nobles Hospital consultant anaesthetist walked north in an anti-clockwise, direction passing no one until race leader Sean Hands emerged at the Lhen. Ironically, Keith was still descending the Sloc with 22 miles to go when news came in that Sean Hands' had crossed the finish line 33 minutes inside Derek Harrison's long-established record time.

In 2007, electronic timing by SPORTident was intoduced to reduce the workload for the numerous time keepers posted around the course.

In the wettest race in living memory 35-year-old Bethany Clague set a new record in 2008 by walking 170 miles over two circuits of the course in less than 48 hours. In the same event, 74-year-old Michael Gray became the oldest-ever finisher recording a time of 23 hours 15 minutes 15 seconds for the 85 miles.

Although only 12 minutes short of becoming the first-ever ladies' Parish Walk champion, Janice Quirk made history in 2009 when she became the first woman to complete the Parish Walk in less than 16 hours.

David Collister and Tony Kneale have the record number of starts at 34 apiece, however Tony, a laundryman at Tromode, has the distinction of starting in every Parish Walk since 1980.

Jock Waddington, a 46-year-old civil servant from Douglas, made history in 2011 when he became the first quadruple winner of the Parish Walk.

Manx Telecom were new sponsors in 2012, a year that produced a record 1,505 starters with 201 making it back to Douglas. In the same event, the first-ever joint winners set a new course record time of 14 hours 42 minutes 32 seconds.

Although the centenary event in 2013 was another wet one, a record number of 215 walkers made it to the finish inside the 24-hour time limit. Four hundred and 80 made it to the halfway mark with record numbers reaching every checkpoint beyond Ballaugh. In the same race, 86-year-old Robert Corkish became the oldest ever starter when he walked as far as Santon.

There have been four different starting points in Douglas since 1960. Upper Church 1960 to 1964, Villa Marina Arcade 1967 to 1986, Villa Marina Gardens 1987 to 2000 and the National Sports Centre 2001 to the present day.

During the same period, there have been nine different starting times: 8:00am, 9:00am, 10:00am, 11:30am, 12 noon, 3:00pm, 5:30pm, 7:00pm and 8:00pm. In 1962 and 1963 the ladies started an hour and a half before the men. A year later, the starting difference was reduced to one hour.

Boundary Harriers took over the running of the event in 1967 which saw the ladies starting five minutes ahead of the men, a format that continued until 1974. The following year saw the ladies setting off 30 minutes before the men, this format continuing until 1992 when a joint starting time was introduced.

Finally, the most outstanding Parish Walk achievement of all time is perhaps that of veteran David Collister who has completed the course on 30 consecutive occasions since 1984. All records are made to be broken however this is one that will almost certainly stand the test of time for years to come.

THE FUTURE

So what does the future hold for the Island's most prestigious and talked about athletic event that continues to capture the public's imagination like no other?

Since its humble beginnings in 1913, when just a dozen took part, this extraordinary event has grown to unimaginable proportions with over 1,500 taking to the roads in 2012 and a record 215 finishing the following year.

Each year, the logistical mountain grows higher with safety issues paramount and always high on the organising agenda. Other than one serious incident in 1968, the event has enjoyed an unblemished safety record – testament to the hard work and total commitment of the organising committee under the strong leadership of race director Ray Cox.

Although race times have improved dramatically over the years, breaking the 16-hour barrier was never thought possible until Albert Johnson accomplished just that in 1967.

Twelve years later, Derek Harrison set a new course record time of 15 hours 20 minutes 51 seconds, a time not improved upon until 2006 when Sean Hands quite literally sprinted around the course some 31 minutes quicker. Since then, only Richard Gerrard, Vinny Lynch and Michael George, have gone under 15 hours, all achieving this magnificent feat in 2012.

The future for the Island's show-piece sporting event looks promising. Another 100 years may seem a long way off but one thing beyond all doubt is that records will continue to be broken and 'never again' quotes spoken!

Parish Walk Winners 1960-2013

Year	Winner	Time
1960	Stanley Cleator	19. 50.30
1961	Henry Harvey	17.10.17
1962	Henry Harvey	16.25.40
1963	Joe Brown	17.04.09
1964	Henry Harvey	16.21.06
1965	No Race	
1966	No Race	
1967	Albert Johnson	15.54.51
1968	Ian Turnbull	8.15.44
1969	Ian Hodgkinson	17.11.25
1970	Dudley Seddon	17.21.49
1971	Graham Young	15.43.12
1972	Derek Harrison	16.19.15
1973	Derek Harrison	16.36.04
1974	John Dowling	16.40.07
1975	Ted Warner	18.49.52
1976	John Cannell	17.28.12
1977	Steve Gardner	19.11.01
1978	Murray Lambden	16.19.37
1979	Derek Harrison	15.20.51
1980	Derek Harrison	16.13.10
1981	John Cannell	16.15.11
1982	John Cannell	15.59.33
1983	John Cannell	16.31.38
1984	Derek Harrison	16.10.17
1985	Willie Corkill	16.29.31
1986	Willie Corkill	17.03.45
1987	Willie Corkill	16.58.33
1988	Martin Lambden	17.12.01
1989	Charlie Weston	18.17.55
1990	Gordon Vale	17.55.10
1991	Charlie Weston	17.46.58
1992	Graham Young	16.38.27
1993	John Cannell	16.11.11
1994	John Cannell	16.13.46
1995	Brian Ashwell	16.37.47
1996	Lee Cain	17.26.29
1997	Chris Flint	17.36.40
1998	Richard Brown	15.59.44
1999	Chris Flint	17.07.46
2000	Peter Kaneen	16.59.54
2001	Robbie Callister	16.59.27
2002	Robbie Callister	16.34.30
2003	Peter Kaneen	15.26.07
2004	Robbie Callister	15.26.31
2005	Robbie Callister	15.24.24
2006	Sean Hands	14.47.36
2007	Robbie Callister	15.36.47
2008	Jock Waddington	15.44.33
2009	Jock Waddington	15.45.56
2010	Jock Waddington	15.18.06
2011	Jock Waddington	15.01.48
2012	Vinny Lynch/ Richard Gerrard	14.42.32
2013	Michael George	14.44.49